2ND EDITION

LOGISTICS MATTERS

ENGLISCH FÜR KAUFLEUTE FÜR SPEDITION UND LOGISTIKDIENSTLEISTUNG

von
Michael Benford
Fritz Michler
Joanne Popp
Isobel Williams

sowie
Justin Ehresman
Sandra Haberkorn
Sabine Steeg-Hintermeier

unter Mitarbeit der Verlagsredaktion

Verfasser/in:	Michael Benford, Bochum
	Fritz Michler, Garbsen
	Joanne Popp, Korntal-Münchingen
	Isobel Williams, Berlin
unter Mitarbeit von:	Justin Ehresman, Ortenberg
Verfasserinnen KMK-Seiten:	Sandra Haberkorn und Sabine Steeg-Hintermeier, Wiesbaden
Berater/innen:	Annekatrin Bürger, Leipzig; Wolfgang Friedhoff, Fulda
Projektleitung:	Andreas Goebel, Kari-ann Warnakulasuriya
Verlagsredaktion:	Menemsha MacBain
Redaktionelle Mitarbeit:	Christiane Knudsen, Nicola Stebbing, Oliver Busch (Wörterverzeichnisse)
Bildredaktion:	Gertha Maly
Layoutkonzept:	finedesign, Berlin
Gesamtgestaltung und technische Umsetzung:	vitaledesign, Berlin
Umschlaggestaltung:	vitaledesign, Berlin
Coverfoto:	Shutterstock.com / Travel mania

Erhältlich sind auch:
Handreichungen für den Unterricht mit MP3-CD und Online-Zusatzmaterialien
ISBN 978-3-06-451648-9

Soweit in diesem Lehrwerk Personen fotografisch abgebildet sind und ihnen von der Redaktion fiktive Namen, Berufe, Dialoge und Ähnliches zugeordnet oder diese Personen in bestimmte Kontexte gesetzt werden, dienen diese Zuordnungen und Darstellungen ausschließlich der Veranschaulichung und dem besseren Verständnis des Inhalts.

www.cornelsen.de

Die Webseiten Dritter, deren Internetadressen in diesem Lehrwerk angegeben sind, wurden teilweise von Cornelsen mit fiktiven Inhalten zur Veranschaulichung und/oder Illustration von Aufgabenstellungen und Inhalten erstellt. Alle anderen Webseiten wurden vor Drucklegung sorgfältig geprüft. Der Verlag übernimmt keine Gewähr für die Aktualität und den Inhalt dieser Seiten oder solcher, die mit ihnen verlinkt sind.

1. Auflage, 2. Druck 2022

Alle Drucke dieser Auflage sind inhaltlich unverändert und können im Unterricht nebeneinander verwendet werden.

© 2019 Cornelsen Verlag GmbH, Berlin

Das Werk und seine Teile sind urheberrechtlich geschützt. Jede Nutzung in anderen als den gesetzlich zugelassenen Fällen bedarf der vorherigen schriftlichen Einwilligung des Verlages. Hinweis zu §§ 60 a, 60 b UrhG: Weder das Werk noch seine Teile dürfen ohne eine solche Einwilligung an Schulen oder in Unterrichts- und Lehrmedien (§ 60 b Abs. 3 UrhG) vervielfältigt, insbesondere kopiert oder eingescannt, verbreitet oder in ein Netzwerk eingestellt oder sonst öffentlich zugänglich gemacht oder wiedergegeben werden. Dies gilt auch für Intranets von Schulen.

Druck und Bindung: Livonia Print, Riga

ISBN 978-3-06-451646-5
ISBN 978-3-06-451647-2 (E-Book)

PEFC zertifiziert
Dieses Produkt stammt aus nachhaltig bewirtschafteten Wäldern und kontrollierten Quellen.
www.pefc.de

Vorwort

Logistics Matters 2nd edition ist eine Neubearbeitung des bewährten Englisch-Lehrwerks für Kaufleute für Spedition und Logistikdienstleistung und wurde für die Ausbildung in Berufsschulen sowie die innerbetriebliche Aus- und Weiterbildung konzipiert.

Das Lehrwerk setzt Englischkenntnisse voraus, die dem Niveau B1 des Europäischen Referenzrahmens *(Common European Framework of Reference)* entsprechen. Es deckt die Themen der aktuellen Lehrpläne der Bundesländer für Englisch in der Berufsschule konsequent ab.

Logistics Matters 2nd edition besteht aus zwölf Units, die flexibel einsetzbar sind. Jede Unit umfasst vier abgeschlossene Lernsituationen, die jeweils in einer Doppelstunde bearbeitet werden können. Eine Unit ist wie folgt aufgebaut:

Foundation: Diese Doppelseite bietet Ihnen mit Grundwissen und elementarem Themenvokabular einen Einstieg in das Thema der Unit.

Part A/B: Diese stark berufsbezogen ausgerichteten Module können je nach Umfang der Inputmaterialien jeweils zwei bis vier Seiten umfassen. Hier werden fachspezifische Schwerpunkte der Unit mithilfe authentischer und aktueller Materialien behandelt.

Communication: Berufliche Kommunikation steht im Fokus des abschließenden *Communication*-Teils. Ein „Das kann ich"-Kästchen – eine Checkliste zur Selbstevaluation – rundet die Unit ab und ermöglicht es den Lernenden, über ihren persönlichen Lernerfolg zu reflektieren.

Alle Lernsituationen sind so konzipiert, dass sie ausgelassen oder zu einem anderen Zeitpunkt behandelt werden können. Somit berücksichtigt die Modulstruktur einer jeden Unit die organisatorische Vielfalt des Englischunterrichts und schafft größtmögliche Flexibilität im Unterricht.

Besonderer Wert wird in diesem Lehrwerk auf **Handlungsorientierung** und direkten Berufsbezug gelegt: Jedes Modul beginnt mit einer branchenspezifischen *Situation* und führt über handlungs- und kompetenzorientierte Lernschritte zu einem Handlungsprodukt. Dieses Lernziel ist jeweils zu Beginn des Moduls mit einem Pfeil gekennzeichnet und ermöglicht so eine schnelle Orientierung.

Unterschiedliche Aktions- und Sozialformen ermöglichen zudem den Einsatz von kooperativen Lernformen und fördern **eigenverantwortliches Lernen**.

Um der Heterogenität der Auszubildenden gerecht zu werden, finden sich zahlreiche Aufgaben zur **Binnendifferenzierung** in den Units. Diese sind mit einem Strich unter der Aufgabenziffer gekennzeichnet und verweisen auf editierbare Kopiervorlagen in den Handreichungen, die alternative Bearbeitungsmöglichkeiten für die jeweilige Aufgabe zur Verfügung stellen.

Zur Vorbereitung auf die **KMK-Prüfung** Stufen II (B1) und III (B2) werden anhand von sechs Unterrichtseinheiten und einer kompletten Musterprüfung prüfungsrelevante Materialien und Aufgaben angeboten und so eine systematische Prüfungsvorbereitung ermöglicht.

Grundlegende grammatikalische Strukturen werden durchweg im **situativen Kontext** vermittelt, ergänzt durch eine systematische Grammatikübersicht im Anhang und Übungsmaterialien in den Handreichungen. Zur Erweiterung des berufsrelevanten Wortschatzes werden Themenwortschätze im Anhang angeboten sowie eine umfangreiche *Unit word list* mit allen neuen Wörtern in chronologischer Reihenfolge und eine *A–Z word list*. Außerdem im Anhang stehen Ihnen dort berufsbezogene *Useful phrases,* die eine effektive berufliche Kommunikation erleichtern, und eine Aufstellung der Incoterms®-Regeln zur Verfügung.

Sämtliche Audiomaterialien finden Sie in den Handreichungen für den Unterricht und darüber hinaus geben kurze **Videos** passend zu den Themen kurze Einblicke in das spätere Berufsleben und vermitteln Fachwissen in motivierender Form. Diese Materialien und die dazugehörigen Arbeitsblätter stehen den Lehrkräften online zur Verfügung.

Die Verlagsredaktion sowie das Berater- und Autorenteam wünschen Ihnen viel Erfolg und Freude mit *Logistics Matters 2nd edition*.

Table of contents

Unit		Content	Situation	Language	
1	**Working conditions**				6
	FOUNDATION	My apprenticeship	Writing a description of your apprenticeship	Describing training Asking for information Agreeing and disagreeing Comparing working conditions Expressing obligation Talking about the future Introducing yourself and others Making small talk Meeting and greeting visitors	
	PART A	Working conditions at my company	Creating a page in the employee handbook about working conditions		
	PART B	Working conditions abroad	Discussing the advantages and disadvantages of the dual system of vocational training		
	COMMUNICATION	Introductions and small talk	Looking after visitors		
2	**My workplace**				14
	FOUNDATION	In the office	Making an inventory of office equipment	Describing office activities Talking about likes and dislikes Talking about your company Describing jobs Describing how often sth happens Giving telephone numbers Making a telephone call	
	PART A	An organization chart	Creating a company organization chart		
	PART B	Job profiles	Creating profiles of departments and jobs		
	COMMUNICATION	Telephoning	Taking and leaving messages		
	KMK Exam practice 1				22
3	**My company**				24
	FOUNDATION	Types of companies	Creating a timeline of your company	Talking about different types of companies Giving directions Talking about the past Describing repeated actions Structuring a presentation Giving a presentation	
	PART A	Showing visitors around	Taking visitors on a guided tour of your company		
	PART B	A company profile	Preparing a presentation about your company		
	COMMUNICATION	A short presentation	Giving a presentation about your work		
4	**Supply chain**				32
	FOUNDATION	Logistics in the supply chain	Creating a poster about your company's role in the supply chain	Describing the supply chain Discussing packaging Understanding shipping marks Talking about different types of warehouses Saying what something is used for Using polite language in emails Salutations and complimentary closes in emails	
	PART A	Packaging and labelling	Planning the packaging and labelling of a shipment		
	PART B	Warehousing	Presenting your company's warehouse		
	COMMUNICATION	Emails	Writing an email to a customer		
	KMK Exam practice 2				40
5	**Enquiries and offers**				42
	FOUNDATION	Company services and USPs	Suggesting improvements to the company website	Making comparisons Structuring an offer Following up on the phone Talking about terms of payment Salutations and complimentary closes in letters	
	PART A	Receiving an enquiry	Clarifying the details of an enquiry		
	PART B	Making an offer	Writing an offer		
	COMMUNICATION	The layout of business letters	Writing a letter of enquiry		
6	**Road and rail transport**				50
	FOUNDATION	Overland transport	Preparing a presentation about road and rail transport	Discussing tolls and vehicles Completing forms (CMR and DGN) Understanding tremcards Explaining consequences Understanding weights and measures Making and confirming arrangements Asking polite questions	
	PART A	Shipping dangerous goods	Planning a shipment and briefing a driver		
	PART B	Following standard road freight procedures	Dealing with a customer's request and writing an email		
	COMMUNICATION	Clarifying information on the phone	Exchanging information about a return load		
	KMK Exam practice 3				60

Unit	Content	Situation	Language	
7	**Air transport**			62
	FOUNDATION — Air transport planning	Preparing a checklist for shipping consignments by air	Understanding universal time Using the international alphabet Shipping unit load devices Understanding air waybills Booking flights and accommodation Talking about future possibilities	
	PART A — IATA and TACT	Scheduling an air cargo shipment		
	PART B — Completing an air waybill	Calling to collect data for an air way bill and updating a colleague		
	COMMUNICATION — Business trips	Making arrangements for an OBC trip		
8	**Sea transport**			72
	FOUNDATION — Sea freight planning	Writing a blog post	Discussing different kinds of ships Describing containers Talking about dimensions Understanding shipping documents Issuing a bill of lading Giving dates, days and times	
	PART A — Containers	Recommending a mode of transport		
	PART B — Transport documents	Preparing a transport document		
	COMMUNICATION — Scheduling	Agreeing collection and delivery dates		
	KMK Exam practice 4			84
9	**Orders and payments**			86
	FOUNDATION — Preparing to order	Comparing offers and making a recommendation	Understanding Incoterms® rules Recommending an offer Negotiating terms of payment Structuring an order or acknowledgement Writing prices Understanding an advice of dispatch Giving directions	
	PART A — Evaluating an offer	Preparing a counter-offer		
	PART B — Placing an order	Negotiating terms with a supplier and placing an order		
	COMMUNICATION — Delivery	Writing to change a delivery address and giving directions		
10	**Customer service**			98
	FOUNDATION — Direct contact with customers	Writing guidelines for customer contact	Communicating clearly and politely with customers Describing cultural differences Giving advice Reporting what someone has said Comparing figures Structuring a complaint Apologizing in emails and letters	
	PART A — Cultural differences	Giving advice about intercultural communication		
	PART B — Responding to complaints	Answering a customer's complaint		
	COMMUNICATION — A telephone complaint	Dealing with a telephone complaint		
	KMK Exam practice 5			108
11	**Sustainability and innovation**			110
	FOUNDATION — Innovations in logistics	Presenting your findings	Discussing automation Talking about the future Describing graphs and charts Talking about the electronic AWB Understanding an agenda Writing the minutes of a meeting	
	PART A — Reducing costs and increasing sustainability	Writing a memo about reducing costs		
	PART B — Making companies more efficient	Write a blog post on company changes		
	COMMUNICATION — Meetings	Taking part in a meeting		
12	**A job application**			118
	FOUNDATION — Where do I go from here?	Writing a description of your apprenticeship	Describing your apprenticeship Writing a job advertisement Practising a (telephone) interview Writing an application for a job	
	PART A — Applying for a job abroad	Writing a job advertisement		
	PART B — Interviews	Practising interviews		
	COMMUNICATION — A CV and a covering letter	Writing a job application		
	KMK Exam practice 6	Writing a job application		128

Partner files	130	Terms of payment	179	A–Z word list	230
KMK Mock exam	146	Conversion tables	179	Irregular verbs	253
Grammar	151	Useful phrases	180		
Transcripts	156	Thematic vocabulary	196		
Incoterms® 2010	177	Unit word list	200		

1 Working conditions

FOUNDATION: My apprenticeship

Situation: You are an apprentice at an international logistics company in Berlin whose working language is English. The company is looking for new international trainees.
→ You write a description of your apprenticeship for the trainee section of the website.

1 Describing two apprenticeships

Your line manager asks you to write an English description of your apprenticeship for the website, so you look online for some examples.

A 2))) Read and listen to what Sophie says, then copy and complete the chart.

> Hello. My name is Sophie, I'm 19 years old. I'm from Bremen. I left school last year with the German "Abitur", which is similar to the British A levels. I now work at Bitz Logistics GmbH where I'm training to be a management assistant for freight forwarding and logistics. My apprenticeship lasts for three years. I'm doing a work-based apprenticeship. I work in the office from 9 to 5 and do block release at vocational school every three months. I get a small salary from the company. It's not much, but I still live with my parents, so I don't have expenses like rent or food. My colleagues are great and help me a lot. I'd like to work in one of the company's foreign branches one day.

1	school qualifications		
2	training company		
3	name of apprenticeship		
4	details of apprenticeship	– length	
		– type	
		– hours in company	
		– time at vocational school	
5	who pays her living expenses		
6	hopes for the future		

B 3))) Listen to Robert describing his training and answer these questions.

1. What are Robert's school qualifications?
2. Where does he work?
3. What will Robert be when he qualifies?
4. How long does his apprenticeship last?
5. What type of training course is he doing?
6. How is his training divided between the office and vocational school?
7. Who pays for Robert's course?
8. What does Robert hope for the future?

2 Talking about your apprenticeship

You talk about your apprenticeship with your colleagues.

 Work with a partner from a different training company. Ask and answer questions about your apprenticeship. Use ideas from exercise 1 to structure your conversation.

› *Useful phrases: Describing apprenticeships, page 180*

> 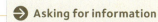 **Asking for information**
>
> **Who** do you work for?
> **What** is the name of your company?
> **Where** is the company located?
> **How many** employees does your company have?

› *Grammar: Questions and short answers, page 151*

3 Reading about the dual education system

You also read online about Germany's dual system of vocational training.

Read the text then answer the FAQs below it.

Most students in Germany complete their school education between the ages of 15 and 18. After that, some of them enter a dual training scheme at a vocational school. With this scheme, an apprentice gets job experience at work and theoretical knowledge of their profession at school.

An apprenticeship usually lasts between 24 and 36 months, depending on the profession. Apprentices spend 50 to 70 per cent of their time working in companies and the rest of the time in the classroom. Depending on the profession, an apprentice may do day release or block release.

The employer is responsible for the apprentice's training and education. They give the apprentices a special apprenticeship contract. The contract protects the apprentice from being fired during the training programme.

Gaining a vocational school qualification gives young workers good chances in their future lives. The qualification standards are the same throughout the whole of Germany, which means that the degree is recognized by every company. Even though the German qualification is not recognized in some countries, the fact that someone has trained in Germany is often enough to get them a good position abroad.

FAQs
1. I would like to work in commerce. How can a dual training scheme help me?
2. Why do some apprenticeships last longer than others?
3. How will my time be split between in-company training and vocational school?
4. My friend is doing block release and I am doing day release. Why aren't we doing the same thing?
5. Who is responsible for my training?
6. Can my employer stop my training before I've finished my apprenticeship?
7. I might have to move to a different town after I qualify. How will my qualification help me find a new employer?
8. I would like to work abroad. How will my qualification help me get a job?

4 Writing about your apprenticeship

It is time to write about your apprenticeship for the trainee information page on your company website.

Write a short description of your training. Give your name, age and say where you are from. Then structure the rest of your description as below. Write about 150 words.

- your school qualifications
- where you work
- what you are training to be
- a short explanation of the dual system
- a short description of your apprenticeship (block/day release; hours in the office / at school)

› *Thematic vocabulary: Training and apprenticeships, page 196*
› *Useful phrases: Describing apprenticeships, page 180*

PART A: Working conditions at my company

Situation: Bitz Logistics GmbH employs many people from all over the world. Your manager asks you to prepare information about the company working conditions for the international employees and apprentices.
→ You create a section for the employee handbook about the working conditions at your training company.

1 Describing ideal working conditions

Your manager first tells you to brainstorm some ideas about your ideal working conditions.

A Choose the ten most important factors from the word cloud and add ideas of your own.

hot desking   medium-sized company   subsidized travel   overtime
open-plan office   canteen   smart clothes   small company   quiet office
shift work   big company   flexitime   customer contact
business English   company smartphone   job-sharing
company car   dress code   busy office   home office

B 👥 Discuss your list with a partner. What points do you agree and disagree on? Give reasons.

C Conduct a class survey and find the five most important points. Explain why they are important to you.

> → **Agreeing and disagreeing**
> In my opinion, / I think a busy office is really important.
> – I agree with you. / Yes, I think you're right.
> – I disagree / don't agree. I think … is more important.

2 Comparing conditions

You listen to a podcast in which two people who work in logistics, Lisa and Lukas, answer interview questions about their individual working conditions.

A 🔊)) Listen to the two interviews and make notes on the following points:
- the size of the company
- current department
- working hours, breaks, overtime
- dress code
- business trips
- employees' availability outside working hours
- facilities and benefits offered by the company
- job prospects at the company

B 👥 Find an apprentice in your class from another company or department and interview each other about your working conditions. Use the list of points above.

› *Grammar: Questions and short answers, page 151*
› *Thematic vocabulary: Training and apprenticeships, page 196*

Working conditions Unit 1

3 Looking the part

Bitz Logistics GmbH has three different dress codes for its staff.

A Look at the table below and match the types of jobs to the dress code for each group of employees.

Freight transportation jobs · Office jobs · Warehousing, package handling & distribution jobs

Bitz Logistics GmbH dress codes		
Types of jobs	recommended	not allowed
1	– casual business clothing When meeting clients: – jacket & trousers (m) – suit / trouser suit (f)	– t-shirts, tank tops – jeans, shorts, capris – trainers, flip-flops
2	– jeans, work trousers, overalls – tucked-in shirt or blouse – steel toe shoes/boots – hard hat & safety vest	– loose or frayed clothing – dangling jewellery – high heels or open toe shoes

3	– jeans, work trousers,
	  shorts below the knees
	– tucked-in shirt or blouse
	– closed toe shoes/boots
		– jewellery (except small earrings,
		  wedding rings, medical alert badges)
		– ear buds, Bluetooth devices

B Describe what the people below are wearing. What type of job do you think they have at Bitz Logistics? Who is wearing inappropriate clothing for all three types of jobs?

1

2

3

4

C How similar or different are the dress codes at Bitz Logistics GmbH to ones at your training company? Have a class discussion about the importance of a dress code in the workplace.

4 Describing your working conditions

Now it is time to describe the working conditions in your training company.

Working in small groups, create a page for the employee handbook about the working conditions in your company and present it to the class. Use your answers from the interviews in exercise 2B and add ideas of your own.

PART B: Working conditions abroad

Situation: Bitz Logistics GmbH would like to become more attractive for apprentices, so your line manager asks you to research working conditions and training programmes in different countries.
→ You discuss the advantages and disadvantages of the dual system of vocational training in Germany with other apprentices.

1 Comparing working conditions

As part of your research, you attend a webinar about international working conditions. The presenter puts a diagram on the screen about how much paid free time to expect when working in different countries.

A With a partner, use the list below to guess the names of the countries. Give reasons for your answers.

Austria · Germany · Greece · Japan · UK · USA

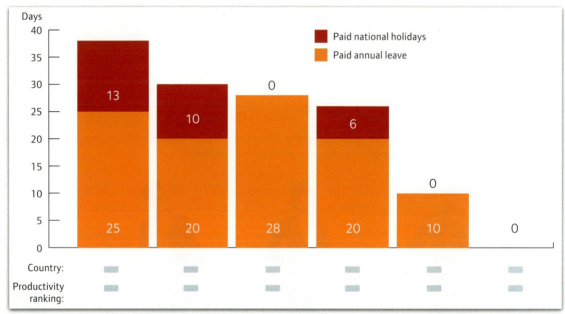

B 5))) Check your answers by listening to what the trainer says about the countries. Put them in order of productivity (1–6).

C 5))) Listen again and complete the phrases from the dialogue with the words you hear.

1 … the only country in which employers ▬ pay their employees for national holidays and annual leave.
2 … they are ▬ to last in our diagram …
3 Germany has the second ▬ number of paid days off work …
4 Which of these two ▬ pay its employees for 28 days' annual leave …?
5 Sorry, it's the UK in ▬ place followed by …
6 … Greece, which has the ▬ productivity.

D Does anything surprise you about the data? Discuss it with your partner and the class.

→ **Expressing obligation**

A German company **has to** give its employees paid annual leave. German employers **have to** pay their employees on national holidays.
An American company **doesn't have to** give its employees paid annual leave.
American employers **don't have to** pay their employees on national holidays.

› *Grammar: Modals and their substitutes, page 155*

Working conditions Unit 1

2 Describing your training

You do some research online and find profiles of two apprentices: Selina from the US and Daniel from the UK. Both are are preparing for a career in logistics.

Hi, I'm Selina Gonzales, I'm 19 and I've always wanted to work in commerce. I finished school at 18 with a high school diploma, I speak Spanish and I'm doing a two-year associate's degree course in business administration at Rockland Community College in New York State. My final grade will be based on my coursework.
In my fourth semester, I'll do an internship at a company. Studying at a two-year college from home is a lot cheaper than going to a four-year college in a different city. I live at home for free and get help from my folks with the tuition fees, too. I also have time to work part-time in a convenience store, so I won't be in debt when I graduate. With my associate's degree I can either get a good job or do a bachelor's degree. My career goal is to be a logistics and procurement manager.

I'm Daniel Chandler, I'm 19 and I left school last year with two A levels. I wanted to learn about commerce and I didn't like the idea of going to uni and getting into debt, so I'm earning money by doing a work-based intermediate apprenticeship in business administration at Southampton Freight Ltd. I have an assessor from Eastleigh College, and she regularly visits me at my workplace. She talks to my line manager and gives me homework, which I upload to my electronic portfolio. My employer pays my college fees. There's no time limit or final examination because my grades are based on my assessor's reports and my coursework. I hope to complete the apprenticeship next year and then do an advanced apprenticeship with day release at Eastleigh College. This will take me another year and improve my chances of a better job, but my long-term goal is to be a shipping administrator.

Infobox

Nach Abschluss der Sekundarstufe II (evtl. mit *high school diploma* [gleicht dem dt. Abitur]) besuchen viele nordamerikanische Schüler/innen ein *community college*. Dies ist eine zweijährige Bildungseinrichtung zur Berufsausbildung und Vorbereitung auf ein Hochschulstudium. Der dort erworbene Abschluss nennt sich *associate's degree* und kann zum Erwerb eines *bachelor's degree* (Bachelorabschluss) angerechnet werden. Letzterer wird i. d. R. nach einem vierjährigen Studium an einer Hochschule erlangt. In Nordamerika ist eine Lehre (*apprenticeship*) im europäischen Sinne fast ausschließlich in technischen Berufen möglich.

Work with a partner and use the two texts and the notes below to role-play a conversation with Selina (US) and then with Daniel (UK) in which you both talk about your training.

- introductions
- academic qualifications
- current course/job
- finance
- assessment/grades
- future plans

→ **Talking about the future**

I'll do an internship.
I **won't be** in debt.
Will you **study**?

› Grammar: Future with will and going to, page 152

3 Comparing different training systems

You discover that the vocational training systems in industrialized countries vary greatly.

A Take a few minutes to list the pros and cons of the German dual system. Think about:
- how you get theoretical/practical training
- your experience at your company/college
- vocational training in other countries (e.g. UK, USA or a country you know about)

B Make a list of pros and cons on the board and have a discussion about the dual system.

COMMUNICATION: Introductions and small talk

Situation: You are working in the sales department at Bitz Logistics GmbH.
→ **You look after a visitor from England until your supervisor, Ms Müller, is ready to meet him.**

1 Introducing yourself and others to colleagues

The Human Resources department at Bitz Logistics stores information about its employees on computerized personnel files.

A 6))) Listen to the people introducing themselves. Copy and complete the entries in your notebook.

Name: Martyna Nowak
Age: ▬¹
Place of birth: Poland
Job description: ▬²

Name: Halil Özdemir
Age: ▬³
Place of birth: ▬⁴
Job description: training supervisor

Name: Deema Mansour
Age: ▬⁵
Place of birth: Syria
Job description: ▬⁶

Name: Robert Klein
Age: 21
Place of birth: ▬⁷
Job description: ▬⁸

Name: Canan Tolon
Age: ▬⁹
Place of birth: Turkey
Job description: ▬¹⁰

Name: Alexei Melnyk
Age: 29
Place of birth: ▬¹¹
Job description: ▬¹²

B You have three minutes to introduce yourself to the other people in the class.

> **Introducing yourself**
>
> I'm Sophie. I'm **from** Bremen. (NOT: I'm ~~coming~~ from Bremen.)
> I work **at** ABC Logistics. (NOT: I work ~~by~~ ABC Logistics.)
> I'm **an** office manager. / I'm **a** management assistant.
> (NOT: ~~My job is ...~~)

C Introduce one of the people you met to the rest of the class.

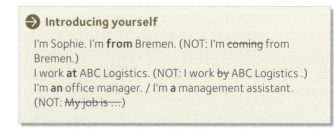

> *Useful phrases: Making introductions page 180*

Working conditions Unit 1

2 Making formal introductions

A Work with a partner. Introduce yourself in a formal way to your partner (a visitor).

B Now formally introduce your partner to another pair. › *Useful phrases: Making introductions, page 180*

3 Making small talk

A In groups, choose suitable topics for small talk in business. Say which topics you should avoid.

holidays   your city/town   religion   the journey to the meeting place

illnesses   sport   politics   the weather   pay   where someone works

B Match the questions (1–5) to the possible responses (a–e).

1 Is this your first time in Berlin?
2 How is your hotel?
3 It's lovely weather, isn't it?
4 How was your journey?
5 Where are you based?

a Yes. It's fantastic. We've been very lucky this year.
b Very nice. I travelled by train this time.
c Yes. I've heard that it's a very interesting city.
d Fine. I have a good view from the window in my room.
e In Scotland. In Edinburgh, in fact.

4 Meeting and greeting the visitor

Now it is time to meet the visitor. You know that the person Ms Müller is expecting is called Mr Brown.

A Work in groups of three. Complete the dialogue. Then close your books and practise the dialogue.

You	*Excuse*¹ me. *Are you*² Mr Brown?
Visitor	Yes, I am.
You	I'm (*own name*). ▬³ do you do? ▬⁴ to Bitz Logistics.
Visitor	Thank you. It's ▬⁵.
You	I'm afraid Ms Müller has been held up, but she'll be here in a few minutes. ▬⁶ your coat?
Visitor	Yes, thank you. Here you are.
You	▬⁷ you like something to drink?
Visitor	Yes, please. I'd like a cup of coffee with milk and sugar.
You	Here you are. Is this your ▬⁸ in Germany?
Visitor	No. I've been here before, but only on holiday.
You	Oh. Here's Ms Müller now. Mr Brown, ▬⁹ Ms Müller.
Ms Müller	▬¹⁰ morning, Mr Brown. Sorry to keep you waiting.
Visitor	No problem. Your assistant has been looking after me very well.

> **Offering help/refreshments**
> Can I take your coat?
> Would you like something to drink?
> Would you like some tea or coffee?

› *Useful phrases: Showing visitors around the company, page 182*

B Write your own dialogue and practise it in your group.

DAS KANN ICH (Unit 1)

– Eine kurze Beschreibung meiner dualen Ausbildung auf Englisch erstellen. (Foundation)
– Informationsmaterial über die Arbeitsbedingungen im Ausbildungsbetrieb gestalten. (Part A)
– Die Vor- und Nachteile des dualen Ausbildungssystems auf Englisch diskutieren. (Part B)
– Englischsprachige Besucher/innen empfangen und jemandem vorstellen. (Communication)

2 My workplace

FOUNDATION: In the office

Situation: You work in the Administration Department of a large logistics company. As your department is moving to new offices next week, your line manager asks you to make an inventory of the office equipment before you move.
→ You make an inventory of the equipment in your office.

1 Thinking about office activities

Before you start your inventory, you think about some of the things you have to do in the office.

A Study the photos (1–6). What are the people doing?

B What equipment do you work with regularly?
What do you (not) enjoy doing?

I use the computer every day. I have to key in data. I enjoy doing that.

> **Talking about likes and dislikes**
>
> I **like making** / **to make** photocopies.
> I **prefer working** / **to work** at the computer.
> I **enjoy meeting** customers. (NOT: I enjoy to meet …)
> I don't **enjoy writing** emails. (NOT: I don't enjoy to write …)

› *Grammar: Verb + infinitive or -ing form, page 153*

My workplace Unit 2

2 Comparing types of offices

On your way to work, you listen to a podcast from Alisha Warner, an office consultant.

> Today, I'd like to compare two very different types of offices: the small office and the open-plan office.

A 7)) Listen and answer the questions.

1. What is the main purpose of an office environment?
2. What is the benefit of working in a small office?
3. How are the work spaces divided in a lot of open-plan administration offices?
4. Why do some employees dislike this kind of office?
5. What are the two advantages of working at a shared table?
6. What are the pros and cons of hot-desking?
7. According to Alisha, why should employees always feel happy and comfortable at their place of work?

VIDEO 1

Watch the video for more information about different types of office.

B What type of office do you prefer to work in? Explain your reasons, using words from the list if necessary.

concentrate on work • quiet • light and airy • loud/noisy • spacious

3 Identifying equipment for meetings

The equipment in the current meeting room has to be handled with care during the move. Your line manager has taken photos so he can check that the equipment is in order when it arrives at the new premises.

A Study the photos and decide what the things are.

1 2 3 4 5 6

B What equipment is in the meeting room at your place of work?

4 Writing an inventory of your office equipment

Now it is time to write an inventory of your office equipment.

👥 Work in a small group. Sit around a table with a large sheet of paper. Write "Inventory of office equipment" in the middle as a title.

Step 1   List the types of equipment you have in your office and meeting room on your corner of the sheet.
Step 2   Discuss your list with the rest of your group. Make a tally list.
Step 3   Use your tally list to write an inventory of the equipment to be taken to the new office premises.
Step 4   Show your inventory to the class.

Computers |||| ||

PART A: An organization chart

Situation: You work for Birkan Logistics GmbH, a logistics company in Essen. You are expecting some English-speaking visitors to the company, so you study the organization chart.
→ You draw an organization chart of your training company.

1 Understanding an organization chart

The chart shows the management and the heads of the departments and sub-departments at Birkan.

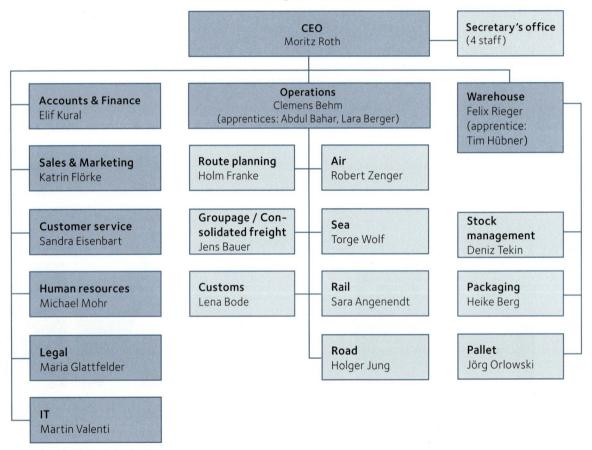

A Find a department or sub-department in the chart for each of the descriptions below.

1. We send invoices to clients and keep track of all the bookkeeping.
2. We take care of storing the goods until they are ready to ship.
3. We arrange local transport in lorries.
4. We deal with customer orders and complaints.
5. We choose the best way to deliver the goods.
6. We're responsible for employing and training people.

My workplace **Unit 2**

B Decide whether the following statements about the organization chart are true or false. Correct the false statements.

1. Moritz Roth is in charge of the company.
2. Felix Rieger coordinates everything involved in shipping goods for customers.
3. Sara Angenendt deals with the consignments that are shipped by aeroplane.
4. Lena Bode organizes paperwork for importing and exporting goods.
5. Jörg Orlowski is in charge of advertising.
6. Martin Valenti is responsible for computer hardware and software.

C Who reports to whom? Use the organization chart to complete the statements.

The Air, Sea, Rail and Road teams all report to ▬¹, who is in charge of ▬². All the heads of department report to one person: the ▬³ of the company. The apprentices all report to Michael ▬⁴. He's the Head of ▬⁵ and is responsible for training. They also report to the heads of the departments and sub-departments. Operations has ▬⁶ sub-departments and the ▬⁷ has three.

2 Talking about your company

Four Birkan Logistics employees are talking about their jobs.

A 8))) Use the information you hear and the organization chart to find out their names, positions and tasks.

B 8))) Listen again and complete the sentences with the words you hear.

1. The people in my department are ▬ for the smooth delivery of goods.
2. Our responsibilities ▬ choosing the appropriate form of transport.
3. My job also ▬ going to trade fairs.
4. I'm in ▬ of planning and supervising the budget.
5. This ▬ analysing sales figures and profit margins.
6. I really ▬ doing my job.
7. My work ▬ understanding how goods are transported.

C Use your answers to exercise 2B to complete the following description.

> I'm in the customer service department and I ▬¹ working there because my work is different every day. My work basically ▬² helping customers who transport their goods with us and often ▬³ speaking English. My boss is ▬⁴ for running the whole department, but I'm in ▬⁵ of all our clients in Scandinavia.

3 Creating your company's organization chart

Now it is time to create an organization chart for your training company.

👥 Work in small groups and draw an organization chart of your company, either as a poster or with suitable software, and present it to the class. Explain who you and the other apprentices in your company report to.

› *Thematic vocabulary: Job titles, page 196; Company departments, page 196*

> **→ Describing your company**
>
> The management is responsible for **running** the company.
> I'm in charge of **arranging** shipments.
> My work includes/involves/entails **speaking** English.

› *Grammar: Gerunds, page 154*

17

PART B: Job profiles

Situation: You work for Walz Forwarders GmbH in Igelsberg. Emma Murphy, an Irish work experience student, asks you for help to learn about the different departments and jobs.
→ You create profiles of departments and jobs at your training company.

1 Describing departments

Emma has to write job profiles for the apprentice file. She first visits eight of the company's departments and makes notes on them.

A Match four of the department names below to the photos.

Accounts & Finance · Customer Service · Human Resources (HR) ·
IT · Legal · Operations · Sales & Marketing · Warehouse

B Translate Emma's notes about six of the departments she visits into German.

1. determine salaries and benefits
2. keep track of items until ready to ship
3. handle documentation
4. deal with complaints and special requests
5. do market research and write reports
6. answer enquiries and make offers
7. acquire new clients through campaigns
8. consolidate different shipments
9. handle all payments and receipts
10. recruit, train and promote staff
11. produce financial reports
12. put consignments on pallets

C Match her notes (1–12) with six of the departments from the list in exercise 1A above.

D 👥 With a partner, discuss the work of the remaining two departments and write a description of what they do. Compare your ideas with those of other pairs. Do you agree?

› *Thematic vocabulary: Job titles, page 196; Company departments, page 196*
› *Useful phrases: Describing jobs and responsibilities, page 180*

My workplace   Unit 2

2 Describing jobs

Emma now interviews some employees and writes down what they say about their jobs.

A 🔊 Guess the missing words in the extracts from six of Emma's interviews, then listen to the recording and check your answers. Which departments do the employees work in?

1. My job ▭ keeping track of financial data and preparing the budget.
2. I'm basically ▭ for finding the best person for the job.
3. I'm in ▭ of everything that goes on in the warehouse.
4. Working in my department ▭ understanding customs regulations.
5. It's my ▭ to make sure that we find new markets and acquire new clients.
6. We ▭ the whole customer service process from beginning to end.

B 🔊 Listen again, write down more facts about the work of the six departments, then expand your notes into whole sentences. Compare them with your neighbour's. Have you missed anything?

C Study the customer service representative's description of her job and use some of the words to complete what the accounting manager says. Make any necessary changes.

Customer service representative

It's my responsibility to make sure our customers get good service. This means paying attention to what our clients want and doing everything I can to meet their needs. Last month, I was in charge of a large project involving a Norwegian customer who needed to begin transporting perishables. I was responsible for the German side. The project involved working closely with the operations department here. I personally oversaw the planning of the schedule and coordinated everything with the client.

Accounting manager

I'm in ▭¹ of the whole accounting department, so I'm personally ▭² for everything that happens there. I ▭³ its daily operations, and my work often ▭⁴ working closely with project managers. I also have overall ▭⁵ for ▭⁶ deadlines for financial reports, which ▭⁷ getting the data ready in good time and ▭⁸ the manpower needed to do the job.

3 Creating a job profile

Now it's your turn to describe your department and the work you do there.

A 👥 Working in small groups, make notes on your department's work and responsibilities, e.g. as a mind map or flow chart, and then write a short text about it, but without naming the department.

B Put the texts on the blackboard/walls of your classroom and read what they say. Guess which department each text describes.

› *Thematic vocabulary: Job titles, page 196; Company departments, page 196*

› *Useful phrases: Describing jobs and responsibilities, page 180*

> **→ Describing how often something happens**
>
> I **often** go to trade fairs.
> My department **sometimes** organizes training courses.
> I'm almost **always** in the warehouse.

› *Grammar: Adverbs of frequency, page 155*

19

COMMUNICATION: Telephoning

> **Situation:** You are doing a work placement at the UK subsidiary of Hamm Trucking GmbH.
> → You call a customer and leave a message.

1 Leaving a voicemail message

Your line manager, Niklas Hartmann, has left you a note asking you to call a customer, Mr Dalton at Esher Engineering, or to leave him a message if he isn't in the office.

A First read the telephone phrases (a–i) and put them in the right order for a phone call or voicemail message.

a Could you ask … (*name*) to call me back / call … ?
b Good morning/afternoon.
c I'd like to speak to / leave a message for … (*name*).
d I'm calling on behalf of … (*name*).
e It's about the …
f My/His/Her number is …
g Thank you. Goodbye.
h The details are as follows: …
i This is … (*name*) from Hamm Trucking UK Ltd.

- Phone Esher Engineering to confirm the delivery of their generators.
- Say that you're calling on my behalf.
- Ask to speak to Roger Dalton. He's the factory manager.
- Tell him that the lorry will be at the factory at 8.30 on Tuesday, 7 June.
- If you only get voicemail, ask Mr Dalton to call me back to confirm the date and time.
- Give him my mobile number (0044 7700 900154). Thanks.

B Work with a partner. Use the phrases (a–i) and the notes above to leave a voicemail message for Mr Dalton. Record your message on your smartphone and play it back to your partner.

2 Understanding voicemail

Mr Dalton was out when you called yesterday and this morning, when you come into the office, you find he has left a message. You pass it on to your line manager, but make three mistakes.

10)) Listen to the recording and find the mistakes in your version of Mr Dalton's message.

While you were out

Caller: Mr Roger Dalton, Esher Engineering

Mr Dalton says that they can't take delivery of the generators on Tuesday, 7 June, but it would work on Wednesday, 8 June, from 7–12 or on Friday, 10 June after 1 o'clock. Please call his secretary on 0044 1632 964022 to confirm one of the dates.

3 Taking phone calls

Before phoning some clients, you check that you know some frequently used telephone expressions.

A Work with a partner and decide how you would say the German phrases (a–j) in English.

a Bleiben Sie bitte dran.
b Der Anschluss ist besetzt.
c Ich stelle Sie durch.
d Das habe ich nicht verstanden. Könnten Sie es bitte wiederholen?
e Buchstabieren Sie bitte Ihren Namen.
f Möchten Sie mit jemand anderem sprechen?
g Ich versuche, Sie zu verbinden.
h Möchten Sie eine Nachricht hinterlassen?
i … (Name) ist im Moment nicht da.
j Wie ist Ihr Name bitte?

B **11))** Listen to Niklas Hartmann's phone call to Esher Engineering and check your answers.

C What extra elements are in the English phrases that are missing in the German?

My workplace   Unit 2

4 Making a phone call

You are back in Germany now and your line manager asks you to phone an English-speaking client.

A   Work with a partner and use the instructions to make a phone call in English.

> **Giving telephone numbers**
> Say each digit separately, except for double digits, e.g. 01233455 = "oh (or zero) one two double-three four double-five".

Partner A: Ferdinand/Megan Pretorius Bloemfontein Steel Ltd, South Africa

Nehmen Sie das Telefongespräch auf Englisch entgegen (Begrüßung, Firmenname, Ihr Name).

Der Anschluss von Herrn Botha ist besetzt. Fragen Sie, ob der/die Anrufer/in jemand anders sprechen möchte.

Sie versuchen, den/die Anrufer/in mit Frau Smit zu verbinden und erklären, dass diese im Moment nicht erreichbar ist. Fragen Sie, ob der/die Anrufer/in eine Nachricht hinterlassen möchte.

Bitten Sie den/die Anrufer/in, seinen/ihren Namen zu buchstabieren.

Fragen Sie nach der Handynummer.

Notieren Sie die Nummer und machen Sie beim Wiederholen einen Fehler.

Schließen Sie das Gespräch höflich ab.

Partner B: You (own name) Hamm Trucking GmbH, Germany

Stellen Sie sich vor und sagen Sie, dass Sie mit Herrn Botha sprechen möchten.

Äußern Sie die Bitte, mit Hannah Smit verbunden zu werden.

Ja, Herr Botha soll Sie auf Ihrem Handy anrufen. Es ist wichtig.

Buchstabieren Sie Ihren Vor- und Nachnamen.

Geben Sie Ihre Handynummer mit Ländervorwahl (+49 …) an.

Korrigieren Sie den Fehler.

Schließen Sie das Gespräch höflich ab.

B   Now improvise a typical telephone dialogue with an English-speaking client who calls the company where you are doing your apprenticeship and wishes to speak to somebody who is not available. Include a message, a telephone number and a name to be spelt.

› *Useful phrases: Telephoning, page 181; Taking telephone calls, page 181*

DAS KANN ICH (Unit 2)
- Eine Bestandsliste der Büroausstattung auf Englisch erstellen. (Foundation)
- Die Struktur meines Ausbildungsbetriebes auf Englisch beschreiben. (Part A)
- Meine Arbeit und meine Abteilung auf Englisch beschreiben. (Part B)
- Eine/n englischsprachige/n Kunden/Kundin anrufen; eine Nachricht hinterlassen. (Communication)

KMK Exam practice 1

1 Produktion: Stufe II (B1)

Situation: Da Ihre Firma sehr stark international agiert und auch viele Zweigstellen im Ausland hat, sind auch Bewerbungen von englischsprachigen Praktikanten/Praktikantinnen und Arbeitnehmern/ Arbeitnehmerinnen sehr erwünscht. Für eine neue internationale Ausbildungs- und Praktikantenmesse plant die Firma einen Messestand und englischsprachiges Infomaterial. Sie werden gebeten, aus Sicht eines Azubis Ihrer Firma wichtige Aspekte in einem Text zusammenzufassen.

Aufgabe: Schreiben Sie einen Bericht, der folgende Punkte beinhaltet:

- kurze Vorstellung der Firma mit wesentlichen Fakten (Standort[e], Produkte/Dienstleistungen, Mitarbeiter/innen, Abteilungen)
- typische Tätigkeiten in der Ausbildung
- Arbeitsbedingungen (Arbeitszeiten, Urlaub, Möglichkeiten der Fortbildung, Verdienstmöglichkeiten, besondere Angebote der Firma)

2 Hörverstehen: Stufe I (A2)

Situation: One of your tasks every morning is to listen to the voicemail messages customers have left on your department's answering machine.

12))) Task: Listen to the telephone messages and write memos for your colleagues including the information on the right.

> - date and time of call
> - who the message is for
> - who the message is from, including the company
> - message for colleague
> - caller's contact details

3 Interaktion: Stufe II (B1)

👥 Work with a partner. **Partner A:** Look here. **Partner B:** Look at File 1 on page 130.

Situation: Sie arbeiten für die Hansen International Spedition GmbH. Ihre Firma bietet ein zuverlässiges Gesamtpaket an Lösungen für Spedition, Transport und Logistik und sorgt für die weltweite Lieferung von Gütern. Sie befinden sich in der Ausbildung und wurden von Ihrem Chef gebeten, einen englischen Praktikanten / eine englische Praktikantin zu begrüßen, der/die für drei Monate in Ihrer Firma arbeiten und Sie in den ersten beiden Wochen im Vertrieb begleiten wird.

Aufgabe: Gestalten Sie in Partnerarbeit einen Dialog auf Englisch mithilfe der folgenden Punkte:

- Begrüßen Sie Ihr Gegenüber und sorgen Sie dafür, dass Ihr Gegenüber sich willkommen fühlt.
- Fragen Sie nach ihrer/seiner Anreise. Betreiben Sie etwas Small Talk.
- Geben Sie Auskunft über Arbeitsabläufe (typische Tätigkeiten, Arbeitszeiten, Pausen usw.) im Vertrieb und über alles, was Ihr/e Gesprächspartner/in wissen möchte. Sie interessieren sich auch für die Firma des Praktikanten / der Praktikantin und seine/ihre dortigen Aufgaben.
- Geben Sie Auskunft über das deutsche Ausbildungssystem.
- Geben Sie Tipps zur Freizeitgestaltung (z. B. Sport, Kultur) und wie der Praktikant / die Praktikantin am besten sein/ihr Deutsch verbessern kann.

4 Mediation: Stufe II (B1)

Situation: Ein wesentlicher Teil Ihrer Arbeit in Ihrer Firma ist es, mit Kunden am Telefon zu kommunizieren und z. B. Termine zu vereinbaren. Daher gibt es in Ihrer Firma Regeln, die man beim Telefonieren beachten sollte.

Aufgabe: Für einen englischen Praktikanten aus Liverpool stellen Sie aus folgendem deutschen Leitfaden eine verkürzte Checkliste auf English zusammen.

Wichtige Regeln bei der Annahme von Telefonanrufen

Identifizieren Sie sich angemessen
Wenn Sie einen Kunden anrufen – egal ob persönlich oder bei einer Nachricht auf dem Anrufbeantworter – melden Sie sich immer mit komplettem Namen und Firmennamen. Darüber hinaus verwenden Sie eine angemessene Begrüßung wie „Guten Morgen" oder „Guten Tag" und vermeiden Sie ein einfaches „Hallo". Dies ist viel professioneller und macht einen besseren Eindruck.

Seien Sie höflich
Vergessen Sie nicht, höfliche Redewendungen wie „danke" und „bitte" zu verwenden und vermeiden Sie Umgangssprache. Das wirkt unprofessionell und unhöflich.

Hören Sie genau zu
Es ist sehr wichtig, dass Sie aufmerksam sind und genau hinhören, was der Anrufer möchte oder worin sein Problem besteht. Es ist ein Unterschied, ob der Kunde ein Prospekt anfordert oder über einen Vorgang verärgert ist. Reagieren Sie angemessen und immer freundlich und bieten Sie Unterstützung an.

Machen Sie sich Notizen
Je nachdem, was in Ihrer Firma üblich ist, machen Sie sich Notizen auf einer dafür vorgesehenen Telefonnotiz oder einem Notizblock. Fragen Sie bei Unklarheiten nach und lassen Sie sich wichtige Begriffe oder Namen buchstabieren, wenn sie aufgrund des Akzentes oder einer schlechten Verbindung nicht gut zu verstehen sind.

„Begleiten" Sie den Anrufer
Je nachdem, was der Anrufer möchte, muss das Gespräch manchmal weiterverbunden werden oder Sie müssen parallel zum Gespräch etwas abklären. Nicht alles kann direkt geklärt und gelöst werden. Verbinden Sie den Anrufer aber nicht einfach weiter und hoffen, dass damit alles erledigt ist, sondern stellen Sie sicher, dass der Anruf zu einem Ergebnis führt.

Bieten Sie Lösungen oder Alternativen an
Wenn eine unmittelbare Lösung des Anliegens oder Problems des Kunden nicht am Telefon erfolgen kann, z. B. weil die gewünschte Person nicht da ist, sorgen Sie dafür, dass der Kunde trotzdem zufrieden auflegt. Kümmern Sie sich darum, dass der Kunde zurückgerufen wird, wenn dies gewünscht und vereinbart wurde, oder sorgen Sie dafür, dass das Anliegen anderweitig erledigt wird.

3 My company

FOUNDATION: Types of companies

Situation: The company where you are doing your apprenticeship now has many international business partners, so it decides to add more information in English to its website.
→ You create a timeline of your company for its English website.

1 Analysing a timeline

You surf the internet and find an article about MAW Logistics plc (SE), a British logistics company.

Read the text and complete the timeline (1–8) opposite.

At the beginning of 2019, Malcolm Williamson, the founder of MAW Logistics plc (SE), was worth £1 million and owned over 2,500 lorries. His road to success hadn't always been an easy one, but he had never given up and had taken every opportunity that he had been given.

Malcom's story began when he bought his first lorry (second-hand) from a local garage in 1965. He wasn't really sure what lay ahead, but he saw the lorry and decided to buy it. He got it for a good price, as the local transport company had run into financial problems and had just gone out of business. In the town of Watchet, where Malcolm lived, there was a big papermill. He offered his services and quickly signed a contract for collecting the bales of wastepaper from the mill and delivering them to the mill's partner in Cheltenham.

One year later, in 1966, Malcolm bought two more lorries and had all three lorries painted in his favourite colours: green and yellow. He also very proudly had the name of his company – MAW Transport – painted on their doors.

In 1968 another new delivery contract meant that the company could expand, and in April 1979 MAW Transport became a private limited company when Malcolm's sons, Joseph and James, joined the company. By 1987 the family had turned MAW Transport Ltd into a medium-sized haulage company with 32 green and yellow lorries.

The company was approached in 2002 by Stigs Transport of Wolverhampton. Stigs Transport were struggling at the time, due to the fuel crisis which had hit their profits, and were looking for a company in the southwest to merge with. The two companies quickly came to an agreement, and the merger was complete. The new, bigger company, now called MAW Transport Ltd, quickly took over the service of the supply chain of a major British supermarket with branches all over the UK. They had so much business that they soon opened their first warehouse in the north of England.

In 2010, MAW Logistics plc (SE) became a public limited company, which sells its shares on the stock market. Now a large multimodal logistics company, it deals with road haulage, rail freight, deep sea and inland waterway transport systems, and has warehousing facilities in the UK, Ireland and the Netherlands.

The company has also diversified slightly in recent years and has two new subsidiaries. Super-fast Transport, which is a special overnight parcel delivery company guaranteeing next day delivery, joined MAW Logistics in 2014. The second subsidiary was founded a year later: Transport Workers Ltd, which is an agency for transport and logistics personnel. Both companies are the perfect addition, and with Transport Workers Ltd, the company no longer has any problems finding staff!

My company   Unit 3

MAW Logistics timeline

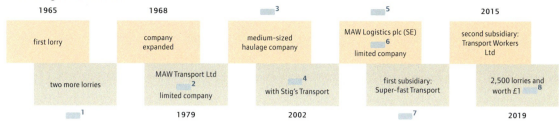

2 Describing your company

You research the different types of company that are mentioned in the text and find these explanations.

Three ways to do business		
UK: Private limited company (Ltd)* **US: Limited liability company (LLC)**	**UK: Public limited company (plc)** **US: Corporation (Corp/Inc)**	**SE Societas Europaea** **(public European company)**
– The company belongs to a closed circle of members. – The members decide what is best for the company. – The members share the profits and can only lose the money they have invested. * In South Africa, Australia and New Zealand: Proprietary limited company (Pty Ltd)	– The company belongs to the shareholders (members of the public). – The directors decide what is best for the company and the shareholders. – The shareholders share the profits and can only lose the money they paid for the shares.	– Type of public limited company that is regulated under EU laws. – Can operate on a European-wide basis. – Can more easily merge with companies in other EU states.

Study the explanations of the three different ways to do business and complete the sentences with the correct information.

1 An SE is regulated under ▇.
2 A private limited company is owned by ▇.
3 An SE can ▇ companies in EU states.
4 A shareholder in a plc gets ▇ of the profit.
5 Members of the public can buy shares in ▇.
6 Bankruptcy is a serious risk for ▇.

> ➜ **Describing types of company**
>
> A public limited company belongs to the shareholders, **who** share the profits. Shareholders can only lose the money **that/which** they paid for the shares if the company goes bankrupt.

› *Grammar: Relative clauses, page 153*

3 Creating a timeline

Your line manager asks you to prepare a timeline for your company's English website.

A   Work in small groups, if possible with people from the same company. Search your company's website for data and visual elements. Find out who bears the risk at your company and include this in your timeline. (If your company is not suitable, choose another local company.)

B   When you have collected enough material, sketch out your timeline on a large sheet of paper. Add suitable images and graphics to make it visually appealing.

C   Complete your timeline and hang it on the wall. Do a gallery walk and give each other points for design, clarity and information. Choose the timeline that gets its message across best.

› *Thematic vocabulary: Company organization, page 196*

PART A: Showing visitors around

Situation: You are getting some work experience at JHP Logistics GmbH, a medium-sized logistics company in Stuttgart that delivers goods for different companies all over the world.
→ You take English-speaking visitors on a guided tour of your training company.

1 Preparing for visitors

As JHP Logistics GmbH often has visitors from abroad, your line manager asks you to prepare an English version of the layout of the company.

Study the diagram and use the words in the box to complete the labelling.

accounting · delivery (in) · distribution (out) · distribution centre · finance · human resources · managing director · pricing · production · project management · quality assurance · sales · showroom · warehouse

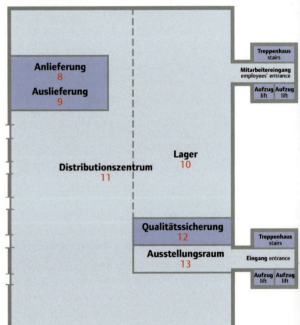

2 Following a tour around a company

To make sure you know suitable English phrases for giving a guided tour, you join two tours around JHP for visitors from abroad.

A 13))) Listen to the two tours and write down the following information:

- who the visitor(s) is (are)
- the starting point of the tour
- the departments visited
- the finishing point

Infobox

British English	American English	
lift	elevator	*Aufzug*
second floor	third floor	2. OG
first floor	second floor	1. OG
ground floor	first floor	*Erdgeschoss*

26

My company Unit 3

B 13)) Read the extracts from the first tour below and guess the missing words. Then listen to the recording again to check your answers.

1 We are ▭ to welcome you to our company.
2 We very much hope you ▭ your stay here.
3 Are there any ▭ before we begin?
4 In that case, we'll ▭ here in the conference room.
5 I'll now ▭ you downstairs to our distribution centre.
6 The gentleman ▭ the left of the window is Mr Nagel.
7 Our next ▭ are the import and export departments.
8 Let's just take the ▭ over here.
9 Let's take a left at the end of the ▭ .
10 Well, that ▭ our tour.

> **Giving directions**
>
> to the left/right of …
> between (the) … and (the) …
> next to (the) …
> opposite (the) …
> upstairs/downstairs
> to take the lift/elevator/
> escalator/stairs to the … floor

C With a partner, practise taking (a) visitor(s) on two or three tours of JHP's offices and distribution centre. Include the following points in your tour:

– choose a starting point, two departments on each floor and a finishing point
– greet the visitor(s) politely
– introduce yourself (full name and position)
– offer to answer questions
– add your own ideas
– finish the tour politely

VIDEO 2
Watch the video to see another company tour.

Begin like this: *Good morning and welcome to … . My name is … . I'm … .*
If you have any questions … .

3 Writing a website post

The Managing Director asks you to write a short article about the Indian delegation's visit to JHP for the company website.

13)) Listen to the first tour again and write a short text including the following information:

Indian company: PABE Transport and Logistics, Mumbai
Representatives: Managing director Tarik Patel and three colleagues
Details of visit: Important business partner in Europe / presentation / tour of company (names of German colleagues and their departments) information about distribution centre / tour of Stuttgart

> **Talking about the past**
>
> A delegation from India **visited** our company last week.
> First of all, we **took** them on a tour of our offices.

> *Grammar: Simple past, page 151*

Begin like this: *Last week we were delighted to welcome a delegation from …*

4 Taking visitors on a tour of your company

Now it's time for you to take some English-speaking visitors on a tour of your own training company.

A Work in small groups from the same training company. Prepare a plan of your company and label the departments in English.

B Find people in your class from another company and use your plan to show them around. Make sure you cover the same points in your tour as in exercise 2C.

> *Useful phrases: Showing visitors around the company, page 182*
> *Thematic vocabulary: Company departments, page 196*

27

PART B: A company profile

Situation: You are getting some work experience at JHP Logistics, a logistics company in Stuttgart. A delegation from India is visiting the company.
→ You give a presentation in English about your company to visitors from abroad.

1 Preparing presentation slides

The head of the distribution centre asks you to find suitable slides to use in a presentation for the visitors.

A You create six slides (A–F). Match them with the headings in the list below.

areas of the distribution centre • company data • distribution centre •
final slide • high-rise warehouse • world market

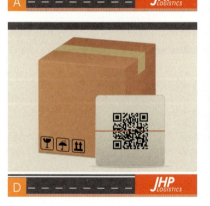

B With a partner, decide in what order the slides should be shown.

C 🔊 14 Listen and write down the order in which the head of the distribution centre describes the slides. Is it the same?

> **→ Describing repeated actions**
>
> We **store** many thousands of pallets of goods.
> We **label** all the packages with a QR code.

› *Grammar: Simple present, page 151*

My company Unit 3

2 Writing a handout

Each visitor from abroad will receive a handout including a profile of JHP Logistics.

A 14))) Listen again and make notes on the company and its distribution centre under the following headings:

- name, location, company statistics
- warehouse
- areas in the distribution centre

B Use your notes to write a profile of the company to add to the handout for the visitors.

> Useful phrases: Describing companies, page 182

> **VIDEO 3**
>
> Watch the video to see another company presentation.

3 Structuring a presentation

Before you write your presentation about your own company, you think about some of the phrases you can use to guide the audience.

Group the expressions that Daniel Nagel uses in his presentation under the headings below.

Welcoming the audience	Introducing your topic	Structuring your presentation	Moving to the next point	Describing visuals	Dealing with questions	Conclusion
Good morning, …						

- … and will then move on to …
- As you can see from this slide, …
- Good morning, ladies and gentlemen and welcome to …
- I'd like to begin by giving you a presentation about …
- I'll be happy to answer any questions you may have.
- I'll start with …
- I work in the … department.
- Many thanks for listening.
- My name is …
- Now if you'd like to ask any questions, I'd be delighted to answer them.
- That was a brief overview of …
- The next thing I'd like to show you are …
- Then at the end …
- This next slide shows …

4 Preparing a presentation

Now it is time to prepare a short presentation about your own training company.

👥 Work with a partner and prepare a presentation about your training company. You can use the following presentation aids:

- a (large colourful, illustrated) poster
- slides or transparencies (maximum of 8 slides)
- some of the company's products
- your own idea(s)

Follow the steps in Communication (pages 30–31) to help you.

> Useful phrases: Giving presentations, page 182; Thematic vocabulary: Company organization, page 196

29

COMMUNICATION: A short presentation

> **Situation:** Some trainees from the UK are soon going to start work at your company.
> → You give a short presentation to the new trainees about your work.

1 Thinking about the contents of a presentation

Your line manager gives you a list of points you should include in your talk.

what the company does • your department • what you do

A Work with a partner. Read the list and decide together what you would like to add to your line manager's list above. Make notes.

B Compare your notes with another pair and decide on the final points you will cover. Make a mind map.

C Agree on the order you will present the contents. Make a numbered list. Write the name and date of your talk at the top of the list.

> Presentation to new trainees: 08.07.20..
> 1 Introduction (self/the company)
> 2
> 3

2 Writing the presentation

A Use your mind map and the list from exercise 1 to write your text. Follow this structure.

Introduction	– Say in a few words what you are going to talk about.
Main part	– Use one paragraph for each topic. – Use signposts to move from one subject to the next.
Conclusion	– Summarize the main ideas. – Invite questions from the audience.

B Check the text together for clarity and correctness as follows:
– Is the information in the text correct? If not, correct it.
– Is the spelling and grammar correct? Use your dictionary and the list of phrases on page 29.

3 Making a prompt card

A presentation comes across best when the presenter looks at the audience and speaks naturally. As it is difficult to do either of these things when you read from a text, you should make yourself a prompt card.

A Follow the steps below.

– Highlight important words and phrases in your text.
– Copy the words and phrases onto an index card.
– Include signposts to structure the ideas.

> - logistics company
> - warehouse
> - apprentice ...

B Practise your presentation in your group, using only your prompt card.

My company Unit 3

4 Giving a presentation

Your presentation will be a success if you study the tips below.

Divide the tips into *Before/During/After the presentation*.

Tips for a great presentation
A   Always face your audience!
B   Decide what visual aids are best for your topic (objects, transparencies, posters, etc.)
C   Decide when it is best to give out handouts (before, during or after the presentation).
D   Do not overload transparencies or slides with information.
E   Do not speak for too long before handing over to your partner.
F   Find out about any cultural differences (e.g. attire, gestures and body language).
G   Give your contact details (e.g. email, website, business card) if appropriate.
H   Make eye contact and do not turn your back on the audience to point to the screen.
I   Offer to answer any questions the audience may have.
J   Practise with a partner before giving the presentation to your audience.
K   Prepare hand-held prompt cards with key words.
L   Speak slowly and freely only using your prompt cards.
M   Start by explaining what the presentation is about.
N   Welcome the audience and introduce yourself/yourselves.

5 Giving your presentation

It is time to give your presentation and to give each other feedback.

A   Decide who is going to speak first in your group. When it is your turn, stand up, look directly at the audience and smile. Then speak freely and clearly using your prompt card. Ask for questions at the end.

B   Give each other feedback using this feedback sheet. Give points from 1 to 3.
(1 point = needs improvement,
2 points = good,
3 points = very good)

› *Useful phrases: Giving presentations, page 182*

Presentation feedback		Points
Content	you covered all the necessary points	
	you used examples to support your points	
Structure	your talk was easy to follow	
	you used useful phrases to structure your talk	
	you summarized the main ideas in your conclusion	
Presentation	you smiled and looked friendly	
	you spoke clearly and freely	
	you looked at the audience when you spoke	
Dealing with questions	you dealt with questions in a friendly manner	
	you answered all the questions clearly	
Overall score for the presentation		/30

DAS KANN ICH (Unit 3)
– Einen informativen Zeitstrahl über meine Firma auf Englisch erstellen. (Foundation)
– Englischsprachige Besucher/innen durch meinen Ausbildungsbetrieb führen. (Part A)
– Meinen Ausbildungsbetrieb englischsprachigen Besuchern/Besucherinnen präsentieren. (Part B)
– Eine kurze Präsentation über meine Arbeit für neue Auszubildende halten. (Communication)

4 Supply chain

FOUNDATION: Logistics in the supply chain

Situation: You work for Henplo Forwarding, a company specializing in food logistics. Henplo has hired a marketing consultant to help grow its customer base. The consultant thinks Henplo should emphasize its role in the supply chain in its advertising.
→ You create a poster about the role of your company in the supply chain.

1 Understanding the supply chain

The consultant sends your company an example of a diagram about supply chains.

A Look at the diagram and match the words (a–h) to the parts of the supply chain (1–8).

a consumer
b distribution
c manufacturer
d processing plant
e procurement
f raw materials
g retailer
h wholesaler

B Match the items from the soya supply chain below to the parts of the supply chain in A.

family picnic · gluten-free bakery company · organic foods wholesaler · organic soya farm · soya mill · supermarket

C Henplo's motto is "From the field to your family". Think about the soya supply chain and say what the motto means.

> **Infobox**
>
> **Supply chain management**
> Supply chain management coordinates every aspect of the supply chain in order to make it more efficient and profitable. Many companies choose to outsource this to other businesses, and some major logistics companies offer it as a part of their range of services.

Unit 4 Supply chain

2 Describing the role of logistics in the supply chain

The consultant sends information about the seven Rs of logistics.

A Match each of the seven Rs with the descriptions below.

1. The customer receives the correct amount of goods.
2. The customer receives the precise items that they need.
3. The goods are not damaged when they arrive.
4. The goods are delivered to the location that the client specified.
5. Transportation is affordable.
6. The goods arrive when the client needs them.
7. The company advertises its services to the right market.

Right product · Right condition · Right quantity · Right time · Right place · Right cost · Right customer

B Henplo's website explains the various services the company offers. Read the excerpt from the website and say which of the seven Rs it includes.

> **Warehousing:** Our temperature and humidity-controlled warehouses are located conveniently around the UK and near major ports in continental Europe. Our warehousing services provide a strategic approach to inventory and reduce your costs by minimizing waste and damage due to improper storage.
>
> **Distribution:** The most important aspect of food logistics is timing. Henplo's years of experience and history of excellence ensure that your goods reach their destination on time and in top condition.
>
> **Just-in-Time Delivery:** In addition to our standard distribution services, Henplo offers JIT delivery – a bonus for perishable items, whose quality depends on speedy delivery.
>
> **Reverse Logistics:** A recall can be an expensive surprise, but Henplo's reverse logistics services minimize the damage. Our tracking software makes sure that no recalled items reenter the supply chain accidentally. We help you manage both the flow of goods and the flow of information to make the process as smooth as possible.

3 Describing your company's role in the supply chain

Now you make a poster showing the role of your training company in the supply chain.

A Form groups from the same training company and make notes about the following points:

- What materials does your company transport? How?
- What is your company's role in the supply chain?
- Is your company involved in procurement or distribution, or both?
- Does your company offer on-demand delivery or play a role in reverse logistics? How so?

B Make a poster showing your company's role in the supply chain. Present it to the class.

> **Infobox**
>
> **On-demand delivery**
> One important service that logistics providers offer their customers is on-demand delivery.
> **Just-in-time (JIT)** is where goods are scheduled for delivery exactly when they will be needed.
> **Just-in-sequence (JIS)**, mainly used in the automobile industry, takes JIT a step further: items arrive at the manufacturer's assembly line when they are needed and in the right order for assembly.

PART A: Packaging and labelling

Situation: Your company, ALEX Logistics, receives an enquiry from Sunlight Productions Ltd. They need to ship equipment from Berlin to the US city of Boston for a new film. Your line manager asks your team to plan the shipment of the equipment.
→ You plan the shipment of different types of goods.

1 Packaging

You familiarize yourself with the different options for packaging items securely.

A Look at the types of external packaging below. Match the terms in the list to pictures 1–9.

antistatic bag · canister · cardboard box · coil · crate · drum · pallet · pallet cage · wooden box

B Now match the types of internal packaging (1–9) to their definition (a–h).

1. packing peanuts
2. bubble wrap
3. cardboard
4. polystyrene foam
5. plastic film
6. foam rubber
7. cold chain boxes
8. wood wool (BE) / excelsior (AE)
9. sack

a. kind of container that keeps goods cold
b. a soft rubber that contains very small bubbles of air
c. a stiff product made of paper, usually brown
d. small pieces of foam
e. a thin continuous piece of plastic
f. a very light soft plastic that is usually white
g. a sheet of plastic which has lots of small air pockets
h. product made of wood shavings
i. a type of large, inexpensive bag

C Choose the appropriate packaging (internal and/or external) for the items below.

1. delicate plants, such as fresh flowers
2. fragile items, such as light bulbs
3. perishable items, such as fruit or meat
4. dry goods, such as tea or flour
5. electronics, such as computer chips

› Thematic Vocabulary: Packaging, page 197

Supply chain   Unit 4

2 Handling marks

An item also needs to be marked correctly to ensure that it is handled properly during transit.

A Match the handling marks (1–8) to what they mean (a–h).

a fragile
b temperature limitations
c this way up
d centre of gravity
e keep dry
f keep away from heat
g handle with care
h do not stack

B Look at the goods in 1C again. Which handling marks would be appropriate for each type of goods?

3 Packaging advice

Mr Novak, an assistant set designer from Sunlight Productions, calls to ask one of your colleagues how to package a sculpture for the set of the film.

A Before you listen to the call, discuss with a partner what you would use to pack a large, heavy statue in order to do the following:

- protect it from getting damaged
- hold it in place during transit
- make sure it is handled properly
- keep it dry if there are changes in temperature

B 15)) Now listen to your colleague's side of the conversation with the customer, Mr Novak. How similar is the advice to yours?

C Mr Novak forgot to take notes during the call, so your colleague asks you to write him an email. Write a short message to Mr Novak explaining which packaging he should use and why. Use the phrases in the box to help.

> **Suggesting packaging solutions**
>
> We suggest using … / surrounding the statue with … to avoid damage in transit / to hold the statue in place / to keep the statue dry.
> You should use a … because the sculpture is so heavy.
> For more protection / extra security …

4 Planning a shipment

Sunlight Productions sends a list of the equipment that needs to be shipped. You advise them on the correct packaging of the items.

- Film equipment: cameras, tripods, microphones, etc. (150 pieces, 1 tonne, 5 m^3)
- Lighting equipment: lights, cable drums, lighting stands, replacement light bulbs
- Stunt cars (5, average length 4 m)
- Food props: sausage (50 kg), tea assortment (5 kg), curry sauce (bottled, 15 l), beer (bottled, 20 cases)
- Other props: 20 street signs (17.5 cm by 83 cm), 20 l artificial blood, 5 kg make-up, 50 l glycerine liquid ("fog juice") for artificial fog

Work in groups. Each group plans the shipment of a different group of the items above. Discuss what packaging and marks are necessary. Then present your ideas to the class.

› *Thematic Vocabulary: Packaging, page 197*

PART B: Warehousing

Situation: You are working in the sales department of ALEX Logistics, a large logistics company that offers its customers both warehousing and transport services. A potential customer is coming to talk to your line manager and asks to see the warehouse facilities. Your line manager asks you to prepare a presentation of the warehouse.
→ You give a presentation of your company's warehouse.

1 Describing a warehouse

To prepare for your presentation, you look at the English words for describing a warehouse.

A Find the English words for the parts of a warehouse (A–K) below.

aisle • cold storage • drive-through pallet rack • floor storage • high-bay shelving • inbound goods • labelling • loading area • outbound goods • pallet rack shelving • pick and pack (picking area)

B Match the equipment used to move goods (1–6) to their descriptions (a–f).

1 forklift
2 lifting platform
3 freight elevator
4 pallet truck
5 crane
6 conveyor belt

a building materials and other heavy objects are moved with this machine's long arm
b materials are transported between floors or levels with this device
c materials are transported between floors in this device
d items are carried on this long loop of material
e this motorized vehicle is powered by diesel, petrol or electricity and used to lift and transport heavy objects
f this vehicle is used to handle pallets

Supply chain Unit 4

2 Working in the warehouse

You decide to ask some colleagues in the warehouse what you should include in your presentation.

16))) Listen to your colleagues describe their work. Match the responsibilities to the jobs.

receiver · forklift operator · picker · loader

A receiver is responsible for guiding lorries, ...

1 guide lorries
2 transport goods to storage
3 check whether items were damaged in transport
4 select items according to the order
5 follow weight distribution plan
6 attend yearly safety courses
7 tag items with RFID tags

> **Infobox**
>
> **RFID tags**
> Radio Frequency Identification (RFID) tags contain a transponder. Information is stored on a small circuit which can be activated by a radio signal with the correct frequency.
> RFID tags have many advantages over barcodes: RFID tags can hold more information than a barcode and the information can be constantly updated. RFID tags can be activated and read from a central point and can be tracked throughout the warehouse. They can be read whether inside or outside the package, and they are not affected by dirt.

3 Preparing for visitors

You next think about the kind of questions visitors might ask about the warehouse and what features they will be interested in. You start by brainstorming possible questions.

A Answer the questions below. Then think of two more questions and ask and answer with a partner.

1 What is the label printer used for?
2 So, what exactly is the RFID reader used for?
3 What items are transported on a forklift?
4 Why are the pallet scales located near the loading bay?
5 How are goods loaded onto lorries?
6 What is required to drive a forklift?

> **→ Describing processes and purposes**
>
> The box **is transported** on the conveyor belt.
> The packages **are opened** with a cutter knife.
> The forklift **is used** for lifting heavy objects.
>
> › *Grammar: Passive forms, page 152*

B Brainstorm features of a warehouse that would be attractive for a customer who wants to store the following products. How can you describe the features to the customer?

Our warehouse is equipped with cold storage. We also offer ...

1 dairy products (e.g. yoghurt) for distribution to regional customers
2 valuable, high-quality bathroom fixtures (e.g. bronze taps and shower heads) for individual or bulk sale to construction and plumbing contractors
3 construction materials (e.g. pallets of roof tiles) for JIT delivery to a nearby building site

4 Presenting your warehouse

You present your company's warehouse to a potential customer.

A Think about the following points:

– What areas does your warehouse have? Who works there? What do they do?
– What kind of shelving/storage do you offer?
– How are goods transported in your warehouse?
– How are goods labelled?
– What advantages do you offer customers?

B Now prepare a presentation of your training company's warehouse and present it to the class.

› *Useful phrases : Giving presentations, page 182; Thematic vocabulary: Warehouses, page 197*

COMMUNICATION: Emails

Situation: You are working in the Sales Department of 5 plus 5 Services, a logistics company that is looking for new customers. Your line manager asks you to arrange a meeting with a consultant.
→ You write an email to the advertising consultant.

1 Giving email addresses over the phone

You check the English for some of the symbols that appear in email addresses.

A Match the symbols (1–6) to the words (a–f).

1 +	4 -	a at	d plus
2 _	5 .	b dot	e number
3 @	6 #	c hyphen	f underscore

B 🔊 17 Listen to your line manager and a customer on the phone. Which email addresses are correct?

1
- a tm.martin@technical-tools.orgnet
- b tmmartin@technical_tools.orgnet
- c tm.martin@technical_tools.orgnet

2
- a maryannbrown@5+5_services.orgnet
- b mary-anne-brown@5+5services.orgnet
- c maryann-brown@5+5services.orgnet

C 👥 Work with a partner. **Partner A:** Look here. **Partner B:** Look at File 2 on page 130.

Dictate these email addresses to Partner B. Check B's answers.

1. DavidMcCarthy+list@co.usa
2. sergei-nikitin@com.ru
3. your own email address
4. the email address of your firm or another email address you often write to

> Can you spell that, please?

> Could you repeat that, please?

2 Writing a subject line

The subject line of an email must state clearly what the email is about.

A 👥 Work with a partner. Study the subject lines (a–f) below and find an email which …

1. is a request for information.
2. gives information about a meeting.
3. asks for assistance.
4. contains new information.
5. announces a change of plan.
6. is a covering letter for a brochure.

a	Subject: Need your help with English
b	Subject: New venue for event on Saturday
c	Subject: Flyer (attached)
d	Subject: Meeting 25.03. Starting time?
e	Subject: Update on project
f	Subject: Agenda

B 👥 With your partner, write suitable subject lines for the following emails.

1. Sorry, I would like to change the date of the meeting to Friday, 12 July.
2. Could you send me information about the presentation, please?
3. I am on holiday from 21.03 till 04.04 inclusive and will answer emails when I return.
4. I am writing to confirm your application for a stand at the Technical Trades Fair. The stand number is C208.
5. As promised, here is the link to the website with tips for writing emails.
6. This is just to let you know that I am interviewing a new export clerk at 12.30.

Supply chain Unit 4

3 Writing an email reply to arrange a meeting

Your line manager shows you the email below and asks you to write a reply for her.

From: Robert Johnson
To: Mary Anne Brown
Subject: advertising campaign meeting

Dear Ms Brown

We have studied the information you sent us about your company and are now ready to discuss our suggestions for your advertising campaign.
We would like to invite you to a meeting in our office on Thursday, 23 October, from 10.00 till 12.30, where we would present our initial ideas to you and your marketing manager, Ms Walker.
Please let us know if the date and time suit you.

Yours sincerely
Robert Johnson

Write the email using your line manager's name. Use a suitable greeting and subject line to reply to Mr Johnson. Include the following points:

- Thank him for the invitation.
- Say that Ms Walker cannot attend on that day. (Apologize and give a reason.)
- Suggest 24th at same time.
- Say that we look forward to the meeting.
- Express hope that the new date is suitable.
- Ask for confirmation soon.

 Using polite language in emails

Could and *would like* are more polite than phrases with *can*, *need* or *want*.
~~Can~~ you let me know by Monday? → **Could** you let …
I ~~need~~ the information today. → I **would like** the …
We ~~want~~ to have a meeting. → We **would like** to …

› *Useful phrases: Writing emails, page 183*

 Salutation and complimentary close in emails

If you do not know the name of the person you are writing to, begin your email with *Dear Sir or Madam*.
If you do not know your business partner well, use a formal salutation and complimentary close.

	Salutation	Complimentary close	
Formal (to unknown person)	Dear Sir or Madam	Yours faithfully	
Formal (to person whose name you know)	Dear Mr/Ms Smith	Kind regards Best regards	Best wishes Yours sincerely
Less formal	Dear Paul / Hi Paula Good morning Paul	Best regards Best	Best wishes All the best

---

DAS KANN ICH (Unit 5)

- Die Rolle meiner Firma in der Lieferkette präsentieren. (Foundation)
- Englischsprachigen Kunden die richtige Verpackung von Sendungen erklären. (Part A)
- Englischsprachigen Kunden die Lagerhalle meiner Firma vorstellen. (Part B)
- Einen Termin per E-Mail vereinbaren. (Communication)

KMK Exam practice 2

1 Hörverstehen: Stufe II (B1)

Situation: Sie machen eine Ausbildung zum Kaufmann / zur Kauffrau für Spedition und Logistikdienstleistung bei Habermann Industrie Service, einem Logistikzentrum für Industriebelieferung. Das Logistikzentrum ist eines der modernsten in Europa, daher kommen häufig Besuchergruppen für geführte Firmenbesichtigungen. Zum Tag der offenen Tür werden viele Interessierte erwartet, auch aus dem europäischen Ausland. Daher werden Mitarbeiter und auch Auszubildende für Besichtigungen geschult. Hierfür wurde ein Mitschnitt der Begrüßung einer englischen Gruppe und der englischen Führung erstellt.

18)) **Aufgabe:** Nachdem Sie selbst an der Führung teilgenommen haben, stellt Ihnen Ihr Ausbildungsleiter den Mitschnitt zur Verfügung und bittet Sie, sich anhand von Leitfragen Notizen zu machen, damit Sie sich besser vorbereiten können. Zur Vorbereitung auf Ihre englische Führung im Logistikzentrum hören Sie den Mitschnitt und machen sich auf Englisch Notizen zu wichtigen Aspekten.

Participants of the tour (remember their names when it's a small group!)	
Location of meeting point (don't forget to send visitors the information in advance)	
Reasons why visitors found their way to the meeting point easily (make sure your visitors find the way!)	
Items the visitors receive during the tour (remember to prepare them ahead of time!)	
General information about the company (carry the company brochure with you – just in case)	
Departments which are mentioned (prepare prompt cards so you don't forget important things)	
Information about the logistics centre (give some interesting facts and figures)	

2 Interaktion: Stufe II (B1)

Work with a partner. **Partner A:** Look here. **Partner B:** Look at File 6 on page 132.

Situation: Together with a lot of other apprentices from different countries, you attend a seminar at the European Apprenticeship Convention with the topic "Modern Warehousing". During the break a young colleague approaches you.

Aufgabe: Role-play a conversation with Partner B. Be prepared to ask and answer questions. You may have to use your imagination and make up possible answers. Use the ideas below to help you.

- Greet him/her properly and introduce yourself
- Exchange information about your company, kind of warehouse management and typical storage products.
- Give feedback about the seminar (content, structure, possible tips and improvements).
- Proceed to the seminar and arrange to meet in the next break.

Logistics Unlimited Ltd.
100 warehouses worldwide
Warehousing and transport systems
High-bay warehouses

3 Produktion: Stufe II (B1)

Situation: Habermann Industrie Service, das Logistikzentrum für Industriebelieferung, möchte Kunden, Lieferanten und Interessierte nun zum Tag der offenen Tür einladen. Ihr Chef bittet Sie, die E-Mail mit der Einladung für englischsprachige Gäste vorzubereiten, und gibt Ihnen dazu einige Informationen.

Aufgabe: Verfassen Sie anhand der Informationen eine E-Mail auf Englisch.

- Tag der offenen Tür mit Besichtigungen am 5. September, 10.00–18.00 Uhr
- Vorführung der Ausrüstung in einem der modernsten Lager Europas
- Präsentationen zum Thema: Lieferung auf Abruf und Just-in-Time
- Hinweis auf angehängten Flyer mit detailliertem Programm
- Bei Interesse an persönlichen Beratungen bitte Termin im Vorfeld vereinbaren (Anruf oder Kontakt direkt über Website möglich).

5 Enquiries and offers

FOUNDATION: Company services and USPs

Situation: You work in the Sales Department of Hanke Logistics International GmbH in Hamburg. Your line manager wants to improve the website in order to attract more customers. She asks you to learn about the company's USPs (unique selling propositions).
→ You make suggestions for improvements to the company website.

1 Looking at a company's website

There is a discussion in the department about how effective the website is. Some colleagues want to highlight the services and USPs better.

A Work in small groups. What do you think is important for a company's website? Consider the following questions, then share your results with the class.

- Who is the website for?
- What is the main purpose of the website? (attracting customers? placing orders? advertising services? …?)
- Which information should appear on the homepage? Which information can be linked to on other parts of the website?

Infobox

USPs
Unique selling propositions are a marketing concept. A USP is a benefit that a company offers which makes it different from – and better than – the competition.

B Look at the homepage below. What information will be especially important or attractive to the customer?

Enquiries and offers   Unit 5

2 Advertising language

You follow the links on the website to pages that describe Hanke's LTL and FTL services.

A Read the texts below and say which of the services or benefits 1–8 the company offers.

1 refrigerated transport
2 live updates on shipment status
3 cross-border FTL services
4 intermodal and multimodal transport
5 low carbon footprint
6 shorthaul regional services
7 invoice auditing
8 small package services

LTL
When it comes to partial-load shipments, Hanke Logistics International gives you three unbeatable benefits. Firstly, our large size allows us to bundle together orders of different scales to make your shipments as efficient as possible. Secondly, we ensure that quality requirements are met at every temperature level: from minus 25 all the way up to plus 25 degrees. And finally, we guarantee maximum planning reliability through daily collections and departures all over Europe, with online tracking for complete transparency. All the essential delivery information is provided to you from the vehicle. It's no wonder we're a market leader in food logistics.

FTL
The fastest transport option on the road is with full truckloads (FTL), and we at Hanke Logistics are specialists in temperature-controlled full truckloads. "Hanke Direct" is a quick, efficient service where goods are shipped directly from the manufacturer to the recipient. "Hanke Direct" uses a system of FTL centres across Europe: from Paris to Prague, London to Lisbon, wherever you need and always direct to the destination.

B Make a list of the adjectives Hanke uses to make their services attractive to customers and say what services they describe.

C Now think of more adjectives that the company could use to describe each of the following: payment options, warehousing, customer service.

3 Comparing companies

Your line manager asks you to find out how Hanke Logistics International is positioned in the market.

A 19))) Copy the chart below. Then listen to the podcast and fill in the missing information.

	Hanke	Lager Group	Carmero SE	Foodster
Turnover (in billion euros)	2.3			2.6
Employees		22,000		28,000
Offices	600	1,850	2,100	580
Countries			123	72
USPs				

B Use your completed chart to compare the companies and describe Hanke's position in the market.

> **Making comparisons**
>
> The company is **as big/large/successful as** …
> The company is **bigger / larger / more successful than** …
> They have **the highest/largest** turnover.
> They have **the second smallest** fleet.
>
> › *Grammar: Comparatives and superlatives, page 154*

4 Improving the website

You are now ready to give the line manager your suggestions for improving the company's website.

Look again at Hanke's USPs and the texts from the company website. Discuss in a group how the website can be improved. Make a list of at least four changes and say why you would make them.

43

PART A: Receiving an enquiry

Situation: You work in the Sales Department of Hanke Logistics International. Your line manager asks you and a colleague to deal with several enquiries.
→ You learn what is involved in an enquiry and call a customer to clarify details.

1 Understanding an enquiry

Before you look at the first enquiry, you review enquiries in English. Enquiries often have a similar structure and must contain certain information or an offer cannot be made.

Use words from the list on the right to translate the enquiries checklist into German.

> **Enquiries checklist**
> 1 source of address
> 2 description of company
> 3 reason for enquiry
> 4 request for quotation
> 5 requirements:
>   – description of goods (type of goods, quantity, packaging, weight, etc.)
>   – place of collection and delivery
>   – mode of transport
>   – expected date of shipment
>   – special requests
>   – terms of payment

Bedarf · Beförderungsart · Beschreibung der Güter · Bitte um (Preis-)Angebot · Beschreibung des Unternehmens · geschätzter Versand-/Verschiffungstermin · Grund für die Anfrage · Zahlungsbedingungen · Ort der Abholung/Lieferung · Quelle der Anschrift · Sonderwünsche

› *Useful phrases: Writing enquires, page 184*

2 Receiving an enquiry

You next look at an enquiry from an Irish company called Belgooly Whiskey Distillers Ltd.

A Read the enquiry and make a list of the points on the checklist that it includes.

Dear Sir or Madam,

We are currently seeking a new forwarder for shipments from the Republic of Ireland to Germany. I see from your website that you specialize in food logistics.

Our product is whiskey. We are the second largest distillery in Ireland and are based in Cork. We would like to start shipping our product (palletized) to a distributor in Germany on a regular basis.

Could you please provide a quotation for us?

If you have any questions, please don't hesitate to contact me.

I look forward to hearing from you.

Yours faithfully,
Mary Moran

B Ms Moran doesn't provide enough information in her email for Hanke to provide a quotation. With a partner, make a list of the details that Hanke will need before they can make an offer.

3 Following up on the phone

You and your colleague, Jan Peters, decide that he will call Ms Moran to enquire about the missing details.

A 20)) Listen to the conversation and correct the mistakes in Jan's notes.

1 *shipment of whiskey from Cork to Halle (Westphalia)*
2 *70 euro pallets, with a height of 2.3 meters each – can use FTL*
3 *delivery by 31 October*
4 *payment option not yet decided*
5 *will contact us about insurance after she speaks to colleague*

B Complete the sentences Jan uses to ask for missing information. Listen again if necessary.

exact destination • how many euro pallets • liability and risk • payment options • pick up the shipment • when you will make the shipment

1 First of all, could you tell me where we would ▬?
2 I'll also need to know the ▬. That will help me calculate distance and time.
3 Can you tell me ▬ the shipment will include? That will help me calculate the space needed.
4 Can I just ask you to give me a rough estimate of ▬?
5 We offer three ▬, but our standard option is net within 30 days of invoice. Would that be acceptable to you?
6 I have one more question. Have you thought about ▬?

C Match sentences 1–6 above to the information Jan asks about (a–f).

a place of delivery
b insurance
c terms of payment
d size of consignment
e place of collection
f expected date of shipment

4 Role-play: Clarifying the details

Hanke has received an enquiry via the contact form on their website, but the customer didn't complete all of the fields. Your line manager forwards you the enquiry and asks you call and clarify the details.

Work with a partner.

Partner A: Look at the enquiry above and make a note of the missing details. Then call Mr/Ms Connell to enquire about the information you need to make an offer.
Partner B: Look at File 3 on page 130. You are Mr/Ms Connell. Answer your partner's questions.

PART B: Making an offer

Situation: You are working in the Fairs and Exhibitions Department of Advens Logistics GmbH. As the spring trade fair season is coming up, the department is quite busy responding to the high volume of enquiries. Your line manager shows you how to write offers to customers.
→ You send an offer to a customer via email.

1 Making an offer

Because you want to review offers in English, your line manager, Katja Brecker, shows you an offer she has written to an English-speaking company in Berlin.

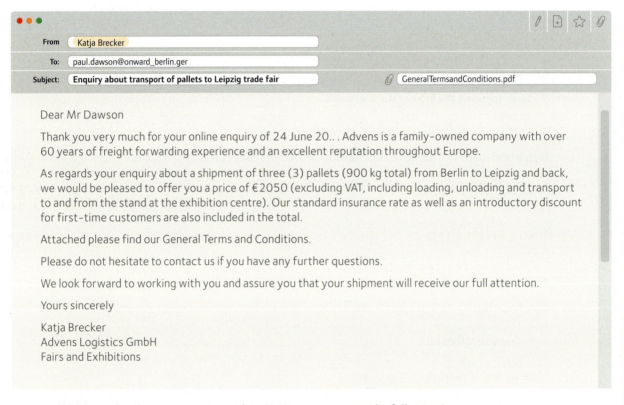

From: Katja Brecker
To: paul.dawson@onward_berlin.ger
Subject: Enquiry about transport of pallets to Leipzig trade fair
Attachment: GeneralTermsandConditions.pdf

Dear Mr Dawson

Thank you very much for your online enquiry of 24 June 20... Advens is a family-owned company with over 60 years of freight forwarding experience and an excellent reputation throughout Europe.

As regards your enquiry about a shipment of three (3) pallets (900 kg total) from Berlin to Leipzig and back, we would be pleased to offer you a price of €2050 (excluding VAT, including loading, unloading and transport to and from the stand at the exhibition centre). Our standard insurance rate as well as an introductory discount for first-time customers are also included in the total.

Attached please find our General Terms and Conditions.

Please do not hesitate to contact us if you have any further questions.

We look forward to working with you and assure you that your shipment will receive our full attention.

Yours sincerely

Katja Brecker
Advens Logistics GmbH
Fairs and Exhibitions

Which words, phrases or sentences does Katja use to express the following?

1. Advens Logistics will make sure the shipment is completed correctly.
2. Katja Brecker is responding to an enquiry about three pallets.
3. The price does not include tax.
4. Katja is offering a reduction in price because Paul Dawson is a new customer.
5. Advens will deliver to and collect the pallets from Onward's stand in the exhibition hall.
6. Additional material was sent with the email.
7. Katja Brecker would be happy to give Paul Dawson more information.

> **Infobox**
>
> **Discounts**
> Discounts, e.g.
> – introductory discounts (first-time customer)
> – quantity discounts (larger numbers/amounts)
> – special discounts (e.g. loyalty, summer sales)
> are deducted from the list price. Discounts granted after payment has been made are called rebates.

Enquiries and offers Unit 5

2 Structuring an offer

When you write an offer, you can usually follow a simple structure.

A Use words from below to translate the checklist.

Anlage(n) · Beschreibung Ihrer Firma/Waren/
Dienstleistungen · Bezug auf Anfrage ·
Geschäftsbedingungen und Rabatte ·
höfliche Schlussformel · Preis · Verkaufsmaterial

> **Offers checklist**
>
> 1 reference to enquiry
> 2 description of your company/goods/services
> 3 sales material
> 4 price
> 5 terms and discounts
> 6 polite ending
> 7 enclosure(s) (letter) / attachment(s) (email)

B Which items from the checklist does Katja's email include?

› Useful phrases: Writing offers, page 185

3 Discussing the details of an offer

Paul Dawson has some questions about the offer and calls Katja to discuss the details.

A 🔊 21 Look at Katja's calculations and listen to the phone call. Are the statements below true or false (or you don't know)? Correct the false statements.

1 The cost for carriage alone is just under €700.
2 Nichols, one of Advens' competitors, offers better rates.
3 Katja offers to lower the administration fee to €70.
4 Katja can offer a discount because there are reduced rates for trade fair customers.
5 Paul is happy with the standard terms of payment.
6 Delivery on the weekend costs extra.

Collection in Berlin and transport to Leipzig exhibition centre warehouse	€390.00
Unloading, storage and transport to stand	€464.00
Collection at stand, storage and loading	€435.00
Administration fee	€89.90
Freight costs from Leipzig exhibition centre to Berlin	€320.00
Insurance (standard rate)	€11.31

B Several terms of payment are mentioned in the conversation. First match these common terms of payment (1–7) to the German equivalents (a–g). Then listen again and note the terms of payment you hear.

1 cash in advance
2 cash on delivery (COD)
3 cash with order (CWO)
4 2% cash discount
5 2% discount for payment within ... days
6 payment on receipt of invoice
7 payment within ... days from date of ...

a Barzahlung bei Auftragserteilung
b Zahlung innerhalb ... Tagen nach ...
c Barvorauszahlung
d Zahlung bei Erhalt der Rechnung
e Barzahlung abzüglich 2 % Skonto
f 2 % Skonto bei Zahlung innerhalb ... Tagen
g Zahlung gegen Nachnahme

› Terms of payment, page 179

4 Writing an offer

The owner of a small tech start-up in Cologne has enquired about shipping goods to a trade fair in Berlin.

Use Katja's notes to send an offer in English.

– Ansprechpartner: Dave Mackey, VrrayTech GmbH, d.mackey@vrraytech.xy
– 13 Paletten Messegut (jeweils 550 kg), Sendung ex Köln, to TechSpecsMesse Berlin.
– 9.900 € inkl. Frachtkosten, Samstagszuschlag, Ladung und Entladung, Zustellung zum Messestand, Regiekosten, Speditionsversicherung und 5 % Rabatt für Aussteller (exhibitors) bei TechSpecs – Zahlung bei Erhalt der Rechnung

COMMUNICATION: The layout of business letters

Situation: You work at Hanke Logistics International GmbH, a forwarder in Hamburg. This week you are helping out in the Pallet Department.
→ You write a letter of enquiry to an English-speaking supplier.

1 Reading an English business letter

Your line manager gives you an example of a letter of enquiry.

A Study the layout and match the parts (1–12) of the letter on page 49 to the labels below (a–l).

a	address/letterhead	d	copies	g	inside address	j	signature block
b	body of the letter	e	date	h	reference initials	k	subject line
c	complimentary close	f	enclosure	i	salutation	l	attention line

B Compare emails and business letters. What are the differences?

2 Writing an English business letter

Your line manager asks you to write enquiries about the purchase of pallets and pallet trucks.

A Complete this text from a letter of enquiry about pallets with the words and phrases below.

attention · delivery · enclosed · enquire · faithfully · look forward · possible ·
quotation · specializing · supplier

Dear Sir or Madam

We understand from your website that you are a ▬▬¹ of wooden and plastic pallets.

We are an international company ▬▬² in food logistics based in Germany with many warehouses throughout Europe (see ▬▬³ brochure).

I am writing to ▬▬⁴ about the purchase and ▬▬⁵ of 500 EPAL 1 Euro pallets for our Hamburg warehouse. As we urgently need the pallets, please let us have a ▬▬⁶ as soon as ▬▬⁷.

Many thanks for your ▬▬⁸ to our enquiry. We ▬▬⁹ to hearing from you soon.

Yours ▬▬¹⁰

B Now write a letter of enquiry about pallet trucks to a wholesaler of warehouse equipment in Spain. Use the correct layout for an English business letter including a suitable salutation and complimentary close.

Contact: Sales Manager, Logistica de Proveedores, Glorieta España, 18, 30004 Murcia, Spain
Product: 15 ABEJA pallet trucks (standard, 540 mm, 2.0 tonnes); 3 ABEJA pallet trucks (long reach, 540 mm, 2.5 tonnes)

› Useful phrases: Writing business letters, page 185
› Thematic vocabulary: Commercial correspondence, page 197

Salutation and complimentary closes in letters

	Salutation	Complimentary close
to a firm	Dear Sir or Madam	Yours faithfully (BE)
		Yours very truly / Cordially yours (AE)
to a person	Dear Mr/Ms Brown Dear Sharon/Martin	Yours sincerely (BE)
		Sincerely yours / Best personal regards (AE)

Enquiries and offers Unit 5

[1] Whey Wholesale Ltd.
267b Dryden Street
London E1 7BT
United Kingdom
+44 (0)20 7946 0109
info@whey_wholesale.brit

[2] 29 April 20..

[3] Our ref: LL/DC

[4] Hanke Logistics International GmbH
Sales Department
Am Zollhafen 48
21107 Hamburg
Germany

[5] For the attention of the Sales Manager

[6] Dear Sir or Madam

[7] **Enquiry about the transport of cheese from Dover to Munich**

[8] We saw your advertisement in this month's "Forwarder Magazine" and see that you specialize in shipping dairy products.

We are a large cheese wholesaler based in London. For a German customer in Munich we need to ship two cheese wheels. The cheese will be shipped on non-standard pallets (66 cm x 66 cm x 15 cm). We would like to use your company for a trial shipment. If your offer is competitive, further shipments are possible.

Please let us have a quotation including your terms of payment.

We look forward to hearing from you soon.

[9] Yours faithfully

[10] *Linda Lambert*

Linda Lambert
Sales Department

[11] cc Vanessa Whitehouse

[12] Enc: Company Magazine

DAS KANN ICH (Unit 5)

- Vorschläge für die Überarbeitung der Firmenwebsite machen und die Marktposition beurteilen. (Foundation)
- Schriftliche und telefonische Anfragen und Angebote auf Englisch erledigen. (Part A)
- Ein Angebot per E-Mail an eine englische Firma schreiben. (Part B)
- Eine schriftliche Anfrage als Brief mit englischem Layout erstellen. (Communication)

49

6 Road and rail transport

FOUNDATION: Overland transport

Situation: You work in the Sales Department at BDI Transport GmbH in Hamburg. Your line manager has asked you to help prepare a short presentation in English about your company's services to a new client from North America who has manufacturing sites all over Europe.
→ You prepare and give a presentation about road and rail transport.

1 Pros and cons of road and rail

First you look at the advantages and disadvantages of road and rail transport.

Work with a partner and draw up a table of the pros and cons of road and rail transport. Use your own ideas and the ones below, then discuss your results with the class.

border controls · door-to-door delivery · express delivery · huge loads · pollution · toll charges · traffic jams

2 Tolls

You take a closer look at toll charges throughout Europe and find the following table showing where on-board units (OBUs) are used and where there are vignettes (V) and/or toll stations (TS).

Country Vehicle weight	Austria	Czech Republic	Germany	France	Belgium	Netherlands	Italy	Poland	Slovenia	Switzerland
≤ 3.5 tonnes	V	V		TS[1] & OBU			TS & OBU		V	V at border
> 3.5 tonnes	OBU	OBU		OBU	OBU		OBU	OBU	OBU	OBU
> 7.5 tonnes	OBU	OBU	OBU	OBU	OBU		OBU	OBU	OBU	OBU

[1] on motorways

A First study the table above, then list the tolls paid for the two trips shown (in red and blue) using:

1 a light van
2 a 10-tonne lorry

B Where will the drivers have to stop and pay?

Road and rail transport Unit 6

3 Talking about road and rail transport

In preparation for your North American visitors, you look at the words and phrases used to describe rail and road transport in North America and the UK and find a comparison on the internet.

> ### When is a car not a car?
>
> The mixture of British English (BE) and American English (AE) used in Europe to describe rail and road transport can be confusing.
>
> **Rail**
> When the Americans say "railroad", the British say "railway". An American "freight train" is a British "goods train". In AE a train has "cars", which can be "passenger cars" or "freight cars". In BE a train has "goods wagons" or "passenger carriages".
>
> **Road**
> A "lorry" is the British word for an American "truck", and in AE the word "cargo" can be used to describe the goods on a truck, train, ship and plane. In BE only ships and planes have a "cargo". An American "box truck" or British "box van" is a van with a box-shaped body. The British often call certain types of box van "Luton vans" because the first vans like this were made in Luton, UK. A "pickup (truck)" and a "forklift (truck)" are the same in AE and BE.
>
> The British call their big lorries HGVs (heavy goods vehicles). One example is an "articulated lorry" or "artic", which has a cab for the driver and a trailer for the goods. The Americans call this a "semi-trailer truck". The containers that they carry are standardized and are called "swap bodies" in AE and BE and also "demountable bodies" in AE. American truck and British lorry drivers both drive "curtainsiders" or "tautliners", which are vehicles with a heavy curtain along each side that is pushed back for loading and unloading and made taut with straps.

Use information from the text to identify the following vehicles in both AE and BE.

4 Giving a presentation

Now it is time for you to give your presentation. Choose one of the options below.

A Give a brief presentation on the road and rail freight services offered by your company.

B Choose a load your company has recently sent abroad by rail or road and describe how it was transported and where it went. If a toll was paid, describe how this was done.

PART A: Shipping dangerous goods

Situation: You are an apprentice at BDI Transport GmbH in Hamburg and your company deals with a wide range of goods, including hazardous materials.
→ Your line manager asks you to help plan some shipments of dangerous goods and to brief a driver who does not speak German.

1 Classifying dangerous goods

First you look at your company's Dangerous Goods Handbook and see the different placards (warning signs), classes and descriptions used.

Placards, classes and descriptions

A Find English words on the placards for the German words below.

ätzend · brandfördernd · entzündlich · feste Stoffe · flüssige Stoffe · gefährlich · Gift · Verschiedenes

B Some of the dangerous materials your company will be shipping are listed below. Choose the correct class and description for each one.

alcohol · arsenic · fireworks · hydrogen · sulphuric acid

2 Understanding a Dangerous Goods Note

BDI Transport GmbH is commissioned to transport a consignment of dangerous goods from the Netherlands to Poland and receives a Dangerous Goods Note (DGN) from the exporter.

A Study the DGN for the consignment opposite and find the information below (1–6). Which warning sign will be needed for the vehicle transporting this load?

1 the exporter
2 the importer
3 the freight forwarder
4 the load
5 the net weight and volume of the goods
6 the shipping clerk's name

B 👥 Your line manager notices that the DGN is incomplete and also contains some errors. Study the form with a partner and guess what is wrong or missing.

Road and rail transport **Unit 6**

MULTIMODAL DANGEROUS GOODS FORM

1. Shipper/Consignor/Sender	2. Transport document number	3. Page 1 of
VAN DYCK OIL BV, ENERGIEWEG 200, 3041 GC ROTTERDAM, NETHERLANDS	3D 214832591000-T63981	1 pages
	4. Shipper's reference	5. Freight Forwarder's reference
	VDO-9761	NE 4021Z
6. Consignee	7. Carrier (to be completed by the carrier)	
G&L RESEARCH, MINIKOWO 187, POZNAŃ, POLAND	BDI TRANSPORT GMBH, PEUTESTRASSE 200, 20539 HAMBURG	

SHIPPER'S DECLARATION
I hereby declare that the contents of this consignment are fully and accurately described below by the proper shipping name, and are classified, packaged, marked and labelled/placarded and are in all respects in proper condition for transport according to the applicable international and national governmental regulations.

8. *This shipment is within the limitations prescribed for:* (Delete non-applicable)	9. Additional handling information
PASSENGER AND CARGO AIRCRAFT CARGO AIRCRAFT ONLY	

10. Vessel/flight no. and date	11. Port/place of loading	12. Port/place of discharge	13. Destination
		–	POZNAŃ, POLAND

14. Shipping marks	*Number and kind of packages; description of goods	Gross mass (kg)	Net mass	Cube (m^3)
	1 TANK, UN 1223, KEROSENE, 3, PG III, (D/E) ENVIRONMEN-TALLY HAZARDOUS	–	832	10.00

15. Container ID no. / vehicle registration no.	16. Seal number(s)	17. Container/vehicle size and type	18. Tare (kg)	19. Total gross mass (including tare) (kg)
STPU747491	STPU747491	–	60	982

CONTAINER/VEHICLE PACKING CERTIFICATE
I hereby declare that the goods described above have been packed/loaded into the container/vehicle identified above in accordance with the applicable provisions (see ADR 2017 5.4.2).
MUST BE COMPLETED AND SIGNED FOR ALL CONTAINER/VEHICLE LOADS BY PERSON RESPONSIBLE FOR PACKING/LOADING

21. RECEIVING ORGANISATION RECEIPT
Received the above number of packages/containers/trailers in apparent good order and condition unless stated heron: REMARKS:

20. Name of company	Haulier's name	22. Name of company (OF SHIPPER PREPARING THIS NOTE)
		VAN DYCK OIL BV
Name/status of declarant	Vehicle reg. no.	Name/status of declarant
		R KAREL SHIPPING CLERK
Place and date	Signature and date	Place and date
		ROTTERDAM 27/8/20..
Signature of declarant	DRIVER'S SIGNATURE	Signature of declarant

*FOR DANGEROUS GOODS: You must specify: UN no., proper shipping name, hazard class, packing group (where assigned) and any other element of information required under applicable national and international regulations

C 22))) Now listen to a telephone conversation in which Laura Stein, your line manager, calls the exporter to correct the DGN. Write down the five changes that must be made.

D Listen again and complete the sentences with the words you hear.

1 If anything is missing or incorrect, the load ▬ be delayed.
2 ▬ see the correct address if you look on our website.
3 If we just ▬ tank, they'll want to know what sort of tank it is.
4 If it's made of plastic, they ▬ accept it.
5 If you need any more information, ▬ be happy to provide it.

53

3 Safety precautions

The load from the Netherlands to Poland is accompanied by a Transport Emergency Card (tremcard) listing the safety equipment to be carried in the cab of the vehicle.

Match the pictures of the emergency equipment (1–9) with words on the tremcard.

TRANSPORT EMERGENCY CARD – Road Transport

UN NO	1275
Class/Division	3
Subsidiary risk	
Packing group	III
ERG-No.	128

Proper shipping name
Kerosene

Personal protective equipment
- Face shield or goggles / light protective clothing
- Protective gloves and footwear
- Eyewash bottle (clean water)

Emergency equipment
- Spill kit (appropriate for the load)
- Plastic or rubber non-sparking shovel / Broom
- Appropriate absorbent or sand

Driver first actions
- Stop the engine
- No smoking allowed / No naked lights
- Put warning signs on road
- Warn road users and others to keep away from the danger area
- Keep upwind
- Inform the police and fire brigade immediately
- Do not try to deal with any fire yourself

4 Role-play: Briefing the driver

Your line manager asks you to brief one of the drivers about a dangerous load.

👥 Work with a partner and use information in your files and on the tremcard above to have a conversation.

Partner A: Look at File 4 on page 131.
Partner B: Look at File 8 on page 133.

> **Explaining consequences**
>
> **If** it**'s** made of plastic, they **won't accept** it.
> **If** there**'s** an emergency, I**'ll notify** the fire brigade.

› *Grammar: Conditional sentences, page 153*

Road and rail transport Unit 6

PART B: Following standard road freight procedures

Situation: You are an apprentice at BDI Transport GmbH in Hamburg and this week you are being shadowed by Linda Clark, an American work experience student from Austin, Texas. Your line manager asks you to deal with a request from a furniture wholesaler in Croatia while at the same time explaining standard road freight procedures to Linda.
→ You deal with the company's request and write an email to confirm arrangements.

1 Euro pallets

You explain to Linda that the load will be sent on Euro pallets. You find an article on the internet explaining how they reduce the turnaround time for goods delivery.

A Read the text and explain in your own words what Euro pallets are and how they speed up trade.

> ## Why Euro pallets?
>
> Not all pallets are the same but all Euro pallets certainly are and since their introduction in 1961 their number has grown to over 500 million. This is because they are exchange pallets, meaning that when the haulier delivers a palletized load, it can be left on the pallet(s). The driver simply picks up as many empty pallets as were used to deliver the load, thereby saving unloading time. Euro pallets are sturdy and can be used many times. European companies pool their Euro pallets, and trucks, containers, forklift trucks and warehouses throughout Europe are designed to handle Euro pallets.
>
> The dimensions of a type 1 Euro pallet are 1,200 mm by 800 mm by 144 mm (width / length / height). Its imperial measurements are 47.24 in (inch) x 31.50 in x 5.70 in. It is made of 11 boards held together by 78 nails. It is approximately 25 kg (55.1 lbs) in weight and can take a load of up to 1,500 kg (3,037 lbs). Euro pallets all have branded markings showing the EPAL logo and giving information about how, where and when the pallet was made. In addition, all Euro pallets must have an EPAL control staple. Any pallet without all these features is not a Euro pallet and could be a fake.

B Find words in the text to label points (a–h) in the diagram.

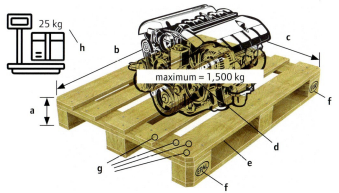

Infobox

Weights and measures
Many English-speaking countries use imperial and metric units in domestic and foreign trade, e.g.:
one inch (1 in / 1") = 2.54 cm
one foot (1 ft / 1') = 30.48 cm
one square foot (1 sq ft / 1 ft^2) = 929.03 cm^2
one cubic inch (1 in^3) = 16.4 cm^3
one pound (1 lb) = 0.453 kg (kilos)

› *Conversion tables, page 179*

C Work with a partner and use the information in your files to describe dimensions and weights.

Partner A: Look at File 9 on page 133. **Partner B:** Look at File 5 on page 131.

Examples:
The pallet is forty-two point two four inches wide and weighs fifty-five point one pounds.
The warehouse is a hundred feet long by fifty feet wide by twenty feet high.

55

2 Understanding a CMR consignment note

Next you look at the CMR note for the load and explain the most important points to Linda.

Study the CMR note and write down the following information.

1. name of the sender
2. name of the consignee
3. the warehouse opening hours in Split
4. documents given to the carrier by the sender
5. number of packages
6. method of packing
7. nature of the goods
8. who will pay for the carriage of the goods

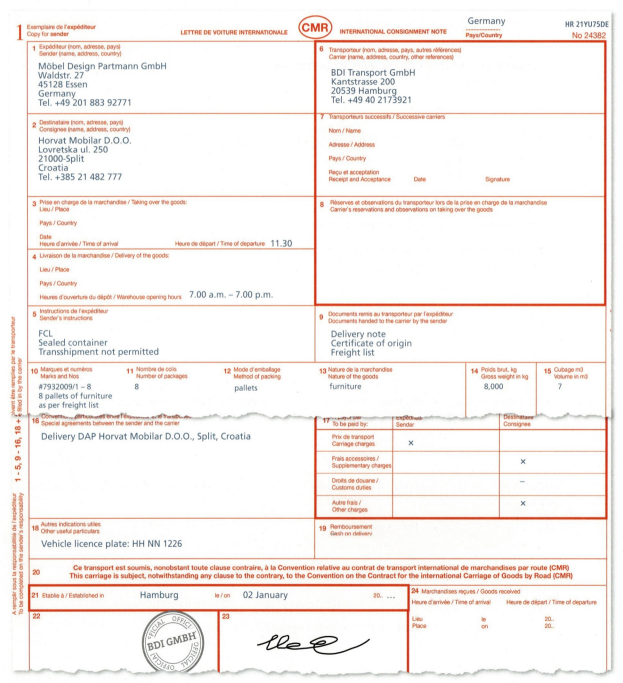

Source: International Road Transport Union (IRU), "IRU CMR Model 2007." Published: 12/01/2017. iru.org/resources/iru-library/iru-cmr-model-2007. Accessed: May 2019

Road and rail transport Unit 6

3 Following procedures

You phone the furniture wholesaler in Split and talk to Bogdan Karić, the warehouse manager, to discuss what changes he wants made to the arrangements for the consignment.

A 23 ») Listen to the dialogue and summarize the changes in your own words. Then read your summary to a partner and correct any errors. Begin your answer like this:

The warehouse manager in Split, Croatia wants us to add goods …

B 23 ») Listen again and complete the sentence below with the words you hear.

1 Is it about the ▭ of furniture?
2 The ▭ from Essen to Split will take the lorry through Zagreb.
3 We would like your lorry to stop in Zagreb on the way and ▭ it up.
4 There's easily enough ▭ for the kitchen furniture.
5 The sender will no longer accept ▭ for the load.
6 Part or all of it could be stolen or ▭.
7 We have a very large ▭ just outside the city.
8 We can add a ▭ to our lorry when it arrives in Zagreb.

C Use the words from B (in the correct form) to complete this report about a different load. Make any necessary changes to the words you use.

> ### Report #11 – Delivery to Spain
> We had to send a ▭¹ of musical instruments from Kiel to Madrid. It was only a small load and we ▭² up the instruments at the sender's warehouse and packed them into a big container at our ▭³ in Hamburg. Our lorry then went on a direct ▭⁴ from Hamburg to Madrid, passing through Belgium and France on the way. As there was still a lot of ▭⁵ in the container, our driver collected more goods in Brussels and Paris, and then in Pamplona, Spain a ▭⁶ with a second container was added. Unfortunately, when the musical instruments arrived in Madrid, some of them were ▭⁷, but according to the terms of delivery, it was not the sender's ▭⁸ to replace them.

4 Confirming arrangements

You hear nothing more about pallets from the warehouse manager at Horvat Mobilar, so the next day you email him as promised.

Write an email including the following points:
– from: you <first name.surname@bdi_transport.ger>, Logistics Department
– to: Bogdan Karić <b.karic@horvat-mobilar.cro>
– reference to yesterday's telephone call
– BDI's vehicle will stop at Zagreb depot
– trailer with container of kitchen furniture will be added
– delivery of kitchen furniture to customer's premises in Split
– request for delivery of kitchen furniture to Zagreb depot by 10 January 20..
– reference to attached invoice
– polite ending

› *Useful phrases: Writing emails, page 183*

COMMUNICATION: Clarifying information on the phone

Situation: You work for SpeedyShipping, a European freight exchange platform based in Berlin. Your job is to match loads with vehicles.
→ You ask for the details of a haulier's vehicle and answer questions about the consignment so you can place a return load.

1 Preparing to place a load

Both you as the freight agent and the haulier need information before a load can be placed, so you both have to ask a lot of questions.

A Use words from below to complete the questions. Sometimes more than one answer is possible.

Do · Does · How · Is · What · When · Where · Who

1 ___'s the deadline for delivery?
2 ___ you want a full truck load or less than a truck load?
3 ___ it have a tail lift or crane?
4 ___ heavy is the load?
5 ___ it a rigid or articulated vehicle?
6 ___ is your vehicle's maximum payload?
7 ___ sort of load is it?
8 ___ is the load to be collected?
9 ___ is the consignee?
10 ___ many pallets will it take?

B Who asks what? Sort the questions above into the following categories.

Questions asked by the freight agent: 2, …
Questions asked by the haulier: 1, …

› Grammar: Questions and short answers, page 151

2 Getting missing information

A haulier phones you to ask why he has not yet heard about a return load.

A 24))) Listen to the telephone dialogue and complete the Return Load form. Write the missing information 1–12 in your exercise book.

Return Load	
Name of haulier:	___1
– contact person:	___2
FTL / LTL	___3
Vehicle description:	___4
– vehicle body (choose one) 5	enclosed ___ curtainsider ___
– vehicle weight	___6
– crane (yes/no)	___7
– tail lift (yes/no)	___8
Available load:	___9
Palletized: (yes/no)	___10
Consignor:	UPM Metal
– location	St Petersburg, Russia
Consignee:	Ryland Engineering
– location	Cork, Ireland
Collection date:	___11
Delivery date:	___12

Road and rail transport   Unit 6

B 24))) Listen again and complete the sentences with the words you hear.

1 Is the name of your company ▬ D – U – double F – E – Y?
2 Did you ▬ confirmation from us?
3 Your request was not ▬.
4 There are some ▬ boxes that still have to be filled in.
5 You didn't ▬ any of the boxes describing your vehicle.
6 ▬ you now give me a description of your vehicle?
7 How much does it ▬?
8 And when is delivery ▬?

> **Asking polite questions**
>
> **Could** you give me the consignee's address?
> What else **would** you like to know?
>
> › Grammar: Modals and their substitutes, page 155

3 Role-play: Matching a load with a haulier

You now have to deal with a return load from Spain.

👥 Work with a partner and role-play the situation shown below. Choose roles, then follow the instructions on your role card. When you have finished, swap roles. The date is 13 March.

Eastvale Bottling Plant
Manchester UK
by 24 March at the latest

No problem, sir!

curtainsider
payload: 25 tonnes
max: 34 Euro pallets

Return load from Spain?

Manchester

Port of Valencia

freight exchange agent

JJK Maquinas S.L., Valencia, Spain
LTL: 15 tonnes of bottling plant machinery on pallets
15 March

haulier
Freight Racer Ltd

Partner A	Partner B
Freight agent / (your own name)	**Haulier, Freight Racer Ltd / (your own name)**
You take a call from a haulier and …	You phone SpeedyShipping and …
– ask him/her to spell his/her name	– explain that you requested a return load from Spain three days ago
– explain that some data is missing on the Return Load form (invent)	– ask why you have received no confirmation
– complete the Return Load form, box by box	– request an LTL
– promise to confirm the details by email	– give the missing information (see diagram)
– finish the call politely	– finish the call politely

DAS KANN ICH (Unit 6)

– Eine Präsentation über Straßen- und Schienentransport halten. (Foundation)
– Einen Gefahrguttransport planen und die Vorschriften für Gefahrgut erklären. (Part A)
– Auf Kundenwünsche eingehen und eine E-Mail zur Bestätigung schreiben. (Part B)
– Fragen zu Nutzfahrzeugen und Ladungen stellen und beantworten. (Communication)

KMK Exam practice 3

1 Mediation: Stufe III (B2)

Situation: Ihre internationale Spedition hat sich unter anderem auf den Transport von gefährlichen Gütern spezialisiert, daher ist der Umgang damit ein wichtiger Teil Ihrer Ausbildung.

Aufgabe: Sie werden gebeten, für Auszubildende und Praktikanten aus Zweigstellen in anderen Ländern, den vorliegenden Text zum Transport von Gefahrgütern in eine englische Checkliste zu übertragen.

Transport von Gefahrgut

Bevor man sich mit Gefahrgut beschäftigt oder es gar transportiert, muss man sich klarmachen, dass diese Stoffe ernste Schäden für Personen, Material und die Umwelt bedeuten können.

Daher ist es wichtig, dass man zunächst identifiziert, welches Gefahrgut vorliegt. Beachten Sie dann entsprechend, wie mit dem Gefahrgut umgegangen werden sollte, und dass angemessene Abläufe eingehalten werden. Die Arbeiten dürfen nur von geschulten Mitarbeitern ausgeführt werden.

Am Anfang steht die sachgemäße Lagerung im Unternehmen, die die gesetzlichen Vorgaben erfüllen muss. Hier geht es unter anderem um die Einteilung von Lagerzonen, Brandschutz, Versicherung und Schulung von Mitarbeitern.

Stellen Sie sicher, dass Schutzausrüstung und Materialien sowie Notfallausrüstung vorhanden sind. Ein wesentlicher Punkt ist auch die angemessene Verpackung bzw. der Container, in dem das Gefahrgut transportiert wird, damit das Paket oder die Lieferung den Versand unbeschadet übersteht.

Nach dem Verpacken muss das Gefahrgut gekennzeichnet werden mit Name, Klasse, Verpackungsmaterial, Menge, Verpackungsanweisungen und Informationen des Hersteller, Versenders und Importeurs.

Die letzte Entscheidung ist dann die Wahl der besten Versandart, die von der Substanz und dem Ziel der Sendung abhängt.

---

2 Produktion: Stufe II (B1)

Situation: Sie arbeiten für Müller & Söhne Logistik und bearbeiten die täglich über das Onlineformular der Firmenwebsite eingehenden Anfragen. Nach der Überprüfung stellen Sie immer wieder fest, dass einigen Anfragen wichtige Infos zur Erstellung eines aussagekräftigen Angebotes fehlen.

Aufgabe: Ihr Chef bittet Sie, eine freundliche E-Mail auf Englisch zu schreiben.

Company Name: SHW Machine Parts
Your Name:
Tel.:
Email: sales@shw.brit
Service (import and/or export):
Mode (air and/or sea):
POL: Wiesbaden
POD: Malta
Date of delivery:
Cargo volume / Dimensions: 10 Euro pallets
Cargo weight:
Description of goods:
Other instructions: Can you please send your general business terms by email?

- Dank für Anfrage
- Fordern Sie höflich die fehlenden Infos an
- Gewünschte AGB werden angehängt
- Bitte um Kontaktaufnahme wegen eines persönlichen Treffens zur Klärung und Unterzeichnung, da Erstkontakt

3 Mediation, Stufe II (B1)

Situation: Sie arbeiten bei der deutschen Niederlassung eines spanischen Spediteurs. Einige Teile Ihrer Homepage sind bislang nur auf Spanisch und Englisch vorhanden. Um stärker auf deutsche Kunden einzugehen, werden Sie gebeten, die USPs und besonderen Services der Firma ins Deutsche zu übertragen.

Aufgabe: Übertragen Sie die wichtigsten Informationen sinngemäß auf Deutsch in die vorbereitete Tabelle.

| PARTNER | WORLDWIDE | NETWORK | CAREER | CONTACT | LANGUAGE |

Specialized services in freight transportation

Expedited Shipping Services are often needed when freight is time-sensitive. Services include 3-day, 2-day and next-day freight services.

Guaranteed Services can be arranged when pick-up or delivery needs to happen on a particular day or at a specific time (before 10 a.m. on a Wednesday or after 6 p.m. on a Tuesday). Ask our freight agents before arranging a shipment, as not all of our carriers offer this service.

Lift Gate Services are often required when there isn't a forklift where goods are meant to be picked up or delivered. These services are available (upon request) with several of our carriers.

Notification Services let you know when to expect pick-up and/or delivery.

Limited Access Pick-ups/Deliveries can be arranged for places that lorries cannot or may not enter (some residential areas, military/government facilities, religious sites, construction sites, schools, etc.). Several of our carriers are equipped for such deliveries.

Dangerous Goods Transport can be arranged with carriers who specialize in the transport of dangerous goods (e.g. fuel, (bio-)chemicals and pharmaceuticals).

Expressversand	
Garantierte Dienstleistungen	
Hubtorservice	
Benachrichtigungsservice	
Abholung und Lieferung bei beschränktem Zugang	
Gefahrguttransport	

7 Air transport

FOUNDATION: Air transport planning

Situation: You are an apprentice at Baumann Air Cargo Logistics GmbH in Frankfurt/Main. Your line manager tells you to check air freight handling procedures for your first shipment to a consignee outside Europe and report back to him. You will be sending a valuable shipment of the latest fashionwear to Tokyo, Japan.
→ You prepare a checklist, including aviation time zones, local time and airport codes, for the load to Japan and some more consignments.

1 Why air freight?

First you review the sort of goods normally sent by air and find an interesting blog post.

> … A load sent from Frankfurt to East Asia by air freight costs €1.84 per kilo and takes 11 hours. The same load sent overland and by ship costs four cents per kilo and takes four weeks. For this reason, only the following are sent as air freight, which can be transported on both passenger planes and air freighters:
> ❶ time-sensitive goods (e.g. "must-have" items such as fashionwear, smartphones, medicines),
> ❷ critical parts needed for production or transport,
> ❸ valuable goods (cash, precious metals, works of art) and
> ❹ perishable, temperature-sensitive goods (food, flowers).

A Work with a partner and decide if the goods below are best sent a) overland / by ship or b) as air freight. Which categories from the text (1–4) are the air freight goods in?

wood · wheat · penicillin · new cars · microprocessors · fresh cherries · coal · a Picasso painting

B Can you think of more examples of the four categories? Make a list and discuss it with your class.

2 Time zones

You review the time zone system used in aviation and find a short explanation of Coordinated Universal Time (UTC), also known as Greenwich Mean Time (GMT), on the internet.

A Study the diagram opposite and work out the UTC time at the following locations when it is 4.00 a.m. in London.

Frankfurt · Moscow · Beijing · Tokyo · Vancouver · New York

Air transport Unit 7

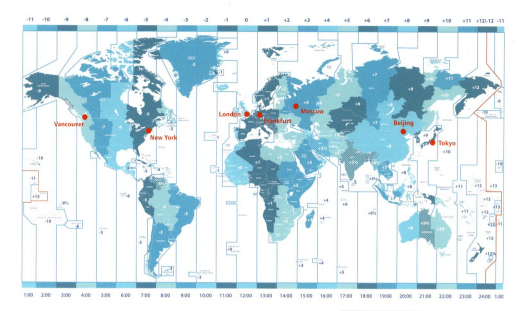

B The flying time from Frankfurt to Tokyo is about 11 hours. What will the local time in Tokyo be if a plane leaves Frankfurt at 11 a.m. and lands in Tokyo 11 hours later? Will it be the same date?

C On the return journey the plane leaves Tokyo at 3 p.m. (15.00 hrs) and lands in Frankfurt 11 hours later. What is the local time in Frankfurt? Will it be the same date?

Infobox

Universal time – some exceptions
Some countries use their own time system. China, for example, covers five meridians but only uses China Standard Time (CST), which is UTC+8. Some countries have daylight saving time (DST) to maximize daylight hours, but this is not the case in Africa or Asia.

3 Airport codes

You receive an email from the Japanese consignee with a poor-quality scan about airport codes and flight times, so you phone to clarify the information.

A 25)) Listen to the phone call and use the international alphabet to write down:

– the three airport codes you hear
– the contact person's email address

Alfa, **B**ravo, **C**harlie, **D**elta, **E**cho, **F**oxtrot, **G**olf, **H**otel, **I**ndia, **J**uliett, **K**ilo, **L**ima, **M**ike, **N**ovember, **O**scar, **P**apa, **Q**uebec, **R**omeo, **S**ierra, **T**ango, **U**niform, **V**ictor, **W**hiskey, **X**-ray, **Y**ankee, **Z**ulu

B Working with a partner, each make a list of all the airport codes you know and dictate them to each other. Swap papers when you have finished and check each other's answers.

4 Finalizing your checklist

Now you are ready to show your line manager your checklists.

A List the time zones and airport codes for the fashionwear to Tokyo.

B You are given some more consignments. Make checklists for the following consignments, and say which of the four categories (see exercise 1 opposite) each one is in.

· roses from Nairobi, Kenya, Jomo Kenyatta Airport to Munich
· medical supplies from Hamburg to Kabul, Afghanistan
· €1 million in cash from London Heathrow to Larnaca, Cyprus
· a jet engine component from Toulouse, France to Sydney, Australia

PART A: IATA and TACT

Situation: You are an apprentice at Ronstadt Air Freight SE, an IATA Cargo Agent in Frankfurt/Main where the company language is English. Your line manager tells you to help a colleague deal with some consignments due for shipment.
→ You use information on the IATA website to check the regulations and schedule shipments with TACT online.

1 Understanding IATA

Your line manager gives you a handout with some facts and figures about IATA.

ABOUT IATA
- global trade association
- since 1945
- offices in 53 countries
- 290 passenger and freight carriers from 120 countries
- 82% of total scheduled traffic
- 250 billion FTK per year
- supports 62.7 million jobs worldwide
- worth $2.7 trillion to the global economy

PRIORITIES

Safety
- airline safety ratings
- accident statistics
- cabin safety

Security
- cargo screenings

Standards
- transportation of dangerous goods, live animals, infectious substances, perishable goods

Environment
- sustainability
- carbon and noise footprint statistics

SERVICES
- simplified paperless electronic payment and clearance system
- currency clearance worldwide
- air cargo market intelligence
- advertising via trade publications, website and newsletters

Study the facts and figures above and answer the questions.

1. How old is IATA?
2. Who are its members?
3. How many people does IATA help to employ directly and indirectly?
4. How does IATA help freight forwarders find a reliable airline?
5. What procedure does IATA support to prevent bombs from being loaded onto planes?
6. What information does IATA provide to enable airlines to monitor pollution levels?
7. How has IATA made it possible for companies to issue and pay invoices more easily?

2 Cargo handling

As an IATA Cargo Agent, you are often asked questions about shipments, so you study the terms used to describe the air freighter that will carry your first load, a unit load device (ULD) of designer clothes.

Use words from the text to label points 1–9 of the diagram.

The long-haul air freighter shown has a capacity of 2,615 m³. It can carry a payload of 53 tonnes and has a range of just over 4,000 km. It has an upward-swinging door over the cockpit for easy loading. A scissor lift is used to load goods, normally in ULDs, into the plane's cargo hold.

The plane has a roller floor so the cargo can easily be pushed into position by only two workers. Although this aircraft is extremely large, with a wingspan of over 60 m, a length of over 56 m and a height of almost 19 m, it can be fully unloaded and loaded in less than an hour.

3 Using TACT

Your company uses *TACT online* to schedule shipments. Under the heading *Documentary requirements* you find out that for security reasons a "precise description" is always required of all items to be shipped as air freight. Descriptions that are imprecise are considered "not acceptable".

Group the descriptions below under the headings "Not acceptable" and "Acceptable". There are six of each.

appliance • carpets • computers • electric saw • electronic goods • flooring • foodstuffs • leather article • machine • oranges • tumble dryer • Western saddle

Infobox

Unit load devices
Air cargo is normally packed using unit load devices (ULDs) which can be pallets or containers contoured to fit into the hold of a passenger or cargo plane. There are almost one million ULDs in service and each one has its own manifest (packing list) and a 10-digit IATA identification code showing its size, type and owner, e.g. AMF 31269 5Y for garments on hangers (GOH) as shown here.

4 Scheduling a consignment with TACT Online

Your first cargo is a consignment of costumes to be flown to New York in a ULD. Your colleague shows you how to enter data on the TACT (Air Cargo Tariff and Rules) website and find out the rates for the shipment.

A First look at the TACT form below and find the English equivalents of these terms.

1. Bestimmungsort
2. Frachtführer
3. frachtpflichtiges Gewicht
4. Gewichtsgebühren
5. Herkunftsort
6. Preisanfrage
7. Stückgut
8. Währung
9. Ware

B 26))) Now listen to your colleague. Look at the form while you listen, and write the missing information 1–15 in your exercise book.

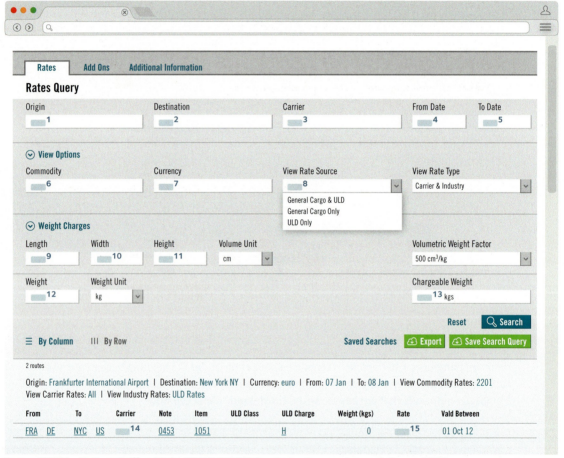

Source: IATA The Air Cargo Tariff and Rules (TACT), *TACT Online*. tact-online.org. Accessed: January 2019

5 Role-play: Scheduling shipments

Your company receives enquiries from exporters about air cargo shipments.

A Role-play a telephone dialogue.

Partner A (cargo agent): Look at File 7 on page 132. **Partner B (exporter):** Look at File 10 on page 134.

B Think of an enquiry that your company has recently received. Make notes on it with your partner and then role-play it in front of your class. Improvise where necessary.

› *Useful phrases: Clarifying details on the phone, page 186*

Air transport   Unit 7

PART B: Completing an air waybill

Situation: You are an apprentice at Ronstadt Air Freight SE, an IATA Cargo Agent in Frankfurt/Main where the company language is English. Your line manager tells you to complete an unfinished air waybill for a colleague who has called in sick.
→ You collect the data on the consignment and use it to complete the air waybill and update your colleague.

1 Preparing an air waybill

First your line manager gives you the shipper's email with information about the consignment.

From: fabrizio.gambino@lorenz-gmbh.ger
To: janine.braun@ronstadt.ger
Subject: Shipment of costumes to Tribeca Opera House, New York
28 Feb 20.., 10:27 GMT+1

Dear Ms Braun

Further to our telephone conversation yesterday, I now wish to confirm our order for shipment of the following goods:

Consignor: Lorenz Costumes GmbH, Andernacher Straße 200, 80993 Munich, Germany
Consignee: Tribeca Opera House, 208 Remsen St, New York, NY10023, USA
From: Frankfurt
To: New York
Goods: opera costumes
Packing: ULD for garments on hangers (GOH)
Delivery: 10 March 20..

Please do not hesitate to contact me should you require further information.

Best regards
Fabrizio Gambino

Dispatch Department
Lorenz Costumes SE
80469 Munich, Germany

Infobox

Shippers, consignors and consignees
The person or company sending the goods is the shipper *(Absender)* or consignor *(Konsignant)*.
The person or company receiving the goods is the consignee *(Empfänger, Konsignatar)*.

Study the email and write down the following in your exercise book.

– the name of the shipper
– the importer
– the airport of departure
– the date of delivery requested

67

2 Adding missing data

Your line manager sends you the unfinished air waybill with a list of more data to add.

A Use the information from the email in exercise 1 and the list below to fill in points 1–9 of the AWB opposite. Write your answers in your exercise book.

AWB no. 81140743

- Pls add this info:
  - FRA – JFK
  - Reserve freight space on flight AC873 on 10 March 20.. and write AC873/10 on AWB
  - For Nature and Quantity of Goods write "CLOTHING AND WEARING APPAREL"
  - For Dimensions or Volume write "AMF 31269 5Y (GOH)"
  - AWB fee is 25.00
  - Date the waybill 3 March 20..

- Phone the shipper and advise him to take out extra insurance for the consignment if it's very valuable. As it stands it's only insured for about €2,500

- Explain there will be fuel and security surcharges

Thx

B 27))) You're unsure about calling the shipper to talk about insurance and surcharges, so you ask your colleague Emily to make the call for you. Listen and complete points A–G on the AWB. (Again, write your answers in your exercise book.)

C 27))) Listen again and complete the sentences with the words you hear.

1. If the costumes were damaged in ▬, you would only get the minimum of about 2,500 euros compensation.
2. That's why I suggest you ▬ out air cargo insurance on the load.
3. The insurance the air carrier offers doesn't cover pre- and on-▬.
4. The ▬ rate for a ULD up to 500 kilos is €1800.
5. We still have the fuel and security ▬ to add.
6. All we have to do now is add up all the ▬.

> **→ Talking about future possibilities**
>
> If the costumes **were** damaged, you **would get** €2,500 compensation. You'**d lose** €47,500 if something **happened** to them.

› *Grammar: Conditional sentences, page 153*

3 Updating a colleague

Write an email to your sick colleague (trevor.bell@ronstadt.ger) telling him about the changes that have been made to the AWB and why. Write in German or English. Start like this in English:

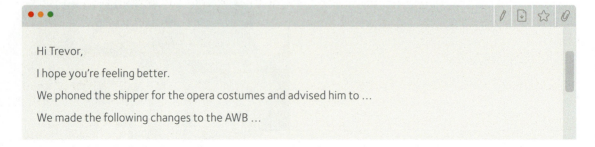

Hi Trevor,

I hope you're feeling better.

We phoned the shipper for the opera costumes and advised him to …

We made the following changes to the AWB …

Air transport Unit 7

Shipper's Name and Address 1	Shipper's Account Number DE478-83206	Not Negotiable Air Waybill Issued By	RONSTADT AIR FREIGHT GMBH CARGO CITY SÜD, GEB:999G 60549 FRANKFURT, GERMANY

Copies 1, 2 and 3 of this Air Waybill are originals and have the same validity.

Consignee's Name and Address 2	Consignee's Account Number US728-21995	It is agreed that the goods described herein are accepted in apparent good order and condition (except as noted) for carriage SUBJECT TO THE CONDITIONS OF CONTRACT ON THE REVERSE HEREOF. All GOODS MAY BE CARRIED BY ANY OTHER MEANS INCLUDING ROAD UNLESS SPECIFIC CONTRARY INSTRUCTIONS ARE GIVEN HEREON BY THE SHIPPER, AND SHIPPER AGREES THAT THE SHIPMENT MAY BE CARRIED VIA INTERMEDIATE STOPPING PLACES WHICH THE CARRIER DEEMS APPROPRIATE. THE SHIPPER'S ATTENTION IS DRAWN TO THE NOTICE CONCERNING CARRIER'S LIMITATION OF LIABILITY. Shipper may increase such limitation of liability by declaring a higher value for carriage and paying a supplemental charge if required.

Issuing Carrier's Agent Name and City RONSTADT AIR FREIGHT GMBH FRANKFURT	Account Information

Agent's IATA Code 23-9 2054/6255	Account No.		

Airport of Departure (Addr. of First Carrier) and Requested Routing	Reference Number	Optional Shipping Information

To 3	By First Carrier RA 018/18	Routing and Destination	To	By RA	To	By	Currency EUR	CHGS Code	WT/VAL PPD X Coll	Other PPD Coll X	Declared Value for Carriage A	Declared Value for Customs NVC

Airport of Destination 4	Requested Flight/Date 5	Amount of Insurance B	INSURANCE – If carrier offers insurance, and such insurance is requested in accordance with the conditions thereof, indicate amount to be insured in figures in box marked "Amount of Insurance".

Handling Information

SCI

No. of Pieces RCP	Gross Weight	kg lb	Rate Class Commodity Item No.	Chargeable Weight	Rate	Charge	Total	Nature and Quantity of Goods (Incl. Dimensions or Volume)
1	100 50	K	U	500	C	C		6 7
1	150						C	

Prepaid C	Weight Charge	Collect	Other Charges AWB FEE 8 (A) D (C) E (C)
	Valuation Charge		
	Tax		
Total Other Charges Due Agent 8			Shipper certifies that the particulars on the face hereof are correct and that insofar as any part of the consignment contains dangerous goods, such part is properly described by name and is in proper condition for carriage by air according to the applicable Dangerous Goods Regulations.
Total Other Charges Due Carrier F			
			Signature of Shipper or his Agent
Total Prepaid G	Total Collect		
Currency Conversion Rates	CC Charges in Dest. Currency	9 Executed on (date)	Frankfurt/Main at (place) Signature of Issuing Carrier or his Agent
For Carrier's Use only at Destination	Charges at Destination	Total Collect Charges	

Source: International Air Transport Association, Cargo Services Conference. Resolution 600a, Attachment 'A' - AIR WAYBILL - TECHNICAL SPECIFICATIONS. *IATA*. iata.org/whatwedo/cargo/Documents/Handbook-links-to-CSC-Resos.pdf Accessed: April 2019

COMMUNICATION: Business trips

Situation: You work for Ronstadt Air Freight SE in Frankfurt/Main. Your line manager tells you to accompany a colleague taking consignments to Ireland and back as an on-board courier (OBC).
→ You make arrangements for an OBC trip.

1 Preparing for the trip

You and your colleague get an email from your line manager with the details.

Please make arrangements for OBC deliveries as follows:

OBC: Hand carry deliveries to and from Hacketstown (near Dublin), Ireland
Article: DNA samples
Category: urgent

Outward journey
Date: 5 May 20..
Pick-up: 7.00 hrs, Institut für Humangenetik, Hardenbergstraße 200, 60327 Frankfurt
Delivery: by 18.00 hrs, to Medlab Services, 96 Water St, Hacketstown, Co. Carlow, Ireland

Return journey
Date/time: 6 May 20..
Pick-up: 10.00 hrs, Medlab Services, 96 Water St, Hacketstown, Co. Carlow, Ireland
Delivery: by 22.00 hrs, to Institut für Humangenetik, Hardenbergstraße 200, 60327 Frankfurt

Samples will be in a lightweight (5 kg) attaché case[1].
There is sometimes flooding in Hacketstown, so a four-wheel drive is advisable.

Thx

[1]Aktentasche

A Read the email and decide which two categories the shipments fall into.

aerospace · automotive · documents · hazardous · hi-tech · medical · pharmaceutical · time-sensitive

B Decide whether the following statements are true or false. Correct the false statements.

1. The courier will check in the attaché case before the flight.
2. The courier has to deliver the samples to Medlab Services at exactly 18.00 hrs.
3. The courier will also bring samples back from Ireland.
4. The courier is advised to travel to the destination and back by public transport.

2 Booking flights

Your colleague phones your company's travel section to book your flights.

28 🔊 Listen to the phone call and complete the flight details. Write the missing information 1–8 in your exercise book.

Date	Flight	Departure	Arrival	Details
5 May 20..	___1	FRA ___2	DUB ___3	class: ___4
6 May 20..	___5	DUB ___6	FRA ___7	class: ___8

Air transport   Unit 7

3 Booking transport and accommodation

You and your colleague next log onto the travel section on your company's intranet to book transport and accommodation in Dublin.

A Look at the list below and decide what you will need for your OBC trip. Make notes in your exercise book.

OBC TRAVEL REQUIREMENTS
Travellers: 1) *Janine Braun*   2) *[Your full name]*

1. Number and type of rooms (single/double/family) required
2. Location (town/city/other)
3. Check-in date
4. Check-out date
5. Hotel / guest house / apartment
6. Facilities (e.g. parking / airport shuttle / Wi-Fi / laundry service)
7. Meals (breakfast / half-board / full-board / self-catering)
8. Other transport needed to final destination (e.g. train / coach / bus / taxi / hire car)

B 29)) After you submit an online form with the information above, your colleague receives a call from the travel section. Listen and compare your notes with the final arrangements. Are there any differences?

C 29)) Who says what? Divide the sentences from the dialogue into what the travel section employee says and what the on-board courier says, then listen again to check your answers.

1. I'm calling about the trip to Dublin.
2. It's an urgent consignment and we don't want any delays.
3. Could you look for accommodation in Hacketstown?
4. That's two return trips costing a total of €82.
5. There's one available from the fifth to the sixth.
6. Please book that for us.
7. Shall I put you down for B&B, half board or full board?
8. We'll take the Farm House.

4 Role-play: Making travel arrangements

Your next flight as an OBC is from Frankfurt to Nice Airport (NCE), France with a time-sensitive automotive part for a rally in Monaco. You call the travel section to make the arrangements.

👥 Work with a partner.
Partner A: Look at File 11 on page 134. **Partner B:** Look at File 14 on page 136.

› *Thematic vocabulary: Business trips, page 197*

DAS KANN ICH (Unit 7)

– Eine Luftfrachtlieferung mit Zielort in einer anderen Zeitzone planen. (Foundation)
– Eine Luftfrachtlieferung mithilfe von IATA und TACT planen. (Part A)
– Einen Luftfrachtbrief vorbereiten und ausfüllen. (Part B)
– Transport und Unterkunft für eine begleitete Sendung planen und buchen. (Communication)

71

8 Sea transport

FOUNDATION: Sea freight planning

Situation: You are doing an apprenticeship at Sea Freight Services GmbH in Hamburg. Your vocational college has an *Azubi-Channel* and wants blog posts in English about typical tasks at work.
→ You write a blog post describing how a consignment was categorized, matched with a suitable vessel and shipped.

1 Why sea freight?

First you do some research on the sort of consignments normally sent by sea and find an article about sea freight on the internet.

Pros and cons of sea freight: About 90% of global trade is transported by ship, but sea freight is not always suitable. Here are some advantages and disadvantages.

Advantages	Disadvantages
Ships can carry • up to 20,000 containers. • dry, liquid or granular bulk (unpackaged) commodities such as wheat, petrol and gravel. • extremely large and/or heavy cargoes. In addition, ships • use a natural, international infrastructure that cost nothing to build. • are cost-effective for distances of 400 km or more. • are environmentally friendly if low-sulphur fuels are used.	Ships are • slow in comparison to other modes of transport (see diagram). • expensive for distances under 400 km. • inflexible (i.e. unsuitable for door-to-door or just-in-time delivery). • sometimes delayed by bad weather. • at risk in areas where there is piracy. • environmentally dangerous if they use high-sulphur fuel (bunker fuel) or break up and cause an oil spill.

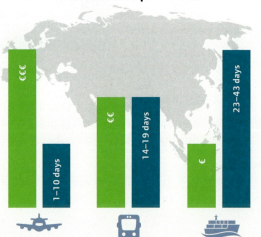

Transit: Europe – Asia (plane: 1–10 days; train: 14–19 days; ship: 23–43 days)

👥 Work with a partner and decide which of the consignments are suitable for sea transport and which are not. Give reasons for your answers in each case.

an ocean liner's propeller • designer clothes for a fashion show • emergency food aid • fresh flowers • iron ore • salt • US$1,000,000 in gold • vegetable oil

Sea transport Unit 8

2 Choosing a suitable vessel

Next you review the different types of vessels available.

Match the pictures (A–F) with the descriptions (1–6).

A

B

C

D

E −25 °C to +25 °C

F

1 A bulk carrier transports unpackaged cargoes that are dropped or poured into its holds.
2 Some container ships can carry more than 20,000 TEU (twenty-foot equivalent units).
3 Crude carriers transport crude oil, e.g. from an oil rig to a refinery.
4 Liquefied gas carriers transport petroleum or natural gas in pressurized tanks.
5 Reefer vessels carry temperature-sensitive cargoes such meat and other perishable goods.
6 Ro-ro (roll-on roll-off) vessels carry vehicles that drive on at one end and off at the other.

3 Placing a load

A school in Essen closed down recently, and your company was commissioned by a local charity to send the furniture to a school in Kinshasa in the Democratic Republic of the Congo (DRC) as cheaply as possible.

Use the information in the table to write a blog post called "Destination Kinshasa". Include:

− why sea freight was preferable to overland transport in this case (price, time)
− the type of vessel and cargo category
− a step-by-step description of how the load was sent from its origin to its destination

Begin like this: *A local charity suggested helping a school in Kinshasa, DRC …*

	PLACE	DISTANCE	TRANSIT TIME	PRICE
🚚	Essen (road haulage)	307 km	9 hours	US$585
📦	Bremerhaven (unloading, loading, export formalities, documentation)		2–4 days	US$178
🚢	Bremerhaven – Matadi, DRC (sea freight, container ship)	9,477 km	22 days	US$2,400
📦	Matadi, DRC (unloading, loading, import formalities, documentation)		1–2 days	
🚚	Kinshasa (road haulage)	329 km	9 hours	US$1,746
			Total	US$4,909
🚚	Essen (road haulage)	9228 km	11 days	
	Kinshasa		Total	US$9,789

PART A: Containers

Situation: You are doing an apprenticeship at Lohmann Sea Freight Services GmbH in Hamburg. Your company is commissioned to ship some medical equipment to Singapore, and your line manager tells you to book container space for the load.
→ You write an email to the consignee recommending a suitable mode of transport.

1 Container handling and stowage

Before booking space, you review how containers are handled at a port and stowed on board a ship.

Use words from the description to label the diagram below (1–6).

Unloading, loading and securing

When a container lorry arrives at an automated port, it first goes through a truck gate where its arrival is recorded and the container is identified electronically. The driver then reverses the lorry under a gantry crane, which picks up the container and stacks it. Later, the gantry crane loads the container onto an automated guided vehicle (AGV). The AGV takes the container to a larger gantry crane, which loads it onto the ship.

To prevent slippage and toppling during sea voyages, containers are locked together with twistlocks at each corner and attached to the deck of the ship with lashing rods.

2 Container dimensions

As customers often ask detailed questions about containers, you study a description on your company's intranet.

Standard sizes

Containers are normally classified by their length, and the most commonly used are 10, 20, 40, 45, 48 or 53 feet long. Most containers are hard-top containers for dry loads (dry containers) and their capacity is measured in twenty-foot equivalent units (TEU). The weight of a container when empty is its tare weight, and the maximum weight it can carry is its payload, net weight or stuffing weight. The tare weight and payload together are the container's maximum gross weight.

Common container dimensions and volumes

	20 ft	40 ft	40 ft high cube
Length	20 ft (6.1 m)	40 ft (12.2 m)	40 ft (12.2 m)
Width	8 ft (2.44 m)	8 ft (2.44 m)	8 ft (2.44 m)
Height	8 ft 6 in (2.59 m)	8 ft 6 in (2.59 m)	9 ft 6 in (2.90 m)
Capacity	1,172 cu ft (33 m^3)	2,377 cu ft (67 m^3)	2,714 cu ft (76 m^3)
TEU*	1	2	2
Tare weight	2,150 kg (4,740 lbs)	3,700 kg (8,157 lbs)	3,800 kg (8,378 lbs)
Payload	24,850 kg (54,785 lbs)	32,500 kg (71,659 lbs)	30,200 kg (66,580 lbs)
Max. gross weight	27,000 kg (59,525 lbs)	36,200 kg (79,807 lbs)	34,000 kg (74,957 lbs)

*A TEU (twenty-foot equivalent unit) is an inexact unit of measurement.

Use information from the text and table to:

1 label the dimensions (a–c) of the container shown here.
2 give the volume of the container shown in three different units.
3 explain whether it is suitable for a load weighing 25,000 kg or not.
4 find the difference between a 40 ft container and a 40 ft high cube container.

20 ft dry container

Infobox

Symbols and abbreviations

'	foot (*pl* feet)	m^3	cubic metre(s)
"	inches(es)	ft^3	cubic foot (*pl* feet)
kg	kilo(s)	lb(s)	pound(s)

The word *foot* has an irregular plural: *feet*
1 ft = one foot   20/40 ft = twenty/forty feet
A 20 ft container = a twenty-foot container
20' × 8' × 8'6" = twenty (feet) by eight (feet) by eight foot six inches

› *Conversion tables, page 179*

3 Container types

Next you check the descriptions of the containers your company uses most.

> ### Common container types
> Containers can be adapted for almost any type of load, but in most cases a hard top (dry) container in a standard size is used. Over-height and/or heavy consignments moved by crane are transported in open-top containers. Flat rack containers without a top or sides are used for over-sized, bulky and/or heavy, weather-resistant loads. Temperature-sensitive cargoes and perishable goods are sent in reefer containers. Organic products that give off condensation are transported in ventilated containers with slats (thin pieces of metal) and openings to let in the air. Bulk containers are used for unpackaged commodities.

A Study the text and label the containers (1–6).

1 — sugar

2 — cocoa beans

3 — steel coils

4 — large saw

5 — clothing

6 — −25 °C to +25 °C — fresh flowers

B Choose a suitable container for the loads below.

a crate measuring 5 m × 2 m × 3.5 m (length/width/height) · coffee beans · computers · frozen meat · grain · steel piping

4 Dealing with an enquiry

Before booking container space, you contact the consignor and receive details of the loads.

Study the email and identify the consignor, consignee, port of loading and port of destination.

Many thanks for your email of 17 January 20... .

The consignments that we wish you to ship from the Port of Rotterdam to the Port of Singapore are:
- 20 m³ of medical equipment (patient monitors, sterilizers, ECG machines)
- 15 m³ of hospital supplies (bedding, bandages, etc.)

Please arrange for these items to be collected at our premises and shipped asap for delivery to:
Singapore University Hospital
1090 Yishun Central, Singapore 768828
Contact: Lee Kuan Tong, Tel. +65 6332 719

We look forward to receiving your confirmation.

Yours sincerely

Mark Walker
Export Sales Manager – Medical Supplies International

Sea transport Unit 8

5 Full container load (FCL) or less than container load (LCL)?

Before contacting the supplier, you find out about the terms that show whether or not consignments may be consolidated with others (groupage consignments). You talk to colleagues about the pros and cons of FCL and LCL shipments and make notes.

Infobox

Container loads
FCL/FCL: full container load with one consignment for one consignee
FCL/LCL: full container load with consignments for more than one consignee
LCL/LCL: less than full container load with consignments for multiple consignees
LCL/FCL: less than full container load with multiple consignments for one consignee

A Copy the table into your exercise book and complete it with the notes below.

	FCL (full container load)	LCL (less than container load)
Cost		
Time		
Risks – theft – damage		

FCL

your goods

LCL

other shippers' goods

your goods

Notes:
1. cheaper for small amounts
2. expensive for small amounts
3. faster, one-stop collection and delivery; one set of documents; faster customs clearance
4. less risk of damage because goods are only handled on collection and delivery
5. less risk of theft because container is locked and unlocked once
6. more risk of damage because of frequent handling for multiple collections and deliveries
7. more risk of theft because container is locked and unlocked multiple times
8. shipper bears entire cost of container
9. shipper shares cost of container
10. slower, multi-stop collection and delivery; multiple sets of documents; slower customs clearance

B Study your table and mark each of the 10 points with A for advantage and D for disadvantage.

6 Recommending a suitable container

You can now reply to Mark Walker at Medical Supplies International and recommend suitable containers for the two loads.

Write an email in your name to Mark Walker (mark.walker@medsint.sng). Include the following points:

- Datum: 19. Januar 20..
- Dank für E-Mail vom 18. Januar 20..
- Empfehlung (FCL- oder LCL-Ladung) für Ladung 1
- Begründung
- Empfehlung (FCL- oder LCL-Ladung) für Ladung 2
- Begründung
- Platz in Containern für beide Ladungen ist inzwischen reserviert
- Abholtermin 25. Januar 20..
- Transitzeit ca. 25 Tage
- Bitte um Bestätigung
- Höflicher Schluss

PART B: Transport documents

Situation: You are doing an apprenticeship at Lohmann Sea Freight Services GmbH in Hamburg, and your company has been commissioned to ship a consignment of medical equipment to a hospital in Singapore.
→ You prepare the transport document needed for a sea freight shipment.

1 Marine transport documents

Your company's intranet has descriptions of the two sea transport documents normally used.

› *Thematic vocabulary: Shipping documents, page 198*

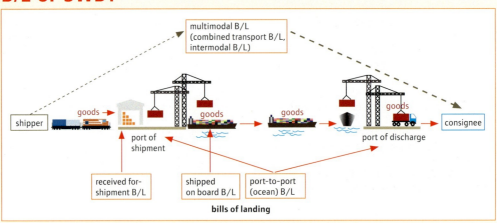

B/L or SWB?

The information needed for goods transported by sea is contained in a bill of lading (B/L) or a sea waybill (SWB).

A **bill of lading** is a receipt for the goods, a contract of carriage and a document of title. It is usually issued by the carrier in triplicate (three originals) on receipt of the goods. The carrier (shipping company) sends the three originals to the shipper (seller) and keeps a copy. The shipper sends the originals to the consignee on the terms agreed, and when the goods reach their destination, the consignee presents one original to the carrier and receives the goods in exchange. After this, the other originals are void.

As a document of title, a B/L is negotiable, meaning that it can be bought and sold while the goods are in transit. A B/L used to transfer ownership in this way is called an order bill of lading.

A received for shipment B/L is issued by the carrier when the goods are on land, waiting to be loaded on a ship. A shipped on board B/L is issued when the goods have been loaded on board the ship. A received for shipment B/L can be converted into a shipped on board B/L after loading. When a port-to-port (or ocean) B/L is used, the carrier is only responsible for the goods during the sea voyage from the port of shipment to the port of discharge. When a multimodal (combined transport / intermodal) B/L is used, the carrier is responsible for the goods for all modes of transport from origin to destination.

A B/L stating that the goods are in apparent good order is said to be clean. This means that the goods and their packaging show no external signs of damage and no items are missing. If there are signs of damage or items are missing, the B/L is said to be foul or claused. A clean, on board bill of lading is often required when payment is made by letter of credit.

A **sea waybill** is a contract of carriage and a receipt for the goods but not a document of title. It is therefore non-negotiable. When an SWB is used, the consignee only has to provide proof of identity to the carrier to obtain the goods, so less time and paperwork are needed. In general, an SWB is used (a) if the shipper knows and trusts the consignee; (b) if the buyer does not wish to sell the goods to another party before they arrive; (c) if the buyer has paid for the goods in advance.

Sea transport Unit 8

A Find the English equivalents of the following German words and expressions in the text and diagram. (The words below are in the same order as the English equivalents.)

1 Konnossement
2 Seefrachtbrief
3 Quittung
4 Beförderungsvertrag
5 Traditionspapier (Eigentumsurkunde)
6 Frachtführer
7 Versender
8 begebbar (übertragbar)
9 Orderkonnossement
10 Übernahmekonnossement
11 Bordkonnossement
12 Löschungshafen
13 in äußerlich gutem Zustand
14 rein
15 unrein
16 Identitätsnachweis

B Study the text and diagram and complete the statements with a, b or c.

1 A bill of lading and a sea waybill have
   a one feature in common. b two features in common. c three features in common.

2 A bill of lading is normally issued by
   a the importer. b the importer's bank. c the shipping company.

3 The holder of the bill of lading has the right to
   a take possession of the goods. b buy the goods. c insure the goods.

4 An order bill of lading
   a cannot be sold. b cannot be used to transfer ownership. c can be bought and sold.

5 A received for shipment B/L is issued when the goods are
   a on board a ship. b on land. c at their destination.

6 A shipped on board B/L can only be issued when the goods have
   a been loaded on a vessel. b reached their destination. c reached the port of discharge.

7 If a consignment is sent to its destination by rail, sea and road, the carrier issues
   a a port-to-port B/L. b an ocean B/L. c a multimodal B/L.

8 If the bill of lading is clean,
   a goods can be missing but not damaged. b no goods show signs of damage or are missing.
   c some goods can show signs of damage but none are missing.

9 If a sea waybill is used, the buyer can obtain the goods if he/she
   a pays the carrier. b proves his/her identity to the carrier. c gives the carrier the original SWB.

10 An SWB is often used in order to
    a save time. b reduce the risk. c avoid customs duties.

79

2 Understanding a bill of lading

Some work has been done on the bill of lading for the medical supplies to Singapore.

LOHMANN SEA FREIGHT SERVICES		**BILL OF LADING FOR OCEAN TRANSPORT OR MULTIMODAL TRANSPORT**	B/L No. 731196330
Shipper MEDICAL SUPPLIES INTERNATIONAL CONDENSATORWEG 500, 1014 AX AMSTERDAM, NETHERLANDS		Booking No. 325001839	
		Export references	
		Onward inland routing (Not part of Carriage as defined in clause 1. For account and risk of Merchant)	
Consignee (negotiable only if consigned "to order", "to order of" a named Person or "to order of bearer") SINGAPORE UNIVERSITY HOSPITAL 1090 YISHUN CENTRAL, SINGAPORE 768828		Notify Party MR LEE KUAN TONG ▭¹	
Vessel MS BARBARA	Voyage No. 1592	Place of Receipt. Applicable only when document used as Multimodal Transport B/L. AMSTERDAM, NETHERLANDS	
Port of Loading ROTTERDAM	Port of Discharge SINGAPORE	Place of Delivery. Applicable only when document used as Multimodal Transport B/L. SINGAPORE UNIVERSITY HOSPITAL	
PARTICULARS FURNISHED BY SHIPPER			
Kind of Packages; Description of goods; Marks and Numbers; Container No./Seal No. 1x 20' STANDARD CONTAINER S.T.C.* STERILIZERS ECG MACHINES ▭³ SHIPPING MARKS ▭⁴ ▭⁵ FREIGHT ▭⁶ L/C NO. ▭⁸ Above particulars as declared by Shipper, but without responsibility or representation by Carrier		Weight ▭² kg	Measurement
Freight & Charges	Rate	Unit	Currency	Prepaid ▭⁷	Collect ▭⁷
Carrier's Receipt. Total number of containers or packages received by Carrier. 15		Place of Issue of B/L ROTTERDAM	**SHIPPED**, as far as ascertained by reasonable means of checking, **IN APPARENT GOOD ORDER AND CONDITION** … Where the bill of lading is negotiable, the Merchant is obliged to surrender one original, duly endorsed, in exchange for the goods. The Carrier accepts a duty of reasonable care to check that any such document which the Merchant surrenders as a bill of lading is genuine and original. If the Carrier complies with this duty, it will be entitled to deliver the Goods against what it reasonably believes to be a genuine and original bill of lading, such delivery discharging the Carrier's delivery obligations. … wherever one original bill of lading has been surrendered any others shall be void.	
Number & Sequence of Original B(s)/L 03 (THREE)		Date of Issue of B/L 29 MAY 20..		
Declared Value		Shipped on-board Date 29 MAY 20..		
Signed for the Carrier Lohmann Sea Freight Services			As Agent(s) for the Carrier	

*said to contain

Sea transport Unit 8

A   Study the document and make notes on the following points:

- consignor
- consignee
- name of vessel
- goods
- port of loading
- port of discharge
- shipped on board or received for shipment B/L
- clean or foul

B   Will the B/L be a port-to-port (ocean) or multimodal B/L for the consignment of medical equipment to Singapore? Give reasons for your answer.

3 Finalizing the details of a B/L

A colleague starts work on the B/L but calls in sick, so you complete the document.

A   30))) Listen to the telephone call to Mark Walker at Medical Supplies International and list the information missing on the B/L opposite (1–8).

B   30))) Listen again and complete the sentences from the dialogue with the words you hear.

1   We have to ▬ the B/L for the shipment.
2   We need more details about the ▬ party.
3   We need to know if it's a ▬ or port-to-port B/L.
4   Do you want us to pick up the consignment at your ▬?
5   So you require ▬ from Amsterdam to Rotterdam.
6   We'd like you to deliver it to the ▬ in Singapore, too.
7   So you also require ▬.
8   And when can we expect the consignment to be ▬?

C   Use your answers from exercise B to complete the text of an email to your colleague. Make any necessary changes to the words.

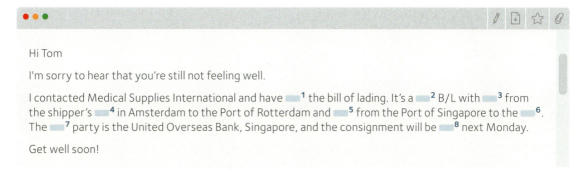

Hi Tom

I'm sorry to hear that you're still not feeling well.

I contacted Medical Supplies International and have ▬¹ the bill of lading. It's a ▬² B/L with ▬³ from the shipper's ▬⁴ in Amsterdam to the Port of Rotterdam and ▬⁵ from the Port of Singapore to the ▬⁶. The ▬⁷ party is the United Overseas Bank, Singapore, and the consignment will be ▬⁸ next Monday.

Get well soon!

4 Issuing a bill of lading

Your colleague is still off sick, so your line manager sends you the data needed to complete another B/L.

Use the following information to complete the bill of lading. (Your teacher will give you a form to fill in.)

Versender: VGO Clothing Ltd, Joydebpur Rd, Gazipur, Bangladesh; Empfänger: Foot-Sprint GmbH, Lange Reihe 400, 28217 Bremen, Germany. Die zu benachrichtigende Person beim Empfänger ist Mr Dieter Dombrowski, Deutsche Bank Bremen, und die Ware wird an Bord des Schiffes MS Cynthia transportiert. Verladehafen ist Chittagong, Löschungshafen Hamburg und Empfangsort Bremen, Deutschland. Gesamt-gewicht der Ware: 2.450 kg; Versandmarkierungen: AJGLK/04195; Fracht bezahlt; Akkreditiv-Nr.: BOB927741; B/L wird in Dhaka ausgestellt.

81

COMMUNICATION: Scheduling

Situation: You are doing an apprenticeship at Lohmann Sea Freight Services GmbH in Hamburg. Your line manager tells you to schedule a consignment of medical equipment from Germany to Singapore.
→ You contact both the consignor and consignee and agree collection and delivery dates.

1 Scheduling collection

Your English line manager, Yvonne Johnson, tells you to email the consignor and finalize collection details. She gives you the following instructions.

- Please send an email in my name to Mark Walker, Export Sales Manager, Medical Supplies International.
- Say collection of medical equipment from their Amsterdam warehouse will be in week 42/43.
- Ask about late collection after 8 p.m.
- Tell Mr Walker to phone Smits Forwarding BV (tel. +31-10-706623) for any last-minute changes.
- Say it's an FCA shipment in a standard 20' dry container with seaworthy packing.
- Get the name and phone number of a contact person at the warehouse in Amsterdam.

> **Giving dates, days and times**
> **at** 6 p.m., **at** lunchtime, **at** the weekend
> **on** Monday, **on** 21 June
> **in** the morning/afternoon/evening,
> **in** week 9, **in** January, **in** 2017

› Incoterms® rules, page 177

Complete your company's standard email for collections to Mark Walker using words and phrases from the notes above.

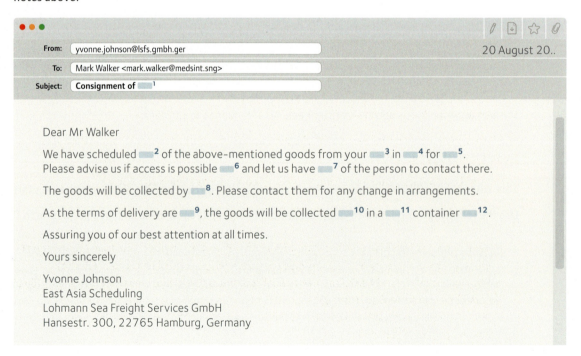

Sea transport Unit 8

2 Re-scheduling delivery

Your line manager tells you to phone the consignee because delivery will be delayed. Before you phone, you make notes on what you are going to say and how to say it as politely as possible.

A Match these basic phrases with the politer versions.

Basic phrases
1. The goods are going to be late.
2. There's nothing we can do about it.
3. I can't say when you'll get them.
4. Your goods will be first off the ship.
5. Sorry about all the trouble.
6. We've no idea what happened.

Politer phrases
a. I can't give you a firm date at the moment.
b. Please accept our apologies for the inconvenience.
c. We're still waiting for an explanation ourselves.
d. I'm afraid delivery of the goods will be delayed.
e. We promise to give your goods priority when unloading the vessel.
f. It's unfortunately due to circumstances beyond our control.

B 31 🔊 Listen to the phone call with Naomi Tan at Singapore University Hospital and note which of the politer phrases (a–f) are used.

3 Writing an email

The weather gets better and you send the consignee details of the new arrangements.

Write an email in your name to Naomi Tan (naomi.tan@uh-singapore.sng).
Use the following information:

- Betreff: Voraussichtliche Ankunftszeit medizinische Geräte
- Datum: 26. Oktober 20..
- Dank für Geduld
- Bezug auf Telefonat am 20. Oktober
- Sturm im Arabischen Meer hat sich verzogen *(to blow over)*
- Schifffahrt hat sich wieder normalisiert *(to be back to normal)*
- voraussichtliche Ankunftszeit der Ware: Ende KW 48
- Bitte um Entschuldigung für die Unannehmlichkeiten
- höflicher Schluss

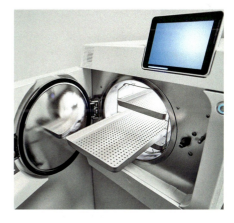

4 Role-play: Discussing schedules over the phone

The bad weather delays another consignment, so you phone the consignee.

👥 Work with a partner. Make sure that you are as polite as possible on the phone. When you have finished, swap roles and repeat the role-play.

Partner A: Look at File 12 on page 134. Partner B: Look at File 15 on page 136.

DAS KANN ICH (Unit 8)

- Ein geeignetes Schiff für verschiedene Ladungen wählen und darüber berichten. (Foundation)
- Einen geeigneten Container für verschiedene Ladungen per E-Mail empfehlen. (Part A)
- Die Eigenschaften und Funktionen eines Seefrachtbriefs (SWB) und eines Konnossements (B/L) verstehen und anwenden. (Part B)
- Mit einem Geschäftspartner höflich und professionell über Abhol- und Liefertermine kommunizieren. (Communication)

83

KMK Exam practice 4

1 Hörverstehen: Stufe II (B1)

Situation: Sie arbeiten in der Logistikabteilung einer englischen Eisengießerei in Chester, die einen zweiten Produktionsstandort in Waco, Texas (USA) unterhält. Sie erhalten den Auftrag, umgehend einen OBC zu buchen, da in den USA aufgrund eines fehlenden mechanischen Ersatzteils ein Produktionsstopp droht. Ihre Kollegin Vivien, die diese Buchungen normalerweise tätigt, hat sich heute krankgemeldet und Sie müssen einspringen. Allerdings hat sie Ihnen eine Sprachnachricht geschickt, um Sie zu unterstützen.

32 🔊 **Aufgabe:** Übertragen Sie das Formular in Ihr Arbeitsheft und füllen Sie es aus.

CLIENT BOOKING FORM

SECTION A	new clients please register here				
	private/commercial: ▭		contact data: ▭		
SECTION B	registered clients please continue here				
requested service:	value courier ☐	handcarry delivery ☐	same-day courier ☐	time-sensitive ☐	temperature-sensitive ☐
category: *(please fill in)*	▭				
hazardous: *(yes/no)*	▭				
packaging of item: ▭ *(attaché case, plastic box, cardboard box)*			**weight (approx.):** ▭		
number of items: ▭		**name/marking of item:** ▭			
supporting documents: *(please fill in)*	▭				
outward journey					
from: ▭			**to:** ▭		
earliest availability of item to be delivered					
date: ▭			**time:** ▭		
submit for instant quote					

2 Mediation: Stufe II (B1)

Situation: Sie bereiten sich auf ein Praktikum in einer englischen Firma vor, die in Liverpool (England) ansässig ist und internationale Logistik im Bereich Verschiffung betreibt. Um einen ersten Überblick über branchenspezifische Organisationen zu bekommen und sich mit Begrifflichkeiten und Abkürzungen vertraut zu machen, übertragen Sie sich den folgenden Text, den Sie im Internet gefunden haben.

Aufgabe: Fassen Sie auf Deutsch die wesentlichen Informationen in einer Tabelle zusammen.

International Maritime Organization
The International Maritime Organization (IMO) belongs to the United Nations, with its 171 member states, and deals mainly with the development and maintenance of a framework that regulates international shipping. To achieve international goals, such as the protection of the environment, it is necessary to reach a common global understanding of technical standards and safety issues.

United Nations Commission on International Trade Law
The abbreviation UNCITRAL stands for the United Nations Commission on International Trade Law. Established in 1966, it focuses on differences between national laws and international conventions. The commission is constantly trying to reach legal agreements, particularly concerning the carriage of goods by sea.

International Organization for Standardization
The International Organization for Standardization (ISO) connects national standards institutes, which are responsible for technical standards, criteria and regulations in a country or state. Its goal is international agreement on how products and materials are manufactured and labelled, so that international trade can rely on established classifications.

World Customs Organization
The WCO is an independent organization, consisting of members from various governments around the world. National customs regulations are compared and evaluated. The overall goal is to achieve as much cooperation on customs issues as possible between member states.

Organisation	Beschreibung/Aufgabenbereich
IMO	
UNCITRAL	
ISO	
WCO	

9 Orders and payments

FOUNDATION: Preparing to order

Situation: You are an apprentice at InterFracht Neumann GmbH in Hamburg where the company language is English. InterFracht will need equipment for a new warehouse in around six months' time. The Purchasing Director gives you a checklist and tells you to compare offers from different suppliers.
→ You compare the terms offered by three suppliers and make a recommendation.

1 Reviewing offers

You receive offers from suppliers in China, Finland and France.

Offer no. 1: Amanda Hei in the Export Sales department at Toprac Ltd in Hong Kong, China sends you an offer via online chat.

Amanda: … We have sold whole warehouse solutions to many European customers and are pleased to offer as follows: Warehouse equipment as specified, US$30,000, FOB Hong Kong, payment by TT* – 50% with order, 50% before loading, guarantee 2 years, delivery 60 days after receipt of order.

InterFracht: Customs duties on goods entering the EU from China will be about 26%, i.e. USD7,800. How much are the shipping charges to Hamburg?

Amanda: Our freight agent can offer you USD1,800 for one 40' container.

*Telegraphic transfer

InterFracht: Thanks. We'll be in touch.

Offer no. 2: Miika Virtanen from FinStore Oy, Oulu, Finland, emails you the offer below.

Product:	Warehouse solution, as per your specifications
Price:	€45,000
Terms of delivery:	CFR Hamburg
Terms of payment:	1/3 with order, 1/3 on delivery, 1/3 within 30 days after delivery
Guarantee:	4 years
Delivery period:	90 days

Offer no. 3: You phone Chantal Goddard, the European Sales Director at Rayonnage Leclerc SA in Metz, France and note down these details.

> total of €45,000, 5 years' guarantee, DAT Hamburg, CWO (cash with order), can deliver in 30 days

Orders and payments Unit 9

Study the offers 1–3 and say which one …

1 will require InterFracht to pay customs duties.
2 includes an exchange rate risk.
3 requires full payment before the goods are shipped.
4 has the longest guarantee and the shortest delivery period.

2 Comparing terms of delivery (Incoterms® rules)

Next you study the Incoterms® rules for the three orders using the definitions on your company's intranet.

FOB – FREE ON BOARD (… named port of shipment) The seller is not responsible for the main carriage of the goods. The seller delivers the goods at their own expense and risk, in the customary packing, cleared for export, on board the vessel selected by the buyer unless otherwise agreed, at the named port of shipment. Thereafter, the buyer bears all the costs and risks of transporting the goods to their destination.

CFR – COST AND FREIGHT (… named port of destination) The seller pays for the main carriage of the goods. The seller delivers the goods at their own expense and risk, in the customary packing, cleared for export, on board the vessel selected by the buyer, at the named port of shipment. The seller pays the transport costs for the goods, excluding transport insurance, up to the named port of destination. The buyer is responsible for insuring the goods for the main carriage and pays all import duties and taxes.

DAT – DELIVERED AT TERMINAL (… named terminal at port or place of destination) Multimodal transport The seller is responsible for the carriage of the goods in the customary packing, cleared for export to the named terminal at the destination by the carrier which they nominate. They bear the risk until the goods have been delivered to the named terminal. The seller is responsible for unloading the goods at the place of destination. The buyer pays all import duties and taxes.

A Study the three definitions and find the English equivalents of the German terms below.

auf eigene Kosten · Bestimmungshafen · Einfuhrzölle und Steuern · frei an Bord · geliefert Terminal · Haupttransport · Kosten und Fracht · übliche Verpackung · Verschiffungshafen · zur Ausfuhr freigemacht

B Copy the checklist into your book and complete it for the remaining offers.

CHECKLIST		Main carriage		Seller bears risks	
Supplier	Incoterms® rule	paid	unpaid	including main carriage	excluding main carriage
Toprac Ltd, Hong Kong, China	FOB Hong Kong		✓		✓

› Incoterms® rules, page 177

C Which of the offers will require a) the importer to insure the goods for the main carriage, b) the seller to pay for unloading at the place/port of destination, and c) the buyer to pay all import duties?

3 Making a recommendation

You are now ready to recommend a supplier.

A Calculate the final price in euros up to the Port of Hamburg / Hamburg Terminal for each offer. If sea freight insurance is necessary, assume the rate will be 0.6% of the insured value (i.e. price + shipping charges).

B Recommend one or two of the three offers. Use the language box to give reasons for your choice.

> **Recommending offers**
>
> I would recommend ordering from / that we order from … (supplier) because …
> Despite … (e.g. the exchange rate risk, currency fluctuation, customs duties), …
> …'s price is … (e.g. almost the same as, far higher/lower than) …'s price.

› Useful phrases: Recommending offers, page 187

PART A: Evaluating an offer

Situation: You are an apprentice at InterFracht Neumann GmbH in Hamburg. Your company needs equipment for a new warehouse in around six months' time and has received an interesting offer, but Alex Horn, the Purchasing Director, wants better terms.
→ You prepare a counter-offer with more favourable terms for your company.

1 Analysing an offer

The Chinese supplier has sent a detailed offer by email.

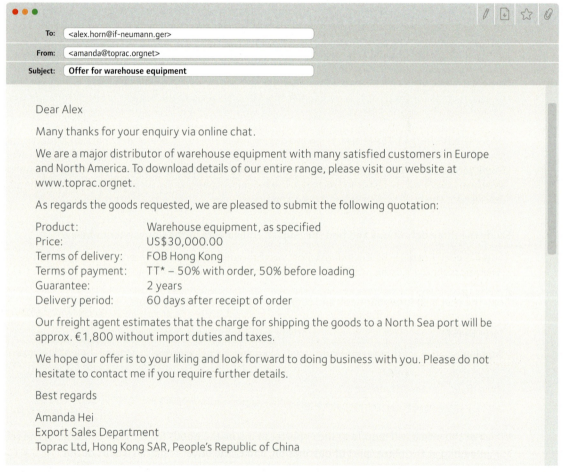

To: <alex.horn@if-neumann.ger>
From: <amanda@toprac.orgnet>
Subject: Offer for warehouse equipment

Dear Alex

Many thanks for your enquiry via online chat.

We are a major distributor of warehouse equipment with many satisfied customers in Europe and North America. To download details of our entire range, please visit our website at www.toprac.orgnet.

As regards the goods requested, we are pleased to submit the following quotation:

Product:	Warehouse equipment, as specified
Price:	US$30,000.00
Terms of delivery:	FOB Hong Kong
Terms of payment:	TT* – 50% with order, 50% before loading
Guarantee:	2 years
Delivery period:	60 days after receipt of order

Our freight agent estimates that the charge for shipping the goods to a North Sea port will be approx. €1,800 without import duties and taxes.

We hope our offer is to your liking and look forward to doing business with you. Please do not hesitate to contact me if you require further details.

Best regards

Amanda Hei
Export Sales Department
Toprac Ltd, Hong Kong SAR, People's Republic of China

*Telegraphic transfer

› *Terms of payment, page 179*

Decide whether the following statements about the email are true or false. Correct the false statements.

1. The total price for shipping the goods to Hamburg will be US$30,000.
2. InterFracht will need to pay for the goods in advance.
3. Toprac will arrange for transport of the goods to a European port.
4. The equipment will arrive early enough to be used in the new warehouse.

Orders and payments   Unit 9

2 Comparing Incoterms® rules

The Purchasing Director wants a C term instead of an F term, so you look up the definitions of the terms most often used by your company on the internet and find the following information sheet.

Incoterms® rules: information sheet

The Incoterms® rules are used by importers and exporters to define the costs and risks of international trade.

Transport costs
If an F term is used, the seller is only responsible for the pre-carriage part of the goods' journey to their destination. In practice, this means that the seller only loads the goods on the first carrier's vehicle (e.g. at the seller's premises) or pays for transporting the goods to a convenient location not too far away (e.g. a nearby port, airport or train station), and loading the goods at that location (e.g. at the port of shipment). The buyer is then responsible for arranging a contract of carriage to transport the goods to their destination and for unloading them when they arrive.

If a C term is used, the seller pays the costs of the main carriage to the destination but not of unloading at the destination. Post-carriage is the buyer's responsibility.

In the case of a D term, the seller pays all transport costs until the goods have reached their destination.

Risk
With an F term, the seller bears the risk until the goods have been handed over to the first carrier, e.g. at the seller's premises, or in the case of FOB until the goods are on board a ship at the port of shipment.

With CPT and CIP, the risk to the seller is the same because it passes to the buyer when the goods have been collected by the first carrier. In the case of CIP, the seller also insures the goods for the main carriage but no longer bears any risk when they have been handed over to the first carrier.

D terms cover all risks until the goods have reached their destination.

Import and export clearance
Export clearance (e.g. export licences, documentation) is arranged and paid for by the seller. Import clearance (e.g. customs duty, import licences and documentation) is arranged and paid for by the buyer. In the Incoterms® 2010 rules there are two exceptions: EXW (the buyer arranges and pays both export and import) and DDP (the seller is responsible).

Copy the table into your book and complete it for the terms CFR, CIF, CIP, DAP and DAT (FCA has been done for you). Refer to the full list of Incoterms® rules on pages 177–178.

B = buyer | S = seller

	Main carriage		Seller bears risk		Seller insures for main carriage	Export clearance		Loading		Import clearance		Unloading	
	paid	unpaid	including main carriage	excluding main carriage		B	S	B	S	B	S	B	S
FCA		✓		✓			✓		✓	✓			✓
CFR													
CIF													

3 Improving the terms of payment

The Purchasing Director wants payment by irrevocable and confirmed letter of credit (L/C) in order to reduce the financial risk. He gives you an information sheet about how an L/C works.

Study the text and put the stages of the transaction in the diagram (A–J) in the order in which they take place (1–10).

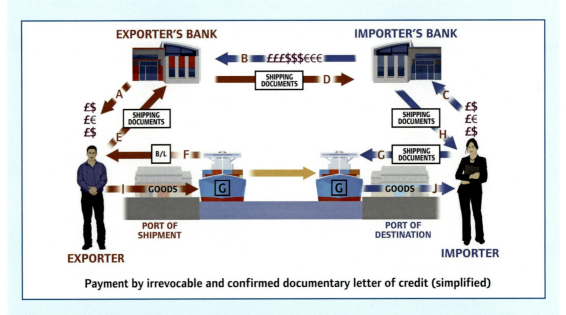

Payment by irrevocable and confirmed documentary letter of credit (simplified)

There are four parties to a payment transaction by irrevocable and confirmed documentary letter of credit (L/C). They are the exporter (seller), the exporter's bank, the importer (buyer) and the importer's bank. At any given time during the transaction, each party has security because they have either the money for the goods or the shipping documents entitling the holder to recover the value of the goods. After the L/C is confirmed, the exporter's bank guarantees to make payment to the exporter if the shipping documents presented are exactly as agreed. The exporter's bank then transfers the documents to the importer's bank and receives payment for them. The importer's bank then hands them over to the importer in exchange for payment in the agreed manner. If the L/C is irrevocable, no changes may be made to the agreement without the consent of all four parties.

The following shows the final 10 stages of payment by L/C in the case of goods sent by sea with a bill of lading (B/L).

1. The exporter gives the goods to the shipping company and they are loaded onto a ship.
2. The exporter receives a B/L, showing he has title to the goods.
3. The exporter now gives the B/L and other documents required for the L/C to his bank.
4. The bank inspects the documents and, if they are in order, pays the exporter as agreed.
5. The exporter's bank now transfers the documents to the importer's bank.
6. The importer's bank pays the exporter's bank.
7. The importer's bank hands the documents over to the importer.
8. The importer makes payment to the importer's bank as agreed.
9. The importer gives the documents to the shipping company at the port of destination.
10. The shipping company gives the importer the goods.

Infobox

Payment by documentary credit is safe but expensive because both banks charge fees for their services.

› *Terms of payment, page 179; Thematic vocabulary: Shipping documents, page 198*

Orders and payments   Unit 9

4 Structuring a counter-offer

You prepare your email to Toprac Ltd by looking at how counter-offers are structured and the type of phrases that are often used.

A First match the sentence halves to make useful phrases for counter-offers.

1	We have seen your offer	a	quarterly settlement, we will be able to place an order.
2	In view of the strong competition in this field	b	if you require further details.
3	Many thanks for the	c	find your approval.
4	Please do not hesitate to contact us	d	we can only order if your price is reduced significantly.
5	We hope that our suggestions	e	note that you are asking 5% more than your competitors.
6	We would ask you to reduce your		
7	Having compared several offers, we	f	for warehouse solutions on the internet.
8	If you are willing to change your terms of payment to	g	minimum order quantity to 50 units for an initial order.
		h	your response to our suggestion.
9	We look forward to receiving	i	above-mentioned offer for warehouse equipment.

B Now match the sentences to the three parts of a counter-offer. (There are three sentences for each category.)

Dear …

1 Reference to initial offer

2 Changes requested

3 Polite ending

Best regards

5 Submitting a counter-offer

The Purchasing Director tells you to draft a counter-offer to Toprac Ltd to be sent in his name.

Use the checklist above and the useful phrases on page 187 to draft a counter-offer as an email to be sent to Amanda Hei at Toprac Ltd. Include the following points:

- sender: Alex Horn (alex.horn@if-neumann.ger), Purchasing Director, InterFracht Neumann GmbH, Mühlenhagen 500, 20539 Hamburg)
- reference to offer dated … (yesterday's date)
- request for change of Incoterms® rules to CFR or CIF Hamburg
- request for payment by irrevocable and confirmed documentary letter of credit
- polite ending

› *Useful phrases: Writing counter-offers, page 187*

VIDEO 4

Watch the video to learn more about orders and shipment.

PART B: Placing an order

Situation: You are an apprentice at InterFracht Neumann GmbH in Hamburg. Your company needs equipment for a new warehouse and has found a potential supplier in Hong Kong. The Purchasing Director shows you how to proceed before placing a larger order with a new supplier.
→ You negotiate terms with the supplier, then place an order for goods.

1 Placing a trial order

Before placing a larger order, your company first places a trial order.

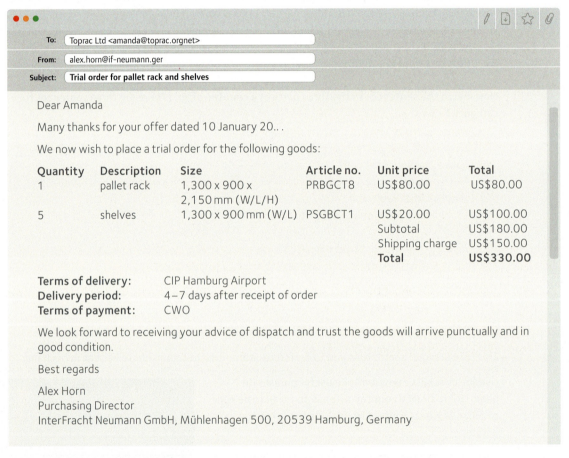

To:	Toprac Ltd <amanda@toprac.orgnet>				
From:	alex.horn@if-neumann.ger				
Subject:	Trial order for pallet rack and shelves				

Dear Amanda

Many thanks for your offer dated 10 January 20…

We now wish to place a trial order for the following goods:

Quantity	Description	Size	Article no.	Unit price	Total
1	pallet rack	1,300 x 900 x 2,150 mm (W/L/H)	PRBGCT8	US$80.00	US$80.00
5	shelves	1,300 x 900 mm (W/L)	PSGBCT1	US$20.00	US$100.00
				Subtotal	US$180.00
				Shipping charge	US$150.00
				Total	US$330.00

Terms of delivery: CIP Hamburg Airport
Delivery period: 4–7 days after receipt of order
Terms of payment: CWO

We look forward to receiving your advice of dispatch and trust the goods will arrive punctually and in good condition.

Best regards

Alex Horn
Purchasing Director
InterFracht Neumann GmbH, Mühlenhagen 500, 20539 Hamburg, Germany

› Incoterms® rules, page 177; Terms of payment, page 179

A Study the order and complete the sentences with a, b or c.
1. For InterFracht Neumann, Toprac Ltd is a) a regular. b) an old. c) a new supplier.
2. The goods will be sent a) by sea. b) by air. c) overland.
3. The goods are insured a) in China only. b) from door to door. c) for the main carriage.
4. Payment is a) in advance. b) on receipt of the goods. c) after receipt of the goods.

B As China is outside the EU, what other costs must InterFracht Neumann expect?

Orders and payments Unit 9

2 Negotiating terms

Your company is satisfied with the samples from Toprac Ltd, so the Purchasing Director phones Ken Wang, the Export Sales Director, to finalize the terms. You listen in and take notes.

A 33))) Listen to the telephone conversation and write notes on the following:

1 the terms of payment
2 third-party inspection
3 the documents that Toprac must give to their bank in Hong Kong
4 the freight agent
5 the costs of the trial order
6 what InterFracht and Toprac must do next

B 33))) Listen again and complete the sentences below with the words you hear.

1 I'm calling about the ▭ order we placed with your company.
2 Are the goods to your ▭?
3 As an ▭ offer we could offer you 30% with order and 70% before loading.
4 We can give you the name of a very good inspection ▭.
5 We have agreed that payment will be by ▭ and confirmed documentary letter of credit.
6 Please ▭ the credit with your bank in Hamburg,
7 We must have a ▭, on board bill of lading.
8 Would you like us to find you a freight agent for the main ▭?
9 We would like you to ▭ the cost of the trial order from the price of our order.
10 All I need from you now is your written ▭ after we place our order …

C You write a post about the new warehouse for your company's intranet. Use eight of your answers to B to fill in the gaps in the text. Make any necessary changes.

Our new warehouse is opening soon, but it took us time to find equipment for it that was to our ▭¹. We eventually found a supplier who made us an attractive ▭² offer, but we wanted some samples first so we placed a ▭³ order to test the quality. It was good, so we agreed payment by ▭⁴ and confirmed letter of credit. The supplier first offered us a received-for-shipment bill of lading, but we needed a ▭⁵, on board B/L for the L/C, which took a little longer. We then agreed on inspection of the goods before loading by an ▭⁶ of our choice and then all we needed to do was ▭⁷ the L/C at our bank in Hamburg. The supplier also agreed to ▭⁸ the price of the samples from the total price, so all in all it was a good deal!

3 Structuring an order

An order usually covers some or all of the points in the checklist.

A Use words from the list below to translate the orders checklist (1–8) into German.

Angaben über die bestellten Waren / Dienstleistungen · Anlage(n)/Anhang/Anhänge · Bestätigung/Versandanzeige · Bezug auf Angebot · höfliche Schlussformel · Internationale Handelsklausel · Liefertermin/-zeit · Lieferung · Preis(e) und Rabatt(e) · Verpackung · Versand · Versicherung · Zahlung

> **Orders checklist**
> 1 reference to offer
> 2 details of goods/services ordered
> 3 price(s) and discount(s)
> 4 delivery
>   – Incoterms® rule   – transport
>   – delivery date/   – packing
>   period   – insurance
> 5 payment
> 6 acknowledgement / advice of dispatch
> 7 polite ending
> 8 enclosure(s) (*letter*) / attachment(s) (*email*)

› *Useful phrases: Writing orders, page 188*

B Choose 12 of the 16 headings in the list to complete the order below.

article no. · cash discount · delivery · description · insurance · packing · payment · quantity · quantity discount · size · subtotal · total · total price · trade discount · transport · unit price

1	2	3	4	5
100	HQ printer	HQ3000	€60.00	€6,000.00
250	Quickchip laptop	QC99	€100.00	€25,000.00
			– 30% ▇6	– €9,300.00
			▇7	€21,700.00
			+ 20% VAT*	€4,340.00
			▇8	**€26,040.00**

▇9: DAP buyer's premises by 30 June 20..
▇10: Sturdy cartons
▇11: 2% 10 days, 30 days net after receipt of invoice
▇12: By road

*value added tax = *Mehrwertsteuer*

Infobox

Structuring an order or acknowledgement
If you are writing about **two or more** items, use a table with headings (see above) to make your order easy to understand. If you are only writing about **one** item, just use headings:
Article: Shelf
Article no.: PSGBCT1
Quantity: 100
List price: US$20.00

Writing prices
Currency symbol first
No space
Comma where there is a point in German
Point where there is a comma in German

€10,500.50

Orders and payments Unit 9

4 Placing an order

The Purchasing Director asks you to place an order for office furniture for the new warehouse with FinStore Oy, a supplier in Finland. You phone them first, then send a written order.

A Work with a partner and role-play the phone call to the Finnish supplier. Use the following instructions.

PARTNER A MIIKA/EMILIA VIRTANEN, FINSTORE OY IN OULU, FINLAND	PARTNER B SIE (EIGENER NAME), EINKAUF, INTERFRACHT NEUMANN GMBH, HAMBURG
– Nehmen Sie den Telefonanruf auf Englisch entgegen (Begrüßung, Firmenname, Ihr voller Name). – Reagieren Sie sehr positiv und fragen Sie, wie viele der Kunde / die Kundin möchte. – Die Ware ist vorrätig. – FCA Preise einschl. Verpackung. – Aufpreis von insgesamt 300,00 € bei Lieferung DAP Hamburg – ⅓ bei Auftragserteilung, ⅓ bei Lieferung, ⅓ innerhalb von 30 Tagen nach Lieferung – Lieferung 4 Tage nach Auftragseingang – Danken Sie für den Auftrag, erklären Sie, dass Sie ihn jetzt schriftlich (*in writing*) brauchen und fragen Sie nach dem Namen und der E-Mail-Adresse des Kunden / der Kundin. – Weitere Fragen? – Danken Sie für die Bestellung und verabschieden Sie sich.	– Stellen Sie sich vor (Ihr voller Name, Firmenname, Ort) und sagen Sie, dass Sie Schreibtische, Bürostühle und Aktenschränke (*filing cabinets*) vom Typ *Trend 3000* bestellen möchten. – Sie brauchen 10 Schreibtische, 10 Bürostühle und 5 Aktenschränke. – Fragen Sie nach den Lieferbedingungen. – Preis für DAP Hamburg Ihr Betriebsgelände? – Danken Sie für die Information und fragen Sie nach den Zahlungsbedingungen. – Lieferzeit? – Sie möchten 10 Schreibtische, 10 Bürostühle und 5 Aktenschränke vom Typ *Trend 3000* bestellen. – Geben Sie Ihren vollen Namen und Ihre E-Mail-Anschrift an (E-Mail: vorname.nachname@if-neumann.ger). – Sie haben keine weiteren Fragen. Sie werden Ihre Bestellung gleich per E-Mail abschicken. – Bedanken Sie sich und verabschieden Sie sich.

B Now place your order (see exercise 4A) in writing. Include the following points in your order:

- heutiges Datum
- Ansprechpartner/in: Herr Miika / Frau Emilia Virtanen in der Verkaufsabteilung
  (E-Mail: miika/emilia.virtanen@finstore.fin; Anschrift: FinStore Oy, Asemakatu 400, 90100 Oulu, Finland)
- Bezug auf Telefongespräch
- Bestellung unsererseits mit Auftrags-Nr. VBFT97 von 10 Schreibtischen vom Typ Trend 3000, Artikel-Nr. DTD3000, Stückpreis 300,00 €, 10 Bürostühlen vom Typ Trend 3000, Artikel-Nr. DTC3000, Stückpreis 500,00 € und 5 Aktenschränken, ebenfalls vom Typ Trend 3000, Artikel-Nr. DTF3000, Stückpreis 200,00 €
- Lieferung: CIP Hamburg innerhalb von 4 Tagen nach Auftragseingang
- Liefergebühr: 300,00 €
- Zahlungsbedingungen: ⅓ bei Auftragserteilung, ⅓ bei Lieferung, ⅓ innerhalb von 30 Tagen nach Lieferung
- Bitte um Auftragsbestätigung und Versandanzeige
- Hoffnung auf pünktliche Lieferung der Ware in gutem Zustand
- höfliche Schlussformel

› *Useful phrases: Writing orders, page 188*

COMMUNICATION: Delivery

Situation: You are an apprentice at InterFracht Neumann GmbH in Hamburg. Your company has ordered some office furniture from a supplier and receives an advice of despatch. Unfortunately, there is a problem with the delivery address.
→ You contact the forwarder, then give the driver directions to the right delivery address and other places.

1 Understanding an advice of dispatch

Your company has received an advice of dispatch from the supplier.

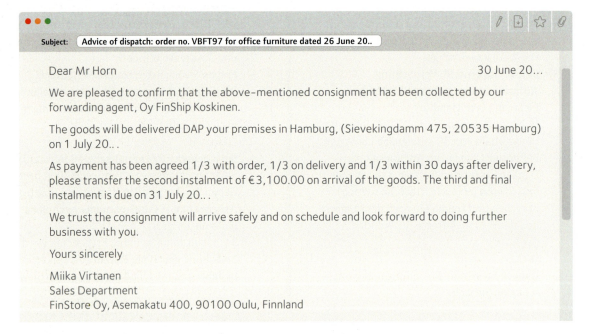

Subject: Advice of dispatch: order no. VBFT97 for office furniture dated 26 June 20..

Dear Mr Horn   30 June 20…

We are pleased to confirm that the above-mentioned consignment has been collected by our forwarding agent, Oy FinShip Koskinen.

The goods will be delivered DAP your premises in Hamburg, (Sievekingdamm 475, 20535 Hamburg) on 1 July 20…

As payment has been agreed 1/3 with order, 1/3 on delivery and 1/3 within 30 days after delivery, please transfer the second instalment of €3,100.00 on arrival of the goods. The third and final instalment is due on 31 July 20…

We trust the consignment will arrive safely and on schedule and look forward to doing further business with you.

Yours sincerely

Miika Virtanen
Sales Department
FinStore Oy, Asemakatu 400, 90100 Oulu, Finnland

Read the advice of dispatch and answer the questions.

1. Where will the shipment be delivered according to the advice of dispatch?
2. Who will deliver it?
3. What is the total price of the shipment and how much has InterFracht Neumann GmbH paid so far?
4. When does FinStore Oy expect InterFracht to make the next payments?

2 Changing the delivery address

When the advice of dispatch arrives, your company realises that the furniture is on its way to the wrong address. Your line manager, Sevda Yavuz, phones the forwarder to change the destination.

A   34 🔊   Listen to the telephone conversation and answer the questions.

1. Where is the consignment now?
2. When is the consignment expected to arrive?
3. How far away is the new destination from the old one?
4. Why can't the driver be contacted?
5. What does the forwarder want InterFracht Neumann to do?
6. How will the driver get written instructions if he comes to the old address?

Orders and payments Unit 9

B Sevda Yavuz asks you to send the Finnish forwarder the new address. Write an email and include the following points.

- Ansprechpartner: Aleksi Heikkinen (aleksi.heikkinen@finship.fin)
- Bezug auf Telefongespräch
- Angabe neuer Lieferadresse: InterFracht Neumann GmbH, Am Genter Ufer 95, 21129 Hamburg
- LWK wird bei Ankunft sofort entladen
- Bei Rückfragen +49 40 108447 anrufen
- Schlussformel

3 Giving directions

The driver of the consignment of furniture can't be reached and arrives at the wrong address.

A 35)) Listen to the first part of the dialogue and complete the sentences with a, b or c.

1 The driver's lorry will be unloaded by a) the driver. b) InterFracht. c) another company.
2 The driver a) doesn't know about. b) knows about. c) doesn't accept the change in plan.
3 The driver will find the new address with a) his navigation system. b) his smartphone. c) your help.

B Use 8 of the 10 words in the box to fill the gaps in diagrams 1–8. Write the answers in your exercise book.

after · ahead · bear · behind · bend · crossroads · roundabout · T-junction · tunnel · turning

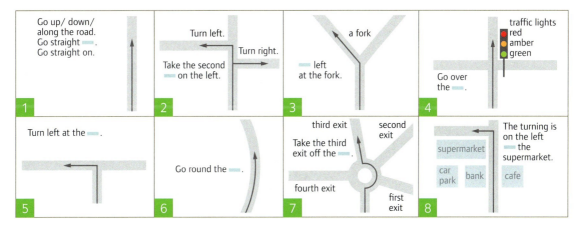

C 36)) Now listen to the second part of the dialogue and check your answers.

4 Role-play: Giving directions

Foreign drivers with better English than German sometimes ask you for directions to local places on foot or to the main roads or motorways.

👥 Work with a partner. Partner A: Look at File 13 on page 135. Partner B: Look at File 22 on page 141.

DAS KANN ICH (Unit 9)

- Verschiedene Angebote vergleichen und schriftlich eine Kaufempfehlung abgeben. (Foundation)
- Ein Gegenangebot mit besseren Konditionen erstellen. (Part A)
- Bessere Bedingungen aushandeln und eine Bestellung aufgeben. (Part B)
- Eine Versandanzeige verstehen und eine Wegbeschreibung auf Englisch geben. (Communication)

10 Customer service

FOUNDATION: Direct contact with customers

> **Situation:** You are part of a team that has been asked to help the Total Quality Management (TQM) Committee develop guidelines for new customer service representatives at ALEX Logistics GmbH.
> → You create guidelines for new employees to help them speak to customers in English.

1 Talking to customers

You read an article about customer service to prepare for a meeting with the committee.

A Before you read the text, think about customer service. In your group, make a list of the most important things to remember when you deal with customers.

B Read the text. Which of your ideas from A does it include?

Customer service for competitive companies

What is customer service? Customer service means helping customers and making sure they are satisfied with your company's services. It can be the difference that gets your company a new, big contract or keeps your customers loyal even when the competition is more innovative or has lower prices. Globalization has made one aspect of customer service far more important than it was in the past: English. Whether or not your company operates internationally, it's very likely that you will have some customers who use English to communicate.

Talking to customers can already be stressful because you are representing your company. Speaking English – especially on the telephone – can be even more of a challenge. If you are someone who is comfortable in English, you're lucky. But if not, it might help to remember that the person you're talking to, especially if that person is not a native speaker of English either, is often just as uncomfortable as you are.

So, how can you have a successful conversation with a customer in English? Here are some tips!

1. Start with the basics: Be polite. Especially when speaking over the phone, politeness is expressed in your words and in your tone, so you need to put the feelings you usually show with a sympathetic smile into words, and soften statements with polite language like "unfortunately" or "I'm sorry". Not doing this can make you seem rude, especially to people from English-speaking countries, who tend to value politeness.
2. Try to make the person that you are talking to feel comfortable. Make sure you know his/her name and use it several times in the conversation. When someone gives his/her name over the phone, take the time to check the spelling right away.
3. Don't rush to get to the point. Speak slowly and clearly, and make small talk if it is appropriate in the situation. You will find that this helps break the ice, especially if the customer is from an English-speaking country like the UK or the USA.
4. Your customer wants to know that you are listening and taking the call seriously. So don't be afraid to ask for clarification or to check that you've understood correctly. Use your active listening skills!
5. Make sure both you and the customer understand and agree on the main points of the conversation. Summarizing important points can also help if the person you're talking to doesn't speak English very well.
6. Last but not least, when you're at the end of the conversation, try to leave a positive final impression.

Customer service   Unit 10

C   Read the text again and answer the questions.

1   How can a small logistics company compete with bigger, more innovative competitors?
2   What role does English play in customer service?
3   Which three strategies can you use to show customers that their needs are important to you?
4   Which two tips from the text are more important when talking to native speakers of English?
5   Which two tips are more important when talking to non-native speakers of English?

D   Look at the following quotes from customer service reps and match them to the tips from the article (1–6).

a   "You're enquiring about shipping fragile goods by air, have I got that right?"
b   "I'm sorry, but I'm afraid we won't be able to do what you're suggesting."
c   "Yes, the weather has been quite bad lately, hasn't it? I hope spring comes early this year!"
d   "I'm just checking on the status of your shipment, Mr Martin. According to the …"
e   "Thanks again for calling. I hope we get the chance to work together again soon."
f   "So, we've agreed on our basic insurance rate for the trial shipment. Let's now look at …"

> **TIP**
>
> **Apologizing and giving bad news**
> - You say "sorry" or "I'm sorry" to apologize to someone when you upset them or bump into them by accident. It is also used to show empathy when you know that someone is in a tough situation, even if the situation isn't your fault.
> - You say "excuse me" to get someone's attention, especially when you want to ask them a question.
> - You can say "pardon" or "excuse me" when you didn't hear or understand what someone said.
> - You say "I'm afraid that …" when giving bad news or telling someone something that they won't like.

2 Being polite

TQM asks your team to review a recording of a customer service call that a customer complained about.

A   37))) Listen to the recording. Why do you think the customer, Ben McIntyre, felt that the customer service representative was impolite? Note down your answers.

B   Now look at the sentences (1–4) from the telephone call. Find more polite ways to say them using the phrases on the right.

1   We are going to deliver your shipment earlier.
2   We can't deliver then.
3   I'm calling to make sure that someone is there on Saturday to unload the goods.
4   We can only deliver on Saturday.

I'm afraid …
We would like to …
Would it be possible to …?
I'm sorry, but it won't be possible to …

3 Guidelines for direct customer contact

TQM asks your team to make a list of guidelines on speaking to customers in English for employees in the customer service department.

A   👥 With a partner, make a list of dos and don'ts for dealing with customers in English. Include useful phrases where possible.

B   👥 Present your guidelines to the class.

Customer service in English – helpful tips
Ask questions when something isn't clear, e.g. "Sorry, but can I just ask a question here?"

99

PART A: Cultural differences

Situation: Your line manager in the Sales Department is sending you and some other trainees to a major trade fair with over 2000 exhibitors and 60,000 visitors from all over the world. The sales manager is looking for new international customers and has asked the trainees to help the trade fair team.
→ You research cultural differences and interact with people from different cultures at the trade fair.

1 Understanding different cultures

As you will be meeting potential customers from all over the world, you think about possible cultural differences you might encounter and discuss them with the other trainees.

A Look at this list of possible behaviours you may observe. Do these behaviours make a good or bad impression on you? Give reasons.

Your (potential) customer …
1 makes a lot of small talk before getting to the main point of the discussion.
2 avoids eye contact with you during your conversation.
3 brings a writing set with expensive pens as a gift for you.
4 is ten minutes late for your meeting.
5 is dressed very informally for the meeting.
6 sits very close to you while you are talking and touches your arm a lot during the conversation.
7 is very formal and makes no jokes or small talk.
8 wants to have some formal agreement in writing before leaving.

Infobox

Different cultures – different behaviour

Everyone is different – people have different personalities and characteristics. But some differences, when they are shared by a group, are cultural. People who belong to the same culture often share similar ideas about what is or is not appropriate. Some of these cultural differences, like ideas about gift-giving or being late or on time, can easily lead to misunderstandings in an international business context.

B Read the information in the box. Then think about the role of culture and look at the behaviours from A again. Do you think that they are cultural, personal or both? Discuss with a partner.

C Discuss your answers with the class.

2 Adapting to different cultures

You decide to find out more about business behaviour in the countries where your company would like to find new customers. You find an article in a blog about international business.

A Read the text opposite, then answer the questions.
1 In which country or countries is business very formal?
2 In which country or countries is business more informal?
3 What is a major difference between business in India and business in the UK?
4 What differences in business behaviour are there between Australia and Portugal?

VIDEO 5

Watch the video to see more about cultural differences.

100

Customer service   Unit 10

Cultural Encyclopedia: Business Culture

India
Business is generally a serious thing in India, so it isn't a good idea to use humour while discussing business with Indian counterparts. It is also common to avoid eye contact. Gift-giving isn't a traditional part of Indian business etiquette.

Turkey
Turkish business people are often very traditional and formal when doing business. It is important to schedule appointments in advance and to be on time to meetings. You may notice that your Turkish business partners make a lot of small talk before starting with serious business.

Portugal
Business can be very formal in Portugal – you should dress nicely for a meeting. In Portuguese business relationships, it is normal to give gifts to customers and business partners. If you refuse a gift, it can be seen as offensive.

Japan
Japanese business etiquette is very formal. This may be most obvious at a first meeting, where the exchange of business cards can feel like a ritual. Japanese people may like more personal space than you are used to – so make sure to apologize if you bump into someone by accident.

United Kingdom
In the UK, an agreement will not normally be final and complete until a written contract has been formally signed and witnessed. British people will probably use humour to make a meeting more comfortable. If you offer a gift, make sure it is just right: if it is too expensive, it might be seen as a bribe; if it is too inexpensive, it might be seen as an insult.

Australia
Australians might seem casual in meetings. They might use language that you think is informal, but don't be fooled: they are still taking the meeting seriously. You can present your business card when you make introductions, but keep it simple: a flashy business card might not make a good impression. People don't usually give gifts as part of business relationships in Australia.

B Work in a group and make a list of advice about doing business in Germany.

3 Dealing with foreign customers

You are now at the trade fair, and you and the other trainees have spent the morning at the stand. During a break, your French colleague, Julie Fortin, tells you about the potential customers she has met so far.

1
Gokul Kumar, FoodTech, Mumbai, India

2
Lina Alves, Bica Coffee, Lisbon, Portugal

3
Dai Miura, Japanese Steel, Kyoto, Japan

4
Greg Bartley, TransEuro Logistics, Bristol, UK

A 38))) Listen and match the descriptions of the meeting below to the potential customers above.

a The meeting went well. Julie's small talk broke the ice with the potential customer.
b The meeting went badly. Julie's jokes didn't make the potential customer feel comfortable.
c Julie thinks that the meeting was fine, but she ran out of business cards.
d Julie didn't have much time and was frustrated by the potential customer's behaviour.

B 38))) Listen again and make a list of Julie's mistakes. Then work with a partner to give her tips and tell her what she could do better next time.

> **Giving advice**
>
> **Make sure you** are on time.
> **Try to** make your partners feel comfortable.
> **It is a good idea to** plan ahead of time.
> **Why don't you** make more small talk?

101

4 Reporting on what people said

When telling you about her morning, Julie also told you some details of her conversations.

Make sentences reporting on what the visitors to the stand said or asked.

1. Ms Alves: "I work for a coffee company."   *Ms Alves said she ...*
2. Mr Kumar: "This is my third visit to this trade fair."
3. Mr Miura: "Do you have any brochures?"
4. Mr Miura: "My supervisor is very interested in your company."
5. Mr Bartley: "Do you have time to talk for a few minutes?"
6. Ms Alves: "When will your line manager call me?"

> **Reporting what someone has said**
>
> "It's nice to meet you."
> → She said it **was** nice to meet me.
> "Where do you work?"
> → He asked where I **worked**.
> "I will contact you soon." → She said she **would contact** us soon.
>
> › *Grammar: Reported speech, page 154*

5 Role-play: At a trade fair

You and the other trainees attend a talk about customer service at the trade fair. After the talk, you introduce yourself to the person next to you, who is from a different culture.

Work in groups of three. Partners A and B choose a behaviour card in your partner file (but don't say which one). Then use the information on your behaviour card and have the conversation below.
Partner A: Look at Partner File 16 on page 137. **Partner B:** Look at Partner File 25 on page 144.

Partner C: During the role-play, observe students A and B. Take notes on the things they say and do. What cultural differences do you notice? What went well in the conversation? What went badly?

Start like this: *When Partner A said that he/she worked for a freight forwarder, Partner B ...*

Partner A

- Begrüßen Sie B.
- Plaudern Sie über das Wetter.
- Sagen Sie, dass Sie für einen Spediteur arbeiten, der sich auf Lebensmitteltransporte spezialisiert hat.
- Sagen Sie, dass Ihre Firma hauptsächlich temperaturkontrollierte Transporte von Obst und Gemüse anbietet. Fragen Sie B nach seiner/ihrer Firma.
- Entschuldigen Sie sich und sagen Sie, dass Sie zum Mittagessen verabredet sind und gehen müssen.
- Antworten Sie höflich, dass das nicht geht, und verabschieden Sie sich.

Partner B

- Erwidern Sie den Gruß.
- Reagieren Sie und machen Sie ein paar Bemerkungen zur Messe. Fragen Sie A nach seinem/ihrem Arbeitgeber.
- Vergewissern Sie sich, dass Sie A verstanden haben, und fragen Sie nach der Dienstleistungspalette der Firma.
- Sagen Sie, dass Ihre Firma auf Gefahrguttransporte in EU-Ländern spezialisiert ist.
- Fragen Sie, ob ein Treffen am Nachmittag möglich wäre.
- Schließen Sie das Gespräch höflich ab.

Customer service Unit 10

PART B: Responding to complaints

Situation: You just started working in the customer service department of ALEX Logistics GmbH. One aspect of your job is dealing with complaints, so you shadow a colleague to learn how to deal with them properly.
→ You look into complaint management at your company and respond to a customer complaint.

1 Different ways to complain

Your colleague asks you to think about the different reasons for complaining.

👥 Work in groups. Describe the last time you made a complaint to a company. What was the problem? How did you make your complaint? What did you do? How did the company react?

2 Making suggestions for improving service

Your colleague has put together a diagram showing the types of complaints the company has received over the past three months. She also shows you some of the negative reviews on the company website.

A Look at the negative reviews (1–6) and match them to the types of complaints shown in the diagram.

1 "Four days late and no explanation! Unacceptable!"
2 "Called the hotline to complain, but they hadn't included an invoice, so I couldn't tell them my customer number!"
3 "What a nightmare. Three weeks later and we are still waiting for 13 of 20 pallets. Never again!"

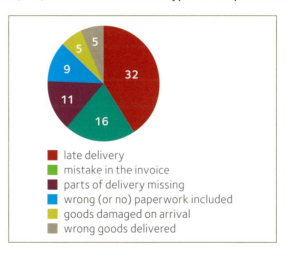

■ late delivery
■ mistake in the invoice
■ parts of delivery missing
■ wrong (or no) paperwork included
■ goods damaged on arrival
■ wrong goods delivered

4 "They delivered quickly, but our furniture was scratched and dented in transit!"
5 "Huge mix-up! Our customer received a package containing computer parts and not the consignment of winter jackets we sent them!"
6 "We were charged for warehousing – but our goods were shipped directly!"

B 👥 Work with a partner. Write a few sentences comparing and contrasting the findings in the pie chart. What were the majority of complaints about? What did the fewest complaints relate to?

C 👥 Discuss who or what might be responsible for each of the problems. Say how things might be improved. Use your ideas to write a short memo to your colleague.

→ **Comparing figures**

The majority of complaints were (about) …
… made up …% of the complaints.
There were **fewer** complaints about …
The **fewest** complaints related to …
… is/was **the same as** … / **higher/lower than** …

› *Grammar: Comparatives and superlatives, page 154*

103

3 Receiving a complaint

Your colleague shows you a complaint from United Sugar.

A Skim the complaint. What category of complaint from the pie chart does it belong to?

To:	customerservice@alexlogistics.ger		07 December 20..
From:	p.hansom@unitedsugar.brit		
Subject:	Shipment number 9230939	Attachment(s)	confirmation9230939.pdf

Dear Sir or Madam

I am writing to inform you that the above-mentioned order has not been delivered to our distributor in Orléans, France.

We enclose copies of all the documents we have regarding this order. You will note that the promised date of delivery was 5 November. The delivery is now two days late.

Please explain why the goods have not been delivered.

Whatever the case may be, you will appreciate that we have customers that are waiting for these goods. We ask that you arrange to deliver the consignment in the next 24 hours as the goods are needed as soon as possible.

We feel sure that you will understand that our future business relationship will depend on how this matter is dealt with.

We expect to hear from you in the very near future.

Best wishes

Peggy Hansom
Sales Department
United Sugar
203-210 Surrey St, Sheffield, S1 2HS, UK

B Read the email and answer the questions.

1. What is the reason for the complaint?
2. Who was supposed to deliver the consignment and when?
3. What information does United Sugar want?
4. Is the problem urgent? Why or why not?
5. How does United Sugar want the logistics company to respond?
6. What consequences could the problem have?

4 Structuring a complaint

Most complaints have a similar structure.

A Use words from the list on the right to translate the complaints checklist (1–6) into German.

> **Complaints checklist**
> 1 Reference to goods
> 2 Description of problem
> 3 Request for explanation
> 4 Consequences for the customer and company
> 5 Request for action
> 6 Polite ending

Bitte um Ergreifung geeigneter Maßnahmen · Bitte um Erklärung · Bezugnahme auf Waren · Darstellung des Problems · Folgen für Kunden und Unternehmen · höfliche Schlussformel

› *Useful phrases: Making/receiving complaints, page 190*

B Look again at the complaint from United Sugar and find examples in the email for each item on the checklist.

Customer service　Unit 10

5 Responding to a complaint

Your colleague responds to the complaint in an email.

Put the parts of his email (A–H) in the correct order.

A   Best wishes

B   We look forward to doing further business with you.

C   Since hearing from you, we have contacted our subcontractor and discovered that the consignment was delivered to the wrong location.

D   Dear Ms Hansom

E   Hans Heinrich Michelsen
    Senior Sales Representative, ALEX Logistics GmbH

F   I hope this solution meets with your approval and would ask you to accept our apologies for the inconvenience.

G   He has informed me that the consignment was delivered this morning, 7 November.

H   If you had any additional costs, we will compensate you for them.

> **Responding to complaints**
>
> I would like to apologize / Please accept my apology for the inconvenience.
> We regret / are sorry to inform you that …
> I'm afraid that / Unfortunately, we will need to delay …
> We will compensate / provide compensation for any further costs.
> I hope that this is acceptable / that this meets your approval.
> Thank you for understanding / for your patience.

› Useful phrases: Responding to complaints, page 191

6 Writing an email reply to a complaint

A large car manufacturer has complained that three consignments have not arrived in time. The consignments were meant to be delivered just-in-time, and the company is losing money because of the delay. In fact, production had to be stopped for three hours. This was the first time in a ten-year business relationship. Your line manager is upset and asks you to respond.

Read the notes from your line manager and respond to the complaint.

15. Oktober
· Lieferverzug an Deutsche Auto AG, Ansprechpartner Holger Schär
· Verzug aufgrund von Problemen bei Subunternehmer
· Wir sind nicht informiert worden.
· Partnerfirma hat einen neune Subunternehmer für ausstehende Lieferungen gefunden
· Lieferung wird am 17.10. um 8 Uhr erfolgen
· Es sollte künftig keine weiteren Probleme mit Lieferungen geben.
· unser Bedauern
· höfliche Schlussformel

COMMUNICATION: A telephone complaint

Situation: You work in the customer service department of Hamburg-based Horn Logistics GmbH.
→ You deal with a telephone complaint.

1 Dealing with complaints on the telephone

Your line manager gives you a list of English phrases for dealing with complaints and tells you to keep it by the phone in case English-speaking customers call.

Match the headings (1–5) to the phrases (a–j). There are at least two phrases for every heading. Some phrases match more than one heading.

1 Apologizing
2 Asking for information
3 Reacting to information
4 Action
5 Ending the call

a Can I just check with you that I've understood everything?
b Could you tell me what it's about, please?
c Could you give me the order number, please?
d I'll have a replacement sent out as soon as possible.
e I'm sorry to hear that.
f Is there anything else I can do for you today?
g Just a moment while I write that down.
h Oh, no. That doesn't sound at all good.
i Thank you for your call. Once again, I'm sorry that there was a problem.
j We're prepared to replace the goods at our expense.

› *Useful phrases: Responding to complaints, page 191*

2 Dealing politely with customers

Olof Bengtsson, a customer from Sweden, calls to complain about a reminder. Your colleague, Anja Wolf, takes the call. Unfortunately, she is not very polite.

A 39))) Listen to the phone call and decide how you would improve it. Make a list.

B 40))) Now listen to how Anja Wolf should have dealt with the phone call with Olof Bengtsson. Which (if any) of your improvements does she make?

> **TIP**
>
> **Making or dealing with complaints on the phone**
> Give your name clearly at the start of the call and write down the name of the person you are speaking to immediately. If necessary, check the spelling of the name.

3 A complaint to a freight forwarder

MedEquip, a medical supplies company in Birmingham, ships many orders with Horn Logistics. The latest consignment has not arrived, so Lucy Hoggs from MedEquip calls to complain. Your colleague Max Jahn answers the phone.

A Look at the phrases (a–h) below and decide who says what – the caller or the person taking the call. (There are four phrases for each speaker.)

a delivery was promised
b How can I help you?
c I will do my best
d it's a shipment of 10
e the exact details
f the shipment number
g to enquire about a shipment
h We can't fulfil our contract

Customer service Unit 10

B Now match the phrases (a–h) with the gaps (1–8) in the text to complete the transcript of the phone call.

Max   Good morning. Horn Logistics, Customer Service Department. Max Jahn speaking.
Lucy   Good morning. This is Lucy Hoggs from MedEquip in Birmingham.
Max   Good morning, Ms Hoggs. ___¹
Lucy   I'm calling ___² of 10 aluminium containers to our warehouse in Liverpool. The consignment was picked up on 18 April and ___³ by 3 May. But, so far, nothing has arrived.
Max   Oh. I'm sorry to hear that. Could you give me ___⁴?
Lucy   Yes. It's DF-54736.
Max   DF-54736. Just a moment, please. I'll check. I'm sorry, Ms Hoggs. I don't seem to have any record of your shipment. Can I just check that I've understood everything? The number is DF-54736 and it was picked up on 18 April. Could you give me ___⁵ of the shipment again, please?
Lucy   Yes, ___⁶ aluminium containers for medical equipment.
Max   Aluminium containers for medical equipment. Ms Hoggs, I'll have to speak to my colleague to find out what the problem is. Can I get back to you later?
Lucy   Well, yes. But I hope it won't take long. ___⁷ until we have the containers.
Max   Yes. I realize that, Ms Hoggs. I'm very sorry about this and ___⁸ to get back to you as soon as possible.
Lucy   Many thanks for your help, Mr Jahn.

> **VIDEO 6**
> Watch the video to see more about dealing with complaints.

C 🔊 41 Now listen and check your answers.

4 Role-play: A telephone complaint

Now you make and deal with a telephone complaint.

A 👥 Work with a partner. **Partner A:** Look here. **Partner B:** Look at File 17 on page 137.

> **Partner A**
> You work for Horn Logistics GmbH.
> You call a subcontractor, Jorge Murano Transportista, in Spain to complain about a consignment that was delivered two days late. In your call, include the following points:
>
> – business relationship for many years – show concern
> – description of the problem   – refund not needed
> – first time mistake   – want guarantee that problem
> – ask for reason(s)   doesn't happen again
>
> Before you make the phone call, check that you know how to deal with complaints in English (exercises 1 and 2).

B 👥 Change roles and do the role-play again using different details.

> **DAS KANN ICH (Unit 10)**
> – Richtlinien für englischsprachige Kundengespräche erstellen. (Foundation)
> – Kulturelle Unterschiede erkennen und ihnen aufgeschlossen begegnen. (Part A)
> – Eine Beschwerde auf Englisch beantworten. (Part B)
> – Mit telefonischen Beschwerden auf Englisch richtig umgehen. (Communication)

KMK Exam practice 5

1 Hörverstehen: Stufe II (B1)

Situation: Sie machen ein Praktikum bei einem englischen Großhändler für Motorrad- und Fahrradzubehör. Für die einzulagernden Waren hat das firmeneigene Außenlager seine Kapazitätsgrenze erreicht. Sie sind der Logistikabteilung zugeteilt und sollen Lösungsmöglichkeiten erarbeiten.
In diesem Zusammenhang stellt Ihnen ihr Kollege Tom telefonisch seine Rechercheergebnisse dar.

42)) **Aufgabe:** Hören Sie sich das Gespräch an und machen Sie sich Notizen.

	Lager 1	Lager 2
Lage		
Platz/Kapazität		
Kosten		
Verfügbarkeit		
Zusätzliche Informationen		
Kontaktdaten		

2 Produktion: Stufe II (B1)

Situation: Sie arbeiten bei einem großen Onlinehändler mit eigener Flotte in Manchester und bemerken, dass Ihre LKW-Trackingsoftware nicht einwandfrei funktioniert. In den letzten Tagen haben Sie sich bereits Notizen gemacht. Sie beschließen, der zuständigen Firma ITlog per E-Mail eine Beschwerde zu schicken. Herr Hunt ist Ihr Ansprechpartner.

Aufgabe: Verfassen Sie eine E-Mail in englischer Sprache. Greifen Sie auf Ihre Notizen zurück.

- GPS-Tracking fehlerhaft (mehrmaliger Absturz in den letzten Monaten, kompletter Neustart erforderlich – Zeit!)
- Notdienst (angeblich 24/7) nur selten erreichbar, nur AB, Rückruf verspätet
- Datenspeicherung müsste für 6 Monate funktionieren, löscht aber teilweise bereits nach 45 Tagen
- Wir erhalten öfters falschen Alarm über Tempoüberschreitungen bei LKW-Fahrern.
- Kartenübersicht über Standorte der Fahrer funktioniert außerhalb GB nicht einwandfrei

3 Mediation: Stufe II (B1)

Situation: Bei einem Praktikum in Irland erhalten Sie ein Coaching für internationale Handelsmessen. Einige der Unterlagen, die Sie erhalten, gefallen Ihnen so gut, dass Sie beschließen, für Ihr Team in Deutschland eine Checkliste zu erstellen. Die Überschriften/Gliederungspunkte für Ihre Liste haben Sie sich schon farbig markiert.

Aufgabe: Lesen Sie den Text und erstellen Sie eine Checkliste auf Deutsch.

Visiting international trade fairs for the first time

International trade fairs offer great opportunities for your company. Establishing international contacts and presenting your products on a global market can rocket your company to the next level.

You should prepare thoroughly. Find fairs that represent a high potential for your business. You can use different sources like trade associations, foreign embassies and consulates, international chambers of commerce and the internet.

Once you have decided on a fair it is vital to book a space early. Trade fairs are always "first-come, first-served", so submit your application for a booth as early as possible, ideally 12 to 18 months before the event.

Then: coordinate shipping arrangements. Don't underestimate the effort! It looks easy because most international trade shows have an official freight forwarder to handle invoicing, arrangements for licenses and declarations, and so on. But you, the exhibitor, have to take care of insurance and prepare all necessary documentation. This can be a nerve-wracking process.

Calculate your budget and be aware that costs of overseas trade fairs can vary. Factors that should be considered include: currency exchange rates, season, extra staff costs and location. Make sure to plan for unexpected costs of at least 20% when you are calculating your budget.

It is also important to check international technical and safety standards! It may be helpful to use a consultant who can advise you on different laws regarding safety and technical requirements.

Last but not least: train your staff! Your company representatives should be prepared to negotiate with international customers. They should also be familiar with the culture of the host country. Role-play possible situations in teams; this may contribute to a confident appearance in what can be an overwhelming situation.

11 Sustainability and innovation

FOUNDATION: Innovations in logistics

Situation: You work for a parcel service company that is planning a smart distribution centre. Your line manager asks you to take part in a working group on innovations in logistics and report back to the group.
→ You research innovations that will affect the logistics industry and present your findings.

1 The autonomous supply chain

You research ideas the company can use in their new smart distribution centre and download a SlideShare presentation about logistics in the future. Unfortunately, the images for the eight slides get mixed up.

A Put the slides above in the right order to match the parts of the text below.

1. An autonomous lorry is going to deliver containers to a …
2. fully automated cargo terminal, which is going to load them onto an …
3. autonomous e-container ship.
4. After the ship is unloaded, a Hyperloop is going to send the containers to a …
5. smart warehouse where the goods are going to be put on …
6. a driverless delivery van and taken to a distribution centre for …
7. delivery to your door by drone …
8. or robot.

B 🔊 43 Now listen to the presentation. What does the presenter mean by "driverless, crewless, noiseless, effortless"? Give examples.

2 The Hyperloop

You want to know more about the Hyperloop and find this information on the internet.

> **The Hyperloop** is an innovative means of transport in which passengers or freight are moved at high speed in a capsule through a system of long tubes. According to current plans, one Hyperloop route is going to run from the Hamburg container terminal to shipyards further inland. Powered by solar energy, the Hyperloop is going to transport freight at a speed of 1,200 km per hour along the route. Experts believe that it will allow freight to be transported more efficiently and will also be more environmentally friendly, which in turn will improve sustainability.

A Read the text and answer the questions.

1 Who and what is going to be able to travel with the Hyperloop?
2 What is the Hyperloop going to move through and what speeds will it be able to reach?
3 What exactly is the Hyperloop going to be used for in Hamburg?
4 What are the advantages of the Hyperloop?

> **→ Talking about the future**
>
> The route **is going to run** from the terminal to shipyards further inland.
> Experts believe that it **will improve** sustainability.

> *Grammar: Future with* will *and* going to, *page 152*

B Do you think the Hyperloop will become reality in Hamburg or elsewhere? If so, will it be an effective means of transporting freight? Tell your partner why/why not.

3 Other new innovations

You find information about three more innovations online.

A Complete the texts with words from below.

collaboration · interconnected · recharge · replaced · transport · vehicles

Smart trucks	Electric motorway	Automated warehouse
Ten years from now, these ___¹ might not look very different from now, but the technology inside them is going to be quite different. Even if not yet self-driving, smart trucks are going to be greener and more ___² (to other trucks and the cloud), leading to greater safety and efficiency.	Electric motorways are going to be the future of road ___³. Hybrid trucks will be able to connect to overhead cables while driving on the motorway. This will save time, as the trucks can drive and ___⁴ at the same time. The technology will also reduce CO_2 emissions and thus be more climate friendly.	People in this type of warehouse are going to be ___⁵ with robots – at least those who find the articles to complete the orders. But people will still pack the articles and do quality control. This robot-human ___⁶ will result in a warehouse that is more efficient, flexible and cost-effective.

B What is your opinion of these innovations? Discuss the advantages and disadvantages with a partner. Think about: cost savings, job security, efficiency, safety, environment.

4 Presenting future technology

Now it's time to present your findings to your line manager and team.

Choose one of the innovations mentioned above (or think on one of your own) and explain why it should be implemented. Give details about how you think it will help your company.

> *Useful phrases: Giving presentations, page 182, Talking about reasons and outcomes, page 192*

PART A: Reducing costs and increasing sustainability

Situation: The logistics company you work for needs to save costs and wants to become more sustainable. Your line manager asks you make suggestions about how this can be accomplished.
→ You write a memo to your line manager suggesting ways for the company to reduce costs and improve sustainability.

1 Rising costs

Your line manager has just returned from a meeting about rising costs. She sends you this memo and the charts.

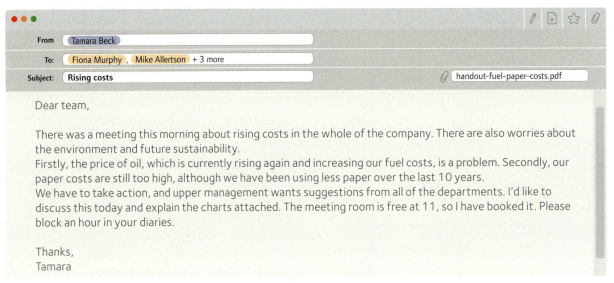

From: Tamara Beck
To: Fiona Murphy, Mike Allertson + 3 more
Subject: Rising costs
Attachment: handout-fuel-paper-costs.pdf

Dear team,

There was a meeting this morning about rising costs in the whole of the company. There are also worries about the environment and future sustainability.
Firstly, the price of oil, which is currently rising again and increasing our fuel costs, is a problem. Secondly, our paper costs are still too high, although we have been using less paper over the last 10 years.
We have to take action, and upper management wants suggestions from all of the departments. I'd like to discuss this today and explain the charts attached. The meeting room is free at 11, so I have booked it. Please block an hour in your diaries.

Thanks,
Tamara

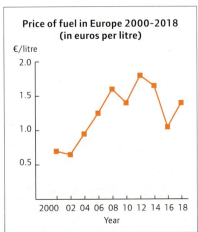
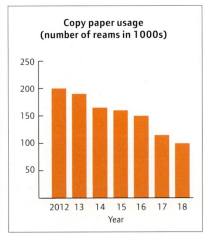
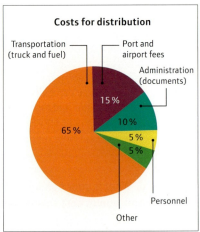

Read the memo and look at the attachments, then answer the questions.

1. Which two costs does the company have to reduce and why?
2. According to the line graph, how much has the price of fuel risen since 2000?
3. Does the bar graph show an increase or a decrease in the amount of paper used?
4. According to the pie chart, which distribution cost is the highest?
5. Why is the team going to meet at 11 a.m.?

Sustainability and innovation   Unit 11

2 Explaining charts

You are at the team meeting and Tamara is about to explain the graphs and charts she sent with the memo.

A Before you listen, match these words and expressions to the diagrams 1–4.

climb • decrease • drop • fall • flatten out • fluctuate • go down • go up • go up and down • increase • level off • remain constant • rise • stay the same

B 44))) Now listen to the meeting and fill in the missing words.

decrease • figures • gradual • levelled off • risen • segment • y-axis

1 The price of fuel has ▬ 70 cents since 2000.
2 On the graph we only have ▬ going back to 2011.
3 The ▬ shows the number of reams of paper.
4 The ▬ up until 2013 was ▬ with a jump in 2014.
5 It ▬ in 2015 and 2016.
6 The biggest ▬ on the pie chart with 65% is for transportation costs.

C 👥 Look at the charts on page 112 again and use information from the meeting and expressions from A to describe one of the graphs or charts in your own words.

› *Useful phrases: Describing graphs and charts, page 192*

3 Mediation: the eAWB

After the meeting, you do some research on how logistics companies can reduce the amount of paper they use. You find this information online and use it to write a memo in English to your line manager.

Read the text and study the graph. Then summarize the most important points in English in a memo to your line manager.

PART B: Making companies more efficient

Situation: You work in the distribution centre of a large international logistics company. The company is going through some changes, and your line manager asks you to prepare a blog post for the intranet summarizing these changes and giving your perspective as an apprentice.
→ You write a summary as a blog post on the company intranet.

1 Things at present

You find these posts on the intranet where people at your company talk about their workplace.

A Look at the posts and sort them into categories. One post fits in two categories.

1. Innovations that have improved efficiency in the workplace
2. New technologies that have not yet been accepted by the workforce
3. Processes that still need to be improved

Selecting goods
In the past, I only had one free hand to pick the goods off the shelves, but now with my smart glasses I have both hands free. The glasses will be made available to everyone soon and will make picking much faster.

Checking driver's hours
I don't like the new smart tachograph at all. Everything you do is recorded, but you still have to remember where you were and why something happened 28 days earlier. I liked the old way better.

Paying in the canteen
Why haven't we started using transponders to pay at the canteen? Everything still has to be paid for with cash and when I go for lunch, I have to get my wallet from my locker first. It's very inconvenient.

Checking work times
We still have an old-fashioned time clock. The time is printed on your card when you arrive and when you leave. It's time for something modern.

Cleaning
Well, I lost my job due to new technology. New robotic cleaning machines were installed last month, and now everything is automatic and I'm no longer needed.

Delivery systems
I used to spend a lot of time waiting for people to open their front doors. Now temporary keyless access opens a car boot and I can deliver a parcel in seconds.

B Complete these comments that other people posted with the correct form of the word in brackets.

1. I doubt the glasses … (give) to everyone any time soon as they're too expensive.
2. … keyless access … (use) all over Germany now? It isn't available yet where I work.
3. All our lorries … (equip) with smart tachographs since the beginning of the year.
4. Time-clock software was … (install) here last month. It's a big improvement.
5. I'm afraid more and more jobs … (lose) in the future due to automation.

> **Talking about facts and processes**
>
> The time **is printed** on your card when you arrive.
> New machines **were installed** last month.
> The glasses **will be made** available soon.
>
> › Grammar: Passive forms, page 152

C Write your own post describing a process at your workplace. Which category in A does it belong to?

Sustainability and innovation Unit 11

2 Future changes

Your company has spent the last months looking at ways to become more efficient, save money and also be more competitive. Today the CEO announces the changes that are going to be implemented.

A 45))) Listen to the CEO. Which improvements does he mention?

same-day delivery • a fitness club • an automated distribution centre • a three-shift plan
time-clock software • a new high-bay shelving system • self-driving delivery vans

B The CEO gives reasons for why the changes are being made and also explains what the outcomes of the changes will be. Match the sentence halves that summarize what he says.

1. Everything is moving faster,
2. In order to make 24/7 delivery possible,
3. By introducing the new plan,
4. The new distribution system will be self-maintaining and self-correcting,
5. A new shelving system will also be built
6. Machines will do more of the heavy and routine work,

a. so mistakes will be a thing of the past.
b. we will introduce a new three-shift plan.
c. which means same-day or overnight delivery is a must.
d. we will be able to reduce your working hours and give you more free time.
e. so workers' health and safety will be improved.
f. which means that we will be able to accommodate more packages.

3 A different opinion

After the announcement, Paul Smith from the works council posts his response on the company intranet.

Read the excerpt and complete the gaps with the words below.

advantage • affect • choose • competitive • efficient • invest • mistakes • personal • skilled

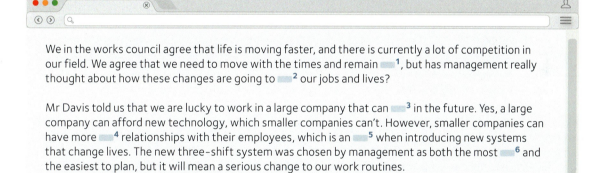

We in the works council agree that life is moving faster, and there is currently a lot of competition in our field. We agree that we need to move with the times and remain ▬¹, but has management really thought about how these changes are going to ▬² our jobs and lives?

Mr Davis told us that we are lucky to work in a large company that can ▬³ in the future. Yes, a large company can afford new technology, which smaller companies can't. However, smaller companies can have more ▬⁴ relationships with their employees, which is an ▬⁵ when introducing new systems that change lives. The new three-shift system was chosen by management as both the most ▬⁶ and the easiest to plan, but it will mean a serious change to our work routines.

There are still a lot of open questions. Will each and every colleague really be able to ▬⁷ the shift that suits them best? Will they really be able to take holiday when they want to? And what about this new autonomous high-speed distribution system? Being self-maintaining and self-correcting is a good thing. And fewer ▬⁸ and better health and safety are also a good thing. But what will happen to employees who aren't ▬⁹ enough to operate the new system? Are there really going to be jobs for everyone? We will continue working to get answers for you.

4 Writing a blog

With all the information you have read and heard, you are ready to write the text for the blog.

Write a short blog post describing the changes that the company is going to make, the reasons for the changes and the expected outcome. Discuss the advantages and disadvantages, and give your opinion.

 Useful phrases: Talking about reasons and outcomes, page 192

115

COMMUNICATION: Meetings

Situation: You work in the HR department of a small company with its own warehouse. You have regular team meetings at which everyone is kept up to date about the department. Team members are also sometimes asked to attend the works council meetings.
→ You take part in a works council meeting about flexitime and write the minutes.

1 An agenda for a meeting

The HR Director, Julia Weiss, has emailed details of the next team meeting to the participants in advance.

Find the words in her email that match the definitions below.

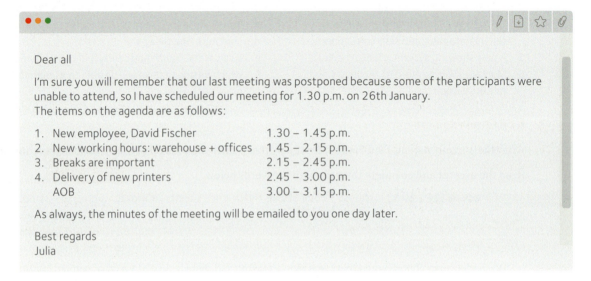

Dear all

I'm sure you will remember that our last meeting was postponed because some of the participants were unable to attend, so I have scheduled our meeting for 1.30 p.m. on 26th January.
The items on the agenda are as follows:

1. New employee, David Fischer   1.30 – 1.45 p.m.
2. New working hours: warehouse + offices   1.45 – 2.15 p.m.
3. Breaks are important   2.15 – 2.45 p.m.
4. Delivery of new printers   2.45 – 3.00 p.m.
   AOB   3.00 – 3.15 p.m.

As always, the minutes of the meeting will be emailed to you one day later.

Best regards
Julia

1 to change to a later date
2 to go to (a meeting)
3 to choose a date
4 the points to be discussed at a meeting
5 extra points discussed at the end of a meeting
6 a record of all the things said or decided at a meeting

2 Attending a meeting

The meeting takes place as planned, but some changes have been made to the agenda.

A 🔊 46 Listen to the meeting and add the new item to the agenda in the correct place.

B 🔊 46 Listen again and complete these sentences from the meeting.

1 Would you go …, please?
2 Would anyone like to … or ask a question?
3 Let's … on to the next topic.
4 I thoroughly … with (name).
5 Can I … in on that?
6 Let's … up the meeting, shall we?

C Now match the sentences above with these topics.

a asking for reactions
b agreeing and disagreeing
c starting a new topic
d asking someone to speak
e finishing the meeting
f asking to speak

› *Useful phrases: Taking part in meetings, page 193*

Sustainability and innovation   Unit 11

3 Checking the minutes of a meeting

The next day you receive the minutes of the meeting. You check the facts against your own notes and notice that there are five mistakes.

 46 Study the minutes, find the mistakes and correct them. Listen to the recording again, if necessary.

Minutes of meeting on 3 January 20..
Attendees: Julia, David, Jürgen, Birgit and Rajiv

1. **New colleague:** David Fuller joined HR today. He only works part-time.
2. **New working hours in the warehouse + offices:** Jürgen Müller gave a presentation on the new working hours in the warehouse. The changeover isn't going to be very easy.
3. **Breaks are important:** Julia reminded us how important our breaks are.
4. **Holiday from last year:** All holiday from last year must be used by the end of September.
5. **Delivery of new printers:** The new printers for the HR department will be delivered next week. No one will be able to print on Monday.

AOB: Date of works council meeting: Monday 3rd February. David Fuller will attend and take the minutes.

4 Taking part in a meeting

David Fuller is off sick on 3 February so you volunteer to take part in the works council meeting and to write the minutes.

A Work in groups of six. Read the situation, then use your role cards to conduct a meeting and come to a decision.

Partners A and B: Look at File 18 on page 138.
Partners C and D: Look at File 21 on page 140.
Partners E and F: Look at File 23 on page 142.

> **VIDEO 7**
> Watch the video to see more about meetings.

› *Useful phrases: Taking part in meetings, page 193*

Situation:
In your company, there are 20 employees in the office and 15 in the warehouse. At the last works council meeting, many employees were in favour of introducing flexitime. Today, there is a meeting between the American General Manager and some staff members to discuss it. Attending the meeting are:

- the General Manager (Partner A)
- the Human Resources Manager (Partner B)
- the Works Council Representative (Partner C)
- an office worker (Partner D)
- a warehouse employee (Partner E)
- an apprentice (Partner F)

B When you have finished, write the minutes of the meeting.

› *Thematic vocabulary: Meetings, page 199*
› *Useful phrases: Negotiating, page 194*

DAS KANN ICH (Unit 11)

– Eine Präsentation über Trends und Innovationen in der Logistik geben. (Foundation)
– In einem Memo die wichtigsten Punkte eines deutschen Textes auf Englisch zusammenfassen. (Part A)
– Über Innovationen und betriebliche Veränderungen in einem Blog schreiben. (Part B)
– An einer Besprechung teilnehmen und ein Protokoll führen. (Communication)

117

12 A job application

FOUNDATION: Where do I go from here?

Situation: You are nearing the end of your course and are thinking about applying for a work placement abroad. You start to think about what you have learned in your apprenticeship and where you might work when you have qualified.
→ You write a description of your apprenticeship for a European job agency.

1 Listening to newly-qualified trainees

You listen to an interview with three newly-qualified trainees. They are talking about the jobs they do and where they would like to find a permanent position.

1 Maren
Logistics manager

2 Garry
Customer services manager

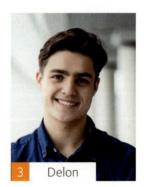

3 Delon
Freight agent

A 47))) **Listen and say what the speakers liked best about their apprenticeship.**

1. Who enjoyed learning from experienced people?
2. Who liked the mixture of going to vocational college and doing practical work?
3. Who enjoyed going to meetings?

B 47))) **Listen again and complete the table with the missing information.**

Name	What I do at work	I'd like to …
Maren	*plan and organize* ▭¹ *by* ▭²	*become a* ▭³
Garry	*calculate* ▭⁴, *and recommend* ▭⁵, *communicate* ▭⁶	▭⁷ *in* ▭⁸
Delon	*anything involving* ▭⁹, *from filling out* ▭¹⁰ *to writing* ▭¹¹	▭¹² *where I can* ▭¹³

A job application   Unit 12

2 Thinking about your skills

You think about the skills you have learned during your apprenticeship.

A   What do you enjoy most about your apprenticeship? What skills are you learning? How do you learn and develop these skills? First make notes on your own.

> **➔ Talking about skills; thinking about possibilities**
>
> I **can** organize a shipment of dangerous goods.
> I'**m able to** work on my own.
> They **might be able to** get a job in the UK.
> You **could** look for work with a cargo airline.

B   👥 Now talk to a partner about the skills you are learning.

› *Grammar: Modals and their substitutes, page 155*

C   👥 Now compare your ideas with another pair and make a list of the skills you are all learning, for example, working with spreadsheets, keying in data, etc. (Keep this list; you will need it for Part A).

D   Report your ideas to the class. In class, make a list in English of the different job titles in your field, e.g. shipping clerk. How can you use the skills you are learning in your preferred area of work?

3 Doing internet research

You search the internet for job opportunities in Europe.

A   👥 Work with a partner. Do internet research to find suitable career prospects in Europe. Make a poster, webpage or PowerPoint presentation showing job offers and companies in your sector. Present your ideas to the class.

B   If you make posters, pin them to the wall and do a gallery walk. Rank the posters using the categories below. Give points from 1–5 for each category.

headline · design · photos/pictures · content · overall effect

4 Reading about the Europass

While you are doing your research online, you come across the European Skills Passport (Europass). You decide to use it to collect your own personal details for applications and your CV.

Download the Europass and start to complete it with your details. (Your teacher has the correct URL.)

> **Infobox**
>
> **The European Skills Passport (Europass)**
>
> This is a standardized CV and language document that can be created online or on your own computer. Potential employers throughout Europe can clearly see your skills and qualifications.
>
> The following sections might be of particular interest to you:
> – **Language Passport** – a self-assessment tool for language skills and qualifications;
> – **Europass Mobility** – a record of skills acquired during a learning experience in a European country;
> – **Certificate Supplement** – a description of skills acquired by holders of vocational training certificates.

5 Describing your apprenticeship

You have contacted an EU job agency asking for help in looking for work experience in Europe. The agent for Germany asks you to write a short description of your apprenticeship in English for the agency file.

Write a short description of your apprenticeship. Before you begin, think about the aspects you should include, e.g. type of training, skills you learned, qualifications you gained, and make notes.

PART A: Applying for a job abroad

Situation: The company you work for is interested in taking on trainees from other countries.
→ You write a job advertisement in English for the position you are leaving.

1 Finding a job

Before you write the advertisement, you think about how you got started in your current position.

Work in groups. Talk to colleagues about how you got started in your job. Make notes and report back to the class.

- Where did you find out about your job?
- How did you apply for the job?
- What qualifications did you have when you applied?

2 Two interesting jobs

Your line manager would like to place an advertisement for your position on an international recruitment agency website. You check the website to get ideas for your advertisement.

Study the two advertisements opposite. What details in them can you use when you write the advert for your job? Think about the following aspects:

- the type of employer
- what the company is looking for
- what the requirements are
- what the company offers
- how to apply

A job application Unit 12

Trainee Forwarding Agent

International freight forwarding company, Hamburg, Germany

As a forwarding agent, you will prepare air waybills, complete export customs entries and classify goods. You will also deal with general administrative work, including invoicing and correspondence.

Requirements:
- min. school leaving certificate
- basic knowledge of MS Office, Excel and Outlook
- fluent German and English and one other language

You should have good written skills and good communication skills.
You should also be a quick learner.

Training period: 3 years, dual system, day release at vocational college 2 days a week

Possibility of being taken on full-time after completing your training

Please submit your application with Ref. number TExCl_14387 here

Trainee Freight Forwarding Agent

Package delivery company, Essen, Germany

Your training in the workplace includes advising customers, planning shipments and optimising routes. You will also negotiate shipping contracts with business partners.

Requirements:
- a recognized school leaving certificate
- good mathematical skills
- fluent German and good English

You should be an accurate worker and be able to work without supervision.
Training takes place over 36 months, including six weeks' block release twice a year.
In the workplace, you will receive continuous support from experienced employees.
Opportunities for follow-up education and promotion within the company.

Please submit your application with Ref. number TCsSp_10732 here.

3 Writing an advertisement for the recruitment agency website

Now you write the advertisement for your current position for the recruitment website.

A Begin with the job title and the training location, then include information about what the successful candidate will do, etc.

B When you have finished, pin your advertisement on the wall and do a gallery walk. Which advert describes your apprenticeship most accurately? Which one sounds like an interesting option for prospective trainees?

› *Useful phrases: Describing jobs and responsibilities, page 180*

121

PART B: Interviews

> **Situation:** You have been shortlisted for a position as a German-speaking junior shipping agent with a British company.
> → You prepare for and practise a telephone interview and a face-to-face interview.

1 Choosing the right candidate

Jennifer Winters, Head of Human Resources at the British company Freight International plc, carries out telephone interviews with candidates who have applied for the job of junior shipping agent.

A 🔊 48 Listen to the interviews and copy and complete the table below.

	Interview 1	Interview 2	Interview 3
Name			
Present employer			
Strengths			
Weaknesses			
Why this job?			
Future plans			
Own questions			

B Discuss the interviews and say which of them were good or bad examples. What did the candidates do right/wrong? Which of the three candidates is the best role model for your own telephone interview?

2 Preparing for a telephone interview

To further prepare yourself for your telephone interview, you read these tips.

Read the text and note down in German the most important tips for your telephone interview.

TIPS FOR YOUR TELEPHONE OR VIDEO INTERVIEW

Be prepared!
- Before the interview you should gather a copy of the job description along with a copy of your letter of application, your CV and your references, and write a list of questions you want to ask the interviewer and a list of your strengths.
- Pin these documents to the wall so that you can check them during the call without having to flick through piles of paper.

On the day of the call
- Place a notebook and a couple of pens beside the phone so you can take notes during the interview.
- Make sure the room you are in is quiet.
- If it is a telephone interview, use a landline where possible. If you have to use your mobile phone, make sure it is fully charged and that you take the call in a place where reception is good.
- If it is a video interview, dress as you would for a face-to-face interview so that you make a good impression. Remember to check that the microphone and video camera on your computer are working before the interview.

During the call
- Concentrate and stay focused. Listen carefully and reply to the interviewer appropriately.
- Be professional and polite. At the end of the call, you can ask, "Do my qualifications meet the company's needs?" However the interview goes, always end with "Thank you for your call." The last few words of a conversation are often the ones that people remember, so always leave a good impression at the end.

A job application Unit 12

3 Role-play: Practising a telephone interview

You and a colleague decide to practise a telephone interview together.

A Work with a partner.

Partner A: You are the interviewer. Look at File 20 on page 139.
Partner B: You are an applicant for the position. Look at File 26 on page 144.

> **Asking for clarification on the telephone**
>
> I'm sorry, could you say that again?
> So, if I understand you correctly, …
> I don't quite understand what you mean by …

› *Useful phrases: Telephoning, page 181*

B With your partner, prepare a dialogue and role-play a telephone interview.

4 Preparing for a face-to-face interview

You listen to a podcast in which an expert gives tips on how to handle face-to-face job interviews.

A What is the expert likely to say? With a partner, brainstorm a list of expressions you might hear and make notes under the headings below.

Here are a few expressions from the podcast to start you off.

Stage 1: Greetings and introductions
arrive at the interview on time

Stage 2: Small talk
talk about the weather

Stage 3: The main part of the interview
talk about yourself

Stage 4: Questions from the candidate
do background research into the company before the interview

Stage 5: Further arrangements and the end of the interview
ask when you can expect to hear from the company again

VIDEO 8
Watch the video to see more about interviews.

B 49))) Now listen and check. How many of your expressions did you hear?

5 Practising for an interview

You and your colleague decide to practise the main part of an interview together.

A First of all, study the list of common interview questions (File 24 on page 143) and how to answer them.

B Work with a partner.

Partner A: Choose one of the job advertisements you read in Part A (page 121) and tell your partner which one you have chosen. Think about the questions the interviewer might ask and how you might answer. Make notes.

Partner B: Study the job advertisement your partner has chosen. Make a list of questions you might ask.

C When you are both ready, role-play the job interview. When you have finished, change roles if you wish.

COMMUNICATION: A CV and a covering letter

Situation: You find out online about the documents which you will need for job applications.
→ You study an English CV and covering letter and write a job application.

1 Reading a website about CVs

You find an interesting website with tips, but the headings have got mixed up.

Work with a partner. Read the tips (1–9) and match them to the headings (a–i).

a	Education and training	d	Personal details	g	Work experience
b	Hobbies and interests	e	References	h	Contact details
c	Personal statement	f	Key skills	i	Further skills

→ TIPS for writing your CV

International CVs

Your CV is a summary of your abilities, work experience, education and qualifications. There is no set format for a British CV but you should keep it short, using clear headings to guide the reader.

1 Give your name and address, telephone number(s) (home/mobile) and email address.

2 This should be a short message that grabs the attention of the reader. Use note form. This helps to keep your CV focused and direct, for example: *Motivated management assistant in freight forwarding.*

3 Here you can summarize your skills and experience which are relevant to the job you are applying for.

4 As a general rule, CVs should be in reverse chronological order, listing the most recent position first. For each position, you should provide the dates of the start and end of employment, the employer's name and address, the job title, the main duties and responsibilities and achievements.

5 Give a brief description of qualifications (school, academic and/or professional). Give the names of schools or colleges in reverse chronological order.

6 Here you should write about common skills gained throughout your education and work experience, such as languages, IT skills, good maths skills or a full, clean driving licence. These skills are of interest for any employer.

7 This feature is optional, but could provide something more personal to discuss at an interview. Be careful about what you write; a dangerous sport or *socializing with friends* may not be what an employer wants to hear!

8 Write your date of birth and nationality under this heading.

9 Due to data protection laws, candidates should not provide referees' names, addresses or any other contact details on CVs, but should state that details are available on request. Always ask your referees' permission before you give someone their contact details.

2 Analysing a CV

You also find an example of a British-style CV online.

Study the CV below. What differences can you find between this CV and a typical German CV?

MARTIN BIENEK
Am Kattenkamp 236, 33611 Bielefeld, Germany
Landline: (+49) 521 3124
Mobile: (+49) 1622 081430
Email: martin.bienek43@hotspot.ger

PERSONAL STATEMENT
Mobile and flexible apprentice mananagement assistant in freight forwarding, in final year of 3-year course, seeking position abroad

KEY SKILLS
Accountancy, Economics
Microsoft Word, Excel
Native speaker of German
Excellent spoken and written English
Good spoken and written Polish

WORK EXPERIENCE
June 20..	Assistant in customer service, London Cargo plc
	Became skilled at interacting with customers from all over the world
July 20..	4-week work placement at Freight AG, doing general office work

EDUCATION AND TRAINING
Since 20..	3-year dual-training scheme at Vocational College and MEB Spedition, Bielefeld, Germany
June 20..	*Abitur* (Final examination similar to A-Levels)
	Main subjects: English, Computer Studies
20..–20..	Primary and secondary education in Bielefeld

FURTHER SKILLS
Full driving licence
First aid certificate

HOBBIES AND INTERESTS
Athletics, football
Training local junior football team

PERSONAL DETAILS
Date of birth: 06 April 20..
Nationality: German

REFERENCES
Available on request

3 Analysing a covering letter

Martin has applied for a job as a freight forwarding and logistics services agent at a company in Ireland.

Read Martin's covering letter on the opposite page and match the parts (1–5) with explanations from the list.

a   asking the employer to invite you for an interview
b   reference to details on your CV
c   reference to the position
d   saying why the applicant is applying for the position
e   stating why the applicant is the best person for the job

4 Writing: An application for a job abroad

You find the following advertisement in a trade magazine and decide to apply for the position.

Prepare your CV and write your application.

German-speaking
Junior Freight Agent
Air Freight

Location: Dublin, Republic of Ireland
Salary: 21,000 euros to 23,000 euros depending on experience

■ **Job description:** duties include
  – selling transport and logistics services
  – arranging shipments, booking cargo space
  – procuring and issuing documents, handling accounts and customs formalities

■ **We are looking for:**
  – relevant vocational school leaving certificate
  – basic knowledge of MS Office
  – fluent German and English

■ **You should be:**
  – confident and personable
  – keen to learn
  – flexible

■ **What we offer:**
  – an excellent working atmosphere
  – optional language training courses
  – good chances of promotion

Please submit your CV together with a covering letter to:
Ms O'Brien, Human Resources, 22 Grand Canal Harbour, Dublin 2, D02 A342

› *Useful phrases: Writing covering letters, page 194*

Am Kattenkamp 236, 33611 Bielefeld, Germany
Phone: (+49) 521 3124, Mobile: (+49) 1622 081430
Email: martin.bienek43@hotspot.ger

20 April 20..

Scott Traders Ltd
Silverbank Industrial Estate
DUBLIN
D11 D4E2
IRELAND

Attn. Mr Haig, Human Resources Director

Dear Mr Haig

Junior Freight Agent

[1] With reference to your advertisement Ref. No. 17673 on the internet, I would like to apply for the post described.

[2] I am very interested in the job you are offering as I feel sure it will give me the opportunity to develop both personally and professionally. I am particularly keen to work in a position which allows me to apply my skills on a daily basis.

[3] As you can see from the enclosed CV, by June of this year I will have completed the final year of a three-year apprenticeship at a Vocational Training College in Bielefeld, Germany. I will then be a fully-qualified freight forwarding and logistics services agent.

[4] As I have practical skills and experience, am flexible, mobile and speak fluent English, German and Polish, I believe I will be a strong member of any team I join and will benefit your company.

[5] My CV is enclosed and I am available for an interview at short notice.

I would very much appreciate it if you would consider my application and hope that you will grant me an interview.

I look forward to hearing from you soon.

Yours sincerely

M. Bienek

Martin Bienek

Encl.

DAS KANN ICH (Unit 12)

- Eine Beschreibung meiner Ausbildung auf Englisch verfassen. (Foundation)
- Eine Stellenanzeige auf Englisch schreiben. (Part A)
- Mich auf ein Bewerbungsgespräch auf Englisch gut vorbereiten. (Part B)
- Bewerbungsunterlagen auf Englisch richtig verfassen und gestalten. (Communication)

KMK Exam practice 6

1 Leseverstehen: Stufe II (B1)

Situation: Sie arbeiten für den Logistikdienstleister Müller in Hanau. Auf eine Stellenanzeige für den Bereich Logistikmanagement hat sich auch ein englischer Interessent (Herr Stuart) beworben. Er spricht gut Deutsch, allerdings ist eines seiner Empfehlungsschreiben auf Englisch. Ihr Chef (Hr. Müller) bittet Sie, dieses für ihn ins Deutsche zu übertragen, und hat Ihnen ein Raster vorbereitet.

Aufgabe: Übertragen Sie das Empfehlungsschreiben anhand des Rasters ins Deutsche.

To whom it may concern

It is with great pleasure that I write this letter of recommendation on behalf of Dennis Stuart.

Dennis has worked for *Logsolution* for almost five years. In his position as a logistics manager, Dennis contributed to the development and international growth of the company by implementing a quality control system and by constantly training employees and improving routines.

He responded to customer needs and built ongoing conversations with both new and established customers. Under his management, delivery times for our customers could be improved significantly.

In his day-to-day work he demonstrates excellent knowledge of documentation and regulations and a deep understanding of road transport. He has strong management skills and a quick, effective approach to problem solving.

His duties included the following tasks:
- Establishing and using IT systems to coordinate transport
- Negotiating with suppliers and customers
- Organizing training courses for staff
- Developing and implementing objectives and strategies for cost reduction and customer satisfaction

Dennis is devoted to his work and shows a deep understanding not only of the business but also of the people he works with. I highly recommend him without reservation.

Hector Rosenberg
Managing Director

Hi, bitte werten Sie mir das Schreiben anhand der folgenden Aspekte aus. VG, Müller

Name Bewerberin/Bewerber	
früheres/aktuelles Beschäftigungsverhältnis	
Dauer letztes Beschäftigungsverhältnis	
zuletzt ausgeübte Position	
Art von Kundenkontakt	
Bereiche von Transportlogistik	
Erfahrung Qualitätskontrolle? Was genau?	
Welche tagtäglichen Aufgaben werden ausdrücklich bescheinigt?	
Soft Skills	

2 Interaktion: Stufe II (B1)

👥 Work with a partner. **Partner A:** Look at File 19 on page 139. **Partner B:** Look at File 27 on page 145.

3 Produktion: Stufe II (B1)

Situation: Sie arbeiten für Express Logistics Ltd. Ihre Unternehmenssprache ist Englisch. Sie nehmen am monatlichen Treffen der Kollegen des Verkaufs teil. Während des Treffens haben Sie Stichpunkte zur Tagesordnung gemacht und müssen diese jetzt noch als Protokoll in ganzen Sätzen auf Englisch formulieren.

Aufgabe: Schreiben Sie auf Englisch ein Protokoll des Treffens.

TAGESORDNUNG 4/20..	
Teilnehmer:	Dr. Fürste; H. Meier; S. Ebert; G. Sonntag; L. Steiner; K. Ostermann
Thema/Anlass:	Monatstreffen

Tagesordnungspunkte (Bericht Dr. Fürste, Abteilungsleiter)	Verantwortlichkeit/Aktion erforderlich?
1. Internetseite soll verbessert werden, neue Services (Kühltransporte, Live-Updates des Versandstatus, niedrige CO2-Bilanz) herausstellen.	S. Ebert: Informationsmail an IT-Abteilung; IT und Marketing: Treffen zur Erarbeitung.
2. Neue Anbieter am deutschen Markt mit ähnlichen Angeboten	G. Sonntag: Vergleich mit Konkurrenzanbietern durchführen, wie ist unsere Marktposition (Umsatz, Arbeitnehmer, Zweigstellen, Länder)?
3. Angebote an Kunden oft nicht vollständig, Beschwerden und Nachfragen per Telefon und E-Mail, dadurch Verlust von Aufträgen möglich!	L. Steiner: Infomail an alle Mitarbeiter, Checkliste zur Erstellung eines Angebotes berücksichtigen!
4. Änderung der Zahlungsbedingungen: zusätzlich zur Zahlung bei Rechnungserhalt auch 3 % Skonto bei Zahlung innerhalb 14 Tagen	K. Ostermann: Information an alle Kunden, Punkt auf der Website ergänzen
5. Dank für geleistete Arbeit im letzten Quartal	

P Partner files

FILE 1: KMK Exam practice 1, exercise 3, Interaktion, page 22

Partner B

Situation: Sie sind ein englischer Praktikant / eine englische Praktikantin aus Liverpool. Dort arbeiten und lernen Sie bei einer englischen Spedition, die Transporte in Großbritannien organisiert. Ihre Firma plant eine Kooperation mit der Hansen International Spedition GmbH. Daher bekommen Sie die Möglichkeit bei der deutschen Firma ein dreimonatiges Praktikum zu absolvieren. Heute treffen Sie dort einen deutschen Auszubildenden, der Sie in den nächsten beiden Wochen betreuen wird.

- Begrüßen Sie Ihr Gegenüber und machen Sie sich bekannt.
- Berichten Sie von Ihrer Anreise. Betreiben Sie etwas Small Talk.
- Fragen Sie nach dem geplanten Arbeitseinsatz und den Arbeitsbedingungen.
- Beantworten Sie Fragen über Ihre Firma und Ihre dortigen Tätigkeiten.
- Informieren Sie sich über typische Merkmale des deutschen Ausbildungssystems.
- Erkundigen Sie sich nach Möglichkeiten der Freizeitgestaltung oder Möglichkeiten, Ihr Deutsch zu verbessern.

FILE 2: Unit 4, Communication, exercise 1C, page 38

Partner B

Dictate these email addresses to Partner A. Check A's answers.

1. beatrice-kuhn@berlin_tools.orgnet
2. Hamish.MacPherson@gov.net.uk
3. your own email address
4. the email address of your firm or another email address you often write to

FILE 3: Unit 5, Part A, exercise 4, page 45

Partner B

You are Henry (or Harriet) Connell from British Snacks plc, Liverpool. A major supermarket chain in southern Germany has just agreed to sell your products. Use the following information to answer the caller's questions.

Collection: The pallets are stored in a warehouse near Calais.
Destination: Munich
Date: First delivery on (choose a date in the near future)
Weight: 15 tonnes
Comment: Shipment must be executed on demand *(auf Anfrage ausgeführt)*.
There will be approx. one delivery of ca. 30 pallets per week, 1 FLT

Partner files

FILE 4: Unit 6, Part A, exercise 4, page 54

Partner A

You are the apprentice. Follow the steps below to have a conversation. (Your partner has the other steps.)

1. Introduce yourself.
3. Tell the driver about the load (kerosene), the container (metal IBC) and the placard (warning sign) to display.
5. The IBC contains 1,000 litres.
6. Give the driver the ADR emergency kit and ask him/her to name and explain the contents.
8. Ask what he/she will do if there is an emergency.
10. Ask what he/she won't do if there is an emergency.
12. Wish him/her a good trip.

FILE 5: Unit 6, Part B, exercise 1C, page 55

Partner B

Situation 1

You are Henry/Henrietta Cooper at PowerTech Electrics Ltd in Colchester, UK. Your company exports electric generators to the European mainland. You phone BDI Transport GmbH in Hamburg and ask about the smallest suitable pallets for the generators listed using either imperial or metric weights and measures (you can decide which to ask about).

Model	Length	Width	Height	Weight
AC Generator type 49A	45 in 1,143 mm	40 in 1,016 mm	32 in 812.8 mm	3,000 lbs 1,360.77 kg
DC Generator type 29D	30 in 762 mm	20 in 508 mm	28 in 711.2 mm	1,000 lbs 453.6 kg
AC/DC Generator type 500X	30 in 762 mm	40 in 1,016 mm	35 in 889 mm	2,750 lbs 1,247.38 kg

Situation 2

You are Linda/Leonard Clark from Austin, Texas. You are on work experience at BDI Transport GmbH in Hamburg and today you are taking phone calls from English-speaking customers. A customer phones you to ask for advice about parcel boxes for their products. Use the table below to make suitable recommendations in metric or imperial weights and measures.

Parcel boxes

Size	Length	Width	Height / Depth
XS	22.5 cm 8.85 in	14.5 cm 5.71 in	3.5 cm 1.38 in
S	25 cm 9.84 in	17.5 cm 6.89 in	10 cm 3.94 cm
M	37.5 cm 14.76 cm	30 cm 11.81 in	13.5 cm 5.31 in
L	45 cm 17.71 in	35 cm 13.78 in	20 cm 7.87 in

FILE 6: KMK Exam practice 2, exercise 2, Interaktion, page 41

Partner B

Together with a lot of other apprentices from different countries, you attend a seminar at the European Apprenticeship Convention with the topic "Modern Warehousing". During the break a young colleague approaches you.

Role-play a conversation with Partner A. Be prepared to ask and answer questions. You may have to use your imagination and make up possible answers. Use the ideas below to help you.

- Greet him/her properly and introduce yourself.
- Exchange information about your company, kind of warehouse management and typical storage products.
- Give feedback about the seminar (content, structure, possible tips and improvements).
- Proceed to the seminar and arrange to meet in the next break.

The Forwarding Agents Inc.
- 70 warehouses all over Europe
- 24/7 operation
- several fully automated warehouses

FILE 7: Unit 7, Part B, exercise 5A, page 66

Partner A

You are a cargo agent (own name) at Ronstadt Air Freight SE, Frankfurt.

- Answer the phone in the usual way (friendly greeting, company name, own name).
- Make sure you understand the caller's name and company name. Check the spelling if necessary.
- Ask about the type of goods. Remember, an exact description is needed for the US authorities.
- You check online and find wooden parquet flooring. Check that that is accurate.
- Find about the sort of container, including how many, dimensions and weight. Note down the information and make sure you wrote everything correctly.
- You check online and find the following information. Tell the caller.

  best rate: €2.68 per kilo
  Royal Canadian Airlines
  Minimum charge €72.43 + €2.68 per kilo
  Next flight is next Monday at 6.45

- Find out what the caller wants to do next, then end the call politely.

FILE 8: Unit 6, Part A, exercise 4, page 54

Partner B

You are Aleksander/Aleksandra Starek, the Polish driver. Follow the steps below to have a conversation. (Your partner has the other steps.)

2   Introduce yourself.
4   Ask how much the IBC contains.
7   Name and explain the contents of the kit (goggles, light clothing, gloves, eyewash bottle, shovel, broom, boots, warning triangles).
9   Use information on the tremcard to explain what you will do if there is an emergency.
11 Use information on the tremcard to explain what you won't do if there is an emergency.
13 Respond politely.

FILE 9: Unit 6, Part B, exercise 1C, page 55

Partner A

Situation 1

You are Linda/Leonard Clark from Austin, Texas. You are on work experience at BDI Transport GmbH in Hamburg and today you are taking phone calls from English-speaking customers. One customer asks you for some advice about pallets. Use the table below to make suitable recommendations using metric or imperial weights and measures.

Type	Length	Width	Height	Weight	Max. load
EPAL 1 / Euro pallet	800 mm 31.50 in	1,200 mm 47.24 in	144 mm 5.70 in	25 kg 55 lbs	1,500 kg 3,037 lbs
EPAL 2	1,200 mm 47.24 in	1,000 mm 39.37 in	162 mm 6.38 in	35 kg 77 lbs	1,250 kg 2,756 lbs
EPAL 3	1,000 mm 39.37 in	1,200 mm 47.24 in	144 mm 5.70 in	30 kg 66 lbs	1,500 kg 3,037 lbs
EPAL 6 / half pallet	800 mm 31.50 in	600 mm 23.62 in	144 mm 5.70 in	9.5 kg 21 lbs	500 kg 1,102 lbs

Situation 2

You are Robert/Roberta Young. You work in the Sales Department at Kran's Outdoor Wear Ltd in Chester, UK. Your company exports sportswear all over Europe. You phone BDI Transport GmbH in Hamburg and ask about the smallest suitable parcel boxes for:
– Urban X rucksack 25 litres (0.88 ft³): height 44 cm x width 35 cm x depth 13 cm (17.3" x 13.8" x 5.2")
– Children's running shoes: length 18 cm x width 8 cm x height 9 cm (7.1" x 3.2" x 3.5")
– Weight training instruction manual: length 20 cm x width 13 cm x depth 1 cm (7.9" x 5.1" x 0.4")

Before you call, decide whether you want to ask about imperial or metric weights and measures.

FILE 10: Unit 7, Part A, exercise 5A, page 66

Partner B

You are an exporter (Sigrid/Simon Berglund) at Quality Hardwood Flooring, Stockholm, Sweden.

- Call the cargo agent at Ronstadt Air Freight SE, Frankfurt and introduce yourself (full name, company).
- You want to ship goods from Stockholm, Sweden to Los Angeles, USA.
- The goods consist of flooring (boards made of wood for making floors). The flooring is loaded on pallets.
- For now you want to ship one container (trial order). Give the cargo agent the details he/she asks for.

  > 120 (length) x 80 (width) x 60 cm (height); weight = 500 kg

- Ask about the airline, total charges and the next available flight. Note down the information and read them back to the agent to make sure they are correct.
- Promise the agent that you will call back today and end the call politely.

FILE 11: Unit 7, Communication, exercise 4, page 71

Partner A

You work as an OBC. (Use your own name.) You have to take an important automotive part to a racing team taking part in a rally in Monaco in three days' time. You have completed your *OBC Travel Requirements* form and get a phone call from the Travel Section. Follow the steps below to have a conversation. (Your partner has the other steps.)

1. Answer the phone (greeting and full name).
3. Ask if everything is now booked for the trip to Monte Carlo.
5. Agree politely.
7. Listen to the available flights and choose the ones you think are best. (You need to be in Monte Carlo by 4 p.m. on the first day and can fly back the next morning.)
9. Ask if there's a hire car available to get from the airport to Monte Carlo.
11. Accept the offer, then ask for half board at a hotel near the city centre in Monte Carlo.
13. Ask for details.
15. Accept the offer.
17. Finish the call politely.

FILE 12: Unit 8, Communication, exercise 4, page 83

Partner A: Consignee

You are Mr Samart / Ms Nin Khamsing, Manager, Banyan Oriental Hotel, Bangkok, Thailand. Follow the steps below to have a conversation about your shipment with an employee at Lohmann Sea Freight Services. (Your partner has the other steps.)

1. Answer the phone (full name, name of hotel, polite greeting)
3. Problem?
5. How long?
7. Big problem! New wing of hotel opening in week 49
9. Ask to be phoned with ETA (estimated time of arrival) as soon as possible (+66 2 890 777)
11. Ask for name and number of caller
13. Thank the caller
14. Polite ending

FILE 13: Unit 9, Communication, exercise 4, page 97

Partner A

Do the three tasks below with your partner.

1. First use the map to practise giving directions to your partner without saying the destination. Do this for three destinations, then change roles.

   Begin like this: You are at starting point 1 on Nordstraße. Go down the road to the crossroads and turn right. At the … turn right/left … Take the … You have reached your destination. Where are you?

2. Now you are in the car park outside your company's warehouse (starting point 6). Give directions to a foreign driver who wants to go to:

   – the supermarket on foot
   – an ATM on foot
   – the A1 motorway
   – the B51 to Münster
   – more destinations chosen by you

3. Now use a map of your local area and improvise being a foreign driver (Georgi Aleksandrov/Maria Aleksandrova) asking for directions to destinations that can be reached a) on foot b) by lorry.

FILE 14: Unit 7, Communication, exercise 4, page 71

Partner B

You are Tim/Tina Jones and work in the travel section.

You have received an *OBC Travel Requirements* form for a trip from Frankfurt to Monte Carlo via Nice Airport (NCE) in France tomorrow. You call the OBC who submitted the form to discuss the arrangements. Follow the steps below to have a conversation. (Your partner has the other steps.)

 2 Introduce yourself (full name, Travel Section). Explain why you are calling (OBC travel requirements for trip to Monte Carlo via NCE).
 4 You first need to go through the details of the flight from Frankfurt to Nice Airport.
 6 Give your colleague the following information and note down the options he/she chooses.

> Two possible flights to Nice tomorrow:
> **either:** 6.50 from FRA to NCE via Paris arriving at 13.10
> **or:** 9.40 from FRA to NCE via Paris arriving at 13.35
> Two possible return flights the next day
> **either:** 10.10 from NCE via Paris arriving at 16.55
> **or:** 12.55 from FRA via Copenhagen arriving at 19.45

 8 Discuss the transfer from Nice Airport to Monte Carlo
10 Better to take the Airport Xpress Bus 110 (every half hour, open return trip €33)
12 All hotels in Monte Carlo are booked up apart from a 5-star hotel for €600 per night. Only available hotel is in Nice.
14 Hotel is a 2-star budget hotel near Nice Airport with breakfast only.
16 Promise to email details and finish the call politely.

FILE 15: Unit 8, Communication, exercise 4, page 83

Partner B

You work at Lohmann Sea Freight Services GmbH, Hamburg. Use your own name and follow the steps below to have a conversation with a consignee from Thailand: Mr Samart / Ms Nin Kamsing from Banyan Oriental Hotel. (Your partner has the other steps.)

 2 Introduce yourself and say reason for calling is consignment of catering equipment
 4 Delay (storm over the Arabian Sea)
 6 Hard to say – weather can change any time
 8 Catering equipment will be first off the ship in Bangkok Port
10 Promise to phone
12 Spell your full name and give your phone number (+49 40 25022)
14 Apologize for the delay
16 Polite ending

FILE 16: Unit 10, Part A, exercise 5, page 102

Partner A

You are visiting a trade fair, where you attend a talk about customer service. After the talk, you introduce yourself to the person next to you.

Choose a behaviour card and use it to role-play the conversation on page 102.

1	2	3
You are from a country where people don't make eye contact.	You are from a country where small talk is very important. It is very rude to talk about business right away.	You are from a country where people are very informal.

FILE 17: Unit 10, Communication, exercise 4, page 107

Partner B

Your work for Jorge Murano Transportista in Spain. You take a call from Horn Logistics GmbH, which uses your company as a subcontractor. They have a problem with a delivery. Use the notes below to reply to the complaint.

- ask what exactly the problem is
- you have a new driver who is making a lot of mistakes
- difficult to get experienced staff
- promise better supervision and training
- refer to long partnership
- offer refund of payment

While you are waiting for Partner A to call, check that you know how to deal with complaints in English (exercises 1 and 2 on page 106).

FILE 18: Unit 11, Communication, exercise 4A, page 117

Partners A and B

Situation: In your company, there are 20 employees in the office and 15 in the warehouse. At the last works council meeting, many employees were in favour of introducing flexitime. Today, there is a meeting between the American General Manager and some staff members to discuss it. Attending the meeting are:
- the General Manager (Partner A)
- the Human Resources Manager (Partner B)
- the Works Council Representative (Partner C)
- an office worker (Partner D)
- a warehouse employee (Partner E)
- an apprentice (Partner F)

	Office	Warehouse
Working hours	7.30 a.m. – 3.30 p.m.	Early shift: 6.00 a.m. – 2.00 p.m. Day shift: 10.00 a.m. – 6.00 p.m.
Break	9.30 a.m. – 9.45 a.m.	15 minutes taken flexibly
Lunch break	12.00 noon – 12.45 p.m.	

Use your role card below and suitable expressions for taking part in meetings to conduct a meeting and come to a decision.

› *Useful phrases: Taking part in meetings, page 193*

Partner A: General Manager

Your opinion on flexitime is neutral and you will decide on the basis of the arguments you hear.
- start the meeting, introduce yourself and ask the participants to introduce themselves
- explain that the meeting is about introducing flexitime
- ask the Works Council Representative to explain why some people want it
- ask if there are any questions
- consult with the HR Manager and come to a decision

Partner B: Human Resources Manager

You are against flexitime because there must always be at least two employees in the warehouse to load and unload lorries early in the morning and late in the afternoon. You would like to introduce shift work in the office to guarantee the necessary paperwork for the lorries all day.
- introduce yourself
- explain your position
- answer your colleagues' questions
- consult with the General Manager and come to a decision

Partner files

FILE 19 : KMK Exam practice 6, exercise 2, Interaktion, page 129

Partner A

Gestalten Sie in Partnerarbeit einen Dialog mithilfe der folgenden Rollenkarte.

> **Situation:** You work for LogInt, a logistics company based in the UK.
> Your company has a stand at an international trade fair and you are responsible for welcoming visitors to the stand. One visitor has an appointment with a manager, but the manager is delayed, so you have to ask the visitor to wait for a little while. Entertain the visitor while he/she is waiting and take care of any problems that occur.
> Be prepared to ask and answer questions. You have to use your imagination to make up possible answers. Use the ideas below to help you:
> – Introduce yourself to the visitor and explain the situation.
> – Offer a refreshment.
> – Engage in small talk (three topics).
> – Calm the visitor when he/she gets annoyed.
> – Try to find a solution for the visitor (possible offers: Internet access? Information material? Voucher for lunch?)

FILE 20: Unit 12, Part B, exercise 3A, page 123

Partner A

There is a job vacancy at Freight International plc. Jennifer/John Winters, Head of Human Resources, calls an applicant for a telephone interview.

You are Jennifer/John Winters. Work with Partner B and role-play the telephone interview. Partner B answers the phone and begins.

> – Introduce yourself.
> – Suitable time for phone call?
> – Ask the candidate to talk about his/her CV.
> – How would the candidate describe himself/herself?
> – How would the candidate's colleagues describe him/her?
> – Is the candidate a team player? Examples?
> – Hobbies?
> – Strengths and weaknesses?
> – Reason for deciding to train as …
> – Expectations of the job?
> – Why should this particular candidate be chosen?
> – Questions?

Swap roles when you have finished.

FILE 21: Unit 11, Communication, exercise 4A, page 117

Partners C and D

Situation: In your company, there are 20 employees in the office and 15 in the warehouse. At the last works council meeting, many employees were in favour of introducing flexitime. Today, there is a meeting between the American General Manager and some staff members to discuss it. Attending the meeting are:
- the General Manager (Partner A)
- the Human Resources Manager (Partner B)
- the Works Council Representative (Partner C)
- an office worker (Partner D)
- a warehouse employee (Partner E)
- an apprentice (Partner F)

	Office	Warehouse
Working hours	7.30 a.m. – 3.30 p.m.	Early shift: 6.00 a.m. – 2.00 p.m. Day shift: 10.00 a.m. – 6.00 p.m.
Break	9.30 a.m. – 9.45 a.m.	15 minutes taken flexibly
Lunch break	12.00 noon – 12.45 p.m.	

Use your role card below and suitable expressions for taking part in meetings to conduct a meeting and come to a decision.

› *Useful phrases: Taking part in meetings, page 193*

Partner C: Works Council Representative

You are in favour of flexitime for the office staff because a lot of the employees need time, e.g. for their children, older relatives, visits to doctors, etc. You would like core time from 9.00 a.m. to 3.00 p.m. with flexible breaks. You don't think that flexitime is a good idea for the warehouse.
- introduce yourself
- explain that flexitime was suggested at the last works council meeting
- ask the other two employees to explain their position and then explain yours
- ask the HR manager a question (invent)

Partner D: office worker

You are married with two children (7 and 9). You would like to start work in the office after 8.00 a.m. after you have taken your children to school. Your husband/wife is a lorry driver and leaves home at 5 a.m., so he/she can't help. When your children are ill, you also need to take them to the doctor's in the morning. You would be happy to make up for a late start by working later in the afternoons when your mother can help out with the children.
- introduce yourself
- explain your position
- ask the HR manager a question (invent)

FILE 22: Unit 9, Communication, exercise 4, page 97

Partner B

Do the three tasks below with your partner.

1. Use the map to practise following directions that your partner gives you. Where do the directions take you? Practise doing this for three destinations, then change roles and give directions to your partner without saying the destination.

   Begin like this: You are at starting point 2 on Bahnhofstraße. Go down the road to the ... and turn left. At the ... turn right/left ... Take the ... You have reached your destination. Where are you?

2. You are a foreign driver (Georgi Aleksandrov/Maria Aleksandrova) and are in the car park outside a company's warehouse (starting point 6). Ask Partner A, who works at the warehouse, for directions to:

   – the supermarket on foot
   – an ATM on foot
   – the A1 motorway
   – the B51 to Münster
   – more destinations chosen by you

3. Use a map of your local area and improvise giving directions to a foreign driver to destinations that can be reached (a) on foot (b) by lorry.

FILE 23: Unit 11, Communication, exercise 4A, page 117

Partners E and F

Situation: In your company, there are 20 employees in the office and 15 in the warehouse. At the last works council meeting, many employees were in favour of introducing flexitime. Today, there is a meeting between the American General Manager and some staff members to discuss it. Attending the meeting are:
- the General Manager (Partner A)
- the Human Resources Manager (Partner B)
- the Works Council Representative (Partner C)
- an office worker (Partner D)
- a warehouse employee (Partner E)
- an apprentice (Partner F)

	Office	Warehouse
Working hours	7.30 a.m. – 3.30 p.m.	Early shift: 6.00 a.m. – 2.00 p.m. Day shift: 10.00 a.m. – 6.00 p.m.
Break	9.30 a.m. – 9.45 a.m.	15 minutes taken flexibly
Lunch break	12.00 noon – 12.45 p.m.	

Use your role card below and suitable expressions for taking part in meetings to conduct a meeting and come to a decision.

› *Useful phrases: Taking part in meetings, page 193*

Partner E: warehouse employee

Your priority is not to be on early shift (6.00 a.m. – 2.00 p.m.) for more than two weeks in a row. If flexitime can guarantee this, you will be in favour of it. You don't mind starting early or finishing late.
- introduce yourself
- explain your position
- ask the HR manager a question (invent)

Partner F: apprentice

You and a lot of other apprentices would like to have flexitime because if you stay out late one night, you can start later the next morning without getting into trouble. You don't like starting work at 6.00 a.m., but you don't mind working until 6.00 p.m.
- introduce yourself
- explain your position
- ask the HR manager a question (invent)

FILE 24: Unit 12, Part B, exercise 5, page 123

Common interview questions	Tips
… about yourself – Tell us about yourself. – How would you describe yourself? – What are your hobbies? – What are your strengths and weaknesses? – Tell us about a mistake you made in the past and how you handled it. – What question would you not like us to ask you?	– Be honest. Show that you are able to use your strengths and indicate that you are working on your "weaknesses". – Be positive. Even if a mistake was made, remember to say that you learned from it. – Say that you hope they do not ask you about a particular department/task as you do not yet have much experience in that department/area. Keep it simple and say something positive.
… about your education, work experience and skills – Why did you choose to train at vocational college? – What responsibilities did you have / do you have during the work placement? / at work? – Please tell me about your present job. – What have you learned in your present job that you think will help you in the position you're applying for with us?	– Talk about the aspects of your education, work experience and skills that are relevant for the job in question. – Talk about a particular project or task which you did successfully.
… about what you know – What languages do you speak? – What computer software are you familiar with?	– Answer honestly. – Be honest. Don't say you know MS Office if you only learned Word, PowerPoint and Excel.
… about your motivation – Why did you apply for this job? – Why do you want to work for this company? – Why do you think you would be a good candidate for this job? – What would you like to achieve in the next five/ten years?	– Show that you have researched the company and know what the job is about. – Stress the positive aspects of the company and the job. – Talk about realistic goals and describe how you would like to progress with your career.
Questions you can ask the interviewer	
– I would like to continue improving my skills. What courses does the company offer? – What kind of training is given to new employees? – Who would I report to? – What are the prospects for promotion? – What are the next stages of the selection process? – When could I start?	

FILE 25: Unit 10, Part A, exercise 5, page 102

Partner B

You are visiting a trade fair, where you attend a talk about customer service. After the talk, you introduce yourself to the person next to you.

Choose a behaviour card and use it to role-play the conversation on page 102.

| 1. You are from a country where the exchange of business cards is very important. | 2. You are from a country where people are very serious. It is rude to smile. | 3. You are from a country where people stand very close to each other when they are having a conversation. |

FILE 26: Unit 12, Part B, exercise 3A, page 123

Partner B

There is a job vacancy at Freight International plc. Jennifer/John Winters, Head of Human Resources, calls an applicant for a telephone interview.

You are the applicant. Work with Partner A and role-play the telephone interview. You begin by answering the phone.

- Introduce yourself.
- Say that this is a suitable time for a phone call.
- Talk about your CV.
- Describe yourself from your own point of view and from that of your colleagues.
- Give examples of how you are a team player.
- Describe your hobbies.
- Describe your strengths and weaknesses.
- Give reasons for choosing this career.
- Describe what you expect from the job.
- Justify why you should be chosen for the job.
- Ask any questions you may have.

Swap roles when you have finished.

FILE 27: KMK Exam practice 6, exercise 2, Interaktion, page 129

Partner B

Gestalten Sie in Partnerarbeit einen Dialog mithilfe der folgenden Rollenkarte.

> **Situation:** You are the logistics manager at a large foundry *(Gießerei)* in Lodz, Poland.
>
> You have an appointment with a manager from LogInt at an international trade fair. You arrive at the LogInt stand on time.
>
> Be prepared to ask and answer questions. You have to use your imagination and make up possible answers. Use the ideas below to help you:
> - Introduce yourself and say you are expected. Show understanding if you have to wait.
> - Ask for a different refreshment.
> - Engage in small talk with the representative.
> - Eventually show annoyance that nothing happens.
> - Accept one of the representative's offers.

# KMK Mock Exam: Stufe II (B1)

Schriftliche Prüfung

Zeit: 120 Minuten
Hilfsmittel: allgemeines zweisprachiges Wörterbuch
Maximale Punktzahl: 100 Punkte

Im Rahmen der schriftlichen Prüfung werden die Aufgabenanteile für die drei Kompetenzbereiche in den meisten Bundesländern wie folgt gewichtet:
Rezeption 40 %
Produktion 30 %
Mediation 30 %

Im Folgenden werden vier Aufgaben vorgelegt, die Sie bearbeiten sollen. Die erste und die zweite Aufgabe beziehen sich auf Ihre Fähigkeit, englische Texte (gesprochene und geschriebene) zu verstehen = **Rezeption**. Bei der dritten Aufgabe wird von Ihnen erwartet, dass Sie ein Schriftstück erstellen = **Produktion** eines englischen Textes. In der vierten Aufgabe sollen Sie Texte von der deutschen oder englischen in die jeweils andere Sprache übertragen = **Mediation**.

Die Prüfung beginnt mit der Hörverständnisaufgabe. Alle weiteren Aufgaben können in beliebiger Reihenfolge bearbeitet werden.

Rezeption I: Hörverstehen   20 Punkte

Situation: Sie werden in drei Monaten ein Praktikum bei dem schottischen Logistikdienstleister SLM antreten. Bei Ihrem Bewerbungsgespräch haben Sie eine andere Praktikantin kennengelernt, die Sie per E-Mail darauf aufmerksam macht, dass Ihr zukünftiger Chef, Mr Fields, heute ein Radiointerview gibt. Sie notieren sich einige Aspekte, um Ihr zukünftiges Arbeitsumfeld und Ihren zukünftigen Chef besser einschätzen zu können.

50))) **Aufgabe:** Machen Sie sich Notizen, indem Sie die Fragen auf Deutsch beantworten.

1. Wie genau wird Mr Fields' Job bezeichnet?
2. Was sagt er über die Berufsaussichten in der Logistik?
3. Wie lang ist er schon bei SLM?
4. An welchem Ort hat er studiert?
5. Was hat er im Studium vertieft?
6. Womit hatte er anfangs im Job am meisten zu kämpfen?
7. Was waren für ihn wichtige theoretische Grundlagen?
8. Was hat ihm am Anfang besonders geholfen?
9. Wo hat er am Anfang Fehleinschätzungen getroffen?
10. Was sagt er über seinen gesellschaftlichen Hintergrund?

Rezeption II: Leseverstehen — 20 Punkte

Situation: Bei der Preisverleihung eines Umweltpreises für Logistikunternehmen werden Sie auf die Firma FisherFreight aufmerksam. Um sich zu informieren und eventuell umweltfreundliche Ideen auch in Ihr Unternehmen einzubringen, werten Sie den folgenden Artikel aus.

Aufgabe: Lesen Sie den Text und füllen Sie das Auswertungsformular aus.

Ziele von FisherFreight:		
	Maßnahme/Maßnahmen	Ergebnis/Ergebnisse
Luftfracht reduzieren		
Verschiffung optimieren		
Verpackung umweltfreundlicher gestalten		
Übergeordnetes Umweltziel:		
Personelle Maßnahme zur Erreichung der Ziele:		

Eco-friendly solutions at FisherFreight

There is no doubt about it, fighting global warming has become a major goal, both in the commercial sector and in private households. At FisherFreight, we too, are doing our part and have put a lot of work and ideas into our overall goal: reducing our CO_2 emissions altogether. We even employ a manager whose job it is to focus on aspects of energy-saving, waste reduction and eco-friendly packaging. This has greatly improved our carbon footprint.

Let's look at some of the steps we have taken in the last seven years:

If we look at all forms of transport, air freight has the greatest environmental impact. At FisherFreight, we wanted to change this and set ourselves the goal of reducing our use of air freight overall. We replanned our global production schedules, made management improvements and began restructuring from air to sea freight. In the last four years, we managed to achieve a 37% reduction of air freight.

Taking a closer look at cargo shipment, we decided to optimize the whole process. We did this in three simple ways: we shortened our shipping routes, increased our use of groupage shipping and improved our load efficiency. This had a positive financial side-effect as well: it really saves a lot of money!

We also needed to make our packaging more environmentally friendly. In the past few years, we have improved the structure and quality of almost all materials used in our packaging in order to improve shipping efficiency and reduce CO_2 emissions. It's not difficult: fitting more goods into a package means a better carbon footprint. We avoid plastic whenever possible. If we cannot avoid bubble wrap, we reuse the plastic. When it comes to using pallets, we try to reduce the amount of scrap wood by making pallets reusable.

Let me give you an example of one of our improvements:

By making the packaging more compact for a product intended for a wholesaler of car parts, we were able to increase the number of units per carton from forty to sixty-two. As you can imagine, this has increased the efficiency of shipping them a great deal, and it saves us (and the wholesaler!) time and money.

Produktion 30 Punkte

Situation: Sie absolvieren Ihre Ausbildung in einer Niederlassung eines deutschen Autoherstellers und sind daran interessiert, ein Praktikum in der Zweigstelle in Abu Dhabi zu machen. Der Leiter der Exportabteilung unterstützt Ihr Vorhaben. Er bittet Sie, ein Anschreiben anzufertigen, welches er an die Personalleiterin international, Frau Julie McArthur, weiterleiten will. Nach Ihrem Gespräch mit ihm finden Sie am nächsten Tag eine Notiz auf Ihrem Schreibtisch.

Aufgabe: Fertigen Sie ein Bewerbungsschreiben an.

Hallo,

nach unserem gestrigen Gespräch habe ich ein paar Tipps für Sie bezüglich Ihres Bewerbungsschreibens. Ihr Brief sollte Folgendes enthalten:

- *Bezug auf mich*
- *Gründe, warum Sie nach Abu Dhabi möchten*
    - *a) beruflich: große Niederlassung; Möglichkeit, sich weiterzuentwickeln*
    - *b) persönlich: Interesse an arabischen Ländern; Vater Bauingenieur, Familie hat einige Jahre in Oman gelebt*
- *Gründe, warum Sie für die Stelle geeignet sind (nennen Sie mindestens zwei „soft skills", Frau McArthur legt darauf sehr großen Wert)*

Vergessen Sie nicht, Ihr Schreiben angemessen und höflich zu beginnen und zu beenden!

Viel Glück!

Mediation 30 Punkte

Situation: Ihre Spedition hat zum ersten Mal eine Einladung zur Logistikmesse „World of Logistics" in Paris erhalten. Ihr Chef bittet Sie, als Entscheidungsgrundlage für eine mögliche Teilnahme die wichtigsten Informationen über die Messe zu ermitteln.

Aufgabe: Lesen Sie die Einladung auf der gegenüberliegenden Seite und fassen Sie die Informationen, die für Ihren Chef wichtig sind (Fakten über die Messe, Teilnehmerzielgruppe, inhaltliche Schwerpunkte und Vorteile bei einer Teilnahme) stichwortartig auf Deutsch zusammen.

Fakten über WOL	—
Zielgruppe Teilnehmer	—
Inhaltliche Schwerpunkte	—
Vorteile bei Besuch der Messe	—

WORLD OF LOGISTICS

Dear Sir or Madam,

We would like to invite you to the WORLD OF LOGISTICS (WOL) trade fair, which takes place in Paris from 27 November to 1 December. The trade fair has proven a great success with people working in logistics, mobility, IT and supply chain management. The first trade fair was held twenty years ago and attracted 100 exhibitors, but by 2019, this figure had risen to 1,200 exhibitors from over 20 different European countries and almost 20,000 visitors, both from the industry and from the general public. We are proud that the WOL has become an established highlight of the year and one of the leading European exhibitions for the transport and logistics industry.

The fair has become the industry's annual meeting place for industry experts and investment decision makers from all over Europe. It is a comprehensive platform where the most important issues affecting the industry today are discussed, and where new innovation potential is brought to light. From leading global players to specialist providers and start-ups, the entire logistics industry can be found at the WOL. The growth in exhibitor numbers and exhibition space at WOL in the past few years as well as the excellent feedback from exhibitors and visitors alike all underline the high quality of this exhibition.

The fair is a platform for firms to showcase a wide range of products and services from the fields of telematics, e-business, telecommunications, intralogistics, warehouse management systems, auto ID, packaging and freight transport systems. Take advantage of this chance to present yourself and your company in a strong and effective manner. You can expect direct feedback on your products from service providers and decision makers from the transport sector, industry and trade associations and put this feedback to good use in further developing your business strategy. WOL is a place to meet and communicate, and offers valuable business opportunities to both exhibitors and visitors. Advance your existing business relationships and establish new contacts with potential clients. Not only will you find more than 1000 exhibitors presenting their products and services on over 25,000 square metres of exhibition space, but first-class speakers will also be giving talks on the latest industry issues in presentations, workshops and discussions. Admission for one day is only €60 including parking, lunch refreshments and a complimentary workshop. Presentations and discussions are free of charge. If you need any assistance with booking a stand or making hotel arrangements, feel free to call our organization team. They will be happy to guide you through the whole process. Please don't hesitate to contact me directly if you have any questions.

Looking forward to meeting you in Paris!

Yours,
Marjorie Duncan

Director Communications WOL

Mündliche Prüfung

Die mündliche Prüfung ist eine Tandem- oder Gruppenprüfung, bei der Sie Gespräche persönlichen und fachlichen Inhalts in der Fremdsprache führen sollen. Sie dauert pro Kandidat/in ca. 25 min. Zur Vorbereitung haben Sie 20 Minuten Zeit.

Phase I: Sie werden gebeten, sich zu persönlichen oder beruflichen Themen (z. B. Vorstellung des eigenen Werdegangs, der Firma und des Aufgabengebietes) zu äußern. Die Kandidaten/Kandidatinnen werden im Wechsel befragt.

Phase II: Im zweiten Teil sollen Sie zusammen mit einem/einer anderen Kandidaten/Kandidatin ein Rollenspiel durchführen. Dazu erhalten Sie vom Prüfer / von der Prüferin Rollenkarten, auf denen eine Situation beschrieben ist, die Sie vorspielen sollen.

Hilfsmittel: allgemeines zweisprachiges Wörterbuch

Interaktion 30 Punkte

Ihre Aufgaben für Phase I könnten wie folgt lauten:

Geben Sie Auskunft über sich anhand folgender Stichworte:

Ihr beruflicher Werdegang:	– Ausbildung, Abschlüsse, Praktika usw.
	– Gründe für diese Berufswahl
Ihre Ausbildungsfirma:	– allgemeines Geschäftsfeld/Spezialisierungsbereiche
	– Anzahl der Beschäftigten, Arbeitsbedingungen usw.
Ihr Arbeitsalltag in der Firma:	– Verwaltungsaufgaben (Beispiele)
	– Vorlieben/Abneigungen
Ihre Pläne für die Zukunft:	– wo Sie in fünf Jahren beruflich gerne wären

Ihre Aufgaben für Phase II könnten wie folgt lauten:

Rollenkarte A

Sie besuchen eine europäische Berufsmesse in Belgien, da Sie sich für ein Praktikum in einem englischsprachigen Land interessieren. Sie schließen in sechs Monaten Ihre Ausbildung als Kaufmann/-frau für Spedition und Logistikdienstleistung ab und sind sich noch nicht sicher, ob Sie in einer internationalen Firma arbeiten oder ein Studium der Logistik anschließen möchten. In jedem Fall erhoffen Sie sich aber eine Verbesserung Ihrer sprachlichen und beruflichen Kenntnisse.

Die Firma *Globotrade* aus England hat einen interessanten Stand. Sie nehmen Kontakt zu einem Repräsentanten / einer Repräsentantin auf, um Fragen bezüglich eines Praktikums zu klären.

Vorab haben Sie sich einen Notizzettel mit den für Sie wichtigsten Aspekten gemacht:

- Leistungsspektrum der Firma?
- Praktikum für sechs Monate möglich?
- Tätigkeit in verschiedenen Abteilungen möglich?
- Logistikabteilung vorhanden?
- Erfahrung mit Praktikanten/Praktikantinnen?
- Bezahlung?
- Unterbringung?

Rollenkarte B

Sie arbeiten für die Firma *Globotrade* aus Birmingham, England und vertreten diese heute auf einer europäischen Berufsmesse in Belgien.

Globotrade ist ein großes Handelsunternehmen, dass sich auf den Vertrieb von Autoreifen (*car tyres*) spezialisiert hat. Diese werden weltweit eingekauft und europaweit vertrieben: per Bahn, per Schiff oder mit einer eigenen Lastwagenflotte. Im Unternehmen arbeiten zurzeit 145 Angestellte, verteilt auf mehrere Abteilungen. Die Logistikabteilung expandiert.

Für Ihre Firma ist das Rekrutieren von Angestellten für die vielen verschiedenen Abteilungen wichtig, da dringend Leute mit Sprachkenntnissen gebraucht werden. Im letzten Jahr haben Sie erfolgreich Praktikanten und Praktikantinnen aus Frankreich und Polen anwerben können, die fest angestellt sind.

Ihre Firma tut einiges dafür, passende Bewerber/innen zu finden. Zwar gibt es keine Bezahlung bei einem Praktikum, aber die Unterbringung in der Nähe der Firma und das Essen in der Kantine sind kostenlos. Darüber hinaus können Interessenten *evening courses* an der nahe gelegenen Berufsschule besuchen.

Ihnen ist es wichtig etwas über die Motivation, die Zukunftspläne und den bisherigen beruflichen/schulischen Werdegang eines Bewerbers / einer Bewerberin zu erfahren.

G Grammar

Simple present

1. I **work** in the Export Department of a logistics company. I **arrange** for goods to be shipped abroad.
2. The company **produces** components for the automobile industry.
3. The company **doesn't ship** its goods to Asia.

- Das *simple present* wird für wiederholte, oft regelmäßige Handlungen in der Gegenwart verwendet.
- Signalwörter: *regularly, sometimes, often, always, normally* usw.
- Manche Verben, die keine Handlung, sondern einen Zustand ausdrücken (*need, like, want, hate, love, know, believe*), stehen (fast) ausschließlich im *simple present*.
- In der 3. Person (*he, she, it, Peter, the firm* usw.) wird ein *-s* angefügt (2).
- Verneinungen werden mit *doesn't/don't* gebildet (3).

Present progressive

1. Our department **is** currently **trying** to find a new supplier.
2. The managers **are negotiating** with a company from Poland right now.

- Das *present progressive* wird gebraucht, wenn man Handlungen beschreibt, die gerade ablaufen oder noch nicht abgelaufen sind.
- Signalwörter: *at the moment, (right) now, just, currently* usw.

Questions and short answers

1. **Do** you **write** a lot of enquiries? – Yes, I **do**. / No, I **don't**.
2. **Did** you **reply** to her email? – Yes, I **did**. / No, I **didn't**.
3. **Can** you **book** the hotel online? – Yes, you **can**. / No, you **can't**.
4. **Is** it easy to use? – Yes, it **is**. / No, it **isn't**.
5. **When/Why/How did** you **find** a new supplier?

- Fragen im *simple present* werden mit *do/does* gebildet (1).
- Fragen im *simple past* werden mit *did* gebildet (2).
- In Sätzen mit Hilfsverben (*is/have/can/will/should/…*) bildet man Fragen, indem man das Hilfsverb des Aussagesatzes vor das Subjekt stellt (3, 4).
- Kurzantworten bestehen aus *yes/no* + Personalpronomen + Hilfsverb (+ *n't*) (1–4).
- Fragewörter stehen immer am Anfang des Fragesatzes (5).

Simple past

1. I **talked** to my line manager about the complaint last week.
2. I **ordered** the new office supplies we need yesterday.
3. What time **did** you **start** work?
4. My first day at work **was** a disaster.

> Eine Liste der unregelmäßigen Verben befindet sich auf S. 253.

- Das *simple past* verwendet man, um auszudrücken, wann etwas geschehen ist (1, 2), oder um über Vergangenes zu berichten (4).
- Signalwörter: *yesterday, last week, two days ago, in 1998, When …?* usw.
- Bei den regelmäßigen Verben wird im *simple past* in allen Personen meist *-ed* angehängt.
- Verneinungen und Fragen werden in allen Personen mit *did/didn't* gebildet.

Past progressive

1 I **was working** in the warehouse last week.
2 I **was talking** to a customer when a colleague **bumped** into me and I **dropped** the phone.

- Mit dem *past progressive* drückt man aus, dass eine Handlung oder ein Vorgang zu einer bestimmten Zeit in der Vergangenheit gerade im Verlauf war (1).
- Es beschreibt oft eine Handlung, die gerade im Verlauf war, als eine zweite Handlung einsetzte. Die zweite Handlung steht im *simple past* (2).

Present perfect

1 We**'ve** just **updated** the organogram on our website.
2 We**'ve** recently **reviewed** our terms and conditions.
3 We **haven't found** out why the delivery was late yet.
4 **Have** you **been able** to decide which route is best?

> Eine Liste der unregelmäßigen Verben befindet sich auf S. 253.

- Mit dem *present perfect* sagt man, dass (nicht wann!) etwas geschehen ist.
- Signalwörter (Zeitadverbien): *this week, already, just, recently, yet* usw.
- Mit *for* (z. B. *for two years*) und *since* (z. B. *since 2015*) drückt man auch aus, wie lange oder seit wann ein Zustand schon andauert.

Future with *will* and *going to*

1 I think the meeting **will take** about two hours.
2 We're running out of pallets. – OK. I**'ll (will) contact** the supplier.
3 We **won't (will not) need** the order until next week.
4 We**'re going to refurnish** all the offices next year.
5 This old computer **is going to break down** soon.

- *Will* wird verwendet, um Vorhersagen zu machen oder Vermutungen über die Zukunft auszudrücken (1).
- *Will* wird für spontane Entscheidungen, Angebote und Versprechen verwendet (2).
- Im gesprochenen Englisch lautet die Verneinung *won't*, ansonsten *will not* (3).
- *Be going to* (+ Infinitiv des Verbs) wird verwendet, um über Pläne oder Absichten zu sprechen (4), oder wenn die Gewissheit (oder ein Anzeichen dafür) besteht, dass etwas geschehen wird (5).

Passive forms

1 The goods **are stored** in our new modern warehouse.
2 The order **was delivered** on Tuesday morning.
3 The shipment **has** already **been dispatched**.
4 The new materials **could be bought** from a local supplier.
5 The equipment **will be installed by** them as part of their customer service.

- Das Passiv wird oft verwendet, wenn man auf eher unpersönliche Art und Weise über Fakten, Vorgänge und Zahlen berichtet.
- Das Passiv wird mit der entsprechenden Form von *be* + Partizip Perfekt (3. Verbform) gebildet. Es können alle Zeiten gebildet werden.
- Passivsätze mit modalen Hilfsverben werden mit einem modalen Hilfsverb + *be* + Partizip Perfekt (3. Verbform) gebildet (4).
- „Von" und „durch" werden in Passivsätzen durch *by* ausgedrückt (5).

Conditional sentences

1. Type 1: **If** there **is** an emergency, I**'ll notify** the fire brigade.
2. Type 2: If there **was** a delay, we **would inform** you immediately.
3. Type 2: I **wouldn't do** that if I **was/were** you.
4. Type 3: If we **had advertised** the service in the right places, we **would have had** more customers.

   - Ein *if*-Satz des Typs 1 drückt eine Bedingung aus, die der Sprecher für durchaus möglich oder wahrscheinlich hält. Der damit verbundene Hauptsatz drückt eine Vorhersage aus, die je nach Situation als Warnung, Versprechen o. Ä. zu verstehen ist (1).
   - Durch einen *if*-Satz des Typs 2 gibt der Sprecher seinem Gesprächspartner einen Ratschlag oder teilt ihm mit, dass er die Erfüllung der Bedingung für unmöglich, unwahrscheinlich (2) oder nicht wünschenswert (3) hält.
   - Ein *if*-Satz des Typs 3 drückt eine nicht mehr erfüllbare Bedingung aus. Die Bedinging bezieht sich auf die Vergangenheit (4).
   - Steht der *if*-Nebensatz an erster Stelle, wird er durch ein Komma vom Hauptsatz abgetrennt (1, 2, 4).

Relative clauses

1. Our customer service agents are the people **who/that deal with customer complaints**.
2. The subcontractor **(which/that) our company uses** is based in Berlin.
3. MegaFreight, **which is our biggest competitor**, offers a similar service at a lower price.

   - Relativpronomen (*who/which/that*) leiten Relativsätze ein.
   - Es gibt den notwendigen und den nicht notwendigen Relativsatz. Notwendige Relativsätze sind für das Verständnis des Satzes unbedingt erforderlich (1, 2) und stehen ohne Komma. Nicht notwendige geben lediglich Zusatzinformationen und werden durch Kommata abgetrennt (3).
   - In notwendigen Relativsätzen kann das Relativpronomen wegfallen, wenn es Objekt ist, d. h. wenn im Relativsatz ein Subjekt steht (2).

Verb + infinitive or *-ing* form

1. I enjoy **working** in a team.
2. I expect **to qualify** as an export assistant in June.
3. I began **working / to work** for the company last year.
4. I'd prefer **to work** from home more often.
5. I'm interested in **getting** some work experience abroad.

   - Auf eine Gruppe von Verben folgt immer die *-ing*-Form (1). Zu diesen Verben gehören: *dislike, enjoy, finish, give up, imagine, involve, keep, mind, miss, practise, recommend, risk, stop, suggest*.
   - Auf eine zweite Gruppe von Verben folgt immer ein *to*-Infinitiv (2). Zu diesen Verben gehören: *afford, agree, arrange, choose, decide, expect, hope, learn, manage, offer, plan, promise, want*.
   - Auf eine dritte Gruppe von Verben kann sowohl die *-ing*-Form als auch ein *to*-Infinitiv folgen (3). Zu diesen Verben gehören: *begin, continue, hate, like, love, prefer, start*.
   - Nach *would hate, would like, would love* and *would prefer* (Kurzform *'d like* usw.) steht nur der *to*-Infinitiv (4).
   - Nach einer Präposition kommt immer die *-ing*-Form (5).

Gerunds

1. **Travelling** from place to place means there is a lot of variety in my job.
2. Do you like **working** in the office?
3. My work consists of **dealing** with orders and shipment.

   - Das Gerundium (= -*ing*-Form des Verbs) kann die Rolle eines Nomens übernehmen.
   - Das Gerundium kann als Subjekt (1), Objekt (2) oder nach Präpositionen (3) verwendet werden.

Comparatives and superlatives

1. The new system is **harder/easier** to use.
2. It's **more expensive than** shipping the goods by rail.
3. It's the **simplest** and **cheapest** offer, but not the **best**.
4. This type of trade fair stand is the **most flexible** solution.
5. The company spent **less** money on advertising last year.
6. The new system is**n't as easy** to update **as** the old one.

   - Einsilbige Adjektive und zweisilbige Adjektive, die auf -*y* enden, steigert man mit -*er*/-*est* (1).
   - Zweisilbige Adjektive, die nicht auf -*y* enden, und alle Adjektive mit mehr als zwei Silben steigert man mit *more/most* (2).
   - Unregelmäßig sind: *good – better – best, bad – worse – worst, little* (wenig) *– less – least, far – farther/further – farthest/furthest* (3, 5).
   - Vergleiche bildet man mit *than* und *(not) as ... as* (2, 6).

Reported speech

1. The customer **said** that they **had received** the shipment.
2. The intern **asked** if she **could take part** in the meeting.
3. My line manager **told** me that the trade fair **is** always **held** in Frankfurt.

   - Man verwendet die indirekte Rede, um zu berichten, was jemand gesagt hat.
   - Steht das einleitende Verb (*ask, say* usw.) in der Vergangenheit, verschieben sich die Verben im Satz entsprechend (1, 2).
   - Wenn das Berichtete immer oder immer noch gültig ist, muss keine Zeitverschiebung erfolgen (3).

Zeitverschiebung bei einleitenden Verben in der Vergangenheit

direkte Rede	indirekte Rede
simple present	simple past
present progressive	past progressive
simple past	past perfect
present perfect	past perfect
will	*would*
can	*could*

Grammar

Adverbs of frequency

1. The trainees **sometimes** attend trade fairs during their training.
2. We have **often** attended sales meetings abroad.
3. The Sales Director is **frequently** away on business.
4. We deliver goods to China **weekly**.

- Häufigkeitsadverbien der unbestimmten Zeit stehen vor dem ersten Hauptverb (1), nach dem ersten Hilfsverb (2) oder nach *to be* (3). Zu ihnen gehören: *already, always, ever, frequently, mostly, never, soon* usw.
- Häufigkeitsadverbien der bestimmten Zeit stehen meistens am Satzende, z. B. *annually, daily, monthly, once, twice, weekly, yearly* (4). Dies gilt auch für *a lot, before, very much, yet*.

Modals and their substitutes

1. I **can** work from home two days a week.
2. I **could** work longer hours if I lived closer to the office.
3. The packaging costs **must** be included in the quotation.
4. You **will be able to** buy the new line of lorries from May onwards.
5. We **won't be allowed to** install the new software on our own.
6. We **should** compare the costs of the different methods of transport.
7. Some items in the consignment were broken and **had to** be replaced.
8. You **mustn't** accept an offer before talking to your line manager.
9. You **needn't** ring the customer. I'll do it in a minute.
10. I **would** like to gain some work experience abroad.

- Modale Hilfsverben wie *can, could, may, would* usw. drücken eine Fähigkeit, eine Erlaubnis, eine Empfehlung, ein Verbot oder einen Wunsch aus.
- Modale Hilfsverben haben in allen Personen die gleiche Form; bei der Verneinung gibt es zusammengezogene Kurzformen.
- Modale Hilfsverben stehen normalerweise in der Gegenwartsform, manche auch in der Vergangenheit. Ersatzverben (*substitutes*) werden benutzt, um alle übrigen Zeiten zu bilden.

Hilfsverb	Ersatzverb
can	*be able to*
could	
may	*be allowed to*
might	
must	*have to*
need not	*don't have to*
shall	
should/ought to	
must not	*not be allowed to*

Transcripts

Track 2: Unit 1, Foundation, exercise 1A

Hello. My name is Sophie, I'm 19 years old. I'm from Bremen. I left school last year with the German "Abitur", which is similar to the British A levels. I now work at Bitz Logistics GmbH where I'm training to be a management assistant for freight forwarding and logistics. My apprenticeship lasts for three years. I'm doing a work-based apprenticeship. I work in the office from 9 to 5 and do block release at vocational school every three months. I get a small salary from the company. It's not much, but I still live with my parents, so I don't have expenses like rent or food. My colleagues are great and help me a lot. I'd like to work in one of the company's foreign branches one day.

Track 3: Unit 1, Foundation, exercise 1B

My name is Robert Klein, I'm 18 years old and I come from Berlin. I left school with Abitur and I now work at ABC Logistics where I'm training to be a forwarding agent. My apprenticeship lasts for two and a half years. It's a work-based apprenticeship. I work in the office three days a week from eight a.m. till four p.m. and I have day-release at vocational school one and a half days a week. The company pays for my course and I also get a small salary. I hope I'll be offered a permanent position in the company when I have finished my training.

Track 4: Unit 1, Part A, exercise 2A

1 Lisa

Mark	Hello, my name is Mark and welcome to my monthly podcast: Working Around the World! We have two guests today. Our first guest is Lisa. Hi Lisa, where are you from?
Lisa	Hi Mark, I'm from Germany.
Mark	So what size company do you work for?
Lisa	I'm an apprentice at a large company. It's a logistics company with branches all over Europe.
Mark	A logistics company? And which department are you in?
Lisa	I'm in warehousing at the moment. This is where we store all the products and coordinate with distribution. But I'll soon be in a different department.
Mark	How many other apprentices are there at your company?
Lisa	I really can't say! It's so big. All I know is that there are ten apprentices who started when I did.
Mark	Wow, OK. Now I need to find out about the hours you work, your breaks and overtime.
Lisa	I work seven hours a day, five days a week.
Mark	So that's 35 hours a week. And when do you start and finish each day?
Lisa	I clock in just before 7 a.m. and clock out at 3 p.m.
Mark	And what about breaks?
Lisa	I usually have an hour's lunch break in the canteen between 12 and 1 p.m.
Mark	Is that all? Don't you have a morning break?
Lisa	Not officially. I just get a cup of coffee when I feel like it.
Mark	I see. And what about overtime?
Lisa	There's no regular overtime, but if there's a big event like an open house, my boss expects everyone to stay late the night before and clear up when it's over. That usually means about 3 hours overtime.
Mark	Ah yes, I see what you mean. Now what about a dress code? Is there one at your company?
Lisa	Oh, yes. We have it in writing and it's quite strict for office staff because they often visit customers all over Europe, but in the warehouse it's pretty relaxed. We can wear jeans, but we have to wear special shoes that have a steel toe reinforcement. And sometimes a safety vest and hard hat.
Mark	Ah yes, of course. Do you sometimes travel to visit customers?
Lisa	Not very often now, but next month when I am in customer service, I'm going to the Czech Republic to visit a customer. I'm really looking forward to that.
Mark	So, as an apprentice you also go on business trips abroad. Nice. We only have a few more questions now. The next one is: when can your boss contact you?
Lisa	Only during working hours. We don't get phone calls or texts outside working hours.
Mark	Not even when you're on standby?
Lisa	Well, apprentices don't have to be on standby in my department, so that never happens.
Mark	I see. Now I need to know about your office. How big is it?
Lisa	Well, there is a large open-plan office in administration with about 30 people in it, so it's never really quiet, but I don't work in there much. And we also hot desk at our company.
Mark	Hot desk? What's that?
Lisa	Office staff don't have their own personal desks in the office. People just take a free desk anywhere and log in. But like I said, I'm almost always in the warehouse these days.
Mark	I see. And what facilities and benefits does your company give its employees?
Lisa	Well, we have a cafeteria, there are free drinks from drinks machines on each floor and we have a snack bar on the ground floor.
Mark	Any benefits?
Lisa	Benefits … just let me think. Ah yes, they pay for my travel ticket and we all have a tablet that we can keep after the apprenticeship… and we get discounts at the nearby outlets.
Mark	Well, that sounds like a very good employer, Lisa. My final questions are whether you want to stay on after your apprenticeship and what job offer you expect.
Lisa	I very much want to stay on and I think I'll get at least a one-year contract when I finish.
Mark	That's it. Thanks for talking to us, Lisa.
Lisa	You're welcome.

2 Lukas

Mark	Hi, this is Mark again with our second guest for today: Lukas. You're also from Germany aren't you, Lukas?
Lukas	Yes, that's right, from Berlin.
Mark	Great. Tell me about the company you work for.
Lukas	It's a small company, a family business with about 20 employees. We make furniture and sell it all over the world.
Mark	And what department are you in?
Lukas	I'm in the logistics department.
Mark	And did you do your apprenticeship there?

Lukas	No, I did that at a really big logistics company. I came here when I finished my apprenticeship.
Mark	I see. And what are the working hours like?
Lukas	Well, officially I work 8 hours a day from Monday to Friday.
Mark	So that's 40 hours per week?
Lukas	Yes, and we all start very early – at 6.30 a.m. – and we have a 30-minute break together at 9 o'clock and then an hour's lunch break at 1 o'clock. We all finish at 4 p.m., normally.
Mark	And do you clock in and out?
Lukas	No, we don't have to. We all come and go at the same time.
Mark	And what about overtime?
Lukas	I do a lot of overtime! We have to meet our delivery deadlines, so I sometimes do up to 8 hours a week of overtime.
Mark	That's a lot. And what about a dress code? Is there one at your company?
Lukas	No, there's no dress code. We can wear whatever we want.
Mark	So, you don't go on business trips?
Lukas	No, never. They need me in the office.
Mark	I see. How does your boss contact you? Does he contact you after work?
Lukas	Oh, yes. By phone or text message or email. He contacts me whenever he needs me. If there's a problem, he phones or texts me after work or at the weekend. I don't mind. That's what it's like in a small company.
Mark	Could you describe your office and the facilities at your company? And any benefits you may get.
Lukas	Office, facilities and benefits … OK, I work in a small office with one other person. We have a hot and cold drinks machine and that's about it.
Mark	And do you have a company phone, tablet or laptop?
Lukas	No, nothing like that.
Mark	Any other benefits?
Lukas	No, not really. Well, come to think of it, I could buy the furniture we make at cost price if I wanted, so that's a big discount.
Mark	Great. And would you like to stay at the company, and if so, what offer do you think your boss will make you?
Lukas	I'm not sure about staying on because it's a very small company. My boss has already said I could get a permanent contract if I wanted to, but I need to think about it.
Mark	That's about all we have time for today. Thanks for joining us.
Lukas	Sure, it was my pleasure.

Track 5: Unit 1, Part B, exercise 1B/C

Presenter	I'm so pleased to be working with an international group today and I think we'll all learn a lot from each other in this session. Remember, if you would like to say something, just click on the microphone icon and everyone will be able to hear you. OK, now you've all had some time to guess the names of the countries and I think some of you will be surprised when you hear the answers. Now let's start with the only country in which employers don't have to pay their employees for national holidays and annual leave. Which one is it?
Participant 1	Japan?
Presenter	I'm afraid not. We hear a lot about the Japanese never taking time off work, but they are second to last in our diagram with ten days' paid annual leave and no paid national holidays.
Participant 2	The US?
Presenter	Exactly! That's why they call the US the "no vacation nation". OK, so we have Japan and the US. Now let's look at the country with most paid holiday and leave. Which one is it?
Participant 2	Germany?
Presenter	Almost! Germany has the second highest number of paid days off work with 30 days in all, but the winner is Austria! It has the highest number of paid days off work with 38 in all. OK, so now we have Japan, the US, Germany and the Austria, so let's look at the two remaining countries – Greece and the UK. Which of these two has to pay its employees for 28 days' annual leave but not for national holidays?
Participant 1	The UK?
Presenter	Exactly! And by the way, that explains why shops in the US and the UK are open 365 days a year, because the national holidays there are unpaid. Now I want to look at productivity in these countries. Which, would you say, has the highest productivity per working hour?
Participant 2	Germany?
Presenter	Almost! Once again it has the second highest. The highest is the US. Then comes Germany and then…?
Participant 1	Austria?
Presenter	Very good! And after that?
Participant 2	Japan?
Presenter	Sorry, it's the UK in fourth place followed by…?
Participant 1	Japan and Greece.
Presenter	That's right. So to sum up: the US has the highest productivity, followed by Germany, Austria, the UK, Japan and Greece, which has the lowest productivity. Let's take a break now and …

Track 6: Unit 1, Communication, exercise 1A

Martyna	Hello. I'm Martyna Nowak. I'm 42. I was born in Poland. I'm a product manager.
Halil	Good morning. My name is Halil Özdemir. I'm 29 years old. I was born in Germany. I'm a training supervisor.
Deema	Good afternoon. My name is Deema Mansour. I'm 19. I was born in Syria. I'm a trainee IT administrator.
Robert	Hello. I'm Robert Klein. I'm 21. I was born in Austria. I'm training to be a forwarding agent.
Canan	Hello. I'm Canan Tolon. I'm 25 years old. I was born in Turkey. I'm a management assistant for office communication.
Alexei	Good morning. My name is Alexei Melnyk. I'm 39 years old. I was born in Ukraine. I'm a software developer.

Track 7: Unit 2, Foundation, exercise 2A

Hello everybody. My name is Alisha Warner and I'm an office consultant. I plan offices in which people should be able to do their work efficiently and happily. For me, the main purpose of a good office environment is to support the people who work there. Whether it's writing, telephoning or computer work, every office should be a nice place to work in. So, today, I'd like to compare two very different types of offices: the small office and the open-plan office. Let's look first at the small office. This is one of the oldest types of offices, a small room which is generally used by one or two people. We all know these offices from visits to public administration buildings. You walk down a long corridor and see one door after another. The doors are closed but you know that someone is in there, working. The benefit of this type of office is that it lets people focus on their work. Most employees who work in a small office say they enjoy being able to concentrate on their work without being interrupted.

In contrast – and it's a big contrast – we have the open-plan office where everyone works together in one big room. There are two ways to set up an open-plan office. First, there's the cubicle set-up. Each desk is hidden by a low partition, and the employees sit in their cubicles and get on with the work. Some employees like this set-up, others say that their open-plan office is noisy and they can't concentrate on what they're doing.

The second set-up is the open-plan office in which there are no partitions at all. You'll often see this kind of thing in start-ups. The desks and workplaces are completely open and everyone can move about easily. Sometimes the employees share one large table. Two big advantages of working at one table are that it supports a sense of community in the workplace and, if employees are working on a team project, they're able to complete it quickly because they can communicate better.

Another idea is hot-desking: the employees don't have their own desk, they just work at any desk that's free. There are pros and cons attached to hot-desking. At the end of the day, each space must be cleared and ready for whoever uses it next, so the office is always neat and tidy. The downside of this is that employees can't put their personal mark on their section of the office. This may result in an office lacking warmth or personality, and feeling uninviting.

So, what's the answer? A small office or an open-plan office? An open-plan office with partitions and cubicles, or a totally open, shared working space? A lot depends on the type of business you do, but whatever your business, employees should always feel happy and comfortable in their place of work. That way, they'll do a better job.

Track 08: Unit 2, Part A, exercise 2A/B

1
The people in my department are responsible for the smooth delivery of goods. Our responsibilities include deciding on the appropriate form of transport (rail, road, etc.) for each consignment and consolidating shipments where possible. We also do all the necessary paperwork and make sure that everything is on schedule.

2
Running advertising to find new customers – that's what I do most of the time. My job also means going to trade fairs, talking to potential customers at our stand and making them offers.

3
I'm in charge of planning and supervising the budget – which is not always so easy. This entails analysing sales figures and profit margins every month and reporting them to the CEO.

4
Hi, I'm an apprentice at Birkan Logistics. I really enjoy doing my job and I learn something new every day. The area I work in is very large but I would say that, to put it simply, my work involves understanding how goods are transported and how to track incoming and outgoing shipments. I'm also learning a lot about coordinating with various customs offices around the world.

Track 9: Unit 2, Part B, exercise 2A/B

1
My job involves keeping track of financial data to preparing the budget. In my department, we also have to know a lot about local, state and federal financial laws and legal requirements.

2
Well, I'm basically responsible for finding the best person for the job. My department also sometimes organizes in-house training courses to help people with work-related problems.

3
I'm in charge of everything that goes on in the warehouse. That means not only preparing goods for shipping, but also safety, scheduling and even the budget.

4
Working in my department means understanding customs regulations and what documents are needed for each shipment. We also have to track freight movements, so we know where the goods are all the time.

5
As the manager of my department it's my responsibility to make sure that we find new markets and acquire new clients. We run advertising in trade magazines and online, and I often go to trade fairs.

6
In my department we oversee the whole customer service process from beginning to end. We send offers, take orders and deal with complaints on the phone or via email.

Track 10: Unit 2, Communication, exercise 2

Hi, this is Roger Dalton from Esher Engineering. Thanks for your message. I'm afraid we'll have to change the date for the delivery of the generators. Our warehouse will be closed for repairs on Tuesday, 7 June, so we can offer you Wednesday, 8 June, any time in the afternoon after 1 o'clock. If that doesn't work for you, you can make the delivery on Friday, 10 June, but only in the morning from 7 to 12. Please confirm one of these dates with my secretary, Sandy. Her number is 0044 1632 960022. Bye for now.

Track 11: Unit 2, Communication, exercise 3B

Receptionist	Esher Engineering, good morning. This is Duncan speaking. How can I help?
Niklas	Good morning, it's Niklas Hartmann from Hamm Trucking UK. Could I speak to Mr Dalton, please?
Receptionist	Just a moment, sir. I'll see if he's in. Please hold the line.
Niklas	Thanks.
Receptionist	I'm afraid his line is engaged. Would you like to call back later?
Niklas	Well, it's pretty important.
Receptionist	In that case, would you like to speak to someone else?
Niklas	How about his personal assistant, Simon Smith?

Receptionist	Simon Smith … I'm trying to connect you …
Niklas	Thanks.
Receptionist	I'm sorry, but Mr Smith is unavailable at the moment.
Niklas	Oh dear … looks like I'm out of luck today.
Receptionist	I could put you through to Mr Dalton's secretary. Perhaps she can help you.
Niklas	Yes, all right.
Receptionist	I'll put you through.
Niklas	Thanks.
Secretary	Hello, Mr Dalton's office, Sandy speaking. How can I help?
Niklas	Hello, I'm trying to get through to Mr Dalton. It's urgent and I hope you can help me. It's about the delivery next week.
Secretary	I see. Who's calling, please?
Niklas	Oh, sorry. I forgot to introduce myself. It's Niklas Hartmann from Hamm Trucking.
Secretary	Nicholas … er … Could you spell your name, please?
Niklas	Yes, certainly. Niklas is my first name. That's N – i – k – l – a – s and my surname is Hartmann spelt H – a – r – t – m – a – n – n.
Secretary	Thanks. I'm afraid Mr Dalton is out all day today. Would you like to leave a message?
Niklas	Yes, all right. Please tell him that we can confirm the delivery of his order on Friday, 10 June, at 2 p.m.
Secretary	I'm sorry, I didn't catch that. Could you repeat that, please?
Niklas	Yes, we can deliver the order on Friday, 10 June, at 2 p.m. …

Track 12: KMK Exam practice 1, exercise 2, Hörverstehen

1

Machine	Tuesday, July 9, 2.40 a.m.
Caller 1	Good evening, this is Derek Stewart from Peters Machine Tools. I am returning the call from Tom Grisham. He was asking for more information about the terms for delivery to Canada. Can he please call me back tomorrow afternoon? I have already sent the paperwork by email, but it makes much more sense to talk about it personally. My number is 001 507 555 0115. Thank you. Goodbye.

2

Machine	Wednesday, November 12, 7.15 a.m.
Caller 2	Hello, my name is Jane Anderson and I am responsible for the International Apprenticeship Fair in Munich. I am not sure whether I have reached the correct department, but we have some questions about your registration for the fair. It would be great if the Human Resources Manager could return my call to talk about details. My number is 0049 89 460990. I'd really appreciate it.

Track 13: Unit 3, Part A, exercise 2A/B

Tour 1

Rau	Good morning, gentlemen. My name is Rolf Rau. I'm the Managing Director of JHP Logistics GmbH, and this morning I'm also your guide. Please come this way. So, welcome to JHP Logistics and to Germany. We are delighted to welcome you to our company. You've had a very long trip here from PABE Transport and Logistics in Mumbai, and we very much hope you enjoy your stay here in Germany.
Patel	Thank you. My colleagues and I would like to thank you for your kind invitation to JHP Logistics. We believe this is the beginning of a long friendship between our two companies and we look forward to having such an important business partner in Europe.
Rau	Thank you, Mr Patel. We are also sure that this is the beginning of a long friendship and look forward to visiting you at your company in India next month. So, are there any questions before we begin? … In that case, we'll start here in the conference room with a short presentation about JHP Logistics, its services and history … Well, that was a brief overview of the company. Are there any questions? No? In that case, I'll now take you downstairs to our Distribution Centre.
Patel	Excuse me, Mr Rau.
Rau	Yes, Mr Patel?
Patel	What is the name of the Head of the Distribution Centre?
Rau	His name is Mr Nagel.
Patel	Mr Nagel. Thank you.
Rau	You're welcome. … Now this is the Distribution Centre. The gentleman to the left of the window is Mr Nagel. He and his team will be able to answer any questions you have about the Distribution Centre. As you can see, straight ahead of us are the lorry bays. The lorries pull in here and deliver the goods that are to be exported and collect the goods that have just arrived from abroad which need distributing both locally and to the rest of Germany. Our next stops are the import and export departments. Let's just take the lift over here … Let's take a left at the end of the corridor and I'll introduce you to the head of our Import Department, Mr Eckert … Now, if we walk to the end of this corridor, we will be in the larger Export Department. Unfortunately, Mrs Kohl, the Head of the Export Department, is on holiday this week, but her deputy can answer any questions you have. Now please follow me to the showroom, which is the last stop of our tour… Well, that concludes our tour. I hope you enjoyed it and if you have any questions, please feel free to ask them. After that we will take you on a tour of Stuttgart, including a visit to …

Tour 2

Klein	Good morning, ladies and gentlemen and welcome to JHP Logistics. My name is Mareike Klein, I work in the Human Resources Department, and we very much hope you will enjoy your time here. There are also other work experience students being shown round the company at the moment. They all speak English or German, and you'll meet them when we finish the tour. I'm your guide for the next hour, so please feel free to ask any questions. So, we're starting our tour here in the Distribution Centre. In front of us you can see where the lorries arrive and behind us all the goods that are waiting to be delivered are stored.
Student 1	May I ask a question?
Klein	Yes, certainly.
Student 1	How many trucks arrive here at the Distribution Centre every day?

Klein	About 30 trucks arrive here every day – that includes weekends, too. Some are delivering goods that need to be exported to other countries. They are stored here for as little time as possible, until they are loaded onto a container which will then be taken either by rail or barge.
Student 2	Excuse me, what's a … uhm … barge?
Klein	It's a boat with a flat bottom used to carry freight on rivers.
Student 2	I see. Thank you.
Klein	So, the goods are then taken by rail or barge to a port, for example Hamburg, or by air from the airport. Other trucks collect goods which have arrived from abroad and will be delivered to companies locally and other destinations in Germany. Some of you will be working alongside our specialists here, and they will show you the procedures you have to follow. Any questions? Yes?
Student 1	How long does it take to …
Klein	So let's now take the lift upstairs to the third floor … OK, now we're on the third floor and I'm going to take you to meet Mr Martin, the head of the Project Management Department, and his team. Good morning, Mr Martin!
Martin	Good morning!
Everyone	Good morning.
Martin	Welcome to the Project Management Department. My name is Matthias Martin and here you will see how customers' orders are turned into projects. Each order has its own project manager who sees the project through from start to finish. Would you like to ask any questions?
Student 2	Yes, I would like to ask a question, please. Which countries do you export to?
Martin	We export all over the world but a lot of our work is in Asia and Africa, and at the moment we're working on a big project for India.
Student 2	Thank you.
Klein	Thanks, Mr Martin. Let's now go on to the Export Department, which is just down the corridor. This is where all the paperwork for the goods that are going to be exported is completed. I can see this department is very busy today, so let's now go to our last stop, which is Mr Rau's office. Mr Rau is our Managing Director, and he's going to tell you something about the history of the company. The Managing Director's office is just down here …

Track 14: Unit 3, Part B, exercise 1C/2A

Good morning, ladies and gentlemen and welcome to JHP Logistics, Germany. We're delighted to have you here in Stuttgart and we hope you will enjoy your visit. My name is Daniel Nagel and I work in the distribution centre. The agenda for today's meeting is in the folder in front of you. Right, I'd like to begin by giving you a presentation about the company. I'll start with some background information and company statistics and will then move on to tell you about our new distribution centre here in Stuttgart. Then at the end, I'll be happy to answer any questions you may have.

As you can see from this slide, JHP Logistics is a medium-sized logistics company with approximately 120 warehouses worldwide. Here in Stuttgart we have a workforce of 158 employees, which includes 15 trainees, and last year our turnover was approximately 5 million euros.

The next slide shows our modern high-rise warehouse. It is 35 metres high and is capable of storing many thousands of pallets of goods. Our warehouse is a manual warehouse, we use forklift trucks to place the goods on the pallets and to collect them when they are needed. On the other hand, the system behind the warehouse is fully automatic, and without this system we wouldn't know where anything is.

We label all the packages with a QR code. The QR code contains information about where the goods have come from, where they are going, dates of delivery, etc. The goods in our warehouse are usually in transit and don't stay there for long.

The next thing I'd like to show you are the four main areas of goods in our distribution centre: There are incoming goods and outgoing goods, then there are goods that will be in our warehouse longer and which go into the storage area. Finally, there are goods that are on hold, which means we can't release them to the customer yet as their payment has not been cleared by the bank.

We have customers all over the world and we deliver to our customers' customers all over the world. It is therefore important that we know exactly which goods are where and when they have to leave our warehouse. It doesn't matter how big or small a delivery is, it will always be handled with respect, and that is something we pride ourselves on – the personal touch.

Right, that was a brief overview of JHP Logistics in Stuttgart. Many thanks for listening. Now if you'd like to ask any questions, I'd be delighted to answer them and then we can go to lunch …

Track 15: Unit 4, Part A, exercise 3B

Well, Mr Novak, for the sculptures you described, I suggest a wooden crate and not a cardboard box. Sculptures of that size have more surface area that can get damaged and need more protection than smaller items. They also weigh more, so their containers need to be stronger.
Well, inside the crate, surround the item with packing material – yes, exactly, like packing peanuts or wood wool.
Hmm, you could use a sheet of polystyrene foam that fits inside the crate and has a cut-out to fit the base of the sculpture. That would hold it in place. And if I were you, I would use another piece of polystyrene to hold the top of the sculpture in place, as well. Make sure you mark the crate with the symbols for "fragile" and "this way up".
No, I absolutely understand why you want more security. For more protection, you can double box the item. So, you package it in a crate, just like we talked about, and put that crate inside a slightly larger wooden crate surrounded by more packing material.
Well, there's one last thing you should think about. There may be changes in temperature during transport which could cause water to condense on the items. If this would be a problem for the sculptures you describe, I would be happy to advise you about drying agents.

Track 16: Unit 4, Part B, exercise 2

1
Well, we receive inbound goods, so that's why we're called receivers. And by we, I mean I work with twelve or so other employees. My colleagues guide lorries into the docks and secure them for unloading. Other colleagues are in charge of unloading. We have

two forklift drivers, but if the items are smaller, they sometimes unload them using a pallet truck or even by hand. I'm responsible for checking to make sure the shipment is correct and none of the items were damaged in transport. If everything is correct, I sign for the goods. And everything that comes off the truck is immediately marked with an RFID tag, so nothing can get lost.

2
I'm a forklift driver. That means I drive a forklift. No, I deliver goods to storage. If they're on pallets, they get stored in the pallet racks. If they're bulky, they are stored on the floor in our special storage area for outsize items. All of the forklift drivers here have licences and we have to attend a forklift safety course once a year. If we don't go on the course, we aren't allowed to drive!

3
I'm a picker. I work at the picking station, but I guess that doesn't mean very much to people who don't work in a warehouse. Picking means selecting goods. So, when a customer wants goods shipped, we collect the items from storage. We switched to paperless picking and packing a long time ago – no more paper! It means that everyone here has been trained on the PC, and I think it makes us much more efficient. Unfortunately, we still don't have dynamic storage – a system that would bring the items to us – so we still have to go and get the items ourselves.

4
I work at the loading station. We're responsible for loading shipments onto the lorries and making sure the shipment is loaded securely. We also have to make sure that the weight is distributed correctly. That sounds like a lot of maths – and I am terrible at maths – but our load planning software makes it all very quick and easy! I've never had a driver complain!

Track 17: Unit 4, Communication, exercise 1B

Manager	I'll just give you my email address. It's t m dot martin at technical underscore tools dot orgnet.
Mary-Anne	Sorry, could you repeat that, please?
Manager	No problem. t m dot martin at technical underscore tools dot orgnet. You can reach me directly with that address.
Mary-Anne	Thank you. Well, my email address is mary hyphen anne hyphen brown at five plus five services dot orgnet.
	The fives are written as numbers. Oh, and my first name, Mary-Anne – Anne is written with an e.
Manager	OK. I'll just read that back to you. Mary hyphen anne hyphen brown at five plus five services dot orgnet. Mary-Anne with a hyphen, the fives written as numbers and Mary-Anne written with an e at the end of Anne.
Mary-Anne	Yes. That's correct.

Track 18: KMK Exam practice 2, exercise 1, Hörverstehen

Guide	Good afternoon. Welcome to Habermann Industrie Service. My name is Josh Duncan. Are you here for the guided tour of the logistics centre?
Ms Clarke	Yes, good afternoon, I'm Janet Clarke from Millerman Inc in Brussels. Nice to meet you.
Mr King	I'm also here for the tour. I'm James King from CarParts Ltd in Dublin.
Guide	Nice to meet you both. Thank you for coming today. I hope you didn't have any difficulty finding us?
Ms Clarke	Not at all, the instructions on your website were very helpful and the signs from the parking lot to the entrance hall were very clear.
Guide	OK, then let's get started. If you have any questions during our tour, please don't hesitate to ask me. Before we start, I would like you to put on the name badges every visitor has to wear. So, we are here at the main building of our company. I will start by giving some general information about our company before we proceed to our logistics centre. Here in Frankfurt lies one of the most modern logistics centres for industrial supply. Habermann Industrie Service covers an area of 150 hectares and it manages the demand for spare parts for more than 25,000 customers on a daily basis.
Mr King	That is very impressive. Is this the company's only location?
Guide	It is definitely the largest location, but we have also smaller branch offices in Stuttgart, Basel and Cardiff. Altogether, we employ around 1800 people and 150 apprentices. Our office building is divided into three floors of 800 m^2 each and is designed in a comfortable, open-plan style to make easier and offer greater comfort.
Ms Clarke	I like the architecture of the building and I am quite impressed by the facilities. Everything seems so new and very modern.
Guide	You're right. We moved here from our old location just last year after the administration building was finished. The logistics centre was completed the year before that. Now our headquarters are based here too. Here in our main building you can find our basic administration with managing director and the departments accounting, human resources, sales and marketing, and purchasing. Now please follow me to our main building of the logistics centre. I have a plan of the whole logistics park for both of you so you can easily see where we are right now.
Mr King	That's very kind of you, thank you.
Ms Clarke	Thank you, I appreciate that.
Guide	Here in the logistics centre, Habermann Industrie Service offers more than 100,000 customer-specific items and industrial spare parts. We have more than 500,000 storage locations altogether with a 10 km conveyor line.
Mr King	I can see vehicles driving without a person behind the wheel!
Guide	You are absolutely right. At Habermann, autonomous systems are a day-to-day reality. In some parts of the warehouses we have changed from manually driven vehicles to a driverless transportation system with Automated Guided Vehicles (AGVs). All work processes are connected through digital networking. At the end of our tour I have prepared a bag with information material and some give-aways from our company. You will also find a voucher for a coffee in our canteen. I hope you enjoyed our tour!

Track 19: Unit 5, Foundation, exercise 3A

Janet   Welcome to European Express, where we take a look at the week's biggest news stories in freight forwarding and logistics. I'm speaking to Will Pennicut, the editor of Forwarder Europe, a journal for specialists in the field of forwarding and logistics. Mr Pennicut, in your latest issue, you published a comparison of the largest logistics companies that specialize in food logistics and found some surprising results.

Will   That's right, Janet. The most remarkable development this year is that Carmero SE has become the market leader – so the company which does the most business. It has the largest turnover – 2.9 billion euros – compared to the Lager Group, whose turnover was slightly lower, 2.71 billion euros, followed by Foodster in third place with 2.6 billion euros. We certainly didn't expect that sort of development for Carmero SE.

Janet   But a turnover of 2.9 billion euros for a company with over 44,000 employees isn't that great, is it? Hanke Logistics International generated 2.3 billion euros with only 12,500 employees.

Will   You make a good point. But Carmero needs more staff than the other companies because they have offices in 123 countries, while Hanke and the Lager Group both work in far fewer countries. Hanke has offices in 30 countries. And the Lager Group, while more competitive, only has offices in 45 countries.

Janet   So, what else makes these companies different from each other?

Will   Well, the Lager Group and Hanke both specialize in road freight, while Carmero and Foodster both specialize in multimodal transport. In my opinion, Foodster is the best option for intermodal road and rail freight. Carmero might be the market leader, but they aren't particularly innovative – not like Foodster.

Janet   So how do you explain Carmero's large market share?

Will   Tradition. Carmero has a long history and an excellent reputation. They built up their company slowly and they provide outstanding customer service.

Janet   And what about Lager and Hanke – what sets them apart from each other?

Will   Lager is particularly proud of their frozen logistics – they have 8,450 lorries on the road, and over 4000 of them are refrigerator lorries. Hanke, on the other hand, is much more flexible. That's a big plus for customers whose needs change from season to season. And, I have to say this for them, Hanke is also much more interested in providing sustainable transport solutions.

Janet   Eco-friendly lorry drivers?

Will   Well, if you want to put it that way, yes.

Track 20: Unit 5, Part A, exercise 3A

Mary   Mary Moran speaking. How can I help you?

Jan   Good morning. This is Jan Peters of Hanke Logistics. I'm calling about your enquiry. You asked for a quotation on a shipment of whiskey?

Mary   Good morning, Mr Peters. I'm glad you called. Yes, we were enquiring about making a shipment of whiskey from Cork to Germany.

Jan   Yes, I have it here. First of all, thank you for your interest. But I'm afraid I can't give you a quotation without some additional information. May I ask you a few questions? The more detailed the information, the more reliable the quotation will be.

Mary   That's not a problem. Go right ahead.

Jan   First of all, could you tell me where we would pick up the shipment?

Mary   The pallets need to be picked up at our factory in Cork.

Jan   Oh, yes, sorry. I see that here now. OK, I'll also need to know the exact destination in Germany. That will help me calculate distance and time.

Mary   The destination in Germany is Halle.

Jan   There are two Halles in Germany, I'm afraid. Do you mean Halle in Westphalia or Halle/Saale?

Mary   Oh, dear. Well, let me see … The postcode is 06108. Does that help?

Jan   Yes, that's great. So, that's Halle/Saale. Can you tell me how many euro pallets the shipment will include? That will let me calculate the space needed.

Mary   There will be 17 euro pallets with a height of 2.3 metres each.

Jan   17 euro pallets, 2.3 metres … So, we'll have the possibility to use FTL … That changes things a bit. Can I just ask you to give me a rough estimate of when you want to make the shipment?

Mary   We'd like the first shipment to arrive in mid-October.

Jan   OK, I'll put down delivery by October 15th, but we can change that later. Now, I'd like to ask you about terms of payment. We offer three payment options, but our standard option is net within 30 days of invoice. Would that be acceptable to you?

Mary   That would be fine.

Jan   OK, I only have one more question. Have you thought about liability and risk?

Mary   I'm afraid I'm going to have to get back to you about that, because I'm not certain. I'll need to talk to my boss first. Would it be all right if I send you an email later?

Jan   That's no problem, I'll leave that blank for now and send you a quotation as soon as we have all of the details.

Mary   I am sorry that the information was incomplete. I hope we'll be able to get things cleared up soon. We're hoping that this will be the start of a long-term relationship.

Jan   Well, that's certainly nice to hear! As soon as you send me that information, I'll let you have the quotation as quickly as possible.

Mary   Thank you very much. Nice talking to you.

Jan   Goodbye, Ms Moran, and thank you again for your enquiry. I hope to hear from you again soon.

Track 21: Unit 5, Part B, exercise 3A

Paul   And how much of the cost is the actual transport to and from Leipzig?

Katja   Well, the carriage costs are about €700, I think. Let me just check … Yes, carriage alone would cost €710.

Paul   OK. So, it's really the loading and unloading that adds to the cost.

Katja   Mmm. Yes and no. The loading and unloading is labour-intensive, of course, but don't forget that we have to store the goods in the centre's warehouse and then bring them to the stand. And then the same again in reverse after the trade fair is over. All of that together comes to around €900.

Paul	I see. Yes, that makes more sense now. What about costs for things like administration and organization? The offer we received from another company – Nichols, I think – included a €70 administration fee.
Katja	Our administration fee is just under €90 – and I'm afraid I can't do much to change that, either. We charge a fixed rate for trade fairs. There's a lot of planning and coordinating that needs to happen behind the scenes to make sure everything goes smoothly.
Paul	I suppose …
Katja	However – and I think you'll be happy to hear this – we're offering new customers a 10% discount this month!
Paul	Well, that is nice to hear! I still have one or two more questions, though.
Katja	That's no problem. Go ahead.
Paul	I'd like to ask about your terms of payment. Nichols is asking for payment after receipt of invoice.
Katja	Yes? That sounds standard.
Paul	Well, do you think we could agree on a longer time period? Say, payment 60 days after receipt of invoice? After the trade fair, half of my employees will be on holiday!
Katja	I'm afraid not, Paul. Because you're a first-time customer, we'll have to insist on payment within 14 days.
Paul	I see. Well. I can understand that. All right, one last question then. What if we need to change the date of delivery to the Sunday before the trade fair instead of the Monday?
Katja	Well, we charge an extra fee for work on weekends.

Track 22: Unit 6, Part A, exercise 2C

Ruben	Goedemorgen, van Dyck Oil. U spreekt met Ruben Karel. Waarmee kan ik u van dienst zijn?
Laura	Good morning. It's Laura Stein from BDI International Transport. Is it all right if we speak English?
Ruben	Yes, that's fine. How can I help?
Laura	Well, I'm phoning about the consignment of kerosene from Rotterdam to Poznan in Poland. Your reference on the DGN is VDO-9761.
Ruben	VDO-9761 … just a moment. Here it is. What would you like to know?
Laura	I've gone through the form and would like to look at some of the details before we collect the load, because if anything is missing or incorrect, the load will be delayed.
Ruben	Yes, I understand.
Laura	Let's start with section 1 of the form. You, as the shipper, are van Dyck Oil BV but I think there's an error in the address. Is it Energieweg 200, 3041 GC Rotterdam, Netherlands?
Ruben	Yes, but not GC, JC. Sorry about that but you'll see the correct address if you look on our website.
Laura	That's how we found out, Mr Karel, but no problem. I've corrected it now. And in section 6 the consignee is G&L Research, Minikowo 187, Poznan, Poland?
Ruben	Yes, that's right.
Laura	Good. Now can we now go to section 14, which is the most important part of the form?
Ruben	Yes, I've got the details here.
Laura	So, in the second box – number and kind of packages – you've written one tank but we need a more exact description. If we just write tank, they'll want to know what sort of tank it is. And if it's made of plastic, they won't accept it.
Ruben	I see. Well, it is a tank but a more exact description would be one metal IBC, which stands for intermediate bulk container.
Laura	One metal IBC … Good, I've put that in the box. As I said, the container would be a problem if we didn't describe it exactly. What about the next box in section 14: Gross mass? The box is empty and we need to complete it with the gross weight of the consignment.
Ruben	It's the same as the next box: Net mass. The net and gross weight are the same so it's 832 kilos in both.
Laura	832 kilos in both.
Ruben	Yes. Look, I'm really sorry about this. I can't understand how we left out the gross weight.
Laura	Don't worry about it, Mr Karel. I do this all day. If people didn't make mistakes, I'd be out of a job. Now shall we just look at the last box in section 14: the cube of goods in cubic metres. Here you have written ten cubic metres. Can that be right?
Ruben	No, it's wrong. It should be one cubic meter. I really do apologize for all these errors.
Laura	No worries. It happens all the time. I only have one more query.
Ruben	And that is?
Laura	Section 19 is the total gross weight (or mass) including the tare, so that should be 832 plus 60, right? I make that 892 but you have 982.
Ruben	Oh no! Someone's mixed up the figures! We were really having a bad day when we filled in this DGN. Please accept my apologies. It should be 892 as you say.
Laura	Well, I'm glad we've got everything sorted out, Mr Karel. Thanks for your help.
Ruben	My pleasure. And if you need any more information, I'll be happy to provide it …

Track 23: Unit 6, Part B, exercise 3A/B

Manager	Horvat Mobilar, halo.
Vanessa	Hallo, it's Vanessa Hartmann from BDI in Hamburg. Could I speak to Mr Bogdan Karić, please?
Bogdan	Speaking. Thanks for calling me back Ms Hartmann. Is it about the consignment of furniture?
Vanessa	Yes, that's right. I understand you would like to make some changes to the arrangements.
Bogdan	Yes, that's right.
Vanessa	I've got the CMR note on the screen in front of me. What would you like us to change, Mr Karić?
Bogdan	The route from Essen to Split will take the lorry through Zagreb, is that right?
Vanessa	Just a moment … Yes, Zagreb is on the way.
Bogdan	Excellent! My company has just ordered some new kitchen furniture from a supplier in Zagreb, so we would like your lorry to stop in Zagreb on the way and pick it up. We have ordered a full container load for the furniture from Essen but I know the container will be half empty, so there's easily enough room for the kitchen furniture, as well.
Vanessa	Just a minute, Mr Karić. Let's just look at the details … The container is sealed, so are you asking us to break the seals in Zagreb?

Bogdan	Yes, you can instruct your driver to do that, can't you? I can give you that in writing.
Vanessa	I'm afraid it isn't that easy, Mr Karić. The Incoterms® rule is DAP Horvat Mobilar, Split, which means that the sender in Essen bears all the risks to the load until the consignee unloads it at its destination in Split. You are the consignee and if you break the seals in Zagreb, the sender will no longer accept responsibility for the load because part or all of it could be stolen or damaged as soon as the container is opened.
Bogdan	I see. Well, I think I have another solution. You also have a depot in Zagreb, don't you?
Vanessa	Yes, that's right. We have a very large depot just outside the city.
Bogdan	In that case, you can pick up a container of kitchen furniture from our supplier in Zagreb and put in onto a lorry that can take two containers. You can then transfer the container of furniture to the new lorry when your lorry arrives in Zagreb and your driver can drive the new lorry with both containers to Split. That would save us a lot of money, Ms Hartmann.
Vanessa	Oh dear Mr Karić, I'm afraid I have to disappoint you again. Transshipment is not permitted.
Bogdan	I'm sorry but I don't understand. What is transshipment?
Vanessa	Transshipment means transferring the load from one lorry to another. The CMR clearly states that transshipment is not permitted.
Bogdan	So what can we do about the kitchen equipment in Zagreb?
Vanessa	I think I have the solution, Mr Karić. We can add a trailer to our lorry when it arrives in Zagreb and put the container of kitchen equipment on it. The driver can then drive the two containers to Split without breaking the seals or transshipment.
Bogdan	Perfect! Thanks for your help, Ms Hartmann. And one more thing, I can see from the pro-forma invoice that you are charging us for pallets, too. This is not necessary. We can give your driver the same number of pallets when he unloads.
Vanessa	I see. Are they Euro pallets, Mr Karić?
Bogdan	I think so. We use them here all the time.
Vanessa	I'm afraid we can't accept local pallets, Mr Karić. We can only exchange Euro pallets. I'll send you the definition of Euro pallets after this phone call.
Bogdan	Thanks. I'll check and get back to you today if we can use our pallets.
Vanessa	OK, Mr Karić. I'll send you written confirmation of the final arrangements by email tomorrow …

Track 24: Unit 6, Communication, exercise 2

Hannah	Good morning and thank you for calling SpeedyShipping. This is Hannah speaking. How may I help you?
Dermot	Good morning. It's Dermot Duffy from Duffy Logistics in Ireland. I'm heading out for Russia now and I'm calling about a return load from St Petersburg to Ireland. I've filled in your online form, but I haven't heard from you yet.
Hannah	Just a moment, sir. Let me just check … Is the name of your company spelt D – U – double F – E – Y?
Dermot	No, that's not right. It's spelt D - U - double F – Y. There's no E.
Hannah	All right, just let me check … when did you fill in the online form, Mr Duffy?
Dermot	I filled it in just before I left Dublin, so it must have been about four days ago.
Hannah	I see. Did you receive confirmation from us to say that your request had been received?
Dermot	I don't know. I left just after I filled in the form and had no time to check.
Hannah	I understand. Just let me see… Well, I think I know what happened, Mr Duffy. You didn't complete the form, so your request was not processed and you didn't receive confirmation.
Dermot	Oh, dear. Yes, I was in a hurry that day.
Hannah	And there are some mandatory boxes that still have to be filled in. You left two of them empty.
Dermot	Oh, I see. Which ones did I leave out?
Hannah	The first one's FTL or LTL. We need to know this before we can match your vehicle with a load.
Dermot	Well, at that time I didn't know because I thought I might have a return load from the factory in St Petersburg. Now I know I'm looking for a full truckload.
Hannah	So you want an FTL. The second piece of information we need is the type of vehicle. You didn't tick any of the boxes describing your vehicle.
Dermot	That's because I wasn't sure which lorry I was taking to Russia.
Hannah	OK, so could you now give me a description of your vehicle, Mr Duffy? Is it a pickup truck, box van, low-loader, artic, curtainsider or lorry with trailer?
Dermot	It's an artic.
Hannah	Enclosed body or curtainsider?
Dermot	Enclosed body.
Hannah	Articulated lorry with an enclosed body … and how much does it weigh?
Dermot	25 tonnes.
Hannah	Crane or tail lift?
Dermot	Tail lift.
Hannah	Good. Just let me check our database. Yes, we have a palletized FTL of 10 tonnes of aluminium to be collected from UPM Metal in St Petersburg for delivery to Ireland.
Dermot	Sounds about right. Where is it to be delivered?
Hannah	Delivery is to Ryland Engineering Limited in Cork.
Dermot	Cork. That's good. I know Cork. And when is it to be collected?
Hannah	The day after tomorrow.
Dermot	And when is delivery by?
Hannah	Ten days from today.
Dermot	That's fine. I'll take it.
Hannah	Excellent, I'll email you our confirmation straight away and this time you'll get it.

Track 25: Unit 7, Foundation, exercise 3A

Tim	Hello, it's Tim Becker from Baumann Air Cargo Logistics in Frankfurt, Germany. I'm phoning about an email with a scan that I got from Mr Ninomiya.
Sayumi	Ah, yes. Mr Ninomiya is my colleague. How can I help you, Mr Becker?
Tim	Well, we can't read the scan very well, so we're not sure which airport to send the consignment of fashion wear to

Transcripts

	next Friday. On the scan the IATA code looks like India – Bravo – Romeo, but that's the code for an airport near Tokyo for holiday flights, I believe.
Sayumi	Yes, India – Bravo – Romeo is Ibaraki Airport and that is not for freight.
Tim	Exactly. We normally send consignments to Narita Airport, and the IATA code for that is November – Romeo – Tango.
Sayumi	Yes, Narita is November – Romeo – Tango, but just let me check to see which one we want, please.
Tim	Yes, certainly.
Sayumi	Thank you for waiting, Mr Becker. We would like the consignment to be sent to Haneda Airport, IATA code Hotel – November – Delta.
Tim	OK, fine. So it's Haneda Airport, Hotel – November – Delta and you'd like it to be delivered next Friday, is that right?
Sayumi	Yes, that's right, Mr Becker. Is there anything else I can do for you?
Tim	Yes, could you let me have your email, so I can contact you if I have another query?
Sayumi	Certainly, Mr Becker. It's Sayumi – dot – Kashiwagi at docomo – dot – jp.
Tim	Could you spell that for me, please?
Sayumi	Yes, certainly. It's Sierra – Alfa – Yankee – Uniform – Mike – India – dot – Kilo – Alfa – Sierra – Hotel – India – Whiskey – Alfa – Golf – India - at – Delta – Oscar – Charlie – Oscar – Mike – Oscar – dot – Juliett – Papa.
Tim	Right, I've got that, Ms Kashiwagi. I'll schedule the consignment to arrive next Friday as planned.
Sayumi	Thank you, Mr Becker. Is there anything else I can do for you?
Tim	No, thanks. Bye for now.
Sayumi	Goodbye, Mr Becker, and have a nice day.
Tim	Thanks, you too.

Track 26: Unit 7, Part A, exercise 4B

Frank	Now to check the rates for the consignment of costumes from Munich to New York we first need to go online. I'll dictate the data to you, and you can enter it. All right?
You	Yes, fine. Shall I log on?
Frank	Yes, please do … OK we're online, so now click on "Rates" … and enter "Munich" under "Origin". Now go to "Destination" and enter "New York" … We should first check that there are rates for this route before we enter any more data.
You	OK. So shall I now click on "Search"?
Frank	Yes that's right…
You	And at the bottom of the page it says: "There are no rates for the requested route", so what do we do now?
Frank	Try another airport.
You	Frankfurt?
Frank	Good idea. Just type in "FRA" and click "Search" again.
You	And it's worked! It says "Frankfurt International Airport" It's offering us rates for this route.
Frank	Excellent. Now we need to enter all the details.
You	So it's from Frankfurt to New York. Carrier?
Frank	Leave it blank. They'll give us one at the end. Now we need to fill in the dates. We want a flight at some time between January the 7th and January the 8th next year.
You	I've entered the dates. What do I put in for "Commodity"?
Frank	We have to be very careful here. We need a precise description. Try "costumes".
You	It says "No results".
Frank	Try "clothing".
You	That's better. It suggests "Clothing and wearing apparel".
Frank	Well that fits costumes for an opera, so click on that.
You	The next box is "Currency".
Frank	Type in "euro".
You	The next box is "View Rate Source" with three options.
Frank	Click on ULD only. We want the costumes in a closed container. We can now enter the dimensions under "Weight Charges". The volume units are in centimetres, so enter two hundred point seven for length … a hundred and fifty-three point four for width and a hundred and sixty-two point six for height. OK?
You	Could you just repeat that to make sure please, Frank?
Frank	Yes, it's two hundred point seven by a hundred and fifty-three point four by a hundred and sixty-two point six.
You	Got it. How about the weight?
Frank	Just enter 100 kg. It doesn't really make much difference.
You	I don't understand. Isn't the weight very important with air cargo?
Frank	Yes, it is, but as the costumes are in a ULD they automatically charge you a standard rate for the volume of the ULD. That's what "Volumetric Weight Factor" means. Look at "Chargeable Weight". It says 500 kilograms, so the price is the same up to 500 kilos.
You	I see.
Frank	All we need to do is click on "Search" again to see what the carrier and the rate is.
You	OK. The carrier is CA. Is that Canadian Air?
Frank	Exactly. And what's the rate?
You	One thousand eight hundred euros.
Frank	So now we know what the rate is, the next step is "Schedules" …

Track 27: Unit 7, Part B, exercise 2B/C

Fabrizio	Lorenz Costumes. You're through to Fabrizio Gambino. How can I help?
Emily	Hello, it's Emily Taylor at Ronstadt Air Freight. I'm calling about the consignment of costumes to New York.
Fabrizio	That's great because we've just finished them. We emailed you the details a few days ago, I believe, and I also talked to someone on the phone about it.
Emily	Yes, that's right but that colleague is off sick, so I just want to check some of the details again if that's all right.
Fabrizio	That's fine.
Emily	And I've just emailed you a copy of the unfinished air waybill for you to look at while we talk.
Fabrizio	Just a moment … yes, it's arrived and … now it's on my screen.
Emily	Good. At the moment you have "NVD" for the "Declared Value for Carriage" and "NIL" for the amount of insurance. That means that if the costumes were damaged in transit, you would only get the minimum of about two thousand five hundred euros compensation.
Fabrizio	€2,500! That's nothing! The costumes are worth €50,000!
Emily	Well, as it stands, you'd lose €47,500 if something happened to them.
Fabrizio	We can't risk losing all that time and work.

165

Emily	I understand, Mr Gambino, and that's why I suggest you take out air cargo insurance on the load.
Fabrizio	Yes, but how much will it cost us?
Emily	We can offer you insurance for the time the consignment's on the plane for less than a hundred euros, but the insurance the air carrier offers doesn't cover pre- and on-carriage.
Fabrizio	So the costumes wouldn't be insured from door to door?
Emily	Exactly.
Fabrizio	So how do we get door-to-door insurance?
Emily	We'll contact an insurer, and they'll send you an offer for door-to-door insurance.
Fabrizio	Great! Thanks.
Emily	Good. So that means that on the air waybill the "Declared Value for Carriage" stays at NVD and the "Amount of Insurance" stays at NIL because you're now going to be taking that out separately.
Fabrizio	Good. Anything else?
Emily	Yes, there are still a few more points to discuss. Did my colleague mention the charges?
Fabrizio	Yes, but he didn't give me any details and said he would get back to me.
Emily	OK, so let's now finalize the charges, shall we? The total weight of your costumes and the container is 150 kilos, and the fixed rate for a ULD up to 500 kilos is €1800, so that makes the charge €1,800. I'll just add all that to the air waybill now … So the "Charge" is €1,800, the "Total" is €1,800 … and again at the bottom … and the "Weight Charge" is also €1,800 prepaid.
Fabrizio	I've got that. Anything else?
Emily	Yes, we still have the fuel and security surcharges to add. They go in the big Other Charges box on the right under the AWB fee of 25. The fuel surcharge is 40 … just let me write that in … and the security surcharge is 15 … 40 and 15 are 55, so we write 55 in the "Total Other Charges Due Carrier" box on the left under "Prepaid".
Fabrizio	OK, I've got that.
Emily	Good. Now all we have to do now is add up all the charges and put the sum in the "Total Prepaid" box.
Fabrizio	So how much does it all come to?
Emily	1,880 … I'll just type that in … and now we really have finished the air waybill.
Fabrizio	Great! And call me any time if you need any more information.
Emily	We will, Mr Gambino. Have a nice day!
Fabrizio	Thanks, you too.

Track 28: Unit 7, Communication, exercise 2

Max	Travel section, Max speaking. How can I help?
Janine	Hi, it's Janine in Frankfurt. I'd like to book two OBC flights for myself and a colleague, please.
Max	Hi Janine. Where are you off to this time?
Janine	Not too far. Dublin on the fifth of May and back on the sixth.
Max	From Frankfurt?
Janine	That's right.
Max	Just a moment … I can get you seats on an Aer Ireland flight on the fifth at 10.55 or 20.55.
Janine	20.55's too late. We'll take the 10.55. When does it arrive in Dublin?
Max	12.15.
Janine	That's fine. We have to be at the destination by 6 p.m., so that gives us plenty of time to pick up a car and so on.
Max	OK, I've got that. Economy or business class? If you want business class, I'll have to give a reason, otherwise we have to book economy.
Janine	Business. It's a time-sensitive, hand-carry shipment and if we fly business class, we won't be bumped.
Max	Yes, they sometimes bump economy passengers if they're overbooked. OK, I'll give the reason as "time-sensitive shipment", and yes, I can see that the flight's already pretty full, so business is best … There we are. Two seats on Aer Ireland flight 650 departing Frankfurt on May the fifth at 10.55 and arriving Dublin at 12.15, business class. Now what about the return flight?
Janine	The next day on the sixth of May.
Max	OK. Just let me check … There's still plenty of room on the 7 o'clock flight to Frankfurt, arriving 10.15. I can get you on that.
Janine	That won't work, I'm afraid, because we have to pick up the return shipment at 10 a.m. Is there a later flight?
Max	Let me just check. There's a flight at 17.00 hours.
Janine	Sounds better. When does it get in at Frankfurt?
Max	Twenty fifteen. Is that too late?
Janine	That should be fine. We have to deliver a return shipment to a destination in Frankfurt by twenty-two hundred hours, so that should work.
Max	Business or economy?
Janine	Business again. It's another time-sensitive shipment.
Max	OK. So that's two seats on Aer Ireland flight 651 departing Dublin at seventeen hundred hours and arriving Frankfurt at twenty fifteen, business class … and now it's booked.
Janine	Good. Thanks for that.
Max	That's what I'm here for. I'll email you your boarding cards and a link for your company smartphones now, so you won't need to print anything out.
Janine	Thanks. Bye for now.
Max	Have a good trip. Bye.

Track 29: Unit 7, Communication, exercise 3B/C

Janine	Ronstadt Air Freight, good morning. This is Janine Braun speaking. How can I help?
Max	Hi Janine.
Janine	Hi Max. Have you booked everything now? It's an urgent consignment and we don't want any delays.
Max	Well almost. Can we just go through the details?
Janine	Yes, fine.
Max	Now you're flying in to Dublin Airport with a colleague on 5 May and staying one night. I've found a very good offer for a 4-star hotel in Dublin city centre, so shall I put you down for that?
Janine	That's a possibility but could you look for accommodation in Hacketstown? That would be better because we have a pick-up there, as well.
Max	OK, fine. Just let me check the local transport links to Hacketstown … yes, you can take the Airport Link Express from the airport to the city centre and a bus to Hacketstown. So that's two return trips costing a total of … €82.
Janine	But we'll have a car, Max, so we won't need to take the Airport Link Express.
Max	I was just coming to that. We always have to book the cheapest option to keep costs down, especially when it

	comes to hire cars, and, as I said, you can get to Hacketstown by public transport and … just let me check … there are three buses a day, so you should be fine.
Janine	Well, I'm not so sure, Max. I've heard that the buses sometimes don't run in that area because of flooding and there may be other delays, so we'll need a car.
Max	I see … OK, just a moment. I can get you a two-door economy-class car from the fifth to the sixth and … there's also a special offer for those dates.
Janine	But if there's flooding and the buses don't run, we'll need a four-wheel drive. These are time-sensitive samples, Max. We can't afford to be late. Can you get us a four-wheel drive?
Max	A four-wheel drive … just a moment … yes, there's one available from the fifth to the sixth … and it's an SUV … with A/C, too.
Janine	Yes, they all have air conditioning but does it have a satnav? That's more important. It's not always so easy to find these places out in the countryside.
Max	Just let me check … yes, it also has a satnav.
Janine	Good. Please book that for us.
Max	All right … and now it's booked. And as regards accommodation, you want something in Hacketstown, right?
Janine	Yes, that's right.
Max	And will you be needing a double or two single rooms?
Janine	Two singles.
Max	All right … and shall I put you down for B&B, half board or full board?
Janine	We'll need an evening meal on the fifth and breakfast on the sixth, so put us down for half board, please. And parking.
Max	OK, anything else, any dietary restrictions or other requirements?
Janine	No dietary restrictions but we'd like WiFi. We should be all right with the mobile network in Dublin, but out in the countryside it could be a problem so we'd like WiFi at the hotel, just to be on the safe side.
Max	So just let me check … There's O'Reilly's Lodge 8 km away from Hacketstown with all the facilities you need but without WiFi. Ah … this looks better … There's Moyne Farm House 10 km from Hacketstown and it has everything, including WiFi, so I can book you two rooms there.
Janine	Sounds good. We'll take the Farm House.
Max	OK, I've booked it for you. Anything else you need?
Janine	That's it, thanks.
Max	Good. I'll email you the details straight away.
Janine	Thanks. Bye for now.
Max	Bye.

Track 30: Unit 8, Part B, exercise 3A/B

Mark	Medical Supplies International, Mark Walker speaking. How can I help?
Vanessa	Hello, it's Vanessa Fischer at Lohmann Sea Freight Services.
Mark	Hi Vanessa. Is it about the shipment of medical equipment to Singapore?
Vanessa	That's right. You were dealing with my colleague, Tom Redford, but he's off sick today, so I'm standing in for him.
Mark	OK. Is everything in place now?
Vanessa	Well, almost. There are just a few points we need to clear up, then we're all set.
Mark	Good. So what do you need to know?
Vanessa	We have to complete the B/L for the shipment. I have it on my screen now and I've sent you a copy, so can you take a look at it with me?
Mark	Yes, fine. The copy's arrived and it's on my screen now.
Vanessa	Good. So, first we need more details about the notify party. That's toward the top of the form, on the right. Do you see it?
Mark	Yes, I do.
Vanessa	Do we have an address for Mr Lee Kuan Tong?
Mark	Just a moment, er – yes, it's United Overseas Bank, Singapore.
Vanessa	So that's United Overseas Bank, Singapore… Good. And now in the section "Particulars furnished by shipper", we need to know the weight of the goods, so how much do they weigh?
Mark	Just under one and a half tonnes. To be precise: one thousand four hundred and seventy-two kilos.
Vanessa	One thousand four hundred and seventy-two kilos, which brings me to the next point. I believe there are three different types equipment in the container but we have no details of the third type.
Mark	Yes, we're also sending anaesthesia machines.
Vanessa	Ana … oh dear, I won't try to say that word because it's too hard, but how do you spell it?
Mark	Anaesthesia?
Vanessa	Yes.
Mark	A – n – a – e – s – t – h – e – s – i – a.
Vanessa	So that's a – n – a – e – s – t – h – e – s – i – a.
Mark	Exactly.
Vanessa	Now the next point is the shipping marks. Do you have them?
Mark	Yes, they are N – S – C – E – slash – 2 – 8 – 4 – 4 – 1.
Vanessa	Just a moment … so that's N – S – C – E – slash – 2 – 8 – 4 – 4 – 1. Is that right?
Mark	Yes, that's right. Anything else you need?
Vanessa	Yes, Full or less than container load?
Mark	Full container load, and we don't want it to be opened before it reaches the consignee.
Vanessa	In that case, I'll add FCL/FCL under the shipping marks … which brings us to freight. My colleague has a cross in the "Collect" box in the next line down on the right but I'm not sure if that's right.
Mark	No, it's wrong. It's freight prepaid.
Vanessa	OK, so it's prepaid … so I'll just add the word "prepaid" after "freight", put a cross on the right under "Prepaid" and delete the cross in the "Collect" box.
Mark	Yes, that's important.
Vanessa	And there's one more important thing to add and that's the L/C number.
Mark	Just a moment. I have it here … the L/C number is UOB 221963.
Vanessa	Ah yes, that's the United Overseas Bank. So it's UOB 221963.
Mark	Yes, that's right. Anything else you need to know?
Vanessa	Just a couple of points. We need to know if it's a multimodal or port-to-port B/L, so do you want us to pick up the consignment at your premises or will you take it to Rotterdam yourselves?

Mark	We'd like you to pick it up for us.
Vanessa	So you require pre-carriage from Amsterdam to Rotterdam … and how about at the other end?
Mark	We'd like you to deliver it to the consignee in Singapore, too.
Vanessa	So you also require on-carriage, making it a multimodal B/L. Right, that would seem to be it.
Mark	Excellent! And when can we expect the consignment to be shipped?
Vanessa	By the end of next week.

Track 31: Unit 8, Communication, exercise 2B

Naomi	University Hospital Singapore, Naomi Tan speaking. How can I help?
You	Hello, it's Tom Stoppel from Lohmann Sea Freight Services in Hamburg.
Naomi	Hello, Mr Stoppel. Are you phoning about the medical equipment?
You	Yes, that's right. I'm afraid delivery of the goods will be delayed.
Naomi	Oh dear! Could you tell me the reason for the delay?
You	It's unfortunately due to circumstances beyond our control because there's a really bad storm over the Arabian Sea.
Naomi	I see but are you able to tell us when we can expect delivery?
You	I can't give you a firm date at the moment, Ms Tan, but we promise to give your goods priority when unloading the vessel and we'll let you know as soon as we have an ETA.
Naomi	ETA?
You	Sorry, estimated time of arrival.
Naomi	All right but could you put that in an email for me? I need to tell my boss what's happening.
You	Most certainly. I'll send you an email immediately.
Naomi	Thanks. And the absolute deadline for us here is week 49. After that we'll be in trouble at the hospital, so can you let us have that ETA as soon as possible?
You	I've noted that, Ms Tan and please accept our apologies for the inconvenience.
Naomi	That's all right under the circumstances. We look forward to receiving your email with the ETA.
You	Thanks, Ms Tan. I'll be in touch again as soon as possible. Bye for now.
Naomi	Bye.

Track 32: KMK Exam practice 4, exercise 1, Hörverstehen

Hi, Claudia, it's Vivien. I'm so sorry, but I'm too ill to come in today. I know there's so much to do right now and I hate to leave you alone, but I can't help it.
I know you haven't done the OBC bookings before. It's really not that difficult, perhaps my hints can help you.
You just open the OBC sheet online, the company is called CLOUDFREIGHT, there's a link under service partner in the drop-down menu.
OK, once you've opened it – it says "Client Booking Form". Now, ignore section A, that's just for new customers and go directly to section B.
Well then, if I remember correctly, the first thing to do is to enter the company's customer number: that's 477195. If you have six digits, you know you're right.
Anyway, after that you move on to tick one of the service options. It's just one small but essential mechanical part, a swivel joint, so it will be carried by hand.
I don't remember what's next now, but somewhere you need to write down how it's packed. That'll be an attaché case and it weighs about one kilo.
Good, that's that. Now go to category: you need to type in the word URGENT.
The export department prepares all the necessary documents: the customs declaration, Patent Certificate and a copy of the NAFTA online registration. NAFTA is spelled N-A-F-T-A.
Now, for the journey itself: Put in today's date. The swivel joint is ready and will be there by nine a.m. at the latest. You don't need to check flights or anything, that's what the OBC service does. But it's important to write down that the flight is from Frankfurt to Dallas/Fort Worth. Just type in the airport codes, which are FRA and DFW.
OK, I think that's it. Please make sure you have made an entry in all options in section B, otherwise you can't submit the form.
Good luck! Call me at home if you need help!

Track 33: Unit 9, Part B, exercise 2A/B

Ken	Toprac Limited, you're through to Ken Wang. How can I help?
Alex	Hello, it's Alex Horn from InterFracht Neumann in Germany. I'm calling about the trial order we placed with your company.
Ken	Ah, yes, Mr Horn. I remember it well. Are the goods to your liking?
Alex	Yes, Mr Wang. They are the kind of thing we're looking for.
Ken	Excellent, Mr Horn. Would you like to place the order you talked about in the online chat? We can still offer you the same price but only for a short time.
Alex	Well, yes and no, Mr Wang. Can we discuss the details first?
Ken	Certainly, Mr Horn.
Alex	The Incoterms® rules are fine, but let's look at the terms of payment. You're asking for 50% with order and 50% before loading. There's an element of risk for us here.
Ken	There is also a risk for us, Mr Horn, but as an introductory offer we could offer you 30% with order and 70% before loading.
Alex	OK, 30% with order and 70% before loading. Yes, that sounds good, but it still means we pay before seeing the goods. I was thinking of payment by letter of credit.
Ken	Yes, we can offer you that, but it still means you pay before seeing the goods.
Alex	Yes, but in this case, we would arrange for a third party to come and inspect the goods before they're loaded.
Ken	We can arrange that for you, Mr Horn. No problem. We can give you the name of a very good inspection agency.
Alex	Thanks Mr Wang, but we already have the name of an inspection agency from the German Chamber of Commerce in Hong Kong. We would use China Quality Focus Ltd.
Ken	That's fine, Mr Horn. China Quality Focus is a good agency. I often recommend them.
Alex	So we have agreed that payment will be by irrevocable and confirmed documentary letter of credit.
Ken	Yes, that's routine for us, Mr Horn. Please open the credit with your bank in Hamburg and we will provide the usual documents to our bank when they contact us.
Alex	Excellent, Mr Wang. Can we just check the documents that you will provide?

Ken	Yes, Mr Horn. We will provide the … uhm … packing list, commercial invoice, certificate of origin and the received for shipment bill of lading.
Alex	That's good, Mr Wang, but we must have a clean, on board bill of lading.
Ken	Clean, on board bill of lading … Yes, we can do that, but it will take a little longer.
Alex	That's fine, Mr Wang, but we still need one more document.
Ken	Which one, Mr Horn? I have listed the four important documents needed.
Alex	The fifth document is a positive inspection report from China Quality Focus Ltd. The inspection agency's report must be included with the other documents to be given to your bank.
Ken	Ah, yes, the inspection report. I have made a note of that, Mr Horn. Would you like us to find you a freight agent for the main carriage?
Alex	Thanks for the offer, Mr Wang, but we already have one over here in Germany.
Ken	I understand. Is there anything else I can do for you, Mr Horn?
Alex	Yes, we would like you to deduct the cost of the trial order from the price of our order. The trial order cost us a total of US$380 with import duties.
Ken	US$380 … Yes, we can do that for you, Mr Horn. That is standard practice.
Alex	Good, so the price is now US$29,620. Thanks, Mr Wang. All I need from you now is your written confirmation after we place our order and a pro-forma invoice so I can open the letter of credit.
Ken	Written confirmation … No problem, Mr Horn. Anything else I can do for you?
Alex	No thanks. That's it for now. We'll now place our order for warehouse equipment in writing and look forward to receiving your confirmation and the pro-forma invoice.
Ken	We'll do that for you, Mr Horn. Thanks for calling.
Alex	My pleasure, Mr Wang. Goodbye for now.
Ken	Goodbye.

Track 34: Unit 9, Communication, exercise 2A

Aleksi	FinShip Oy, haloo?
Sevda	Hello, it's Sevda Yavuz from InterFracht Neumann in Hamburg. I'm phoning about a shipment that will be arriving here soon. I'd like to change the destination.
Aleksi	OK, could I have the order number, please?
Sevda	Yes, it's VBFT97. It's a consignment of office furniture.
Aleksi	Just a moment … VBFT97 … Yes, it's on a lorry on its way to Hamburg at this very moment.
Sevda	I see …
Aleksi	And it should be at your premises in three or four hours' time.
Sevda	Oh dear … that doesn't give us much time to change the destination.
Aleksi	I'm not sure we can do much now, but why do you want to change it?
Sevda	The furniture is for our new warehouse, which hadn't been built when we ordered it. Now we have the new address and that's where we need the furniture.
Aleksi	I see. How far away is the new warehouse from the old one?
Sevda	About 17 kilometres. About 25 minutes by road. Can I give you the new address?
Aleksi	Yes, please.
Sevda	It's Am Genter Ufer 295.
Aleksi	Could you spell that for me, please?
Sevda	Yes, certainly. It's Alfa – Mile – new word – Gold – Echo – November – Foxtrot – Echo – Romeo – new word – Uniform – Foxtrot – Echo – Romeo. The house number is 295.
Aleksi	And it's in Hamburg … Postcode?
Sevda	21129.
Aleksi	All right. Just wait a minute and I'll try to contact the driver on the phone … Just a moment … I'm sorry but I can't get through to him. I think he's on the ferry to Puttgarden and he's probably asleep. Look can you send us an email with the details of the new address in writing? We need it in writing if you change any of the details.
Sevda	Yes, certainly. Could I have your email address, please?
Aleksi	Yes, it's aleksi.heikkinen@finship.fin.
Sevda	Could you spell the first half for me, please? I mean your name.
Aleksi	Yes, certainly. It's Alfa – Lima – Echo – Kilo – Sierra – India – dot – Hotel – Echo – India – Kilo – Kilo – India – November – Echo – November – at – finship – dot – f – i – n.
Sevda	OK, I've got that.
Aleksi	And we'll keep trying to contact the driver and send him a text message with the new address.
Sevda	And if he still comes to the old address?
Aleksi	I'll email the new arrangements to you in Finnish as soon as I get your email. You can then print them out and give them to him if he still comes to the wrong address.
Sevda	OK, great!
Aleksi	And I'll put my phone number on the email, so he can phone me if he's unsure about anything.
Sevda	Very good. Thanks for your help.
Aleksi	My pleasure. Anything else I can do for you?
Sevda	No, thanks. Bye for now.
Aleksi	Bye.

Track 35: Unit 9, Communication, exercise 3A

Driver	Hello, I have a delivery from Finland. Will you unload it now?
You	Hello, you're from FinShip, aren't you?
Driver	Yes, that's right. My lorry is just over there.
You	Well, there's been a change in plan. We need you to drive to a different address.
Driver	Different address? I don't understand. The delivery note says this address. Here, look what it says.
You	Yes, but I have an email from your boss with new instructions. Here you are.
Driver	So there is a new address here in Hamburg. How far is it?
You	Not far. About 17 kilometres.
Driver	I'm sorry but my navigation system is not working properly and there is roadwork everywhere.
You	No problem. If you like, I can sit in the cab with you and give you directions.
Driver	That is a very good idea! Please come this way.

Track 36: Unit 9, Communication, exercise 3C

You	What's your name?
Driver	Georgi. Just call me Georgi.
You	So, Georgi, just go straight ahead for a bit. It's a long road … Now take the second turning on the left.
Driver	Second turning on the left.
You	In a moment it's a bit tricky because there's a fork. You can see it up there. Here we are. Now bear left at the fork.
Driver	At the fork … bear left … OK. And now where do I go?
You	Just go straight ahead for a bit. Can you see those traffic lights ahead?
Driver	Yes, I can see them at the crossroads.
You	And they're green, so go over the crossroads and soon we'll have to turn left … Now we're coming to a T-junction where we have to go left or right, so turn left at the T-junction and then go down that road for a few kilometres.
Driver	And now?
You	There's a bend coming up, so go round the bend and then it's a bit more complicated.
Driver	All right.
You	Up ahead there's a big roundabout, so take the third exit off the roundabout and we're almost there.
Driver	Third exit off the roundabout.
You	Not far now. Now you need to slow down a bit because it's just up here. Can you see the shoe shop, bank and supermarket on the left?
Driver	Yes, I can see them.
You	Well, the turning is on the left after the supermarket.
Driver	On the left after the supermarket. And now?
You	I have good news for you, Georgi. We've arrived!

Track 37: Unit 10, Foundation, exercise 2A

Andrea	Hi, this is Andrea Kießling from ALEX Logistics. Am I speaking to Ben McEnroe?
Ben	This is Ben McIntyre.
Andrea	Yes, yes. I'm calling about your shipment with us … number LZ-095-325, which is due for delivery at your premises on Monday. I'm calling to inform you about a change in delivery. We're expecting bad weather in the region and we are going to deliver your shipment earlier, so that there is no disruption in delivery. Will there be someone at your premises on Saturday to unload the goods?
Ben	I'm sorry. Hang on. I didn't quite get all of that. Which shipment was that?
Andrea	LZ-095-325.
Ben	And you want to deliver on Saturday instead of Monday? Because of bad weather? That's news to me, I haven't heard about any big storm. Saturday? That would be very inconvenient … Are you certain you can't deliver on Monday?
Andrea	No. We can't deliver then.
Ben	I see.
Andrea	I'm calling to make sure that someone is there on Saturday to unload the goods.
Ben	Would it be possible to deliver on Friday?
Andrea	There's no chance of that. We can only deliver on Saturday. The bad weather is making everything very difficult for us.
Ben	I understand that, it's just that it will be difficult for us to arrange for someone to be here on Saturday.

Track 38: Unit 10, Part A, exercise 3

It's been a busy morning, hasn't it? I can't believe how full it's been. And I've met so many interesting people. For example, this morning I talked to Gokul Kumar from … uhm … FoodTech – they're based in Mumbai. To show respect, I wanted to give him one of our give-aways, so I gave him our writing set. The nicer one, you know. I wanted him to have something on his desk that reminds him of us. But … I don't think he liked me very much. I tried to make him feel comfortable, gave him a coffee, you know, and made a few jokes about Germany, but he didn't laugh. And I don't think he'll get in contact with us. I just don't have a good feeling about the whole thing. I was a bit disappointed.

Later I had tea with Lina Alves from Lisbon, which is kind of funny as she works for a coffee company. I think that meeting went a bit better. She was much more relaxed. We sat over in the corner of the stand and talked a lot about Lisbon – I told her that I had visited Lisbon last year and I liked it a lot. At the end of our conversation she gave me some nice chocolate. I really enjoyed the meeting with her, and she said she would contact us soon.

And, oh, I also talked to someone from Japan! I had a long conversation with a man from Japanese Steel in Kyoto. I have his card here somewhere … Ah, here. His name was Dai Miura. I gave him my business card as well. He said that they wanted to start selling to firms in Eastern Europe and that they were looking for a company with a lot of experience in sea freight. While we were talking, his supervisor came by and said hello. Unfortunately, I had run out of business cards because the stand was so crowded all morning. But Mr Miura has my card, so I don't think that will be a problem.

The last person I talked to was Greg Bartley from TransEuro Logistics in Bristol. He talked a lot! But, it was funny, he never wanted to talk about business. He told me about his flight here, that it was delayed. We talked about the weather and the trade fair and how busy it is, much busier than last year, and so many more visitors from North America … I was in a hurry, so I asked him if we could meet again tomorrow. We made an appointment, but a few minutes ago I checked my emails and there was one from him cancelling the meeting. So, I guess that didn't go so well either.

Track 39: Unit 10, Communication, exercise 2B

Anja	Wolf.
Olof	Oh. Hello. Erm. Do you speak English?
Anja	Yes.
Olof	Oh. Good. This is Olof Bengtsson calling from Swedish Matches. Is that Horn Logistics in Hamburg … the customer service department?
Anja	Yes.
Olof	And, erm, who am I speaking to, please?
Anja	Wolf.
Olof	Ah. Ms Wolf. Erm. Is, erm, are you the correct person to take a complaint about a payment?
Anja	What's the problem?
Olof	It's about my shipment of matches from Östersund to Warsaw. I have just received a reminder for the payment of the shipment. This was a trial shipment and you can be sure that I paid the invoice the day after receipt.
Anja	What's your customer number?
Olof	Let me see … erm … it's 942761.

Anja	OK. I can't do anything at the moment. I'll get it sorted after lunch.
Olof	So, will you phone me back? My phone number is …
Anja	It's here on the display.
Olof	0046 63 57 564?
Anja	Yes, Mr Bengton.
Olof	And my name is Bengtsson. You will be sure to look into this? Well, thank you very much.

Track 40: Unit 10, Communication, exercise 2B

Anja	Guten Morgen. Horn Logistics, Verkaufsabteilung. Anja Wolf am Apparat.
Olof	Oh. Hello. Erm. Do you speak English?
Anja	Yes, of course. How can I help you?
Olof	Oh. Good. This is Olof Bengtsson calling from Swedish Matches. Is that the customer service department?
Anja	Yes, this is the customer service department, Mr Bengtsson. My name's Anja Wolf.
Olof	Ah. Mrs, erm, Ms Wolf. Hmm. Is, erm, are you the correct person to take a complaint about a payment?
Anja	It depends on what it's about. Could you give me some details, please?
Olof	It's about my shipment of matches from Östersund to Warsaw. I have just received a reminder for the payment of the shipment.
Anja	Oh, I'm sorry to hear that. Could you give me your customer number, please?
Olof	Let me see … erm … it's 942761.
Anja	Just a moment, please. Right. 942761. I have it here. Shipment of two containers. And you say that you received a reminder?
Olof	That is correct. I am sorry, but I have to say that I am disappointed. This is a trial shipment and you can be sure that I paid the invoice the day after receipt.
Anja	Oh, dear. I'm extremely sorry to hear that you've had so much trouble. I'm sure my manager would like to discuss this with you. Can I ask her to phone you immediately when she comes in to work tomorrow?
Olof	Yes, All right. I'll be in my office till 2 p.m., so she should call me there. The number is 0046 129 546 993.
Anja	Let me repeat it to you, please. 0046 129 546 993. Yes. You'll get a call tomorrow, Mr Bengtsson.
Olof	Could you tell me your manager's name, please?
Anja	It's Mia Richter.
Olof	Mia Richter. Good, Thank you very much, Ms Wolf.
Anja	You're welcome, Mr Bengtsson. Thank you for calling. Goodbye.
Olof	Goodbye.

Track 41: Unit 10, Communication, exercise 3C

Max	Good morning. Horn Logistics, Sales Department. Max Jahn speaking.
Lucy	Good morning. This is Lucy Hoggs from MedEquip in Birmingham.
Max	Good morning, Ms Hoggs. How can I help you?
Lucy	I'm calling to enquire about a shipment of 10 aluminium containers to our warehouse in Liverpool. The consignment was picked up on 18 April and delivery was promised by 3 May. But, so far, nothing has arrived.
Max	Oh. I'm sorry to hear that. Could you give me the shipment number?
Lucy	Yes. It's DF-54736.
Max	DF-54736. Just a moment, please. I'll check. I'm sorry, Ms Hoggs. I don't seem to have any record of your shipment. Can I just check that I've understood everything? The number is DF-54736 and it was picked up on 18 April. Could you give me the exact details of the shipment again, please?
Lucy	Yes, it's a shipment of 10 aluminium containers for medical equipment.
Max	Aluminium containers for medical equipment. Ms Hoggs, I'll have to speak to my colleague to find out what the problem is. Can I get back to you later?
Lucy	Well, yes. But I hope it won't take long. We can't fulfil our contract until we have the containers.
Max	Yes. I realize that, Ms Hoggs. I'm very sorry about this and I will do my best to get back to you as soon as possible.
Lucy	Many thanks for your help, Mr Jahn.

Track 42: KMK Exam practice 5, exercise 1, Hörverstehen

Hi, there, Tom here. Sorry, I was very busy this morning, now you're away. Well, I guess the old answering machine will do…

I haven't finished all my research yet, but here's what I've found out so far.

There are two options in the region. The first warehouse is only about 400 metres away, so it's actually in the direct neighbourhood of our warehouse. It's rather big, 600 square metres, and in good condition. It was renovated recently and is completely equipped with thermal insulation. It will be available next spring. My contact person was a Mr Miller, a very friendly person, and he showed me the whole place. I'm not an expert but it looks good. By the way, Mr Miller is in the picture and you can call him directly to receive more information. That would be 07700 900156.

The second warehouse I looked at was in Chester, about one mile away from the company. It consists of two parts that could be connected, so it would either be 200 square metres or 450 square metres. The good thing is that we could rent it straight away as there is no tenant at the moment. But frankly, the place looks rather shabby and it was dirty – perhaps we need to look somewhere else. Anyway, I have no contact person for that warehouse yet, apart from the estate agent who gave me the address. The facility manager of the place didn't call me back, so I just went there on my own.

That's why I suggest writing an official email. You can find all the information on the website of Benson Warehousing, the email address is benson@spaceplace.brit, that's B-E-N-S-O-N at spaceplace dot B-R-I-T.

Oh, and last but not least: prices! Benson is 35 pounds per square metre, per quarter. The agent had a list for me. The other one, you know, the one nearby, is 160 pounds per square metre, per year.

OK, that's all for now. You said you needed the information quickly. If you have questions, or if I've forgotten anything, just call me on my mobile.

Have a nice day!

Track 43: Unit 11, Foundation, exercise 1B

Welcome to my presentation about the autonomous supply chain. I'll try and keep it short as I know you're all very busy.

Driverless, crewless, noiseless, effortless – these are going to be the keywords of the future. Let me show you what I mean. As you can see on this slide, this is an autonomous lorry – "driverless" – which is on its way to a fully automated cargo terminal. The lorry will get its information about where to go from vehicles close to it. After the autonomous lorry delivers the containers to the port, the containers will be loaded onto the autonomous e-container ship by an automated crane that moves around the port controlled by a computer. So, with all this automation – the lorry, the container ship, the crane – this is where "crewless" is going to be the keyword. Not having a large crew of workers to carry out these routine jobs will save time and money.

Now let's look at what happens after the ships have been unloaded. Here you see that a Hyperloop is going to deliver the containers to a smart warehouse. This will be a "noiseless" process – our next keyword – even though the Hyperloop reaches very high speeds. So, now we are in the smart warehouse where the goods are put on shelves – by robots, of course. These same robots will later take the goods from the shelves when they are ready for delivery. To do this, the robots are going to read the QR codes on the goods, so they know what goes where and when, and then load the goods onto driverless delivery vans (there's "driverless", again). These vans will deliver your goods to the final logistics hub, so to another warehouse or a distribution centre. For the last mile – that's what we call the movement of the goods to the final destination – drones or robots are going to deliver the goods to the customers' premises or homes. This will again save time and money, and the process is going to be – and here's the final keyword for today – "effortless".

Thanks for listening to my brief presentation about the autonomous supply chain. Are there any questions?

Track 44: Unit 11, Part A, exercise 2B

Thank you all for attending this meeting at such short notice. Have you all got copies of the charts? Great.

Let's take a look at the first graph which shows the price of fuel in Europe between 2000 and 2018. As you can see the price of fuel has risen 70 cents since 2000. Since 2006 it has cost more than 1 euro and hasn't gone below that amount. Naturally we can do nothing about the fuel prices, but we can strategically plan our deliveries and the methods of transport we use. It is cheaper for us to use less fuel and also better for the environment. So, I'd like one of you to look into things we can do. Fiona, could you do that please? Thanks.

Moving on to the second graph. We all know that if we reduce the amount of paper we use, we also lower CO_2 emissions. Unfortunately, on the graph we only have figures going back to 2012 as you can see on the x-axis of the graph. The y-axis shows the number of reams of paper we use per year in thousands. As you can see, the decrease up until 2013 was gradual with a jump in 2014. Then it levelled off in 2015 and 2016 with another big decrease in 2017. So, Rani, could you look into that and see what reasons you can find for the drop, please? Thank you. And I'd also like one of you to look into the electronic air waybill. How effective is it in saving paper, what the benefits are, etc. Who would like to do that? Any volunteers? Ah, good, thank you.

The pie chart is just to give you some background information about what makes up the distribution costs. This enables us to look for other areas where we can both reduce costs and also increase sustainability. As you can see the biggest segment on the pie chart with 65% is for transportation costs. This includes not only fuel but also all the costs for our fleet of trucks – tax, motorway tolls, maintenance, etc. I think there are developments in truck technology that will mean we can reduce costs and also help the environment. Mike, can you see what you can find out to help us here, please?

OK, now I'd like to tell you a few more things about my meeting this morning.

Track 45: Unit 11, Part B, exercise 2A

Good morning, ladies and gentlemen. Before I get started, I just want to thank you for attending this meeting today. Not all the changes we want to make will be popular, but we believe they are the right way forward for us. In order to stay competitive, all companies must invest in the future and innovate. And luckily, as a large international company, we can start investing in the future now.

Everything is moving faster these days, and when people place orders, they want their products as soon as possible. This means same-day or overnight delivery is a must. So, starting in August, we will be operating 24 hours a day, seven days a week. To make 24/7 delivery possible, we will introduce a new three-shift plan, with the first shift from 6 a.m. to 2 p.m., the second shift from 2 p.m. to 10 p.m. and the third shift from 10 p.m. to 6 a.m. By introducing the new shift plan, we will be able to reduce your working hours, and you can select a shift that fits with your lifestyle and personal life. This means, for example, that you can have more free time after work, partners can have more flexibility when looking for employment, and family life can improve. There will be meetings with all employees affected to help find the best shift that suits each one of you.

To make distribution more efficient, we are also going to upgrade to a new autonomous distribution system. The new distribution system will be self-maintaining and self-correcting, so mistakes will be a thing of the past. It does mean that the warehouse will have to be refitted in July. A new high-bay shelving system will also be built at that time. It will take less space, which means that we can accommodate more packages. The turnaround, turnover, handling and transshipment of packages will be faster. As machines will do more of the heavy and routine work, your health and safety will be improved and the number of days lost at work due to illness can be reduced. This will result in a higher level of reliability.

Track 46: Unit 11, Communication, exercise 2A/B

Julia   Good morning everybody and welcome to today's meeting. There has been one change to the agenda as we need to talk about any holiday you have left over from last year. I think we should do that after we've talked about breaks. OK, you all know who I am, but I'd like to introduce you to our new colleague who started today, David Fischer. He will be working part-time for the first three months, and from April he will increase to full-time. Welcome to the HR department, David. You are the first item on today's agenda would you like to introduce yourself?

David	Sure. I'm David Fischer and I finished my training and passed all my exams in November. As Julia just said, I came on board today, so I'm the new boy in the office. I'm really looking forward to working here.
Julia	Thanks for that, David. Would the others like to introduce themselves to David? Jürgen, would you go first, please?
Jürgen	Hi. I'm Jürgen Müller. I'm head of the warehouse. I'm here to talk about the new working hours in the warehouse from next month.
Julia	Thanks, Jürgen. Rajiv?
Rajiv	Good morning. My name is Rajiv Mittal. I'm a trainee in my second year. I've already worked in the export and import departments, and I have been working in HR for the last four months.
Julia	Many thanks, Rajiv. Our next topic is the new working hours in the warehouse and the offices, so would you go ahead please, Jürgen?
Birgit	Hold on, Julia. Hi David, I'm Birgit Beutel and I also work in the HR department and I'm in the works council, too.
Julia	Sorry, Birgit. OK, Jürgen, over to you.
Jürgen	Certainly, Julia. As you all know, there are going to be new working hours in the warehouse … To conclude, I would say that all the colleagues in the warehouse seem happy with the new hours they will be working.
Julia	Many thanks, Jürgen. Would anyone like to comment or ask a question? … OK, if not then let's move on to the next topic, which is the importance of breaks. Can you say something about this please, Birgit?
Birgit	Yes, I'd like to show you a short presentation on how important breaks are for health, safety and efficiency …
Julia	Thank you, Birgit. Very interesting. Uhm, Birgit, you also wanted to tell us something about leftover holiday from last year.
Birgit	Yes, just a reminder to those of you who have holiday left from last year. It has to be used by the end of March this year. That shouldn't be a problem as Easter is at the end of March, too.
Julia	Thanks, Birgit. Everyone, please let me know if you have any problems organizing your holiday. Right, the next topic is the delivery of the new printers. Rajiv?
Rajiv	There will be four new printers delivered next week. One colour printer and three black and white ones. Unfortunately, it means no one will be able to print anything on Tuesday. Sorry.
Julia	That's not very good news!
Birgit	I thoroughly agree with Julia.
Jürgen	Can I come in on that, Birgit … Julia?
Julia	Go ahead, Jürgen.
Jürgen	There is no problem. You can use the printers in the warehouse on Tuesday. You will have to come downstairs to collect your printouts, but at least you will be able to print the most important things.
Julia	Thank you, Jürgen for that. So, we've covered item breaks and holiday, and now item no. 5, delivery of the new printers, and we've spoken about the new working hours in the warehouse and offices, so we've covered all the items on today's agenda. Let's wrap up the meeting, shall we? Or is there any other business?
Birgit	I just have one final point. The next works council meeting will be on Monday 3rd February. Has anyone got time to attend the meeting with me, please? We need someone to take the minutes for us.
David	I can attend with you, Birgit.
Birgit	Great, thanks.
Julia	Thank you, David. Well, that would seem to be it. You'll be getting the minutes by email tomorrow. Many thanks everyone for your input …

Track 47: Unit 12, Foundation, exercise 1

1: Maren

Presenter	Hello, and welcome to this week's podcast. This week, we're talking to a group of people who have recently gained their business qualifications. Let's start with you, Maren. Would you like to introduce yourself?
Maren	OK. I'm Maren, and I've just completed my apprenticeship as a logistics manager.
Presenter	What did you like best about your apprenticeship?
Maren	I liked the mixture of going to vocational college and doing practical work.
Presenter	What do you do at work?
Maren	I plan and organize shipments by sea and air.
Presenter	Right. Now, what about the future? What would you like to do in the future?
Maren	I'd like to become a logistics coordinator.
Presenter	Well, all the best, Maren.

2: Garry

Garry	My name's Garry and I'm a customer services manager.
Presenter	OK. What did you enjoy most about your apprenticeship, Garry?
Garry	I enjoyed going to meetings.
Presenter	Apart from going to meetings, what else do you do in your job?
Garry	Well, I usually work on my own. I calculate prices for shipments, recommend insurance policies and communicate with international business partners.
Presenter	Sounds as if the work is quite varied. Now that you've finished your training, where do you go from here?
Garry	Oh, that's easy. I'd like to get another qualification in Business Administration for Transportation and Logistics.
Presenter	Oh. That's great!

3: Delon

Presenter	Hello. Can you tell us your name and something about your apprenticeship?
Delon	Yes. My name's Delon, and I've just qualified as a freight agent.
Presenter	What did you like best about your apprenticeship?
Delon	I enjoyed learning from experienced people.
Presenter	What does a freight agent do at work?
Delon	Basically, it's anything involving freight! You organise transport, advise customers … It's a lot of office work, really. So it can be anything from filling out forms to writing offers.
Presenter	Hmm. Now that you've qualified, what about the future? Where would you like to work?
Delon	I'd like to find a job abroad where I can use my English.
Presenter	That sounds good.

Track 48: Unit 12, Part B, exercise 1A

Interview 1: Tobias Klein

Tobias Hallo?
Jennifer Good evening. Am I speaking to Tobias Klein?
Tobias Wer ist das? Ich versteh' nichts. Bist du das Kati?
Jennifer This is Jennifer Winters. I'm the Recruitment Manager at Freight International plc. Am I speaking to Mr Tobias Klein?
Tobias Oh! Oh yes! Freight International plc. Yes, I understand. Yes, my name is Tobias Klein. Please wait a moment. I must go outside …
Jennifer Is this a good time to call you, Mr Klein?
Tobias Yes! It's very good! No problem, Mrs Winter. We can talk in a moment. Just let me go outside with my mobile …
Jennifer I can't hear you very …
Tobias Thank you for calling me, Miss Winters! I am very happy to answer your questions!
Jennifer Could you tell me what job you're doing at the moment, Mr Klein?
Tobias Yes, I'm an Azubi – I mean a trainee, but I've finished now, so I'm not, but I was … but I'm still at Argo in Frankfurt!
Jennifer I see … I think we … problem … signal strength.
Tobias Strength? Yes, I have strengths, Mrs Winter. I am very good at work and at school and at football because I am a team player.
Jennifer I see … And what about your weaknesses?
Tobias Weaknesses? I sometimes forget important things … but I now use the reminder function on my mobile. That helps.
Jennifer And why do you want a job at Freight International, Mr Klein?
Tobias I've always wanted to work in Manchester. It has a famous football team and very nice people.
Jennifer We are in London, Mr Klein, but that doesn't really matter now. Could you tell me something about your plans for the future?
Tobias Well, I want a well-paid job so I can be independent and free.
Jennifer I see. Are there any questions you would like to ask about the job, Mr Klein?
Tobias I'm sorry. I didn't hear what you said, Miss Winter. The signal is very bad and the battery of my mobile is almost …

Interview 2: Bianca Tiemeyer

Bianca Tiemeyer?
Jennifer Good morning. Am I speaking to Bianca Tiemeyer?
Bianca Yes, that's right.
Jennifer This is Jennifer Winters. I'm the Recruitment Manager at Freight International plc. Is this a good time to talk to you for a few minutes about your application for the post of a German-speaking junior shipping agent?
Bianca Yes, I'm at work but I have permission to use the office phone because it's my father's company – Tiemeyer Freight in Dortmund.
Jennifer Oh I see. Now I've studied your CV and would like to know a little more about you. Would you like to take me through your CV?
Bianca Well, I think the CV says everything, really. I haven't got a copy in front of me now, but it lists my skills and abilities. I went to the States for a year, so my English is very good.
Jennifer And what other strengths do you have?
Bianca Other strengths? That's a standard question isn't it? Anyway, I would say I have all the usual strengths – I'm punctual, so I'm reliable, honest, hard-working and so on.
Jennifer I see. And weaknesses?
Bianca That's a very good question. Weaknesses … Well, perhaps I expect too much from other people. My own standards are very high, and I suppose it's unfair to want everyone to be perfect.
Jennifer And why do you want this job in particular?
Bianca Why this job? Well, I think I'm probably best qualified for it. My grades at school were very good and I'd like to work abroad for a few years.
Jennifer I see. What are your future plans, Miss Tiemeyer? Where do you see yourself in five years' time?
Bianca I really can't say. It depends whether I like this job or not. If I like it, I'll stay on for a few years. It depends on the people, really.
Jennifer Do you have any questions you wish to ask?
Bianca That's another standard question, isn't it? Actually, I do have one question. Would you help me to find a good flat? I want something comfortable and not too far from the company.
Jennifer I'll pass the question on, Miss Tiemeyer. Is there anything else you'd like to know?
Bianca No, that's all, thanks. When will I hear from you?
Jennifer Within the next 48 hours. Thanks for answering my questions. Goodbye.
Bianca Bye.

Interview 3: Sebastian Hartmann

Sebastian Hartmann?
Jennifer Good evening. Am I speaking to Sebastian Hartmann?
Sebastian Yes, that's right.
Jennifer This is Jennifer Winters. I'm the Recruitment Manager at Freight International plc. Is this a good time to talk to you for a few minutes about your application for the post of a German-speaking junior shipping agent?
Sebastian Yes, evenings are fine.
Jennifer Good. I've studied your CV and would like to know a little more about you. Would you like to take me through it?
Sebastian Yes, certainly. I would say one of my skills is the ability to work in a team and get the best out of myself with the help of others. That's one of the reasons why my team won the Team Project Management Competition. I also organized a programme for some Norwegian visitors to the company last year. It was great fun and they've invited me back to Norway next summer. And I learned a lot about living and working in the UK when I worked for a freight-forwarding company in York. I saw very good customer services there and would like to offer the same standard myself.
Jennifer So, in a nutshell, what would you say your strengths are?
Sebastian Teamwork, taking the initiative, working independently and understanding what the customer wants.
Jennifer And what about your weaknesses?
Sebastian I'm sure I have many but I would say a lack of experience. That's why I want to start work now.
Jennifer What made you apply for this job?

Sebastian	The skills listed are exactly what I have learned in my traineeship. There is also a link with Germany, so I feel I can make a special contribution. And I like working in the UK, so I see it as the perfect opportunity.	Pat	That's it. Now, let's move on to the main part of the interview. You'll be asked questions by one or more interviewers.
Jennifer	What are your plans for the future?	Presenter	The interview might be conducted by more than one person?
Sebastian	I hope to develop in the job. I want to gain experience and then perhaps study for higher qualifications in the evening. London is a good place for that.	Pat	That's correct. Sometimes there's a panel of interviewers. Now, preparation for this part is extremely important. Think about the questions you might be asked and make a list. You'll definitely be asked to talk about yourself. Perhaps the interviewer will ask you about your strengths and weaknesses. Write down the questions – and think about how you're going to answer. And always remember to relate your answers to the job on offer.
Jennifer	Would you like to ask any questions yourself?		
Sebastian	Yes, on your website it says you sometimes send employees to India or East Asia, for example. Would this be an option for me?		
Jennifer	Not in the first year, but if you stay longer, you can apply to be posted overseas. Many young people do this. Any other questions?	Presenter	Yes, that's important. Keep focused on the job. What should a candidate do if he or she doesn't understand a question?
Sebastian	That was the most important one, thanks.	Pat	If you don't understand a question, ask the interviewer to clarify. You can say: "Could you explain what you mean by … ?" – whatever it is. A good interviewer will ask the question again in a slightly different way.
Jennifer	In that case we'll be in touch again within 48 hours and thank you for answering my questions.		
Sebastian	My pleasure. Goodbye.		
Jennifer	Goodbye, Mr Hartmann.		

Track 49: Unit 12, Part B, exercise 4B

Presenter	Thanks for coming along to talk to us today, Pat.	Presenter	Hmm. I hope so. Now, earlier you mentioned questions from the candidate. I remember my very first interview. I had no idea what to ask.
Pat	My pleasure. It's nice to be here.		
Presenter	Good. Now, today you're going to give us advice about how to prepare for an interview.	Pat	Oh, dear. Some preparation would have helped. It's important to do some background research into the company before you go for the interview. Find out about the company's most recent developments and the future prospects of the company you hope to work for. Go to the firm's home page on the internet, read the business section of your newspaper, or look through business magazines. As you're doing your research, note down any questions that occur to you concerning the company. You should also, of course, prepare some questions about the job itself. Then, when you're asked if you have any questions, this is your chance to show your interest in the company and the job.
Pat	Correct. I'm going to go through each of the five stages of a job interview and talk about how candidates can prepare themselves. So, stage one, greetings and introductions. That's perhaps the easiest part of the interview, but it still needs some preparation. First of all, you should find out where the interview location is and how to get there so that you arrive in good time. Try to give yourself enough time to relax and calm down. You should also make sure that you're wearing appropriate clothes.		
Presenter	First impressions count. Would you advise people to buy new clothes specially for the interview?		
Pat	No, not particularly. Your clothes need to be appropriate for the job, clean and smart, that's all. They don't have to be new.	Presenter	Right. Be prepared with questions about the company and the job! And that's the end of the interview and you can say goodbye.
Presenter	Right. What about body language at the start of the interview?	Pat	Well, not quite. Before the interview comes to an end, the interviewer usually says when the candidate can expect to hear from the company or if there's to be a further interview or a test – hmm – say, in the form of an assessment centre evaluation. So, only after these arrangements have been made, is your last task as a candidate to say thank you and goodbye. Again, a good, firm handshake and a smile, and that's it.
Pat	Body language is important. Walk into the room as confidently as possible, shake hands and make eye contact. Don't be shy. Look directly at the interviewer or interviewers. You'll be asked to take a seat, and there will be a bit of small talk.		
Presenter	Talking about the weather, your journey, that kind of thing?		
Pat	That's right. There might also be a question about where you live or your hobbies.	Presenter	Well, thank you, Pat, for these very helpful interviewing tips. I'm sure our listeners have learned a lot today and that they'll be able to put your tips to good use in their interviews. Now, next week's podcast is about …
Presenter	Some people find it difficult to make small talk, even in their own language. What advice can you give us there, Pat?		
Pat	I think the best thing to do is to simply get into the habit of making small talk in English with a colleague or a friend.		
Presenter	That's a good idea. Practise making small talk whenever you can.		

Track 50: KMK Mock exam, Rezeption I, Hörverstehen

Interviewer With us today is Mr Fields who is a logistics manager at SLM. And I would like to ask you, Mr Fields, to tell us something about your job.

Mr Fields OK, I'm going to talk about my field of work and also my passion: logistics. As you probably know, logistics is one of the largest and most important branches in Great Britain. And if you're interested in this sector, let me tell you straight away: your job opportunities in this sector are very good – both nationally and internationally – and it's really interesting work as well!

Interviewer How long have you been working at SLM?

Mr Fields I have been there for seven years now.

Interviewer Can you summarize in a nutshell what a logistics manager has to do?

Mr Fields Uhm, I would say … as a manager of logistics you have to take on organizational and managerial tasks. Does that sound too simple?

Interviewer It sounds very concise and I'm curious what it implies. Shall we start at the beginning? I know you earned a degree in Manchester. But when you started working, were you prepared for the difficulty and complexity of the job?

Mr Fields Was I prepared for my work, hmm …? Well, in my course of study I specialized in the development of distribution strategies. But I also acquired more general knowledge. For example, I learned how to organize production and transportation procedures and how to optimize an enterprise economically. We were taught that to be successful as a manager you need business management skills as well as specialized logistics expertise.
At the beginning of my career, I probably struggled most with personnel management. I honestly had to "learn the language" and be very strict and consistent in my communication. You don't learn that in theory. You have to be able to present and negotiate in international meetings, but at the same time you have to deal with frustrated and angry lorry drivers.

Interviewer Did theory teach you any managerial skills?

Mr Fields It did, in a way. Let me give you some examples of things we learned that I found most helpful. I think the most helpful topics were quality control and supply-chain management.
Now, I know that sounds a bit boring, but it isn't when you apply all these theoretical aspects in practice. And believe me, in my first weeks I was very happy to have at least the background knowledge, because the day-to-day challenges can be quite overwhelming for a beginner. So, yes, I would say I was prepared for the things that you can prepare for, if that makes sense.

Interviewer Was there anything in particular that helped you when you were getting started?

Mr Field I was quite lucky because I had good basic knowledge of both air and sea freight and that came in handy. But nobody will start a new job or position without making mistakes.

Interviewer Can you give us an example of a mistake that you made at the beginning of your career?

Mr Fields As I said before: communication is vital. One of the biggest misjudgements I made in the beginning was to underestimate the importance of social skills – and I'm not talking about being able to make small talk or speak in meetings. No, I'm talking about communicating well with the people that work for you. I had to learn the hard way that you can only be as good as the people that work for you. Don't get me wrong, I come from a working-class background. I understand the problems of my workers but still – I really needed to communicate the good and the bad, the achievements as well as the problems, and that's not easy.

Interviewer Thank you very much for your openness, and I can only agree: everybody makes mistakes, but it's important that we learn from them.

Incoterms® rules

As trade becomes more and more global, goods travel further and further, crossing geographical, cultural and language barriers on their way. For this reason, it is essential that importers and exporters agree to use the same terms of reference.

In 1936 the International Chamber of Commerce in Paris invented a set of International Commercial Terms (Incoterms® rules) to define importers' and exporters' rights and obligations, such as transport costs, risk, insurance, customs duty, documentation, loading and unloading. Since then the Incoterms have been revised eight times to keep up with developments in the field of international trade and translated into many different languages. The last revision was in 2020. There are now eleven Incoterms, seven of which can be used for any mode or combined modes of transport, e.g. truck, train, ship or rail. The other four are used for ship or inland waterway transport only. The Incoterm DAT* from the 2010 rules can, however, also still be used if required.

RULES FOR ANY MODE OR MODES OF TRANSPORT

1
EXW (EX WORKS)
Ab Werk
The seller makes the goods available at his premises. The buyer bears all the costs and risks of transporting the goods to their destination.

2
FCA (FREE CARRIER)
Frei Frachtfuhrer
The seller loads the goods on board the first carrier's vehicle. The buyer bears all the costs and risks of transporting the goods to their destination.

3
CPT (CARRIAGE PAID TO)
Frachtfrei bis
The seller bears all the costs and risks until the goods are handed over to the first carrier. He pays the transport costs, without insurance, for the main carriage to the named destination. The buyer insures the goods for the main carriage and bears all other costs.

4
CIP (CARRIAGE AND INSURANCE PAID TO)
Frachtfrei versichert bis
The seller bears all the costs and risks until the goods are handed over to the first carrier. He pays the transport costs, including all-risk insurance, for the main carriage to the named destination. The buyer bears all other costs.

5
DAP (DELIVERED AT PLACE)
Geliefert benannter Ort
The seller bears all the costs and risks until the goods have reached their destination. The buyer is responsible for import duties and unloading the goods.

6
DPU (DELIVERED NAMED PLACE UNLOADED)
Geliefert benannter Ort entladen
The seller bears all the costs and risks until the goods have reached the named place and is also responsible for unloading them. The buyer bears all other costs.

7
DDP (DELIVERED DUTY PAID)
Geliefert Zoll bezahlt
The seller bears all the costs and risks until the goods have reached their destination, including import duties. The buyer is responsible for unloading the goods.

> ***DAT** (DELIVERED AT TERMINAL) (Incoterms® 2010)
> The seller delivers when the goods, once unloaded from the arriving means of transport, are placed at the disposal of the buyer at a named terminal at the named port or place of destination. "Terminal" includes a place, whether covered or not, such as a quay, warehouse, container yard or road, rail or air cargo terminal. The seller bears all risks involved in bringing the goods to and unloading them at the terminal at the named port or place of destination.

RULES FOR SEA AND INLAND WATERWAY TRANSPORT

8
FAS (FREE ALONGSIDE SHIP)
Frei Langsseite Schiff
The seller delivers the goods alongside the ship at the port of shipment. The buyer bears all the costs and risks of transporting the goods to their destination.

9
FOB (FREE ON BOARD)
Frei an Bord
The seller delivers the goods on board the ship at the port of shipment. The buyer bears all the costs and risks of transporting the goods to their destination.

10
CFR (COST AND FREIGHT)
Kosten und Fracht
The seller delivers the goods on board the ship at the port of shipment. He pays the transport costs, without insurance, for the main carriage to the port of destination. The buyer insures the goods for the main carriage and bears all other costs.

11
CIF (COST, INSURANCE AND FREIGHT [… named port of destination])
Kosten, Versicherung und Fracht
The seller bears all the costs and risks until the goods are delivered on board the ship at the port of shipment. He pays the transport costs, including basic insurance, to the named port of destination. The buyer bears all other costs.

"Incoterms" is a trademark of the International Chamber of Commerce (ICC).

Terms of payment

payment in advance	Vorauszahlung/Vorkasse
cash with order (CWO)	Barzahlung bei Auftragserteilung
payment by irrevocable and confirmed documentary (letter of) credit	Zahlung durch unwiderrufliches und bestätigtes Dokumentenakkreditiv
documents against payment (D/P) / cash against documents (CAD)	Kasse gegen Dokumente
cash on delivery (COD)	gegen Nachnahme
⅓ with order, ⅓ on delivery, ⅓ within 30 days after delivery	⅓ bei Auftragserteilung, ⅓ bei Lieferung, ⅓ innerhalb von 30 Tagen nach Lieferung
payment within 60 days from date of invoice	Zahlung innerhalb von 60 Tagen nach Rechnungsdatum
10 days 2%, 30 days net	Zahlung innerhalb 10 Tagen abzüglich 2 % Skonto oder innerhalb 30 Tagen netto
payment on receipt of goods	Zahlung bei Erhalt der Waren
payment on receipt of invoice	Zahlung bei Rechnungserhalt
documents against (three months') acceptance (D/A)	Dokumente gegen (Dreimonats-)Akzept
open account terms with monthly/quarterly settlement	offenes Zahlungsziel mit monatlicher/vierteljährlicher Abrechnung

Conversion tables

Distance

1 inch (in)	= 2.54 centimetres
1 foot (ft)	= 30.48 centimetres
1 yard (yd)	= 0.9144 metres
1 mile (mi)	= 1.609 kilometres
1 centimetre	= 0.3937 inches (⅜ inch)
1 metre	= 39.37 inches (3 feet, 3 ⅜ inches)
1 kilometre	= 0.62137 miles

Area

1 square inch (in^2)	= 6.452 square centimetres
1 square foot (ft^2)	= 0.0929 square metres
1 square mile (m^2)	= 2.59 square kilometres
1 square centimetre	= 0.155 square inches
1 square metre	= 10.764 square feet
1 square kilometre	= 0.3861 square miles

Mass/Weight

1 ounce (oz)	= 28.35 grams
1 pound (lh)	= 0.453 kilograms
1 UK ton ('long ton')	= 1,016 kilograms
1 US ton ('short ton')	= 907 kilograms
1 gram	= 0.035 ounces
1 kilogram	= 2 pounds, 3.3 ounces

Volume

1 UK pint (pt)	= 0.568 litres
1 UK quart (qt)	= 1.137 litres
1 UK gallon (gal)	= 4.546 litres
1 US pint	= 0.473 litres
1 US quart	= 0.946 litres
1 US gallon	= 3.785 litres
1 cubic inch (in^3)	= 16 cubic centimetres
1 cubic foot (ft^3)	= 0.03 cubic metres

U Useful phrases

Describing apprenticeships — Unit 1

- I work for … (name of employer) in … (place).
- I'm in the first/second/third/last year of my apprenticeship.
- I go to vocational training college on day release every … (e.g. Monday and Tuesday).
- … on block release for six weeks/three months twice/three times a year.
- I decided to train as a management assistant in logistics and freight forwarding because I like arranging national and international transport services.
- My apprenticeship lasts/takes three years/is three years long.

- Ich arbeite für … (Name des Arbeitgebers) in … (Ort).
- Ich bin im ersten/zweiten/dritten/letzten Jahr meiner Ausbildung.
- Ich gehe jeden … (z. B. Montag und Dienstag) in die Berufsschule zum berufsbegleitenden Unterricht.
- … habe Blockunterricht für sechs Wochen / drei Monate zwei-/dreimal im Jahr.
- Ich entschied mich, eine Ausbildung zum/zur Kaufmann/Kauffrau für Spedition und Logistikdienstleistungen zu machen, weil ich gerne nationale und internationale Transportdienstleistungen organisiere.
- Meine Ausbildung dauert drei Jahre / geht drei Jahre lang.

Making introductions — Unit 1

Greeting people you do not know
- Good morning/afternoon/evening. I'm …
- How do you do? My name is …
- Nice/Pleased to meet you.
- Nice to meet you, too.
- Excuse me. Are you …?
- Yes, I am. / No, I'm not. I'm …
- Welcome to …
- Thank you. It's nice to be here.

- Guten Morgen/Tag/Abend. Ich bin …
- Freut mich. Mein Name ist …
- Es freut mich, Sie kennenzulernen.
- Ganz meinerseits.
- Entschuldigung. Sind Sie …?
- Ja, das bin ich. / Nein, das bin ich nicht. Ich heiße …
- Herzlich willkommen bei/in …
- Dankeschön. Es ist schön, hier zu sein.

Introducing people
- This is … . / These are my colleagues, John and Mary.
- I'd like to introduce … from the … department.

- Das ist … . / Das sind meine Kollegen, John und Mary.
- Darf ich Ihnen … aus der …-Abteilung vorstellen?

Making small talk
- I hope you're well.
- … is such a beautiful city!
- The weather is so good today!
- Did you have a good trip/flight?

- Ich hoffe, es geht dir/Ihnen gut.
- … ist so eine schöne Stadt.
- Das Wetter ist heute so schön.
- Hattest du / Hatten Sie eine gute Reise / einen guten Flug?

Describing jobs and responsibilities — Unit 2

- I work in a team of management assistants.
- I report directly to the …
- I arrange for goods to be shipped abroad.
- I make sure our products get to our customers.
- It's my responsibility to obtain the necessary shipping documents.

- Ich arbeite in einem Team von Managementassistenten/assistentinnen.
- Ich bin dem/der … direkt unterstellt.
- Ich organisiere den Güterversand ins Ausland.
- Ich stelle sicher, dass unsere Produkte bei unseren Kunden/Kundinnen ankommen.
- Ich bin dafür verantwortlich, die benötigten Lieferpapiere zu besorgen.

Useful phrases

– I am responsible for maintaining our customer database.	– *Ich bin dafür verantwortlich, die Kundendatenbank zu pflegen.*
– Working in my department means understanding customs regulations.	– *Für die Arbeit in meiner Abteilung ist es wichtig, die Zollvorschriften zu kennen.*
– I work fixed hours/a 39-hour week.	– *Ich habe feste Arbeitszeiten / eine 39-Stunden-Woche.*
– I do a lot of overtime	– *Ich mache viele Überstunden.*

Telephoning — Unit 2

Identifying yourself

– Good morning. My name's …	– *Guten Morgen. Ich heiße …*
– Good afternoon. This is … from … (company).	– *Guten Tag. Hier spricht … von … (Firma).*
– Good evening. I work for …	– *Guten Abend. Ich arbeite bei …*

Explaining the reason for your call

– I'm enquiring about …	– *Ich möchte mich nach … erkundigen.*
– I'd like some information on …	– *Ich hätte gern nähere Informationen zu …*

Asking for a person/department

– I'd like to speak to Mr/Ms …	– *Ich würde gerne (mit) Herrn/Frau … sprechen.*
– Could you put me through to the … department, please?	– *Könnten Sie mich bitte zur …-Abteilung durchstellen/ weiterleiten?*

Saying what you want to do

– Can I leave a message?	– *Kann ich eine Nachricht hinterlassen?*
– I'll call again later.	– *Ich rufe später noch einmal an.*
– Could you ask Mr/Ms … to call me back?	– *Könnten Sie Herrn/Frau … bitten, mich zurückzurufen?*

Ending the call

– Thank you for your help/assistance.	– *Vielen Dank für Ihre Hilfe/Unterstützung.*
– You're welcome.	– *Gern geschehen. / Bitte sehr.*
– Goodbye.	– *Auf Wiederhören.*
– Have a nice day/evening.	– *Einen schönen Tag/Abend noch.*

Taking telephone calls — Unit 2

– Who's calling, please?	– *Wie ist Ihr Name bitte?*
– Could you spell your name, please?	– *Könnten Sie bitte Ihren Namen buchstabieren?*
– I'm sorry, I didn't understand. Could you repeat that, please?	– *Es tut mir leid, ich habe das nicht verstanden. Könnten Sie das bitte wiederholen?*
– I'll put you through.	– *Ich stelle Sie durch.*
– I'm trying to connect you.	– *Ich versuche, Sie zu verbinden.*
– Please hold the line.	– *Bleiben Sie bitte dran.*
– I'm afraid the line is engaged.	– *Der Anschluss ist leider besetzt.*
– I'm sorry, … (name) is unavailable at the moment.	– *Es tut mir leid, aber … (Name) ist im Moment nicht da.*
– Would you like to speak to someone else?	– *Möchten Sie mit jemand anderem sprechen?*
– Would you like to leave a message?	– *Möchten Sie eine Nachricht hinterlassen?*

Showing visitors around the company — Unit 3

Giving a tour of the company
- Let's start by visiting …
- Here we have the … department.
- On the left/right, you can see …
- This is where we make/dispatch …

- Lassen Sie uns bei/beim/in/im … beginnen.
- Hier ist die …-Abteilung.
- Zu Ihrer Linken/Rechten sehen Sie …
- Hier stellen wir … her / versenden wir …

Asking for and giving directions
- Could you tell me the way to …, please?
- Yes, certainly.
- Go down the corridor until you get to …
- Take the first/second/last door on your right.
- Turn right at the end of the corridor.

- Könnten Sie mir bitte sagen, wie ich nach/zur/zum … komme?
- Ja, selbstverständlich.
- Gehen Sie den Flur entlang, bis Sie zur/zum … kommen.
- Nehmen Sie die erste/zweite/letzte Tür rechts.
- Biegen Sie am Ende des Flurs rechts ab.

Offering help/refreshments
- Can I take your coat?
- Would you like something to drink?
- Would you like some tea/coffee/water?

- Möchten Sie Ihren Mantel ablegen?
- Darf ich Ihnen etwas zu trinken anbieten?
- Möchten Sie Tee/Kaffee/Wasser?

Describing companies — Unit 3

Describing your company
- We are based/located in … (country/city).
- Our headquarters are in … (country/city).
- The company was founded in … (year).
- We are in the … industry.
- We are a multinational/local/small company/business.
- We are a start-up.
- We have branches/subsidiaries/offices in … (country)/all over the world.
- We have … (number) employees.
- We are a privately-owned company/corporation.

- Wir sind in … (Land/Stadt) ansässig.
- Unser Hauptsitz befindet sich in … (Land/Stadt).
- Das Unternehmen wurde im Jahr … gegründet.
- Wir sind in der …-Branche (tätig).
- Wir sind ein internationales/regionales/kleines Unternehmen / ein kleiner Betrieb.
- Wir sind ein Start-Up(-Unternehmen).
- Wir haben Filialen/Tochterfirmen/Büros in … (Land) / überall auf der Welt.
- Wir haben … (Anzahl) Angestellte.
- Wir sind ein Privatunternehmen/eine Privatgesellschaft.

Talking about the company's products/services
- We make/produce/manufacture …
- We distribute …
- We offer/provide …
- We make sure the goods get from A to B.

- Wir produzieren/erzeugen …/stellen … her.
- Wir vertreiben …
- Wir liefern … / bieten … an.
- Wir stellen sicher, dass die Güter von A nach B geliefert werden.

Giving presentations — Unit 3

Introduction
- My name is … and this is my partner, …
- We are apprentices at … in Germany.
- This morning, I'm/we're going to talk about …
- Our topic today is …

- Mein Name ist … und das ist mein/e Partner/in, …
- Wir sind Auszubildende bei … in Deutschland.
- Heute spreche ich/sprechen wir über …
- Das heutige Thema lautet …

Useful phrases

Structure
- I've divided my presentation into three main parts, as follows: …
- First/Firstly, … / Second/Secondly, … / After that/Then …

- Ich habe meine Präsentation in drei (Haupt-)Teile gegliedert, und zwar …
- Erstens, … / Zweitens, … / Anschließend/Dann …

Signposts
- To begin with, …/Next, …/Now …
- The next topic I'm going to talk about is …
- Now I'd like to move on to …

- Zuerst, …/Als Nächstes, …/Jetzt …
- Das nächste Thema, das ich behandeln/über das ich sprechen möchte, lautet …
- Jetzt möchte ich zum Thema … übergehen.

Handouts
- I've prepared a few things/handouts for you to take away.
- I hope you'll find these copies of the graphics useful.

- Ich habe etwas/Handouts für Sie zum Mitnehmen vorbereitet.
- Ich hoffe, dass Sie diese Kopien der Grafiken nützlich finden.

Conclusion
- Before I finish my presentation, I'd just like to mention …
- I'd like to go over the main points again.
- Finally, …/In conclusion, …/In summary, …

- Bevor ich meinen Vortrag beende, möchte ich … kurz erwähnen.
- Ich möchte die Hauptpunkte/Hauptargumente nochmals kurz darlegen.
- Zum Schluss …/Abschließend …/Zusammenfassend …

Questions/Thanking the audience
- Are there any questions?
- We have time for a few questions/one last question.
- Well, that's the end of my presentation.
- Thank you for your attention/for listening.

- Gibt es/Haben Sie noch Fragen?
- Wir haben noch Zeit für ein paar Fragen/eine letzte Frage.
- Damit bin ich am Ende meiner Präsentation angelangt.
- Vielen Dank für Ihre Aufmerksamkeit/fürs Zuhören.

Writing emails	Unit 4

Salutation
- Dear Sir or Madam (*formal*)
- Dear Mr/Ms Smith (*formal*)
- Dear Paul (und Paula)
- Good morning, Paul (*less formal*)
- Hi/Hello Paula (*less formal*)

- Sehr geehrte Damen und Herren,
- Sehr geehrter Herr / Sehr geehrte Frau Schmidt,
- Lieber Paul (, liebe Paula),
- Guten Morgen Paul,
- Hallo Paula,

Complimentary close
- Regards/Best regards/Best wishes/Yours sincerely (*formal*)
- Best regards/Best/Best wishes
- All the best (*less formal*)

- Mit freundlichen Grüßen / Freundliche Grüße
- Viele Grüße / Mit freundlichen Grüßen
- Alles Gute / Herzliche Grüße

Opening sentence
- I'm just writing to … (*formal*)
- Just a quick note/message to … (*less formal*)

Ich schreibe Ihnen, um zu / weil …
Nur eine kurze Mitteilung/Nachricht, um zu …

Conclusion
- I look forward to your reply/to hearing from you. (*formal*)
- Many thanks in advance. (*formal*)
- I hope to hear from you soon. (*less formal*)

- Ich freue mich auf Ihre Antwort.
- Vielen Dank im Voraus.
- Ich freue mich, bald von Ihnen/dir zu hören.

Writing enquiries — Unit 5

Source of address

- We have seen your company's advertisement in the current edition of ... (name of publication) and are most interested in your products/services.
- We note from your company's website that you are specialized in ...
- You have been recommended to us by ... (name of the person/company).

Description of your company

- We are a rapidly growing/leading forwarder/transporter/importer/exporter of ... with excellent business contacts all over ... (region/country) and beyond.
- Our company is a major/well-established (German) transporter of ... (goods) both at home and abroad.
- We have many long-standing customers all over Europe.

Your requirements

- Please send us a favourable quotation for these items/for ... (products).
- We would welcome a quotation for ...
- Please let us have your export price list.
- ... including all discounts granted
- Please also let us know if you would like to provide samples.
- ... including details of your terms of delivery and payment.
- Details of your terms of delivery and payment would also be appreciated.
- We would be grateful if a representative could call on us.
- How soon would you need delivery?

Polite ending

- We are looking forward to working with you soon.
- We look forward to hearing from you soon/in the near future.
- We look forward to your early reply with interest.

- Wir haben Ihre Anzeige in der aktuellen Ausgabe von ... (Name der Veröffentlichung) gesehen und interessieren uns sehr für Ihre Produkte/Dienstleistungen.
- Wir haben auf der Homepage Ihres Unternehmens gesehen, dass Sie auf ... spezialisiert sind.
- Sie wurden uns von ... (Name der Person/Firma) empfohlen.

- Wir sind ein schnell wachsender/führender Spediteur/Transporteur/Importeur/Exporteur für ... mit hervorragenden Geschäftskontakten in ganz ... (Region/Land) und darüber hinaus.
- Unser Unternehmen ist ein bedeutender/gut eingeführter (deutscher) Spediteur von ... (Waren/Dienstleistungen) im In- und Ausland.
- Wir haben viele langjährige Kunden in ganz Europa.

- Bitte schicken Sie uns ein passendes (Preis-)Angebot für diese Artikel / für ... (Produkte).
- Wir hätten gerne ein (Preis-)Angebot für ...
- Bitte senden Sie uns Ihre Export-Preisliste zu/lassen Sie uns Ihre Export-Preisliste zukommen.
- ... einschl. aller gewährten Rabatte
- Bitte teilen Sie uns auch mit, ob Sie Muster/Proben zur Verfügung stellen möchten.
- ... einschl. Einzelheiten über Ihre Liefer- und Zahlungsbedingungen.
- Bitte lassen Sie uns Informationen zu Ihren Liefer- und Zahlungsbedingungen zukommen.
- Wir wären dankbar, wenn uns ein/e Außendienstmitarbeiter/in besuchen könnte.
- We schnell/bald benötigen Sie die Lieferung?

- Wir freuen uns darauf, bald mit Ihnen zu arbeiten/zusammenzuarbeiten.
- Wir hoffen auf baldige Antwort. / Wir freuen uns auf Ihre Antwort.
- Wir sehen Ihrer baldigen Antwort mit Interesse entgegen.

Useful phrases

Writing business letters — Unit 5

Salutation
– Dear Sir or Madam (*to a firm*)	– *Sehr geehrte Damen und Herren,*
– Dear Mr/Ms Brown	– *Sehr geehrte/r Herr/Frau Brown,*
– Dear Sharon	– *Liebe Sharon,*

Complimentary close
– Yours faithfully (*BE: to a firm*)	– *Mit freundlichen Grüßen*
– Yours very truly / Cordially yours (*AE: to a firm*)	– *Mit freundlichen Grüßen*
– Yours sincerely (*BE*)	– *Mit freundlichen Grüßen*
– Sincerely yours / Best personal regards (*AE*)	– *Mit freundlichen Grüßen / Beste Grüße*

Writing offers — Unit 5

Reference to enquiry
– As agreed in our telephone conversation of this morning (of today) …	– *Wie heute (Morgen) telefonisch vereinbart …*
– We were delighted to receive your enquiry dated … about our … services.	– *Wir waren sehr erfreut, Ihre Anfrage vom … über unser(e) … Dienstleistungen zu erhalten.*
– I am pleased to let you have details of our offer in writing.	– *Gerne lasse ich Ihnen ein schriftliches Angebot zukommen.*
– Many thanks for the above-mentioned enquiry/your enquiry dated …	– *Wir danken für Ihre oben genannte Anfrage / Ihre Anfrage vom …*

Description of your company/services
– We are a major distributor of …	– *Wir sind ein bedeutender Großhändler für …*
– … with an excellent reputation throughout Europe.	– *… mit einem hervorragenden Ruf in ganz Europa.*
– We have many satisfied customers throughout Western Europe and North America.	– *Wir haben bereits viele zufriedene Kunden überall in Westeuropa und Nordamerika.*

Sales material
– A brochure on … / Our current catalogue and price list is/are attached/enclosed for your information.	– *Zu Ihrer Information ist/sind ein Prospekt über … / unser aktueller Katalog und eine aktuelle Preisliste angehängt/beigefügt.*
– To download details of our services together with our export price list, please visit our website at …	– *Um Einzelheiten über unsere Dienstleistungen und unsere Export-Preisliste herunterzuladen, besuchen Sie bitte unsere Homepage unter …*

Price
– As regards the goods requested, we are pleased to submit the following quotation: …	– *Was die gewünschten Waren betrifft, freuen wir uns, Ihnen folgendes Angebot zu unterbreiten: …*
– Please find attached our quotation/our terms and conditions.	– *Anbei senden wir Ihnen unser Angebot/unsere Geschäftsbedingungen.*

Terms and discounts
– Our prices are quoted FOB Hamburg.	– *Unsere Preise verstehen sich FOB Hamburg.*
– Delivery will be made CIP Frankfurt Airport / DDP your premises.	– *Die Lieferung erfolgt CIP Flughafen Frankfurt / DDP Ihren Geschäftsräumen.*
– A quantity discount of … % is granted on orders for …	– *Bei Abnahme von … wird ein Mengenrabatt von … % gewährt.*
– Our terms of payment for an initial order are CWO.	– *Bei Erstauftrag kann lediglich bar bei Auftragserteilung gezahlt werden.*
– Our usual terms of payment are ⅓ with order and ⅔ by irrevocable and confirmed documentary letter of credit.	– *Unsere üblichen Zahlungsbedingungen sind ⅓ bei Auftragserteilung und ⅔ per unwiderruflichem und bestätigtem Dokumentenakkreditiv.*

– ... or, with favourable references, 10 days 3%, 30 days net.	– ... oder, bei günstigen Referenzen, 3 % Skonto bei Zahlung innerhalb von 10 Tagen, netto bei Zahlung innerhalb von 30 Tagen.
– Regular customers may be granted preferential terms.	– Stammkunden können wir ein Angebot zu günstigen (Zahlungs-)Konditionen/Vorzugsbedingungen machen.
– If regular orders are placed with our company, open account terms may be granted.	– Wenn unserer Firma regelmäßige Aufträge erteilt werden, kann ein offenes Zahlungsziel gewährt werden.
Delivery	
– within ... days after receipt of order	– innerhalb von ... Tagen nach Auftragseingang
– Delivery is made within approx. 30 days after receipt of order.	– Die Lieferung erfolgt innerhalb von ca. 30 Tagen nach Auftragseingang.
Polite ending	
– We look forward to receiving your order.	– Wir freuen uns auf Ihren Auftrag.
– We hope our offer is to your liking ...	– Wir hoffen, dass unser Angebot Ihnen zusagt ...
– ... and look forward to doing business with you.	– ... und freuen uns auf die Zusammenarbeit.
– Please do not hesitate to contact us if you require further details.	– Bitte zögern Sie nicht, uns zu kontaktieren, wenn Sie weitere Einzelheiten benötigen.

Clarifying details on the phone	Unit 6
Repeating what somebody says	
A: We can deliver everything by Thursday.	A: Wir können alles bis Donnerstag liefern.
B: Thursday. Right.	B: Donnerstag, in Ordnung.
Asking for clarification	
A: My address is 23 Fairfield Gardens.	A: Meine Adresse lautet 23 Fairfield Gardens.
B: Sorry. Did you say 23 or 33?	B: Entschuldigung, sagten Sie 23 oder 33?
Reading something back	
A: My number is 01622082148.	A: Meine Nummer lautet 01622082148.
B: I'll just read that back to you. 01622082148.	B: Ich wiederhole: 01622082148.
– Can you just read that back to me?	– Könnten Sie das bitte wiederholen?
– Can I just check that? It's ...	– Kann ich das kurz kontrollieren/überprüfen? Es ist ...

Making travel arrangements	Unit 7
Booking flights and trains	
– I'd like to enquire about flights to ...	– Ich möchte mich über Flüge nach ... erkundigen.
– I would like to reserve ...	– Ich möchte ... reservieren (lassen).
– Could I please have a one-way/return (train) ticket to ...?	– Ich hätte gerne eine einfache Fahrt / eine Rückfahrkarte nach ... .
– I would like to buy a flight/return flight to ...	– Ich möchte einen einfachen Flug / einen Rückflug nach ... kaufen.
– Do you want to fly business class or economy?	– Möchten Sie Business oder Economy fliegen?
– You are booked on flight ... on 6 June.	– Sie sind auf Flug ... am 6. Juni gebucht.
– Your flight departs at 7 a.m. and arrives at 9 a.m.	– Ihr Flug startet um 7 Uhr und landet um 9 Uhr.
– You should check in at least two hours before your flight.	– Sie sollten mindestens zwei Stunden vor Abflug einchecken.
– Please reserve me a window/an aisle seat on the 9.15 a.m. train to York.	– Bitte reservieren Sie mir einen Fensterplatz/ Gangplatz im Zug nach York um 9:15.
– Would you like a first-class or a second-class ticket?	– Möchten Sie eine Fahrkarte erster Klasse oder zweiter Klasse?

Useful phrases

Booking hotels or conference rooms

– I'd like to book a single/double room.	– Ich möchte ein Einzel-/Doppelzimmer buchen.
– I'd like to reserve a suite for two nights from 6 to 8 June.	– Ich möchte eine Suite für zwei Nächte vom 6. bis zum 8. Juni reservieren.
– Is breakfast included in the price?	– Ist Frühstück im Preis inbegriffen?
– We require a conference room for 25 people.	– Wir benötigen ein Tagungsraum für 25 Leute.
– Could you please send me confirmation of the booking?	– Könnten Sie mir bitte eine Buchungsbestätigung schicken?
– We regret to inform you that we have to cancel the booking.	– Leider müssen wir Ihnen mitteilen, dass wir die Buchung stornieren müssen.
– Is there a discount for …?	– Gibt es einen Rabatt für …
– I'd like to reserve a table for two at 7 p.m on the evening of 6 June.	– Ich möchte einen Tisch für zwei Personen um 19 Uhr am 6. Juni reservieren.

Recommending offers — Unit 9

– I would recommend ordering from … (supplier) because …	– Ich würde empfehlen, dass wir/Sie bei … (Lieferant) bestellen, weil …
– I/we recommend that we order from … (supplier) because …	– Ich/wir empfehle/empfehlen, dass wir bei … (Lieferant) bestellen, weil …
– If we order from…, we'll have to pay … (e.g. import duty and … / for transport from … to …)	– Wenn wir bei … (Lieferant) bestellen, müssen wir … (z. B. Einfuhrzoll und … / für den Transport von … nach …) bezahlen.
– As the price is quoted in … (currency, e.g. US dollars) … it might … (change/rise), so …	– Da der Preis in … (Währung, z. B. US-Dollar) ausgewiesen ist, könnte er (sich) noch … (ändern/steigen), daher …
– Despite … (e.g. the exchange rate risk, currency fluctuation, customs duties), I recommend …	– Trotz … (z. B. des Wechselkursrisikos, der Kursschwankungen, der Zollgebühren) empfehle ich …
– The … supplier's price is … (e.g. almost the same as, far / a lot / …% higher/lower than) the …'s price.	– Der Preis des …-Lieferanten ist (z. B. fast der gleiche wie, weit/viel/… % höher/niedriger als) beim …-Lieferanten.

Writing counter-offers — Unit 9

Reference to offer

– Many thanks for your email/offer for … dated …	– Vielen Dank für Ihre E-Mail / Ihr Angebot über … vom …
– Having seen your offer on the internet and spoken to you on the telephone …	– Nachdem wir Ihr Angebot im Internet gesehen und mit Ihnen telefoniert haben …
– We have seen your offer for … on the internet.	– Wir haben Ihr Angebot über … im Internet gesehen.

Changes requested

– We have checked the details of your offer …	– Wir haben die Einzelheiten Ihres Angebots geprüft …
– In view of the strong competition in this field …	– Angesichts der starken Konkurrenz auf diesem Gebiet …
– We will be in a position to place an order with your company.	– Wir sind in der Lage, Ihrem Unternehmen einen Auftrag zu erteilen.
– If you are willing to change your terms of delivery to …	– Wenn Sie bereit sind, Ihre Lieferbedingungen in … zu ändern.
– … and your terms of payment to ….	– … und Ihre Zahlungsbedingungen in …

Polite ending

– We hope that our suggestion(s) find your approval.	– *Wir hoffen, dass unser Vorschlag / unsere Vorschläge Ihre Zustimmung findet/finden.*
– … and look forward to hearing from you soon.	– *… und freuen uns auf Ihre baldige Antwort.*
– Please do not hesitate to contact us if you require further details.	– *Bitte zögern Sie nicht, uns zu kontaktieren, wenn Sie weitere Einzelheiten benötigen.*

Writing orders — Unit 9

Reference to offer

– Many thanks for your offer dated …	– *Vielen Dank für Ihr Angebot vom …*
– Having seen your offer on the internet and spoken to you on the telephone …	– *Nachdem wir Ihr Angebot im Internet gesehen und mit Ihnen telefoniert haben …*
– We have seen your offer for … on the internet.	– *Wir sind im Internet auf Ihr Angebot von … aufmerksam geworden.*

Details of goods/services ordered

– We now wish to place an order/a trial order for the following goods:	– *Wir möchten einen Auftrag/Probeauftrag über folgende Waren erteilen:*
– [*Headings*] Quantity/Description/Size/Article no.	– *[Überschriften] Menge/Beschreibung/Größe/Artikel-Nr.*

Price(s) and discount(s)

– [*Headings*] Unit price/List price/Catalogue price/Total	– *[Überschriften] Stückpreis/Listenpreis/Katalogpreis/Gesamt*
– Subtotal/Total price	– *Zwischensumme/Gesamtpreis*
– 19% VAT (value added tax)	– *19 % USt./MwSt. (Umsatzsteuer/Mehrwertsteuer)*

Delivery

– delivery date/period	– *Liefertermin/-zeit*
– within 10 days after receipt of order	– *innerhalb von 10 Tagen nach Auftragserhalt*
– by 30 June 20..	– *bis zum 30. Juni 20..*

Payment

– CWO	– *Barzahlung bei Auftragserteilung*
– 30% in advance, 70% after completion	– *30 % im Voraus, 70 % bei Fertigstellung*
– ⅓ with order, ⅓ on delivery, ⅓ within 30/60/90 days after delivery	– *⅓ bei Auftragserteilung, ⅓ bei Lieferung, ⅓ innerhalb von 30/60/90 Tagen nach Lieferung*
– by transfer to our a/c at … (bank)	– *per Überweisung auf unser Konto bei … (Geldinstitut)*
– by bank transfer	– *per Überweisung*
– 2% 10 days, 30 days net after receipt of invoice	– *2 % Skonto bei Zahlung innerhalb von 10 Tagen, netto bei Zahlung innerhalb von 30 Tagen nach Rechnungserhalt*

Acknowledgement/Advice of dispatch

– We look forward to receiving your advice of dispatch.	– *Wir freuen uns, Ihre Versandanzeige zu erhalten.*
– Please send us your confirmation of order and advice of dispatch in the near future.	– *Bitte schicken Sie uns Ihre Auftragsbestätigung und Versandanzeige in den nächsten Tagen zu.*

Polite ending

– We trust the goods will arrive punctually and in good condition …	– *Wir vertrauen darauf, dass die Ware pünktlich und in gutem Zustand ankommt …*
– … and will place further/regular orders if they sell well.	– *… und werden weitere/regelmäßige Aufträge erteilen, wenn sie sich gut verkauft.*

Advice of dispatch/delivery — Unit 9

Reference to goods ordered
- Many thanks for your order dated … for the above-mentioned … (goods).
- The goods will be collected by us this afternoon/this evening/tomorrow and flown/sent to … (location).
- We are pleased to confirm that the above-mentioned … (consignment/goods)
- … has/have now been sent to you by container.

Mode of transport
- The goods will be shipped by cross-Channel ferry from the Hook of Holland to Felixstowe …
- … and then delivered franco to your premises by road.
- The goods will be despatched to you on (Airline) Flight No. … on …
- … on (Airline) Flight No. … leaving Munich Airport at 10.00 am on June 15 … .
- They will be delivered to you by lorry

Terms of delivery
- Delivery will be made … (e.g. CIP Cologne-Bonn Airport on (Airline) Flight No. … /CIF Dover) franco to your premises/warehouse in … (location).
- The goods will be delivered … (Incoterms® rule, e.g. DPU, DDP) your warehouse/premises in … (location) on … (date).

Estimated time of arrival
- The goods are expected to reach your warehouse by the end of the month.
- in approx. 3 weeks' time

Packing
- The goods have been packed in sturdy cases (marked …).
- The goods have been packed in sturdy cartons with the usual marks.

Payment
- Please make payment by transferring the sum of … to our account no. … at … (name of bank) in … (location).
- As payment ⅓ with order, ⅓ on delivery and ⅓ within 30 days after delivery has been agreed, …
- Please transfer the second instalment of € … on receipt of the goods. The third and final instalment is due on …
- We have instructed our correspondent bank, the Midland Bank in Ipswich, to release the documents to you on payment/acceptance of our draft for € … .

- *Vielen Dank für Ihren Auftrag vom … für die oben genannte(n) … (Ware/-n).*
- *Wir werden die Ware heute Nachmittag/heute Abend/morgen abholen und dann nach … (Ort) fliegen (lassen)/schicken.*
- *Wir freuen uns zu bestätigen, dass die oben genannte(n) … (Lieferung/Güter) …*
- *… Ihnen jetzt per Container zugesandt worden ist/sind.*

- *Die Waren werden mit der Kanalfähre von Hook van Holland nach Felixstowe geschickt …*
- *… und dann per Straße frei Ihren Geschäftsräumen geliefert.*
- *Die Waren werden Ihnen mit dem (Fluggesellschaft) Flug Nr. … am … zugeschickt.*
- *… mit dem (Fluggesellschaft) Flug Nr. … ab Flughafen München um 10.00 Uhr am 15. Juni … .*
- *Sie werden Ihnen per Lkw geliefert.*

- *Die Lieferung erfolgt CIP Flughafen Köln-Bonn mit dem (Fluggesellschaft) Flug Nr. … /CIF Dover) frei Ihren Geschäftsräumen / Ihrem Lager in … (Ort).*
- *Die Waren werden am … (Datum) … (Incoterms®-Regel, z. B. DPU, DDP) Ihrem Lager / Ihren Geschäftsräumen in … (Ort) geliefert.*

- *Die Waren sollen bis Ende des Monats Ihr Lager erreichen.*
- *in ca. 3 Wochen*

- *Die Güter wurden in festen Kisten verpackt (mit der Markierung …).*
- *Die Ware wurde mit den üblichen Markierungen in festen Kartons verpackt.*

- *Wir bitten um Überweisung des Betrags von … auf unser Konto mit der Nr. … bei (Geldinstitut) in … (Ort).*
- *Da Zahlung ⅓ bei Auftragserteilung, ⅓ bei Lieferung, ⅓ innerhalb von 30/60/90 Tagen nach Lieferung vereinbart wurde, …*
- *Bitte überweisen Sie nach Erhalt der Ware die zweite Rate von … €. Die dritte und letzte Rate ist am … fällig.*
- *Wir haben unsere Korrespondenzbank, die Midland Bank in Ipswich, angewiesen, die Dokumente bei Zahlung / Akzept unseres Wechsels über … € an Sie herauszugeben.*

- The shipping documents for the documentary credit (air waybill, commercial invoice, packing list, insurance certificate) have now been handed over to our bankers and payment (of ... [amount]) has been received.

Polite ending
- We trust that the goods will arrive punctually and in good condition.
- We trust the consignment will arrive safely and on schedule and look forward to doing further business with you.
- ... and look forward to receiving further orders.

– *Die Versanddokumente für das Dokumentenakkreditiv (Luftfrachtbrief, Handelsrechnung, Packliste, Versicherungsschein) sind nun unserer Bank übergeben worden und die Zahlung (in Höhe von ... [Betrag]) ist erfolgt.*

– *Wir vertrauen darauf, dass die Ware pünktlich und in gutem Zustand ankommt.*
– *Wir vertrauen darauf, dass die Sendung sicher und gemäß Zeitplan ankommen wird, und freuen uns darauf, weitere Geschäfte mit Ihnen zu tätigen.*
– *... und freuen uns darauf, weitere Aufträge zu erhalten.*

Making/receiving complaints — Unit 10

Reference to goods
- The above-mentioned goods were delivered on ... and forwarded to our customers all over Germany/Europe.
- We regret to inform you that they/we are dissatisfied with them.

– *Die oben genannten Waren wurden am ... geliefert und unseren Kunden überall in Deutschland/Europa zugestellt.*
– *Leider müssen wir Ihnen mitteilen, dass sie/wir damit unzufrieden sind.*

Description of problem
- On examining the goods/When they opened the boxes, we/our customers discovered that ...
- ... some of the articles were missing
- ... some/all of the articles/appliances were dirty/discoloured/(badly) damaged.
- We enclose/attach photographs of these items for your information.
- We received the wrong consignment.
- We were wrongly charged for ...
- The delivery has not arrived.

– *Bei Prüfung der Ware / Beim Öffnen der Kartons, stellten wir / unsere Kunden fest, dass ...*
– *... einige der Artikel fehlten.*
– *... einige/alle Artikel/Geräte verschmutzt/verfärbt/(stark) beschädigt waren.*
– *Wir fügen zu Ihrer Information Fotos dieser Artikel bei.*
– *Wir haben die falsche Lieferung erhalten.*
– *Uns wurde(n) fälschlicherweise ... berechnet.*
– *Die Lieferung ist nicht erfolgt/angekommen.*

Request for explanation
- Please explain why our order was so poorly executed/how this could happen.
- We would welcome your explanation of the damage incurred during transit.
- Please explain why the goods have not been delivered.

– *Bitte erklären Sie, warum unser Auftrag so schlecht ausgeführt wurde / wie dies passieren konnte.*
– *Wir würden eine Erklärung (von Ihnen) für den während der Überfahrt/Überführung entstandenen Schaden begrüßen.*
– *Bitte erklären Sie (mir/uns), warum die Ware noch nicht geliefert wurde.*

Request for action
- We must therefore insist that you ...
- We must therefore ask you to ...
- ... deliver the consignment in the next 24 hours.

– *Wir müssen daher darauf bestehen, dass Sie ...*
– *Wir müssen Sie deshalb bitten, ...*
– *... die Lieferung innerhalb der nächsten 24 Stunden zu liefern.*

Polite ending
- We feel sure you will appreciate that ...
- ... our future business relationship will depend on how this matter is dealt with.

– *Sie werden sicherlich dafür Verständnis haben, dass ...*
– *... die Fortsetzung unserer Geschäftsbeziehung davon abhängt, wie diese Angelegenheit geregelt wird.*

Useful phrases

– We trust you will deal with this matter without delay.	– Wir vertrauen darauf, dass Sie sich unverzüglich mit dieser Angelegenheit befassen werden.
– We expect to hear from you in the very near future.	– Wir erwarten, recht bald von Ihnen zu hören.
– We look forward to receiving your comments on this matter without delay.	– Wir freuen uns auf Ihre unverzügliche Stellungnahme zu dieser Angelegenheit.

Responding to complaints — Unit 10

Acknowledgement of complaint
- We have (just) received your email/letter regarding the above-mentioned consignment of …
- Your complaint is now being investigated.

– Wir haben (soeben) Ihre E-Mail / Ihren Brief bezüglich der oben erwähnten Lieferung von … erhalten.
– Ihre Beschwerde wird jetzt geprüft.

First expression of regret
- We are sorry to hear the consignment was delayed and that some of the goods were damaged.
- … and are dismayed to hear that the consignment is unsatisfactory.

– Es tut uns leid zu hören, dass die Sendung verzögert eintraf und dass einige der Waren beschädigt waren.
– … und es tut uns (sehr) leid zu hören, dass die Lieferung unzufriedenstellend ist.

Action taken
- Since hearing from you,/receiving your email, …
- … we have contacted our subcontractor …
- … we have investigated the matter and discovered/found out that …
- … there was an error in our dispatch section.
- … the consignment was delivered to the wrong location.

– Nach Erhalt Ihrer Nachricht/E-Mail …
– haben wir unseren Subunternehmer kontaktiert.
– … haben wir die Angelegenheit untersucht und herausgefunden, dass …
– … es einen Fehler in unserer Versandsabteilung gab.
– … die Lieferung an den falschen Ort / die falsche Stelle geliefert wurde.

Solution
- The missing… (articles)/Replacements will be delivered to you carriage paid within 24/48 hours.
- The consignment will be delivered within 24 hours.
- We will compensate you for any additional costs incurred.

– Die fehlenden … (Artikel) / Ersatzgeräte werden Ihnen innerhalb 24/48 Stunden frachtfrei geliefert.
– Die Lieferung wird Ihnen innerhalb 24 Stunden geliefert.
– Wir werden Sie für alle zusätzlich anfallenden Kosten entschädigen.

Second apology
- Please accept our apologies for this.
- In the meantime, please accept our apologies for the inconvenience caused (which was due to circumstances beyond our control).
- We assure you it will not happen again.

– Wir entschuldigen uns vielmals.
– Bitte nehmen Sie unsere Entschuldigung für die Unannehmlichkeiten an (die durch Umstände außerhalb unserer Kontrolle verschuldet wurden).
– Wir versichern Ihnen, dass es nicht wieder vorkommen wird.

Polite ending
- We hope this suggestion/solution will find your approval.
- We look forward to doing further business with you.

– Wir hoffen, dass dieser Vorschlag / diese Lösung Ihre Zustimmung finden wird.
– Wir freuen uns darauf, weitere Geschäfte mit Ihnen zu tätigen.

Talking about reasons and outcomes — Unit 11

Giving reasons

– This innovation is going to help the company because …	– *Diese Innovation wird der Firma helfen, weil …*
– This idea will save money because …	– *Diese Idee spart Geld, weil …*
– This technology is good for the environment because …	– *Diese Technologie ist umweltfreundlich, weil …*
– I think it is a good/bad idea because …	– *Ich denke, es ist eine gute/schlechte Idee, weil …*
– The reason why it will work is …	– *Der Grund, warum es funktionieren wird, ist …*

Talking about outcomes

– This means … is a must.	– *Das heißt, dass … ein Muss ist.*
– In order to do this, we need to …	– *Um dies umzusetzen, brauchen wir …*
– In order for us to make this possible, …	– *Um dies möglich zu machen, … / Damit wir dies möglich machen können, …*
– By introducing this new plan, we will be able to …	– *Durch die Einführung dieses neuen Plans werden wir in der Lage sein, …*
– …, which means, there will be more …	– *…, was bedeutet, dass es mehr … geben wird.*
– This results in …	– *Daraus folgt, dass …*

Describing graphs and charts — Unit 11

– The graph/chart shows/presents …	– *Die Grafik/Das Diagramm zeigt … / stellt … dar.*
– The horizontal/vertical axis has a scale from … to …	– *Die horizontale/vertikale Achse hat eine Skala von … bis …*
– The x-axis/y-axis is divided into … units/sections each representing …	– *Die X-Achse/Y-Achse ist unterteilt in … Einheiten/Abschnitte, die jeweils … darstellen.*
– The number of … decreased slightly last month.	– *Die Zahl der … ging im letzten Monat leicht zurück.*
– The number of … jumped sharply in June.	– *Die Zahl der … stieg im Juni stark an.*
– They reached their peak in August, then levelled off.	– *Sie erreichten ihren Höhepunkt im August und pendelten sich dann ein.*
– … accounted for about/roughly/approximately one third of all … .	– *… machten etwa/annähernd/ungefähr ein Drittel aller … aus.*
– Deliveries to China made up just over/under one tenth of our business.	– *Lieferungen nach China machten etwas über/unter ein Zehntel unseres Geschäfts aus.*
– The biggest segment on the pie chart shows …	– *Das größte Stück im Kreisdiagramm zeigt …*
– The figures fluctuated at the beginning of the year.	– *Die Zahlen schwankten am Anfang des Jahres.*
– There was an increase / a decrease last year.	– *letztes Jahr gab es eine Steigerung / einen Rückgang.*
– Sales figures remained constant through 2018.	– *Die Verkaufszahlen blieben im Verlauf des Jahrs 2018 konstant.*
– The amount climbed steadily.	– *Die Menge stieg stetig an.*
– The figures dropped suddenly in June.	– *Die Zahlen sind in Juni plötzlich gefallen.*

Taking part in meetings — Unit 11

Starting the meeting
- Good morning everybody and welcome to …
- The first item on today's agenda is …

- Guten Morgen miteinander und willkommen zu …
- Der erste Punkt auf der heutigen Tagesordnung lautet …

Asking someone to speak
- Would you go ahead, please?
- Can you give us a brief update?

- Würden Sie / Würdest du bitte anfangen?
- Könnten Sie / Könntest du uns ein kurzes Update geben?

Asking for reactions
- Would anyone like to comment or ask a question?
- Are there any issues?

- Hat jemand dazu einen Kommentar abgeben oder eine Frage?
- Gibt es Fragen oder Probleme?

Asking for opinions
- What do you think about …?
- What's your opinion of/view on …?

- Wie denken Sie / denkst du über …?/Was hältst du / halten Sie von …?
- Wie ist deine/Ihre Meinung (dein/Ihr Standpunkt) zu …?

Expressing a point of view
- It seems to me (that) …
- In my opinion, …
- From what I can see, …

- Mir kommt es so vor, als ob …
- Meiner Meinung nach …
- Was ich hier sehe, ist … / Nach dem, was ich hier sehe, …

Asking to speak
- Could I just say that …?
- Can I come in on that?

- Darf ich (kurz) anmerken, dass …?
- Darf ich dazu etwas sagen?

Agreeing
- Yes, I agree.
- I thoroughly agree with … (name).

- Ja, ich stimme zu/ich bin (damit) einverstanden.
- Ich stimme … (Name) völlig/absolut zu.

Disagreeing politely
- (I'm afraid) I don't agree with … (name).

- Ich stimme ich … (Name) da (leider) nicht zu. / Ich kann … (Name) da (leider) nicht zustimmen.

- I agree up to a point, but …
- Actually,/In fact, I think (that) …

- Ich stimme bis zu einem gewissen Punk zu, aber …
- Eigentlich/Tatsächlich/Vielmehr denke ich, dass …

Starting a new topic
- Let's move on to the next topic, which is …
- The next point is …

- Lassen Sie uns / Lass uns mit dem nächsten Thema fortfahren, es ist …
- Der nächste Punkt ist …

Promising action
- I'll pass that on to …
- We'll get back to you.

- Ich werde das an … weiterleiten.
- Wir werden auf Sie/dich zurückkommen.

Finishing the meeting
- Let's wrap up the meeting with …
- Well, that would seem to be it.

- Lassen Sie uns / Lass uns das Meeting mit … zum Abschluss bringen.
- Gut, das war's/wär's dann.

Negotiating	**Unit 11**

Direct approach
- Are you prepared to …?
- Can you reduce the price by … (e.g. €20)?
- Will you increase … (e.g. production) by …?
- Are you able to guarantee … (e.g. delivery)?
- Do you accept these terms?

- *Sind Sie bereit, …?*
- *Können Sie den Preis um … (z. B. 20 €) reduzieren?*
- *Werden Sie … (z. B. die Produktion) um … steigern?*
- *Können Sie … (z. B. die Auslieferung) garantieren?*
- *Akzeptieren Sie diese Bedingungen?*

Indirect approach
- We need to talk about …
- … is a problem for us.
- … (e.g. our competitors) are …% cheaper.
- We're thinking of ordering more/less …
- We need a maximum/minimum of …
- How much more … can you produce?

- *Wir müssen über … sprechen.*
- *… ist ein Problem für uns.*
- *… (z. B. unsere Konkurrenz) ist/sind … % günstiger.*
- *Wir denken darüber nach, mehr/weniger … zu bestellen.*
- *Wir brauchen ein Maximum/Minimum von …*
- *Wie viel mehr … können Sie herstellen?*

Offering help
- We can help you with …
- We can give you … if you can …
- I suggest that you …

- *Wir können Ihnen mit … helfen.*
- *Wir können Ihnen … geben, wenn Sie … (können).*
- *Ich schlage vor, (dass) Sie …*

Accommodating changes to the offer
- I have some room to move.
- OK. I'm prepared to offer you that.
- Yes, I think we can do that for you.

- *Ich habe etwas Spielraum.*
- *In Ordnung. Das kann ich Ihnen gern anbieten.*
- *Ja, ich denke, dass wir das für Sie tun können.*

Refusing what the client asks for
- I'm sorry, but the price that I quoted you is the best I can do.
- No. I'm afraid I can't do that.
- Well, I can't offer you … . But what I can do is …

- *Es tut mir leid, aber der Preis, den ich Ihnen angeboten habe, ist nicht weiter verhandelbar.*
- *Nein, das kann ich leider nicht tun.*
- *Ich kann Ihnen kein/-e … anbieten. Ich kann (Ihnen) jedoch …*

Writing covering letters	**Unit 12**

Opening phrases
- With reference to your advertisement in … (newspaper) of … (date), …
- I would like / wish to apply for the above-mentioned position/post of … (job).

- *Bezugnehmend auf Ihre Annonce/Ausschreibung in … (Zeitung) vom … (Datum), …*
- *Hiermit möchte ich mich für die oben genannte Stelle als … (Berufsbezeichnung) bewerben.*

Education, training, present employment
- I attended … (school/college) for … (length of time).
- I studied … (subjects) at vocational school in … (place) from … (date) to … (date).
- At present I am working for a/an … (type of company) as a/an … (job).
- I will complete my period of training on … (date).

- *Von … bis … besuchte ich … (Schule/Hochschule).*
- *An der Berufs(fach)schule in … (Ort) lernte/belegte ich … (Fächer) von … (Datum) bis … (Datum).*
- *Zurzeit arbeite ich bei einem/einer … (Firmenbezeichnung) als … (Berufsbezeichnung).*
- *Am … (Datum) werde ich meine Ausbildung abschließen.*

Useful phrases

Closing paragraph

- I enclose/Enclosed is my CV (*BE*)/résumé (*AE*)/a list of my qualifications and experience.
- I am available for interview at your earliest convenience.
- I hope you will consider my application favourably and …
- … (I) look forward to hearing from you in the near future.

- *Anbei finden Sie meinen Lebenslauf / eine Übersicht meiner Qualifikationen und Erfahrungen.*
- *Für ein Vorstellungsgespräch stehe ich Ihnen jederzeit gern zur Verfügung.*
- *Über eine positive Antwort/Rückmeldung würde ich mich sehr freuen und …*
- *… (ich) freue mich darauf, bald von Ihnen zu hören.*

Thematic vocabulary

Training and apprenticeships — Unit 1

A levels	Abitur, Abiturfächer
apprentice	Auszubildende/r, Lehrling
apprenticeship	Lehre, Ausbildung
block release	Blockunterricht (an der Berufsschule)
certificate	Zeugnis, Diplom
course	Studiengang
coursework	schriftliche Arbeit(en)
day release	tageweise Freistellung zur beruflichen Weiterbildung
degree	Abschluss
diploma	Abschlusszeugnis
final grade	Abschlussnote
grade	Note
internship	Praktikum
job experience	Berufserfahrung, praktische Erfahrung
living expenses	Lebenshaltungskosten
part-time	Teilzeit
to qualify	einen/den Abschluss machen
qualification	Qualifikation, Abschluss
salary	Gehalt
school leaving certificate	Schulabschluss
school qualification	Schulabschluss
theoretical	theoretisch
to train (to be a …)	eine Ausbildung (zum/zur …) machen
trainee	Auszubildende/r
training company	Ausbildungsbetrieb
training course	Ausbildung
training supervisor	Ausbildungsleiter/in
vocational college/school	Berufsschule, Berufsfachschule
vocational training	Berufsausbildung
work experience	Praktikum
workplace	Arbeitsplatz

Job titles — Unit 2

accountant	Buchhalter/in
accounting manager	Buchhaltungsleiter/in
chief executive officer (CEO)	Vorstandsvorsitzende/r, Geschäftsführer/in
colleague	Kollege, Kollegin
commercial director	kaufmännische/r Leiter/in
employee	Arbeitnehmer/in, Beschäftigte/r
employer	Arbeitgeber/in, Unternehmer/in
factory manager	Betriebsleiter/in, Werksleiter/in
head of department	Abteilungsleiter/in
industrial management assistant	Industriekaufmann/-frau
IT management assistant	Informatikkaufmann/-frau
legal adviser	Justiziar/in
line manager	(direkte/r) Vorgesetzte/r
management assistant for freight forwarding and logistics	Kaufmann/-frau für Spedition und Logistikdienstleistung
manager	Manager/in
managing director	Geschäftsführer/in
office management assistant	Kaufmann/-frau für Büromanagement
personal assistant (PA)	Persönliche/r Assistent/in
production manager	Produktionsleiter/in
project manager	Projektleiter/in
purchasing director/manager	Einkaufsleiter/in
receptionist	Empfangsmitarbeiter/in
specialist	Fachmann/-frau
staff	Personal
technician	Techniker/in
warehouse manager	Lagerleiter/in

Company departments — Units 2–3

accounting / accounts (department)	Buchhaltung
administration	Verwaltung
board (of directors)	Geschäftsführung, Vorstand
department	Abteilung
distribution (department)	Vertrieb
finance (department)	Rechnungswesen
financial controlling (department)	Controlling
head office/headquarters	Zentrale
human resources (HR) (department)	Personal(abteilung)
labelling	Bezeichnung, Etikettierung
legal department	Rechtswesen
management	Geschäftsleitung, Geschäftsführung
manufacturing	Fertigung, Herstellung
material delivery	Materialanlieferung
press	Presse
pricing (department)	Kalkulation
project management	Projektleitung
quality assurance/management (department)	Qualitätssicherung
reception	Rezeption, Empfang
research and development (R&D) (department)	Forschung(s-) und Entwicklung(sabteilung)
warehouse	Lager(halle)

Company organization — Unit 3

(general) partnership	Personengesellschaft, offene Handelsgesellschaft (OHG)
limited company (Ltd) / closed corporation	Gesellschaft mit beschränkter Haftung (GmbH)
limited partnership	Kommanditgesellschaft (KG)
public limited company (plc) / open corporation	Aktiengesellschaft (AG)
share	Aktie
shareholder	Aktionär/in, Teilhaber/in
sole proprietor/trader	Einzelunternehmer/in

Thematic vocabulary

Packaging — Unit 4

antistatic bag	Antistatik-Beutel
bag	Tasche (groß); Beutel (klein)
barrel	Fass, Tonne
basket	Korb
bottle	Flasche
box	Kasten, Kiste, Schachtel
bubble wrap	Luftpolsterfolie
can, tin	Dose
canister	Kanister
carton	Karton
centre of gravity	Schwerpunkt
crate	Kiste
delicate	empfindlich
Do not stack.	Nicht belasten! Nicht stapeln!
drum	Tonne
dry goods	Trockengüter, Trockenware(n)
electronics	elektronische Geräte
external packaging	Außenverpackung
fragile	zerbrechlich
foam rubber	Schaumgummi, Moosgumi
handle with care	Vorsicht, zerbrechlich! Zerbrechliches Packgut!
handling marks	Handhabungskennzeichen, Versandzeichen
internal packaging	Innenverpackung
Keep dry.	Vor Nässe schützen!
Keep away from heat.	Vor Hitze schützen!
packet	Paket
pallet	Pallette
pallet cage	Gitterboxpallette
packing peanuts	Verpackungschips, Füllchips
perishable	verderblich
plastic film	Plastikfolie
polystyrene	Styropor
roll	Rolle
rubber	Gummi
sack	Sack
sea container	Seecontainer
This way up	Hier oben
tube	Tube
wood shavings	Holzspäne
wood wool (BE) / excelsior (AE)	Holzwolle
wooden box	Holzkiste

Warehouses — Unit 4

aisle	Gang
cold storage	Kühllager, Kühlhaus
conveyor belt	Förderband
crane	Kran
drive-through pallet rack	Durchfahrregal
floor storage	Bodenlager
forklift	Gabelstapler
high-bay shelving	Hochregallager
inbound goods	Wareneingang, eingehende Ware
labelling	Etikettierung, Etikettieren
loader	Belader/in
loading area	Ladefläche, Ladezone
outbound goods	Warenausgang, ausgehende Ware
pallet rack shelving	Palettenregal
pick and pack (picking area)	Kommissionierzone
picker	Komissionierer/in
receiver	Warenannehmer/in
shelving	Regallager
storage	Lagerung, Lager

Commercial correspondence — Unit 5

address	Adresse
addressee	Empfänger/in
to attach sth	anhängen
attachment	Anhang
attention (attn)	zu Händen
attention line	Zeile „zu Händen"
(Best) Regards	Viele Grüße, Mit freundlichen Grüßen
Best wishes	Mit freundlichen Grüßen
body	Haupttext
complimentary close	Schlussformel
date	Datum
Dear Sir or Madam	Sehr geehrte Damen und Herren,
to enclose	beifügen
enclosure (enc)	Anlage
inside address	Innenadresse
letterhead	Briefkopf
paragraph	Absatz
reference (ref)	Zeichen
registered mail/post	Einschreiben
salutation	Anrede
sender	Absender
signature block	Signatur
signature	Unterschrift
subject (line)	Betreff(zeile)
Yours faithfully	Mit freundlichen Grüßen
Yours sincerely	Mit freundlichen Grüßen

Business trips — Unit 7

accommodation	Unterkunft, Unterbringung
air-conditioned	klimatisiert
air conditioning	Klimaanlage, Klimatisierung
appointment	Termin
arrival	Ankunft
to attend sth	etw besuchen, an etw teilnehmen
to cancel	absagen, stornieren
to check in	sich anmelden, einchecken
to check out	sich abmelden, auschecken
conference centre	Tagungszentrum, Kongresszentrum
connecting flight	Anschlussflug
departure	Abreise, Abflug
dining room	Speisesaal
excess	Selbstbehalt
front desk	Rezeption
insurance cover	Versicherungsschutz

meeting room	Sitzungszimmer, Konferenzraum	rail consignment note	Bahnfrachtbrief
mileage	(enthaltene) Kilometer	receipt	Erhalt; Empfangsbescheinigung
one-way flight	einfacher Flug	shipping note (S/N)	Schiffszettel, Warenbegleitschein
passenger	Passagier/in	single administrative document	Einheitspapier
to postpone	verschieben		
reception	Empfang, Rezeption	waybill (WB)	Frachtbrief
receptionist	Empfangsmitarbeiter/in		
request	Bitte, Anfrage		
requirement	Anforderung		
reservation	Reservierung, Buchung		
return flight	Hin- und Rückflug		
shuttle	Zubringer		
smoke-free	rauchfrei		
trade fair	Messe		
travel expenses	Reisekosten, Reisespesen		

Trade fairs — Unit 10

booth	(Messe-)Stand
brochure	Broschüre, Prospekt
event	Veranstaltung
exhibition hall	Messehalle, Ausstellungshalle
fair	Messe
flyer	Faltblatt
giveaway	Werbegeschenk
to hand sth out	etw austeilen, etw ausgeben
loyalty card	Kundenkarte
sales literature	Verkaufsprospekte, Informationsmaterial
stand	(Messe-)Stand
trade fair	Fachmesse, Branchenmesse
venue	Veranstaltungsort

Shipping documents — Unit 9

advice of dispatch	Versandanzeige
air freight	Luftfracht
air waybill (AWB)	Luftfrachtbrief
approval: on approval	zur Ansicht, auf Probe
bill of lading (B/L)	Seefrachtbrief, Konnossement
bonded warehouse	Zollverschlusslager
cargo	Ladung, Fracht
cargo space	Frachtraum
certificate of origin (C/O)	Ursprungszeugnis
chamber of (industry and) commerce	(Industrie- und) Handelskammer
combined transport waybill	kombinierter Warenbegleitschein
commercial invoice	Handelsrechnung
consignment note [road or rail]	Frachtbrief [Straßen- oder Bahn-]
consignee	Empfänger/in
consignor	Absender/in, Versender/in
consular invoice	Konsularrechnung, Konsultatsfaktura
contract of carriage	Beförderungsvertrag
customs clearance	Zollabfertigung
customs declaration	Zollinhaltserklärung
customs invoice	Zollrechnung, Zollfaktura
dangerous goods certificate	Gefahrgutbescheinigung
delivery note	Lieferschein
destination; port of destination	Bestimmungsort; Bestimmungshafen
export licence	Exportlizenz
forwarder's certificate of receipt (FCR)	Spediteurübernahmebescheinigun
freight	Fracht
freight rates	Frachttarife
import licence	Einfuhrgenehmigung
to take out insurance	eine Versicherung abschließen
insurance certificate (IC)	Versicherungsschein, -police
to insure goods against a risk	Ware gegen ein Risiko versichern
to issue	ausstellen, ausfertigen
loss; total or partial loss	Verlust; Gesamt- oder Teilverlust
packing list	Packliste
pro forma invoice (P/I)	Proforma-Rechnung

Complaints — Unit 10

apology	Entschuldigung
to cancel sth	etw stornieren
compensation	Entschädigung
credit note	Gutschrift
damaged	beschädigt
dented	verbeult
dirty	verschmutzt
discoloured	verfärbt
discrepancy	Unstimmigkeit, Diskrepanz
dissatisfied	unzufrieden
delayed	verspätet
faulty	mangelhaft, defekt
free of charge	unentgeltlich, kostenlos
inconvenience	Unannehmlichkeiten
late	verspätet
mix-up	Durcheinander, Verwechselung
to overcharge sb	jdm zu viel berechnen
to query sth	etw infrage stellen, etw anzweifeln
to reimburse sb	jdm Geld zurückzahlen, jdm entschädigen
reimbursement	Rückerstattung
to remit	überweisen
to replace sth	etw ersetzen
replacement	Ersatz
to resolve sth	etw lösen
scratched	verkratzt
soiled	beschmutzt
statutory	gesetzlich vorgeschrieben
unsatisfactory	unzulänglich, unbefriedigend
warrenty period	Gewährleistungszeit

Thematic vocabulary

Describing graphs — Unit 11

bar chart	Säulendiagramm
chart	Diagramm
decrease	Abnahme, Rückgang
to decrease	abnehmen, zurückgehen
drastic(ally)	drastisch
drop	Fall, Rückgang
to drop	fallen, zurückgehen
figures	Zahlen
financial year	Geschäftsjahr
to flatten out	auf gleichem Stand bleiben
graph	Diagramm, Kurve
to hit a maximum	einen Höchstwert/-stand erreichen
increase	Zunahme, Anstieg
to increase	zunehmen, ansteigen
to level off	sich einpendeln
line graph	Liniendiagramm
minimum	Tiefstwert, Tiefstand
output	Produktion
pie chart	Tortendiagramm
quarter	Quartal
quarterly	vierteljährlich, Quartals-
to recover	sich erholen
to remain constant	gleich bleiben
to rise	steigen, ansteigen
sales figures	Umsatzzahlen, Verkaufszahlen
unit	Einheit, Stück
volume of sales	Umsatzvolumen
x-axis	X-Achse
y-axis	Y-Achse

Meetings — Unit 11

absence	Abwesenheit
absentee	Abwesende/r
agenda	Tagesordnung
any other business (AOB)	Verschiedenes
audience	Publikum
body language	Körpersprache
to call a meeting	eine Sitzung einberufen
to circulate sth	etw (an alle) verteilen
conference	Tagung, Konferenz
conference room	Besprechungsraum, Sitzungssaal
contact details	Kontaktdaten
to cover	(Thema) behandeln
date	Termin
eye contact	Blickkontakt
to face sb	sich jdm zuwenden, jdn anschauen
feedback	Reaktion(en), Rückmeldung(en)
gesture	Geste
to get a message across	eine Botschaft vermitteln
graphic	Grafik
handout	Arbeitsblatt, Broschüre
to highlight	hervorheben
index card	Karteikarte
invitation	Einladung
item on the agenda	Tagesordnungspunkt
minutes	Protokoll
to participate	teilnehmen
participant	Teilnehmer/in
to point to sth	auf etw deuten, auf etw zeigen
presenter	Redner/in, Vortragende/r, Moderator/in
prompt card	Moderationskarte
report	Bericht
to reserve	reservieren
screen	Leinwand, Bildschirm
slide	Folie
to take place	stattfinden
to take the chair / to be in the chair	die Sitzung leiten
talk/lecture	Vortrag
transparency	(Overhead-)Folie, Dia
to turn one's back on sb	jdm den Rücken zuwenden

1–12 Unit word list

Dieses Wörterverzeichnis enthält alle neuen Wörter aus *Logistics Matters 3rd Edition* in der Reihenfolge ihres Erscheinens (Seitenzahlen sind angegeben). Nicht angeführt sind die Wörter aus dem Grundwortschatz. Wörter aus den Hörverständnisübungen sind mit einem T (Transkript) und Wörter aus den *Partner files* mit einem P gekennzeichnet. Die Zahl am linken Rand gibt die Seitenzahl an.

Abkürzungen	AE = amerikanisches Englisch	jdm = jemandem	pl = plural noun
	BE = britisches Englisch	jdn = jemanden	sb = somebody
	etw = etwas	jds = jemandes	sth = something

UNIT 1

6	condition [kənˈdɪʃn]	Bedingung
	working conditions pl [ˌwɜːkɪŋ kənˈdɪʃnz]	Arbeitsbedingungen
	apprenticeship [əˈprentɪʃɪp]	Lehre, Ausbildung
	apprentice [əˈprentɪs]	Auszubildende/r, Lehrling
	logistics [ləˈdʒɪstɪks]	Logistik
	trainee [treɪˈniː]	Auszubildende/r, Lehrling
	section [ˈsekʃn]	Bereich, Abschnitt
	line manager [laɪn ˈmænɪdʒə]	(direkte/r) Vorgesetzte/r
	description [dɪˈskrɪpʃn]	Beschreibung, Darstellung
	similar (to sth) [ˈsɪmələ]	(einer Sache) ähnlich
	A levels pl [ˈeɪ levlz]	Abitur, Abiturfächer
	to train to be a … [ˈtreɪn tə bi ə]	eine Aubildung zum/zur … machen
	freight forwarding [ˈfreɪt fɔːwədɪŋ]	Spedition(swesen)
	management assistant for freight forwarding and logistics [ˌmænɪdʒmənt əsɪstənt fə ˌfreɪt fɔːwədɪŋ ənd ləˈdʒɪstɪks]	Kaufmann/-frau für Spedition und Logistikdienstleistung
	to last (for …) [lɑːst]	dauern
	block release [ˌblɒk rɪˈliːs]	Blockunterricht *(an der Berufsschule)*
	vocational school [vəʊˌkeɪʃənl ˈskuːl]	Berufsschule
	salary [ˈsæləri]	Gehalt
	expenses pl [ɪkˈspensɪz]	Kosten, Auslagen
	rent [rent]	Miete
	colleague [ˈkɒliːg]	Kollege/-in
	branch [brɑːntʃ]	Niederlassung, Filiale
	school qualification [ˌskuːl kwɒlɪfɪˈkeɪʃn]	Schulabschluss
	training company [ˈtreɪnɪŋ kʌmpəni]	Ausbildungsbetrieb
	details pl [ˈdiːteɪlz]	Einzelheiten, Angaben
	living expenses pl [ˈlɪvɪŋ ɪkspensɪz]	Lebenshaltungskosten
	hope [həʊp]	Hoffnung

T	forwarding agent [ˈfɔːwədɪŋ eɪdʒənt]	Spediteur/in, Kaufmann/-frau für Spedition und Logistikdienstleistung
	day release [ˈdeɪ rɪliːs]	tagweise Freistellung zur beruflichen Weiterbildung
	(training) course [kɔːs]	Ausbildung
	permanent [ˈpɜːmənənt]	unbefristet

	to qualify [ˈkwɒlɪfaɪ]	einen/den Abschluss machen
	to divide sth [dɪˈvaɪd]	etw aufteilen
7	to structure sth [ˈstrʌktʃə]	etw aufbauen, etw strukturieren
	to be located in … [bi ləʊˈkeɪtɪd ɪn]	in … sein/liegen
	dual education system [ˌdjuːəl edʒuˈkeɪʃn sɪstəm]	duale Ausbildung
	vocational training [vəʊˌkeɪʃənl ˈtreɪnɪŋ]	Berufsausbildung
	to enter a scheme [ˌentər ə ˈskiːm]	an einem Programm teilnehmen
	job experience [ˌdʒɒb ɪkˈspɪəriəns]	Berufserfahrung, praktische Erfahrung
	theoretical [θɪəˈretɪkl]	theoretisch, Theorie-
	knowledge [ˈnɒlɪdʒ]	Wissen, Kenntnisse
	profession [prəˈfeʃn]	Beruf
	depending on [dɪˈpendɪŋ ɒn]	je nach
	contract [ˈkɒntrækt]	Vertrag
	to protect sb/sth from sth [prəˈtekt frəm]	jdn/etw vor etw schützen
	to fire sb [ˈfaɪə]	jdn entlassen
	to gain sth [geɪn]	etw erlangen, etw erwerben, etw gewinnen
	standard [ˈstændəd]	Maßstab, Anforderung, Norm
	throughout … [θruːˈaʊt]	in ganz …
	degree [dɪˈgriː]	Abschluss
	to recognize sth [ˈrekəgnaɪz]	etw anerkennen
	even though [ˈiːvn ðəʊ]	auch wenn
	to train [treɪn]	eine Ausbildung machen
	position [pəˈzɪʃn]	Stelle, Stellung
	abroad [əˈbrɔːd]	im/ins Ausland

Unit word list

commerce	[ˈkɒmɜːs]	Handel, Wirtschaft
to split sth	[splɪt]	etw aufteilen
in-company	[ˌɪn ˈkʌmpəni]	betriebsintern
explanation	[ˌekspləˈneɪʃn]	Erläuterung
to be responsible for sth	[bi rɪˈspɒnsəbl fə]	für etw zuständig sein, für etw verantwortlich sein
to create sth	[kriˈeɪt]	etw entwerfen, etw erstellen
to brainstorm	[ˈbreɪnstɔːm]	Ideen sammeln
medium-sized	[ˈmiːdiəm saɪzd]	mittelgroß, mittelständisch
to subsidize	[ˈsʌbsɪdaɪz]	subventionieren, bezuschussen
overtime	[ˈəʊvətaɪm]	Überstunden
smart	[smɑːt]	(Kleidung:) elegant, schick
open-plan office	[ˌəʊpənplæn ˈɒfɪs]	Großraumbüro
flexitime	[ˈfleksitaɪm]	Gleitzeit
shift work	[ˈʃɪft wɜːk]	Schichtarbeit
company car	[ˈkʌmpəni kɑː]	Firmenwagen
dress code	[ˈdres kəʊd]	Kleiderordnung
to give reasons for sth	[ˌgɪv ˈriːznz fə]	etw begründen
to conduct sth	[kənˈdʌkt]	etw durchführen
survey	[ˈsɜːveɪ]	Umfrage
in my opinion	[ɪn maɪ əˈpɪnɪən]	meiner Meinung nach
to compare sth (to sth)	[kəmˈpeə]	etw (mit etw) vergleichen
individual	[ˌɪndɪˈvɪdʒuəl]	persönlich, individuell
current	[ˈkʌrənt]	aktuell, momentan
department	[dɪˈpɑːtmənt]	Abteilung
working hours pl	[ˌwɜːkɪŋ ˈaʊəz]	Arbeitszeit(en)
break	[breɪk]	Pause
business trip	[ˈbɪznəs trɪp]	Geschäftsreise
availability	[əˌveɪləˈbɪləti]	Verfügbarkeit
facilities pl	[fəˈsɪlətiz]	Einrichtungen, Anlage(n), Ausstattung
benefits pl	[ˈbenɪfɪts]	Zusatzleistungen, Sozialleistungen
job prospects pl	[ˈdʒɒb prɒspekts]	berufliche Perspektiven
monthly	[ˈmʌnθli]	monatlich
host	[həʊst]	(Talkshow-)Moderator/in
size	[saɪz]	Größe
warehousing	[ˈweəhaʊzɪŋ]	Lagerung, Lagerhaltung, Lagerwesen
to store sth	[stɔː]	etw lagern
to coordinate with sb	[kəʊˈɔːdɪneɪt wɪð]	sich mit jdm abstimmen
distribution	[ˌdɪstrɪˈbjuːʃn]	Vertrieb, Versand, Distribution
to clock in/out	[ˌklɒk ˈɪn/ˈaʊt]	ein-/ausstempeln
canteen	[kænˈtiːn]	Kantine
morning break	[ˈmɔːnɪŋ breɪk]	Frühstückspause
official(ly)	[əˈfɪʃl]	offiziell
to feel like sth	[ˈfiːl laɪk]	Lust auf etw haben
event	[ɪˈvent]	Veranstaltung
open house	[ˌəʊpən ˈhaʊs]	Tag der Offenen Tür
to clear up	[ˌklɪər ˈʌp]	aufräumen
in writing	[ɪn ˈraɪtɪŋ]	schriftlich, in Schriftform
quite	[kwaɪt]	ziemlich
strict	[strɪkt]	streng
staff	[stɑːf]	Mitarbeiter/innen, Personal
pretty	[ˈprɪti]	ziemlich
relaxed	[rɪˈlækst]	locker, entspannt
steel toe	[ˈstiːl təʊ]	Stahlkappe
reinforcement	[ˌriːɪnˈfɔːsmənt]	Verstärkung
safety vest	[ˈseɪfti vest]	Sicherheitsweste
hard hat	[ˌhɑːd ˈhæt]	Schutzhelm
customer service	[ˌkʌstəmə ˈsɜːvɪs]	Kundenbetreuung, Kundendienst
Czech Republic	[tʃek rɪˈpʌblɪk]	Tschechische Republik
text (message)	[tekst]	SMS
standby	[ˈstændbaɪ]	Bereitschaft
administration	[ədˌmɪnɪˈstreɪʃn]	Verwaltung
to log in	[ˌlɒg ˈɪn]	sich einloggen
drinks machine	[ˌdrɪŋks məˈʃiːn]	Getränkeautomat
ground floor	[ˌgraʊnd ˈflɔː]	Erdgeschoss
travel ticket	[ˈtrævl tɪkɪt]	Monatskarte, Jahreskarte (ÖPNV)
discount	[ˈdɪskaʊnt]	Rabatt, Skonto
nearby	[ˈnɪəbaɪ]	in der Nähe, nahegelegen
(retail) outlet	[ˈaʊtlet]	(Einzelhandels-)Geschäft
whether	[ˈweðə]	ob
to stay on	[ˌsteɪ ˈɒn]	bleiben, dableiben
job offer	[ˈdʒɒb ɒfə]	Stellenangebot
at least	[ət ˈliːst]	mindestens, zumindest
That's it.	[ðæts ˈɪt]	Das war's.
You're welcome.	[jɔː ˈwelkəm]	Bitte (sehr). Gern geschehen.
family business	[ˈfæməli bɪznəs]	Familienunternehmen
furniture	[ˈfɜːnɪtʃə]	Möbel
lunch break	[ˈlʌntʃ breɪk]	Mittagspause
delivery	[dɪˈlɪvəri]	Lieferung, Zustellung
deadline	[ˈdedlaɪn]	Frist, Fertigstellungstermin
to meet a deadline	[ˌmiːt ə ˈdedlaɪn]	eine Frist einhalten
to text sb	[tekst]	jdm eine SMS schicken
I don't mind.	[aɪ dəʊnt ˈmaɪnd]	Ich habe nichts dagegen.
Come to think of it …	[ˌkʌm tə ˈθɪŋk əv ɪt]	Wenn ich es mir recht/genau überlege …
at cost price	[ət ˌkɒst ˈpraɪs]	zum Selbstkostenpreis
offer	[ˈɒfə]	Angebot
to join sb	[dʒɔɪn]	(Radio-/TV-Sendung:) bei jdm zu Gast sein
It was my pleasure.	[ɪt wəz ˌmaɪ ˈpleʒə]	Es war mit ein Vergnügen. Gern geschehen.

9	to **look the part** [ˌlʊk ðə ˈpɑːt]	entsprechend *(rollengerecht)* aussehen		to **be pleased to do sth** [bi ˌpliːzd tə ˈduː]	sich freuen, etw zu tun, etw gern tun
	to **match sth to sth** [ˈmætʃ tə]	etw einer Sache zuordnen	T	**session** [ˈseʃn]	Unterrichtseinheit
	recommended [ˌrekəˈmendɪd]	empfohlen		**surprised** [səˈpraɪzd]	überrascht, erstaunt
				I'm afraid … [aɪm əˈfreɪd]	leider
	freight [freɪt]	Fracht, Frachtgut		to **take time off (work)** [teɪk ˌtaɪm ˈɒf]	sich frei nehmen
	transportation [ˌtrænspɔːˈteɪʃn]	Transport, Beförderung		**second to last** [ˌsekənd tə ˈlɑːst]	vorletzte/r/s
	package [ˈpækɪdʒ]	Paket		**vacation** AE [vəˈkeɪʃn]	Urlaub, Ferien
	package handling [ˈpækɪdʒ hændlɪŋ]	Stückguthandhabung, Pakethandling		**winner** [ˈwɪnə]	Sieger/in
	allowed [əˈlaʊd]	zulässig, erlaubt		**remaining** [rɪˈmeɪnɪŋ]	übrige/r/s
	casual [ˈkæʒuəl]	*(Kleidung:)* leger		**by the way** [ˌbaɪ ðə ˈweɪ]	übrigens
	suit [suːt]	Anzug; Kostüm		**unpaid** [ˌʌnˈpeɪd]	unbezahlt
	trouser suit [ˈtraʊzə suːt]	Hosenanzug		**per** [pə]	pro
	trainers *pl* [ˈtreɪnəz]	Turnschuhe, Sportschuhe		**working hour** [ˌwɜːkɪŋ ˈaʊə]	Arbeitsstunde
	to **tuck the shirt in** [tʌk ðə ʃɜːt ˈɪn]	das Hemd in die Hose stecken		**once again** [ˌwʌns əˈgen]	erneut
	blouse [blaʊz]	Bluse		to **sum up** [tə ˌsʌm ˈʌp]	zusammenfassend (gesagt)
	boots *pl* [buːts]	Stiefel		to **take a break** [ˌteɪk ə ˈbreɪk]	eine Pause machen
	loose [luːs]	*(Kleidung:)* weit			
	frayed [freɪd]	zerfranst		to **express sth** [ɪkˈspres]	etw äußern, etw ausdrücken
	dangling [ˈdæŋglɪŋ]	herabhängend, baumelnd		**obligation** [ˌɒblɪˈgeɪʃn]	Verpflichtung
	jewellery [ˈdʒuːəlri]	Schmuck		**profile** [ˈprəʊfaɪl]	Porträt, Profil
	high heels *pl* [ˌhaɪ ˈhiːlz]	hochhackige Schuhe	11	to **prepare for sth** [prɪˈpeə fə]	sich auf etw vorbereiten
	open-toe [ˌəʊpən təʊ]	zehenfrei		**career** [kəˈrɪə]	(berufliche) Laufbahn, Karriere
	closed-toe [ˈkləʊzd təʊ]	*(Schuh:)* geschlossen		**diploma** [dɪˈpləʊmə]	Abschlusszeugnis
	earring [ˈɪərɪŋ]	Ohrring		**associate's degree** [əˈsəʊʃiəts dɪgriː]	US-Berufsschulabschluss
	wedding ring [ˈwedɪŋ rɪŋ]	Ehering		**course** [kɔːs]	Studiengang
	medical alert badge [ˌmedɪkl əˈlɜːt bædʒ]	Notfallanhänger		**business administration** [ˈbɪznəs ədmɪnɪstreɪʃn]	Betriebswirtschaft
	ear buds *pl* [ˈɪə bʌdz]	In-Ear-Kopfhörer		**grade** [greɪd]	Note
	device [dɪˈvaɪs]	(elektronisches) Gerät		**final grade** [ˌfaɪnl ˈgreɪd]	Abschlussnote
	inappropriate [ˌɪnəˈprəʊpriət]	unangemessen		**coursework** [ˈkɔːswɜːk]	schriftliche Arbeit(en)
	clothing [ˈkləʊðɪŋ]	Kleidung		**internship** [ˈɪntɜːnʃɪp]	Praktikum
10	**attractive** [əˈtræktɪv]	reizvoll, attraktiv		**for free** [fə ˈfriː]	umsonst
	to **research sth** [rɪˈsɜːtʃ]	etw recherchieren		**folks** [fəʊks]	Leute; (AE) Eltern
	advantage [ədˈvɑːntɪdʒ]	Vorteil		**tuition fees** *pl* [tjuˈɪʃn fiːz]	Studiengebühren
	disadvantage [ˌdɪsədˈvɑːntɪdʒ]	Nachteil		**part-time** [ˌpɑːtˈtaɪm]	Teilzeit
	to **attend sth** [əˈtend]	an etw teilnehmen, etw besuchen		**convenience store** AE [kənˈviːniəns stɔː]	lang geöffneter Laden (oft mit Tankstelle), Mini-Markt
	presenter [prɪˈzentə]	Redner/in, Vortragende/r, Moderator/in		to **be in debt** [bi ɪn ˈdet]	Schulden haben, verschuldet sein
	diagram [ˈdaɪəgræm]	Grafik, Diagramm		to **graduate** [ˈgrædʒueɪt]	den Abschluss machen
	screen [skriːn]	Leinwand, Bildschirm		**goal** [gəʊl]	Ziel
	to **guess sth** [ges]	etw erraten		**procurement** [prəˈkjʊəmənt]	Beschaffung, Einkauf
	Austria [ˈɒstriə]	Österreich		**specialist** [ˈspeʃəlɪst]	Fachmann/-frau, Experte/-in
	Greece [griːs]	Griechenland		to **get into debt** [ˌget ɪntə ˈdet]	sich verschulden
	national holiday [ˌnæʃnəl ˈhɒlədeɪ]	landesweiter Feiertag		to **earn sth** [ɜːn]	etw verdienen
	annual leave [ˌænjuəl ˈliːv]	Jahresurlaub		**intermediate** [ˌɪntəˈmiːdiət]	mittlere/r/s
	productivity [ˌprɒdʌkˈtɪvəti]	Produktivität		**assessor** [əˈsesə]	Betreuer/in, Gutachter/in
	ranking [ˈræŋkɪŋ]	Einstufung, Bewertung		to **upload** [ˌʌpˈləʊd]	hochladen
	trainer [ˈtreɪnə]	Ausbilder/in		**portfolio** [pɔːtˈfəʊliəʊ]	Arbeitsmappe
	order [ˈɔːdə]	Reihenfolge			

Unit word list

	fee [fiː]	Gebühr
	limit [ˈlɪmɪt]	Beschränkung, Begrenzung
	final examination [ˌfaɪnl ɪgzæmɪˈneɪʃn]	Abschlussprüfung
	report [rɪˈpɔːt]	Gutachten, Bericht
	advanced [ədˈvɑːnst]	fortgeschritten, weiterführend
	to improve sth [ɪmˈpruːv]	etw verbessern
	long-term [ˌlɒŋˈtɜːm]	langfristig
	administrator [ədˈmɪnɪstreɪtə]	Leiter/in, Manager/in
	introductions pl [ˌɪntrəˈdʌkʃnz]	Bekanntmachen, Vorstellen
	academic [ˌækəˈdemɪk]	akademisch, schulisch, Schul-, universitär, Universitäts-
	qualification [ˌkwɒlɪfɪˈkeɪʃn]	Abschluss, Qualifikation
	finance [ˈfaɪnæns]	Finanz(en)
	assessment [əˈsesmənt]	Beurteilung, Bewertung, Einschätzung, Urteil
	to discover sth [dɪˈskʌvə]	etw entdecken, etw feststellen
	industrialized country [ɪnˌdʌstriəlaɪzd ˈkʌntri]	Industrieland, -staat
	to vary [ˈveəri]	variieren, sich unterscheiden
	pros and cons pl [ˌprəʊz ənd ˈkɒnz]	Argumente dafür und dagegen, Vor- und Nachteile
	practical [ˈpræktɪkl]	praktisch, Praxis-
	e.g. [ˌiː ˈdʒiː]	z. B.
	board [bɔːd]	(Wand-)Tafel
12	to look after sb/sth [lʊk ˈɑːftə]	sich um jdn/etw kümmern
	supervisor [ˈsuːpəvaɪzə]	Vorgesetzte/r, Chef/in
	Human Resources (HR) [ˌhjuːmən rɪˈsɔːsɪz]	Personal(abteilung)
	to store sth [stɔː]	etw (Daten usw.) speichern
	computerized [kəmˈpjuːtəraɪzd]	elektronisch, Computer-
	personnel [ˌpɜːsəˈnel]	Personal, Mitarbeiter/innen
	personnel file [ˌpɜːsəˈnel faɪl]	Personalakte
	to introduce sb/oneself to sb [ˌɪntrəˈdjuːs tə]	jdn/sich jdm vorstellen
	entry [ˈentri]	Eintrag
	place of birth [ˌpleɪs əv ˈbɜːθ]	Geburtsort
	job description [ˈdʒɒb dɪskrɪpʃn]	Stellenbeschreibung
	training supervisor [ˈtreɪnɪŋ ˌsuːpəvaɪzə]	Ausbildungsleiter/in
	Syria [ˈsɪriə]	Syrien
	Turkey [ˈtɜːki]	Türkei
T	Poland [ˈpəʊlənd]	Polen
	product manager [ˌprɒdʌkt ˈmænɪdʒə]	Produktmanger/in
	management assistant for office communications [ˈmænɪdʒmənt əˌsɪstənt fər ˈɒfɪs kəmjuːnɪˈkeɪʃnz]	Kaufmann/-frau für Bürokommunikation
	software developer [ˈsɒftweə dɪveləpə]	Software-Entwickler/in
13	formal(ly) [ˈfɔːml]	formell, förmlich
	suitable [ˈsuːtəbl]	geeignet, passend
	to avoid sth [əˈvɔɪd]	etw vermeiden, etw umgehen
	illness [ˈɪlnəs]	Krankheit
	politics [ˈpɒlətɪks]	Politik
	journey [ˈdʒɜːni]	Fahrt, Anreise
	meeting place [ˈmiːtɪŋ pleɪs]	Treffpunkt
	pay [peɪ]	Bezahlung, Gehalt
	response [rɪˈspɒns]	Antwort, Reaktion
	to be based in … [bɪ ˈbeɪst ɪn]	seinen Sitz in … haben, in … sein
	fantastic [fænˈtæstɪk]	phantastisch, toll
	to be lucky [bɪ ˈlʌki]	Glück haben
	view [vjuː]	Aussicht, Blick
	in fact [ɪn ˈfækt]	genau genommen, tatsächlich, eigentlich
	to be called [bɪ ˈkɔːld]	heißen
	Excuse me. [ɪkˈskjuːz miː]	Verzeihung. Entschuldigung.
	to hold sb up [ˌhəʊld ˈʌp]	jdn aufhalten
	coat [kəʊt]	Jacke, Mantel
	to keep sb waiting [kiːp ˈweɪtɪŋ]	jdn warten lassen
	refreshment [rɪˈfreʃmənt]	Erfrischung(sgetränk)

UNIT 2

14	workplace [ˈwɜːkpleɪs]	Arbeitsplatz
	inventory [ˈɪnvəntri]	Bestandsliste
	equipment [ɪˈkwɪpmənt]	Geräte, Ausstattung, Ausrüstung
	to enjoy doing sth [ɪnˈdʒɔɪ]	etw gern tun
	to key sth in [ˌkiː ˈɪn]	etw (am Computer) eingeben
	data pl [ˈdeɪtə]	Daten
	likes and dislikes pl [ˌlaɪks ən ˈdɪslaɪks]	Vorlieben und Abneigungen
	photocopy [ˈfəʊtəʊkɒpi]	Fotokopie
15	consultant [kənˈsʌltənt]	Berater/in
T	efficient(ly) [ɪˈfɪʃnt]	effizient
	purpose [ˈpɜːpəs]	Zweck, Absicht
	environment [ɪnˈvaɪrənmənt]	Umgebung, Umfeld
	to support sb/sth [səˈpɔːt]	jdn/etw unterstützen
	generally [ˈdʒenrəli]	normalerweise, im Allgemeinen
	public [ˈpʌblɪk]	öffentlich
	building [ˈbɪldɪŋ]	Gebäude
	corridor [ˈkɒrɪdɔː]	Flur, Gang
	benefit [ˈbenɪfɪt]	Vorteil, Nutzen
	to focus on sth [ˈfəʊkəs ɒn]	sich auf etw konzentrieren
	to concentrate (on sth) [ˈkɒnsntreɪt]	sich (auf etw) konzentrieren
	to interrupt [ˌɪntəˈrʌpt]	unterbrechen, stören

in contrast (to sth) [ɪn ˈkɒntrɑːst]	im Gegensatz (dazu/zu etw)	management [ˈmænɪdʒmənt]	Geschäftsleitung, Geschäftsführung
to set sth up [ˌset ˈʌp]	etw einrichten, etw planen, etw aufbauen	head of department [ˌhed əv dɪˈpɑːtmənt]	Abteilungsleiter/in
cubicle [ˈkjuːbɪkl]	Kabuff, Arbeitsplatz (im Großraumbüro)	sub-department [ˈsʌb dɪpɑːtmənt]	Unterabteilung
set-up [ˈsetʌp]	Anordnung, Einrichtung, System	CEO (Chief Executive Officer) [ˌsiː iː ˈəʊ]	Vorstandsvorsitzende/r, Geschäftsführer/in
to hide sth [haɪd]	etw verbergen	secretary [ˈsekrətri]	Sekretär/in
partition [pɑːˈtɪʃn]	Trennwand	accounts (department) [əˈkaʊnts]	Buchhaltung
to get on with one's work [ˌget ˌɒn wɪð wʌnz ˈwɜːk]	seine Arbeit machen	sales (department) [seɪlz]	Verkauf(sabteilung)
noisy [ˈnɔɪzi]	laut	legal department [ˌliːgl dɪˈpɑːtmənt]	Rechtsabteilung
to share sth [ʃeə]	sich etw teilen, etw gemeinsam nutzen	operations (department) [ˌɒpəˈreɪʃnz]	Betrieb(-sabteilung)
to support sb/sth [səˈpɔːt]	jdn/etw fördern	route planning [ˈruːt plænɪŋ]	Routenplanung
sense of community [ˌsens əv kəˈmjuːnəti]	Gemeinschaftssinn	groupage freight [ˈgruːpɪdʒ freɪt]	Sammelgut
to communicate [kəˈmjuːnɪkeɪt]	kommunizieren	consolidated freight [kənˈsɒlɪdeɪtɪd freɪt]	Sammelgut
to be attached to sth [bi əˈtætʃt tə]	mit etw verbunden sein	customs [ˈkʌstəmz]	Zoll
to clear a space [klɪər ə ˈspeɪs]	einen Platz räumen	air freight [ˈeə freɪt]	Luftfracht
neat and tidy [ˌniːt ən ˈtaɪdi]	sauber und ordentlich	sea freight [ˈsiː freɪt]	Seefracht
		rail freight [ˈreɪl freɪt]	Bahnfracht
downside [ˈdaʊnsaɪd]	Nachteil, Schattenseite	road freight [ˈrəʊd freɪt]	Straßenfracht
to put your personal mark on sth [pʊt jɔː ˌpɜːsnl ˈmɑːk ɒn]	einer Sache seinen persönlichen Stempel aufdrücken	warehouse [ˈweəhaʊs]	Lager
		stock management [ˌstɒk ˈmænɪdʒmənt]	Bestandsführung, Lagerverwaltung
to result in sth [rɪˈzʌlt ɪn]	zu etw führen, etw ergeben	packaging [ˈpækɪdʒɪŋ]	Verpackung
to lack sth [læk]	etw nicht haben	pallet [ˈpælət]	Palette
warmth [wɔːmθ]	Wärme	invoice [ˈɪnvɔɪs]	Rechnung
personality [ˌpɜːsəˈnæləti]	Persönlichkeit	client [ˈklaɪənt]	Kunde/Kundin
uninviting [ˌʌnɪnˈvaɪtɪŋ]	wenig einladend	to keep track of sth [ˌkiːp ˈtræk əv]	den Überblick über etw behalten
shared [ʃeəd]	gemeinsam	bookkeeping [ˈbʊkkiːpɪŋ]	Buchhaltung, Buchführung
to depend on sth [dɪˈpend ɒn]	von etw abhängen, auf etw ankommen	to take care of sth [ˌteɪk ˈkeər əv]	sich um etw kümmern, etw bearbeiten, etw erledigen
to feel comfortable [ˌfiːl ˈkʌmftəbl]	sich wohlfühlen	goods pl [gʊdz]	Ware(n), Güter
		to ship sth [ʃɪp]	etw versenden, etw verschicken
according to [əˈkɔːdɪŋ tə]	gemäß, entsprechend, zufolge	to arrange (for) sth [əˈreɪndʒ]	etw veranlassen, etw organisieren, etw planen
to dislike sth [dɪsˈlaɪk]	etw nicht mögen, etw nicht leiden können	transport [ˈtrænspɔːt]	Transport, Beförderung, Verkehr
airy [ˈeəri]	luftig	lorry BE [ˈlɒri]	Lastwagen
spacious [ˈspeɪʃəs]	geräumig	to deal with sth [ˈdiːl wɪð]	sich um etw kümmern, sich mit etw befassen
to identify [aɪˈdentɪfaɪ]	identifizieren, bestimmen	customer [ˈkʌstəmə]	Kunde/Kundin
to handle sth with care [ˌhændl wɪð ˈkeə]	etw mit Vorsicht behandeln	order [ˈɔːdə]	Auftrag, Bestellung
move [muːv]	Umzug	complaint [kəmˈpleɪnt]	Reklamation, Beschwerde
to be in order [bi ɪn ˈɔːdə]	in Ordnung sein	to deliver sth [dɪˈlɪvə]	etw zustellen, etw liefern
premises pl [ˈpremɪsɪz]	Geschäftsräume, Betriebsgelände	to employ sb [ɪmˈplɔɪ]	jdn einstellen, jdn beschäftigen
sheet (of paper) [ʃiːt]	Blatt (Papier)	to train sb [treɪn]	jdn schulen, jdn ausbilden
title [ˈtaɪtl]	Titel, Überschrift	17 statement [ˈsteɪtmənt]	Aussage
tally list [ˈtæli lɪst]	Abhakliste, Strichliste	true [truː]	zutreffend, richtig
16 organization chart [ˌɔːgənaɪˈzeɪʃn tʃɑːt]	Organigramm	false [fɔːls]	unzutreffend, falsch
to draw [drɔː]	zeichnen	to be in charge of sth [bi ɪn ˈtʃɑːdʒ əv]	für etw zuständig sein, für etw verantwortlich sein

Unit word list

to **coordinate** sth [kəʊˈɔːdɪneɪt]	etw miteinander abstimmen, etw koordinieren
to **be involved in** sth [bɪ ɪnˈvɒlvd ɪn]	mit etw zu tun haben
consignment [kənˈsaɪnmənt]	Sendung, Lieferung
aeroplane [ˈeərəpleɪn]	Flugzeug
paperwork [ˈpeɪpəwɜːk]	Formalitäten, Unterlagen, Papierkram
to **import** sth [ɪmˈpɔːt]	etw einführen, etw importieren
to **export** sth [ɪkˈspɔːt]	etw ausführen, etw exportieren
advertising [ˈædvətaɪzɪŋ]	Werbung
to **report to** sb [rɪˈpɔːt tə]	jdm unterstehen

T
smooth(ly) [smuːð]	reibungslos
responsibility [rɪˌspɒnsəˈbɪləti]	Aufgabe, Zuständigkeit, Verantwortlichkeit, Verantwortung
to **include** sth [ɪnˈkluːd]	etw umfassen, etw einschließen, etw beinhalten
appropriate(ly) [əˈprəʊpriət]	angemessen, passend
form of transport [ˌfɔːm əf ˈtrænspɔːt]	Transportart
to **consolidate** sth [kənˈsɒlɪdeɪt]	etw zusammenfassen, etw konsolidieren
to **make sure** [ˌmeɪk ˈʃʊə]	sicherstellen, gewährleisten, dafür sorgen
schedule [ˈʃedjuːl]	Zeitplan
on schedule [ɒn ˈʃedjuːl]	planmäßig, termingerecht, pünktlich
to **run advertising** [ˌrʌn ˈædvətaɪzɪŋ]	Werbung schalten
trade fair [ˈtreɪd feə]	Fachmesse, Branchenmesse
potential [pəˈtenʃl]	möglich, potenziell
stand [stænd]	(Messe-)Stand
to **supervise** sth [ˈsuːpəvaɪz]	etw überwachen, etw beaufsichtigen, etw kontrollieren
budget [ˈbʌdʒɪt]	Etat, Budget
to **entail** sth [ɪnˈteɪl]	etw mit sich bringen
to **analyze** [ˈænəlaɪz]	analysieren
sales figures pl [ˈseɪlz fɪɡəz]	Umsatzzahlen, Verkaufszahlen
profit margin [ˈprɒfɪt mɑːdʒɪn]	Gewinnspanne
to **report** sth **to** sb [rɪˈpɔːt tə]	jdm etw melden
area [ˈeəriə]	Bereich, Gebiet
to **put** [pʊt]	formulieren, sagen
to **put it simply** [tə ˌpʊt ɪt ˈsɪmpli]	vereinfacht gesagt
to **involve** sth [ɪnˈvɒlv]	etw beinhalten, etw umfassen
to **transport** sth [trænˈspɔːt]	etw befördern, etw transportieren
to **track** sth [træk]	etw verfolgen, etw nachverfolgen
incoming [ˈɪnkʌmɪŋ]	eingehend
outgoing [ˈaʊtɡəʊɪŋ]	ausgehend

shipment [ˈʃɪpmənt]	Sendung
various [ˈveəriəs]	verschiedene
customs office [ˌkʌstəmz ˈɒfɪs]	Zollamt, Zollstelle
task [tɑːsk]	Aufgabe
to **run** sth [rʌn]	etw leiten
Scandinavia [ˌskændɪˈneɪviə]	Skandinavien

18
job profile [ˈdʒɒb prəʊfaɪl]	Stellenprofil
(freight) forwarder [ˈfɔːwədə]	Spediteur, Spedition
work experience [ˈwɜːk ɪkspɪəriəns]	Praktikum
file [faɪl]	Akte
to **determine** sth [dɪˈtɜːmɪn]	etw festlegen, etw bestimmen
item [ˈaɪtəm]	Artikel
to **handle** sth [ˈhændl]	etw bearbeiten, etw erledigen
documentation [ˌdɒkjumenˈteɪʃn]	Papiere, Unterlagen, Dokumente, Dokumentation
special request [ˌspeʃl rɪˈkwest]	Sonderwunsch
market research [ˌmɑːkɪt rɪˈsɜːtʃ]	Marktforschung
enquiry [ɪnˈkwaɪəri]	Anfrage
to **acquire** sb [əˈkwaɪə]	jdn akquirieren
campaign [kæmˈpeɪn]	(Werbe-)Kampagne
payment [ˈpeɪmənt]	Zahlung
receipt [rɪˈsiːt]	Beleg, Quittung, Empfangsbestätigung
to **recruit** [rɪˈkruːt]	(Personal) einstellen
to **promote** sb [prəˈməʊt]	jdn befördern
financial report [faɪˌnænʃl rɪˈpɔːt]	Finanzbericht

19
extract [ˈekstrækt]	Auszug, Ausschnitt
recording [rɪˈkɔːdɪŋ]	Aufzeichnung, Aufnahme
financial data pl [faɪˌnænʃl ˈdeɪtə]	Finanzdaten
to **prepare** sth [prɪˈpeə]	etw ausarbeiten, etw erstellen
regulations pl [ˌreɡjuˈleɪʃnz]	Vorschriften
process [ˈprəʊses]	Verfahren, Ablauf, Prozess

T
state laws pl [ˌsteɪt ˈlɔːz]	Landesgesetze
federal laws pl [ˌfedərəl ˈlɔːz]	Bundesgesetze
legal requirements pl [ˌliːɡl rɪˈkwaɪəmənts]	gesetzliche Bestimmungen, rechtliche Vorgaben
in-house [ˌɪn ˈhaʊs]	betriebsintern
work-related [ˈwɜːk rɪleɪtɪd]	arbeitsbezogen
to **prepare** sth [prɪˈpeə]	etw vorbereiten
safety [ˈseɪfti]	Sicherheit
scheduling [ˈʃedjuːlɪŋ]	Disposition, Terminplanung
even [ˈiːvn]	sogar
freight movement [ˈfreɪt muːvmənt]	Güterbewegung, Transport

market	[ˈmɑːkɪt]	Markt
trade magazine	[ˈtreɪd mægəziːn]	Fachzeitschrift
to oversee sth	[ˌəʊvəˈsiː]	etw überwachen, etw beaufsichtigen
via	[ˈvaɪə]	per
to expand sth	[ɪkˈspænd]	etw ausweiten, etw erweitern
to miss sth	[mɪs]	etw übersehen
customer service representative	[ˌkʌstəmə ˌsɜːvɪs ˌreprɪˈzentətɪv]	Kundenberater/in, Kundenbetreuer/in
accounting manager	[əˈkaʊntɪŋ mænɪdʒə]	Buchhaltungsleiter/in
to pay attention to sth	[ˌpeɪ əˈtenʃn tə]	auf etw achten
to meet sb's needs	[ˌmiːt ˈniːdz]	jds Anforderungen erfüllen, jds Bedürfnissen entsprechen
involving sb	[ɪnˈvɒlvɪŋ]	mit jdm
Norwegian	[nɔːˈwiːdʒən]	norwegisch
perishables pl	[ˈperɪʃəblz]	verderbliche Güter
to work closely with sb	[ˌwɜːk ˈkləʊsli wɪð]	eng mit jdm zusammenarbeiten
daily operations pl	[ˌdeɪli ɒpəˈreɪʃnz]	Tagesgeschäft
overall	[ˌəʊvərˈɔːl]	Gesamt-
in good time	[ɪn ˌɡʊd ˈtaɪm]	rechtzeitig
manpower	[ˈmænpaʊə]	Arbeitskräfte
to be one's turn	[bi wʌnz ˈtɜːn]	an der Reihe sein
flow chart	[ˈfləʊ tʃɑːt]	Flussdiagramm
to name sth	[neɪm]	etw nennen, etw benennen
blackboard	[ˈblækbɔːd]	Wandtafel
20 work placement BE	[ˈwɜːk pleɪsmənt]	Praktikum
subsidiary	[səbˈsɪdiəri]	Niederlassung
trucking	[ˈtrʌkɪŋ]	Lkw-Transport, Spedition
to leave a message	[ˌliːv ə ˈmesɪdʒ]	eine Nachricht hinterlassen
voicemail	[ˈvɔɪsmeɪl]	Mailbox
engineering	[ˌendʒɪˈnɪərɪŋ]	Technik, Maschinenbau
to call back	[ˌkɔːl ˈbæk]	zurückrufen
on behalf of sb	[ɒn bɪˈhɑːf əv]	für jdn, in jds Namen
as follows	[əz ˈfɒləʊz]	wie folgt
to confirm sth	[kənˈfɜːm]	etw bestätigen
generator	[ˈdʒenəreɪtə]	Generator
factory manager	[ˈfæktəri mænɪdʒə]	Betriebsleiter/in, Werksleiter/in
factory	[ˈfæktəri]	Fabrik, Werk
mobile BE	[ˈməʊbaɪl]	Handy, Mobiltelefon
to pass sth on	[ˌpɑːs ˈɒn]	etw weiterleiten
caller	[ˈkɔːlə]	Anrufer/in
to take delivery of sth	[ˌteɪk dɪˈlɪvəri əv]	etw in Empfang nehmen
to take a (phone) call	[ˌteɪk ə ˈkɔːl]	ein Gespräch entgegennehmen

T	to work	[wɜːk]	funktionieren
	for now	[fə ˈnaʊ]	einstweilen
	frequent(ly)	[ˈfriːkwənt]	häufig
	expression	[ɪkˈspreʃn]	Ausdruck
T	Speaking.	[ˈspiːkɪŋ]	(Telefon:) Am Apparat.
	line	[laɪn]	Leitung
	to hold the line	[ˌhəʊld ðə ˈlaɪn]	(Telefon:) am Apparat bleiben
	engaged	[ɪnˈɡeɪdʒd]	(Telefon:) besetzt
	case	[keɪs]	Fall
	personal assistant	[ˌpɜːsənl əˈsɪstənt]	persönliche/r Assistent/in
	to connect	[kəˈnekt]	verbinden
	to be unavailable	[bi ˌʌnəˈveɪləbl]	(Telefon:) nicht zu sprechen sein
	to be out of luck	[bi ˌaʊt əv ˈlʌk]	kein Glück (mehr) haben
	to put sb through	[ˌpʊt ˈθruː]	(Telefon:) jdn durchstellen
	to get through to sb	[ˌɡet ˈθruː tə]	zum jdm durchkommen
	urgent(ly)	[ˈɜːdʒənt]	dringend
	to spell	[spel]	buchstabieren
	first name	[ˈfɜːst neɪm]	Vorname
	surname	[ˈsɜːneɪm]	Nachname
	to catch sth	[kætʃ]	etw verstehen, etw mitbekommen
	to be missing	[bi ˈmɪsɪŋ]	fehlen
21	digit	[ˈdɪdʒɪt]	Ziffer
	separate(ly)	[ˈseprət]	einzeln, separat
	except for	[ɪkˈsept fə]	außer
	instruction	[ɪnˈstrʌkʃn]	Anweisung
	steel	[stiːl]	Stahl
	to improvise	[ˈɪmprəvaɪz]	improvisieren
	to be available	[bi əˈveɪləbl]	(Telefon:) zu sprechen sein
	to include sth (in sth)	[ɪnˈkluːd]	etw (in etw) aufnehmen

UNIT 3

24	business partner	[ˈbɪznəs pɑːtnə]	Geschäftspartner/in
	timeline	[ˈtaɪmlaɪn]	Zeitachse, Zeitschiene
	to surf the internet	[ˌsɜːf ði ˈɪntənet]	im Internet surfen
	opposite	[ˈɒpəzɪt]	gegenüber
	founder	[ˈfaʊndə]	Gründer/in
	worth	[wɜːθ]	wert
	to own sth	[əʊn]	etw besitzen
	the road to success	[ðə ˌrəʊd tə sʌkˈses]	der Weg zum Erfolg
	to take an opportunity	[ˌteɪk ən ɒpəˈtjuːnəti]	eine Chance nutzen
	garage	[ˈɡærɑːʒ]	Autowerkstatt
	truck	[trʌk]	Lastwagen, Lkw
	to lie ahead (of sb)	[ˌlaɪ əˈhed]	vor jdm liegen, (jdm) bevorstehen

Unit word list

to run into problems	[ˌrʌn ɪntə ˈprɒbləmz]	Probleme bekommen
to go out of business	[gəʊ ˌaʊt əv ˈbɪznəs]	das Geschäft aufgeben, zumachen
papermill	[ˈpeɪpəmɪl]	Papierfabrik
service	[ˈsɜːvɪs]	Dienst, Dienstleistung
to sign	[saɪn]	unterzeichnen
to collect sth	[kəˈlekt]	etw abholen
wastepaper	[ˈweɪstpeɪpə]	Altpapier
bale	[beɪl]	Ballen
mill	[mɪl]	Fabrik, Werk
to paint sth	[peɪnt]	etw lackieren
proud(ly)	[praʊd]	stolz
to expand	[ɪkˈspænd]	expandieren
private limited company (Ltd)	[ˌpraɪvət ˌlɪmɪtɪd ˈkʌmpəni]	Gesellschaft mit beschränkter Haftung (GmbH)
to join a company	[ˌdʒɔɪn ə ˈkʌmpəni]	in ein Unternehmen eintreten, zu einem Unternehmen kommen
to turn sth into sth	[ˈtɜːn ɪntə]	etw zu etw machen, etw in etw umwandeln
haulage company	[ˈhɔːlɪdʒ kʌmpəni]	(Straßen-)Spedition(sfirma), Frachtfuhrunternehmen
to approach sb	[əˈprəʊtʃ]	an jdn herantreten, auf jdn zukommen
to struggle	[ˈstrʌgl]	in Schwierigkeiten stecken, zu kämpfen haben
due to	[ˈdjuː tə]	aufgrund von, wegen
fuel crisis	[ˈfjuːəl kraɪsɪs]	Ölkrise
to hit sth	[hɪt]	etw (schwer) treffen
profit	[ˈprɒfɪt]	Gewinn, Profit
to merge	[mɜːdʒ]	fusionieren
to come to an agreement	[ˌkʌm tu ən əˈgriːmənt]	handelseinig werden
merger	[ˈmɜːdʒə]	Fusion
supply chain	[səˈplaɪ tʃeɪn]	Lieferkette, Versorgungskette
major	[ˈmeɪdʒə]	groß, bedeutend, wichtig
public limited company (plc)	[ˌpʌblɪk ˌlɪmɪtɪd ˈkʌmpəni]	Aktiengesellschaft (AG)
share	[ʃeə]	Aktie
stock market	[ˈstɒk mɑːkɪt]	Aktienmarkt
multimodal	[ˌmʌlti ˈməʊdl]	multimodal
to deal with sb/sth	[ˈdiːl wɪð]	mit jdm/etw zu tun haben
road haulage	[ˈrəʊd hɔːlɪdʒ]	Güterkraftverkehr, Straßentransport
deep sea transport	[diːp ˌsiː ˈtrænspɔːt]	Hochseeschifffahrt
inland waterway transport	[ˌɪnlænd ˈwɔːtəweɪ trænspɔːt]	Binnenschifffahrt
Netherlands	[ˈneðələndz]	Niederlande
to diversify	[daɪˈvɜːsɪfaɪ]	sich diversifizieren
slight(ly)	[slaɪt]	geringfügig, etwas
in recent years	[ɪn ˈriːsnt jɪəz]	in den letzten Jahren
overnight	[ˌəʊvəˈnaɪt]	über Nacht
parcel delivery	[ˈpɑːsl dɪlɪvəri]	Paketzustellung
to guarantee sth	[ˌgærənˈtiː]	etw garantieren
to found sth	[faʊnd]	etw gründen
agency	[ˈeɪdʒənsi]	Agentur
perfect addition	[ˌpɜːfɪkt əˈdɪʃn]	optimale Ergänzung
to mention sth	[ˈmenʃn]	etw erwähnen, etw nennen
limited liability company (LLC) AE	[ˌlɪmɪtɪd ˌlaɪəˈbɪləti kʌmpəni]	Gesellschaft mit beschränkter Haftung (GmbH)
to belong to sb	[bɪˈlɒŋ tə]	jdm gehören
closed	[kləʊzd]	geschlossen
circle	[ˈsɜːkl]	Kreis
to invest	[ɪnˈvest]	investieren
Corporation (Corp/Inc) AE	[ˌkɔːpəˈreɪʃn]	Aktiengesellschaft (AG)
shareholder	[ˈʃeəhəʊldə]	Aktionär/in
public	[ˈpʌblɪk]	Öffentlichkeit
member of the public	[ˌmembər əv ðə ˈpʌblɪk]	Privatperson, Einzelperson
director	[dəˈrektə]	Vorstand
to be regulated under EU laws	[bi ˌregjuleɪtɪd ʌndər ˌiː juː ˈlɔːz]	EU-Recht unterliegen
to operate	[ˈɒpəreɪt]	geschäftlich tätig sein
bankruptcy	[ˈbæŋkrʌpsi]	Konkurs
serious	[ˈsɪəriəs]	ernst, schwer, groß, erheblich
risk	[rɪsk]	Gefahr, Risiko
to go bankrupt	[gəʊ ˈbæŋkrʌpt]	Pleite gehen
visual(ly)	[ˈvɪʒuəl]	visuell
element	[ˈelɪmənt]	Bestandteil, Element
to bear sth	[beə]	etw (Risiko, Kosten) tragen
to collect sth	[kəˈlekt]	etw sammeln
to sketch sth out	[sketʃ ˈaʊt]	etw (vor)zeichnen
graphic	[ˈgræfɪk]	Grafik
appealing	[əˈpiːlɪŋ]	ansprechend
gallery walk	[ˈgæləri wɔːk]	Galerierundgang
clarity	[ˈklærəti]	Klarheit, Deutlichkeit
to get a message across	[get ə ˌmesɪdʒ əˈkrɒs]	eine Botschaft vermitteln
to show sb around	[ʃəʊ əˈraʊnd]	jdn herumführen, jdm (etw) zeigen
guided tour	[ˌgaɪdɪd ˈtʊə]	Führung
layout	[ˈleɪaʊt]	Grundriss, Anordnung, Plan
labelling	[ˈleɪblɪŋ]	Bezeichnung, Etikettierung
conference room	[ˈkɒnfərəns ruːm]	Besprechungsraum
works council	[ˌwɜːks ˈkaʊnsl]	Betriebsrat
stairs pl	[steəz]	Treppe, Treppenhaus
entrance	[ˈentrəns]	Eingang
tour	[tʊə]	Rundgang
to join sth	[dʒɔɪn]	sich einer Sache anschließen, bei etw mitmachen

starting point ['stɑːtɪŋ pɔɪnt]	Ausgangspunkt
finishing point ['fɪnɪʃɪŋ pɔɪnt]	Endpunkt

T

managing director [ˌmænɪdʒɪŋ dəˈrektə]	Geschäftsführer/in
guide [gaɪd]	Führer/in
this way [ˈðɪs weɪ]	hier entlang
to be delighted [bɪ dɪˈlaɪtɪd]	sich sehr freuen, (hoch) erfreut sein
sb enjoys sth [ɪnˈdʒɔɪz]	jdm gefällt etw, jd genießt etw
stay [steɪ]	Aufenthalt
kind [kaɪnd]	freundlich, nett
invitation [ˌɪnvɪˈteɪʃn]	Einladung
connection [kəˈnekʃn]	Kontakt, Verbindung
to turn sth round [ˌtɜːn ˈraʊnd]	etw (Unternehmen usw.) wieder auf Kurs bringen, etw sanieren
to provide sb with sth [prəˈvaɪd wɪð]	jdm etw bieten, jdn mit etw versorgen
to be glad (to do sth) [bɪ ˈglæd]	sich freuen(, etw zu tun)
brief [briːf]	kurz, knapp
overview [ˈəʊvəvjuː]	Überblick
downstairs [ˌdaʊnˈsteəz]	(nach) unten
distribution centre [dɪstrɪˈbjuːʃn sentə]	Vertriebszentrale, Distributionszentrum
gentleman [ˈdʒentlmən]	Herr
straight ahead [ˌstreɪt əˈhed]	geradeaus
lorry bay BE [ˈlɒri beɪ]	Ladebucht
to pull in [ˌpʊl ˈɪn]	einfahren, heranfahren
to distribute sth [dɪˈstrɪbjuːt]	etw vertreiben, etw versenden
both … and [ˌbəʊθ ənd]	sowohl … als auch
lift BE [lɪft]	Aufzug, Fahrstuhl
to take a left/right [ˌteɪk ə ˈleft/ˈraɪt]	links/rechts abbiegen
deputy [ˈdepjəti]	Stellvertreter/in
showroom [ˈʃəʊruːm]	Ausstellungsraum, Verkaufsraum
stop [stɒp]	Station, Halt
to conclude sth [kənˈkluːd]	etw beschließen, etw beenden
to feel free to do sth [fiːl friː tə ˈduː]	etw ruhig tun, gern etw tun können
lady [ˈleɪdi]	Dame
to store sth [stɔː]	etw aufbewahren
to load sth [ləʊd]	etw verladen
barge [bɑːdʒ]	Lastkahn
port [pɔːt]	Hafen
destination [ˌdestɪˈneɪʃn]	Zielort, Bestimmungsort
to work alongside sb [ˌwɜːk əˈlɒŋsaɪd]	mit jdm arbeiten
to follow a procedure [ˌfɒləʊ ə prəˈsiːdʒə]	sich an eine Vorgehensweise halten
upstairs [ˌʌpˈsteəz]	(nach) oben
to see sth through [ˌsiː ˈθruː]	etw (Projekt) durchgehend betreuen

elevator AE [ˈelɪveɪtə]	Aufzug, Fahrstuhl

27

to give directions [ˌgɪv dəˈrekʃnz]	den Weg beschreiben, den Weg erklären
escalator [ˈeskəleɪtə]	Rolltreppe
polite(ly) [pəˈlaɪt]	höflich
including [ɪnˈkluːdɪŋ]	mit, einschließlich
representative [ˌreprɪˈzentətɪv]	Vertreter/in
to label sth [ˈleɪbl]	etw bezeichnen, etw etikettieren
to cover sth [ˈkʌvə]	etw (Thema) behandeln

28

slide [slaɪd]	(Präsentation:) Folie
heading [ˈhedɪŋ]	Überschrift, Rubrik
high-rise warehouse [ˌhaɪ raɪz ˈweəhaʊs]	Hochregallager
turnover [ˈtɜːnəʊvə]	Umsatz
approximately (approx.) [əˈprɒksɪmətli]	ungefähr, zirka
market share [ˌmɑːkɪt ˈʃeə]	Marktanteil
goods on hold [ˌgʊdz ɒn ˈhəʊld]	Sperrlager
storage [ˈstɔːrɪdʒ]	Lagerung, Lager

T

agenda [əˈdʒendə]	Programm, Tagesordnung
folder [ˈfəʊldə]	Mappe, Ordner
background [ˈbækgraʊnd]	Hintergrund
statistics [stəˈtɪstɪks]	Statistik(en)
to be happy to do sth [bɪ ˈhæpi tə duː]	etw gern tun
workforce [ˈwɜːkfɔːs]	Belegschaft, Arbeitskräfte
to be capable of sth [bɪ ˈkeɪpəbl əv]	zu etw in der Lage sein
manual [ˈmænjuəl]	händisch, von Hand bedient
forklift (truck) [ˈfɔːklɪft ˈtrʌk]	Gabelstapler
to place sth [pleɪs]	etw platzieren, etw setzen
on the other hand [ɒn ði ˈʌðə hænd]	andererseits
fully automatic [ˌfʊli ɔːtəˈmætɪk]	vollautomatisch
to contain sth [kənˈteɪn]	etw enthalten
in transit [ɪn ˈtrænzɪt]	unterwegs, auf dem Transportweg
to release sth [rɪˈliːs]	etw freigeben
not … yet [nɒt ˈjet]	noch nicht
to clear a payment [ˌklɪər ə ˈpeɪmənt]	eine Zahlung freigeben, eine Zahlung abrechnen
therefore [ˈðeəfɔː]	daher, folglich
to pride onself on sth [ˈpraɪd ʌnself ɒn]	auf etw (besonders) stolz sein
personal touch [ˌpɜːsənl ˈtʌtʃ]	persönliche Note

repeated [rɪˈpiːtɪd]	wiederholt

29

to receive sth [rɪˈsiːv]	etw bekommen, etw erhalten
handout [ˈhændaʊt]	Arbeitsblatt, Broschüre
to guide [gaɪd]	leiten, führen
audience [ˈɔːdiəns]	Publikum
visuals pl [ˈvɪʒuəlz]	visuelle Hilfsmittel
to deal with sb/sth [ˈdiːl wɪð]	mit jdm/etw umgehen, sich mit jdm/etw befassen

	conclusion [kənˈkluːʒn]	Schluss
	aid [eɪd]	Hilfsmittel
	colourful [ˈkʌləfl]	bunt, farbenfroh
	illustrated [ˈɪləstreɪtɪd]	bebildert, illustriert
	transparency [trænsˈpærənsi]	(Overhead-)Folie, Dia
30	contents [ˈkɒntents]	Inhalt
	introduction [ˌɪntrəˈdʌkʃn]	Einleitung
	structure [ˈstrʌktʃə]	Aufbau, Struktur
	signpost [ˈsaɪnpəʊst]	orientierender Hinweis in einer Präsentation
	to summarize sth [ˈsʌməraɪz]	etw zusammenfassen
	to invite sth [ɪnˈvaɪt]	zu etw auffordern, um etw bitten
	correctness [kəˈrektnəs]	Richtigkeit
	spelling [ˈspelɪŋ]	Rechtschreibung
	prompt card [ˈprɒmt kɑːd]	Moderationskarte
	to come across [ˌkʌm əˈkrɒs]	wirken
	either [ˈaɪðə]	beide/s, eine/r/s (von zweien)
	to highlight [ˈhaɪlaɪt]	hervorheben
	index card [ˈɪndeks kɑːd]	Karteikarte
31	to divide sth into sth [dɪˈvaɪd ɪntə]	etw in etw unterteilen/ aufteilen
	to face sb [feɪs]	sich jdm zuwenden, jdn anschauen
	visual aids pl [ˈvɪʒuəl eɪdz]	visuelle Hilfsmittel
	to overload sth [ˌəʊvəˈləʊd]	etw überladen
	to hand over to sb [ˌhænd ˈəʊvə tə]	an jdn übergeben
	attire [əˈtaɪə]	Kleidung
	gesture [ˈdʒestʃə]	Geste
	body language [ˈbɒdi læŋgwɪdʒ]	Körpersprache
	contact details pl [ˈkɒntækt diːteɪlz]	Kontaktdaten
	business card [ˈbɪznəs kɑːd]	(geschäftliche) Visitenkarte
	eye contact [ˈaɪ kɒntækt]	Blickkontakt
	to turn one's back on sb [ˌtɜːn wʌnz ˈbæk ɒn]	jdm den Rücken zuwenden
	to point to sth [ˈpɔɪnt tə]	auf etw deuten, auf etw zeigen
	key word [ˈkiː wɜːd]	Stichwort
	feedback [ˈfiːdbæk]	Reaktion(en), Rückmeldung(en)
	improvement (to sth) [ɪmˈpruːvmənt]	Verbesserung (von/an etw)
	to support sth [səˈpɔːt]	etw (Argumentation) untermauern
	manner [ˈmænə]	Art (und Weise)
	overall score [ˌəʊvərˌɔːl ˈskɔː]	Gesamtpunktzahl

UNIT 4

32	to specialize in sth [ˈspeʃəlaɪz ɪn]	sich auf etw spezialisieren
	food logistics [ˈfuːd lədʒɪstɪks]	Lebensmittellogistik
	to hire sb [ˈhaɪə]	jdn beauftragen, jdn engagieren
	to grow the customer base [ˌgrəʊ ðə ˈkʌstəmə beɪs]	den Kundenstamm ausbauen/erweitern
	to emphasize sth [ˈemfəsaɪz]	etw betonen, etw herausstellen
	manufacturer [ˌmænjuˈfæktʃərə]	Hersteller/in, Produzent/in
	processing plant [ˈprəʊsesɪŋ plɑːnt]	Aufbereitungsanlage, Verarbeitungsanlage
	raw materials pl [ˌrɔː məˈtɪəriəlz]	Rohstoffe, Rohmaterial(ien)
	retailer [ˈriːteɪlə]	Einzelhändler/in
	wholesaler [ˈhəʊlseɪlə]	Großhändler/in
	gluten-free [ˈgluːtn friː]	glutenfrei
	bakery [ˈbeɪkəri]	Bäckerei
	organic [ɔːˈgænɪk]	Bio-
	soya mill [ˈsɔɪə mɪl]	Sojamühle
	aspect [ˈæspekt]	Seite, Gesichtspunkt, Aspekt
	in order to [ɪn ˈɔːdə tə]	um ... zu
	profitable [ˈprɒfɪtəbl]	rentabel, wirtschaftlich, gewinnbringend
	to outsource sth [ˈaʊtsɔːs]	etw auslagern
	range of services [ˌreɪndʒ əf ˈsɜːvɪsɪz]	Dienstleistungsangebot
33	condition [kənˈdɪʃn]	Zustand
	quantity [ˈkwɒntəti]	Menge
	amount (of sth) [əˈmaʊnt]	Menge (an etw)
	precise [prɪˈsaɪs]	genau
	damaged [ˈdæmɪdʒd]	beschädigt
	to specify sth [ˈspesɪfaɪ]	etw (genau) angeben
	affordable [əˈfɔːdəbl]	erschwinglich
	to advertise sth [ˈædvətaɪz]	etw bewerben, für etw Werbung machen
	excerpt [ˈeksɜːpt]	Auszug, Ausschnitt
	humidity [hjuːˈmɪdəti]	Feuchtigkeit
	convenient(ly) [kənˈviːniənt]	praktisch, (verkehrs)günstig
	strategic(ally) [strəˈtiːdʒɪk]	strategisch
	approach (to sth) [əˈprəʊtʃ]	Herangehensweise (an etw), Konzept (für etw)
	to minimize sth [ˈmɪnɪmaɪz]	etw minimieren
	waste [weɪst]	Abfall
	damage [ˈdæmɪdʒ]	Beschädigung(en), Schaden, Schäden
	improper [ɪmˈprɒpə]	unsachgemäß
	excellence [ˈeksələns]	Spitzenleistungen
	to ensure sth [ɪnˈʃʊə]	etw sicherstellen, etw gewährleisten
	on time [ɒn ˈtaɪm]	pünktlich
	in addition to sth [ɪn əˈdɪʃn tə]	zusätzlich zu etw
	bonus [ˈbəʊnəs]	zusätzlicher Vorteil

perishable items *pl* [ˌperɪʃəbl ˈaɪtəmz]	verderbliche Waren	inexpensive [ˌɪnɪkˈspensɪv]	preiswert, kostengünstig, billig
speedy [ˈspiːdi]	schnell, zügig	internal packaging [ɪnˌtɜːnl ˈpækɪdʒɪŋ]	Innenverpackung
reverse logistics [rɪˌvɜːs ləˈdʒɪstɪks]	Rücknahmelogistik	delicate [ˈdelɪkət]	empfindlich
recall [ˈriːkɔːl]	Rücknahme, Rückruf	plant [plɑːnt]	Pflanze
to recall sth [rɪˈkɔːl]	etw *(Produkt)* zurückrufen	fresh [freʃ]	frisch
to reenter the supply chain [rɪˈentə ðə səˈplaɪ tʃeɪn]	wieder in die Lieferkette gelangen	fragile [ˈfrædʒaɪl]	zerbrechlich
		light bulb [ˈlaɪt bʌlb]	Glühbirne
		meat [miːt]	Fleisch
accidentally [ˌæksɪˈdentəli]	versehentlich	dry goods *pl* [ˈdraɪ gʊdz]	Trockengüter, Trockenware(n)
flow of goods [ˌfləʊ əv ˈgʊdz]	Warenfluss	flour [ˈflaʊə]	Mehl
		electronics *pl* [ˌɪlekˈtrɒnɪks]	elektronische Geräte
flow of information [ˌfləʊ əv ɪnfəˈmeɪʃn]	Informationsfluss		
		35 handling marks *pl* [ˈhændlɪŋ mɑːks]	Handhabungskennzeichen, Versandzeichen
on-demand delivery [ɒn dɪˌmɑːnd dɪˈlɪvəri]	bedarfsgerechte Lieferung, Lieferung auf Abruf	to mark sth [mɑːk]	etw kennzeichnen
How so? [ˌhaʊ ˈsəʊ]	Inwiefern?	limitation [ˌlɪmɪˈteɪʃn]	Begrenzung, Beschränkung, Unter-/Obergrenze
to be scheduled for delivery [bi ˌʃedjuːld fə dɪˈlɪvəri]	(zu einem bestimmten Zeitpunkt) geliefert werden (sollen)	temperature limitations *pl* [ˈtemprətʃə lɪmɪteɪʃnz]	zulässiger Temperaturbereich
sequence [ˈsiːkwəns]	Folge, Abfolge, Reihenfolge	This way up [ˌðɪs ˌweɪ ˈʌp]	Hier oben
assembly [əˈsembli]	Montage	centre of gravity [ˌsentər əv ˈgrævəti]	Schwerpunkt
assembly line [əˈsembli laɪn]	Montagelinie, -kette, -band	Keep dry. [ˌkiːp ˈdraɪ]	Vor Nässe schützen!
34 labelling [ˈleɪblɪŋ]	Etikettierung, Etikettieren	Keep away from heat. [kiːp əˈweɪ frəm ˈhiːt]	Vor Hitze schützen!
to familiarize onself with sth [fəˈmɪliəraɪz wʌnself wɪð]	sich mit etw vertraut machen, sich in etw einarbeiten	to handle sth [ˈhændl]	etw handhaben, etw behandeln
to package sth [ˈpækɪdʒ]	etw verpacken	Handle with care. [ˌhændl wɪð ˈkeə]	Vorsicht, zerbrechlich! Zerbrechliches Packgut!
secure(ly) [sɪˈkjʊə]	sicher, fest	Do not stack. [duː nɒ ˈstæk]	Nicht belasten! Nicht stapeln!
external packaging [ɪkˌstɜːnl ˈpækɪdʒɪŋ]	Außenverpackung	type of goods [ˌtaɪp əv ˈgʊdz]	Warenart
antistatic bag [æntiˌstætɪk ˈbæg]	Antistatik-Beutel	advice [ədˈvaɪs]	Rat, Ratschlag, Ratschläge, Empfehlung(en)
canister [ˈkænɪstə]	Kanister	sculpture [ˈskʌlptʃə]	Skulptur
cardboard [ˈkɑːdbɔːd]	Pappe	film set [ˈfɪlm set]	Filmkulisse
coil [kɔɪl]	Rolle, Spule	to hold sth in place [ˌhəʊld ɪn ˈpleɪs]	etw halten, etw fixieren
crate [kreɪt]	Transportkiste		
drum [drʌm]	Trommel	transit [ˈtrænzɪt]	Transport
pallet cage [ˈpælət keɪdʒ]	Gitterboxpalette	proper(ly) [ˈprɒpə]	sachgemäß, richtig
wooden box [ˌwʊdn ˈbɒks]	Holzkiste	**T** to suggest sth [səˈdʒest]	etw vorschlagen
packing peanuts *pl* [ˈpækɪŋ piːnʌts]	Verpackungschips, Füllchips	surface area [ˈsɜːfɪs eəriə]	Oberfläche
bubble wrap [ˈbʌbl ræp]	Luftpolsterfolie	protection [prəˈtekʃn]	Schutz
polystyrene [ˌpɒliˈstaɪriːn]	Styropor	to weigh [weɪ]	wiegen
plastic film [ˌplæstɪk ˈfɪlm]	Plastikfolie	to surround sth with sth [səˈraʊnd wɪð]	etw mit etw umgeben
rubber [ˈrʌbə]	Gummi		
foam rubber [ˌfəʊm ˈrʌbə]	Schaumgummi, Moosgummi	packing material [ˌpækɪŋ məˈtɪəriəl]	Verpackungsmaterial
cold chain [ˈkəʊld tʃeɪn]	Kühlkette	cut-out [ˈkʌtaʊt]	Aussparung
wood wool *BE* [ˈwʊd wʊl]	Holzwolle	to fit [fɪt]	passen
excelsior *AE* [ekˈselsɪə]	Holzwolle	sth fits sth [fɪts]	etw passt ein etw hinein
container [kənˈteɪnə]	Behälter	base [beɪs]	Fuß, Sockel
bubble [ˈbʌbl]	Blase	if I were you [ɪf ˌaɪ wə ˈjuː]	an Ihrer Stelle
stiff [stɪf]	steif, starr, fest		
foam [fəʊm]	Schaum	security [sɪˈkjʊərəti]	Sicherheit
continuous [kənˈtɪnjuəs]	endlos	to double box sth [ˈdʌbl bɒks]	etw zweifach in einer Kiste verpacken
wood shavings *pl* [ˈwʊd ʃeɪvɪŋz]	Hobelspäne		

Unit word list

to **condense** [kən'dens]	sich niederschlagen, kondensieren	
to **advise sb** [əd'vaɪz]	jdn beraten	
drying agent ['draɪɪŋ eɪdʒənt]	Trockenmittel, Trocknungsmittel	

solution [sə'luːʃn]	Lösung	
extra ['ekstrə]	zusätzlich	
tripod ['traɪpɒd]	Stativ	
tonne [tʌn]	Tonne	
cable drum ['keɪbl drʌm]	Kabeltrommel	
lighting stand ['laɪtɪŋ stænd]	Leuchtenstativ	
replacement [rɪ'pleɪsmənt]	Ersatz	
average ['ævərɪdʒ]	Durchschnitt	
props *pl* [prɒps]	Requisiten	
sausage ['sɒsɪdʒ]	(Brat-)Wurst, Würstchen	
assortment [ə'sɔːtmənt]	Auswahl, Zusammenstellung	
bottled ['bɒtld]	in Flaschen	
case [keɪs]	Kasten, Kiste	
street sign ['striːt saɪn]	Straßenschild	
by [baɪ]	mal	
artificial [ˌɑːtɪ'fɪʃl]	künstlich, Kunst-	
glycerine ['glɪsriːn]	Glyzerin	
liquid ['lɪkwɪd]	Flüssigkeit	
fog [fɒg]	Nebel	
juice [dʒuːs]	Saft	
36 **aisle** [aɪl]	Gang	
cold storage [ˌkəʊld 'stɔːrɪdʒ]	Kühllager, Kühlhaus	
drive-through pallet rack [ˌdraɪv θruː 'pælət ræk]	Durchfahrregal	
floor storage ['flɔː stɔːrɪdʒ]	Bodenlager	
high-bay shelving [haɪ ˌbeɪ 'ʃelvɪŋ]	Hochregallager	
inbound goods *pl* [ˌɪnbaʊnd 'gʊdz]	Wareneingang, eingehende Ware	
loading area ['ləʊdɪŋ eəriə]	Ladefläche, Ladezone	
outbound goods *pl* [ˌaʊtbaʊnd 'gʊdz]	Warenausgang, ausgehende Ware	
pallet rack shelving [ˌpælət ræk 'ʃelvɪŋ]	Palettenregal	
to **pick** [pɪk]	kommissionieren	
picking area ['pɪkɪŋ eəriə]	Kommissionierzone	
lifting platform ['lɪftɪŋ plætfɔːm]	Hebebühne	
freight elevator ['freɪt elɪveɪtə]	Lastenaufzug, Warenaufzug	
pallet truck ['pælət trʌk]	Palettenhubwagen	
crane [kreɪn]	Kran	
conveyor belt [kən'veɪə belt]	Förderband	
building materials *pl* ['bɪldɪŋ mətɪəriəlz]	Baustoffe, Baumaterial	
level ['levl]	(Gebäude:) Ebene, Etage	
loop [luːp]	Schleife, Schlaufe	
motorized ['məʊtəraɪzd]	motorisiert	
vehicle ['viːəkl]	Fahrzeug	

to **power sth** ['paʊə]	etw antreiben, etw mit Energie versorgen	
petrol BE ['petrəl]	Benzin	
electricity [ɪˌlek'trɪsəti]	Strom, Elektrizität	
to **lift sth** [lɪft]	etw anheben, etw hochheben	
37 **(warehouse) receiver** [rɪ'siːvə]	Warenannehmer/in	
forklift operator [ˌfɔːklɪft 'ɒpəreɪtə]	Gabelstaplerfahrer/in	
picker ['pɪkə]	Kommissionierer/in	
loader ['ləʊdə]	Belader/in	

T
to **receive sth** [rɪ'siːv]	etw in Empfang nehmen	
to **secure sth** [sɪ'kjʊə]	etw sichern	
to **unload** [ˌʌn'ləʊd]	entladen	
by hand [baɪ 'hænd]	von Hand	
to **sign for sth** ['saɪn fə]	etw quittieren	
immediately [ɪ'miːdiətli]	sofort, unverzüglich	
RFID tag [ɑːr ˌef eɪ ˌdiː 'tæg]	RFID-Etikett	
bulky ['bʌlki]	sperrig	
outsize items *pl* [ˌaʊtsaɪz 'aɪtəmz]	Sperrgut, überdimensionierte Ware(n)	
license ['laɪsns]	Genehmigung, Führerschein	
once [wʌns]	einmal	
to **be allowed to do sth** [bi ə'laʊd tə duː]	etw tun dürfen	
picking station ['pɪkɪŋ steɪʃn]	Kommissionierplatz	
to **select sth** [sɪ'lekt]	etw auswählen	
to **switch to sth** ['swɪtʃ tə]	auf etw umstellen	
paperless picking [ˌpeɪpələs 'pɪkɪŋ]	beleglose Kommissionierung	
to **train sb on sth** ['treɪn ɒn]	jdn an etw schulen	
unfortunately [ʌn'fɔːtʃənətli]	bedauerlicherweise, leider	
loading station ['ləʊdɪŋ steɪʃn]	Ladestation, Verladestation	
to **distribute sth** [dɪ'strɪbjuːt]	etw verteilen	
maths [mæθs]	Mathematik	
load planning ['ləʊd plænɪŋ]	Ladeplanung, Verladeplanung	
to **complain** [kəm'pleɪn]	sich beschweren, sich beklagen	

weight distribution ['weɪt dɪstrɪbjuːʃn]	Gewichtsverteilung	
to **tag sth** [tæg]	etw etikettieren	
radio-frequency identification (RFID) [ˌreɪdiəʊ ˌfriːkwənsi aɪdentɪfɪ'keɪʃn]	Funkerkennung	
circuit ['sɜːkɪt]	Schaltkreis	
radio signal ['reɪdiəʊ sɪgnəl]	Funksignal	
frequency ['friːkwənsi]	Frequency	
constantly ['kɒnstəntli]	ständig	
to **update sth** [ˌʌp'deɪt]	etw aktualisieren	
to **affect sth** [ə'fekt]	etw beeinträchtigen	

feature ['fi:tʃə]	Merkmal, Eigenschaft, Besonderheit	
label printer ['leɪbl prɪntə]	Etikettendrucker	
reader ['ri:də]	Lesegerät	
scales pl [skeɪlz]	Waage	
to require sth [rɪ'kwaɪə]	etw erfordern, etw verlangen	
to equip sth with sth [ɪ'kwɪp wɪð]	etw mit etw ausstatten	
dairy products pl ['deəri prɒdʌkts]	Milchprodukte	
valuable ['væljuəbl]	wertvoll	
fixtures pl ['fɪkstʃəz]	Armaturen	
tap [tæp]	Wasserhahn	
bulk sale ['bʌlk seɪl]	Massenverkauf, Großhandelsverkauf	
construction contractor [kən'strʌkʃn kəntræktə]	Bauunternehmen, Bauunternehmer/in	
plumbing contractor ['plʌmɪŋ kəntræktə]	Klempnereibetrieb	
roof tile ['ru:f taɪl]	Dachziegel	
building site ['bɪldɪŋ saɪt]	Baustelle	
shelving ['ʃelvɪŋ]	Regallager	

38
to arrange sth [ə'reɪndʒ]	etw (Termin usw.) vereinbaren	
to appear [ə'pɪə]	vorkommen, auftauchen	
dot [dɒt]	Punkt	
hyphen ['haɪfn]	Bindestrich, Minus	
underscore ['ʌndəskɔ:]	Unterstrich	
to dictate [dɪk'teɪt]	diktieren	
firm [fɜ:m]	Firma	
subject line ['sʌbdʒɪkt laɪn]	Betreffzeile	
to state [steɪt]	angeben, erklären, sagen, darlegen, sagen	
request (for sth) [rɪ'kwest]	Bitte (um etw)	
assistance [ə'sɪstəns]	Hilfe, Unterstützung	
to announce [ə'naʊns]	ankündigen	
change of plan [ˌtʃeɪndʒ əv 'plæn]	Planänderung	
covering letter ['kʌvərɪŋ letə]	Anschreiben, Begleitschreiben	
brochure ['brəʊʃə]	Prospekt	
venue ['venju:]	Veranstaltungsort	
flyer ['flaɪə]	Faltblatt	
to attach [ə'tætʃ]	(E-Mail:) anhängen	
update (on sth) ['ʌpdeɪt]	aktuelle Informationen (zu etw), aktueller Überblick (über etw)	
inclusive [ɪn'klu:sɪv]	einschließlich	
application (for sth) [ˌæplɪ'keɪʃn]	Antrag (auf/für etw)	
trade [treɪd]	Gewerbe, Branche	
fair [feə]	Messe	
to let sb know sth [ˌlet 'nəʊ]	jdm etw mitteilen, jdm Bescheid sagen	
to interview sb ['ɪntəvju:]	mit jdm ein Vorstellungsgespräch führen	
export clerk ['ekspɔ:t klɑ:k]	Außenhandelskaufmann/-frau	

39
reply (to sth) [rɪ'plaɪ]	Antwort (auf etw)	
to study sth ['stʌdi]	sich etw genau ansehen	
suggestion [sə'dʒestʃən]	Vorschlag	
to invite sb [ɪn'vaɪt]	jdn einladen	
initial ideas pl [ɪˌnɪʃl aɪ'dɪəz]	erste Ideen	
to suit sb [su:t]	jdm passen	
Yours sincerely [ˌjɔ:z sɪn'sɪəli]	(Brief:) Mit freundlichen Grüßen	
greeting ['gri:tɪŋ]	(Brief:) Anrede	
to reply (to sth) [rɪ'plaɪ]	(auf etw) antworten, (etw) beantworten	
to apologize [ə'pɒlədʒaɪz]	sich entschuldigen	
confirmation [ˌkɒnfə'meɪʃn]	Bestätigung	
salutation [ˌsælju'teɪʃn]	(Brief:) Anrede	
complimentary close [ˌkɒmplɪˌmentri 'kləʊz]	(Brief:) Schlussformel	
Dear Sir or Madam [dɪə ˌsɜ:r ɔ: 'mædəm]	(Brief:) Sehr geehrte Damen und Herren,	
Yours faithfully [ˌjɔ:z 'feɪθfəli]	(Brief:) … und verbleiben mit freundlichen Grüßen	
(Best) Regards [rɪ'gɑ:dz]	(Brief:) Viele Grüße, Mit freundlichen Grüßen	
Best wishes [ˌbest 'wɪʃɪz]	(Brief:) Mit freundlichen Grüßen	

UNIT 5

42
unique selling proposition (USP) [juˌni:k 'selɪŋ prɒpəzɪʃn]	Alleinstellungsmerkmal	
to attract sb [ə'trækt]	jdn anlocken, jdn ansprechen, jdn anziehen	
to consider sth [kən'sɪdə]	etw in Betracht ziehen, über etw nachdenken, etw berücksichtigen	
to place an order [ˌpleɪs ən 'ɔ:də]	einen Auftrag erteilen, eine Bestellung aufgeben	
competition [ˌkɒmpə'tɪʃn]	Konkurrenz	
especially [ɪ'speʃəli]	besonders	
less than truckload [ˌles ðən 'trʌkləʊd]	Teilladung (Lkw)	
full truckload [ˌfʊl 'trʌkləʊd]	Komplettladung (Lkw)	
transshipment [træns'ʃɪpmənt]	Umladung	
fuss [fʌs]	Heckmeck, Gedöns, Theater	
hub [hʌb]	Knotenpunkt, Drehkreuz	
convenience [kən'vi:niəns]	günstige Lage	
freight capacity ['freɪt kəpæsəti]	Frachtkapazität, Laderaum	
competitive price [kəm'petətɪv praɪs]	günstiger Preis	

43
refrigerated transport [rɪˌfrɪdʒəreɪtɪd 'trænspɔ:t]	Kühltransport	
shipment status ['ʃɪpmənt steɪtəs]	Sendungsstatus, Versandstatus	
cross-border ['krɒs bɔ:də]	grenzübergreifend	
intermodal transport [ɪntəˌməʊdl 'trænspɔ:t]	kombinierter Verkehr, intermodaler Transport	

Unit word list

carbon footprint [ˌkɑːbən ˈfʊtprɪnt]	CO₂-Fußabdruck	
shorthaul [ˈʃɔːthɔːl]	Kurzstrecken-Rechnungsprüfung	
invoice auditing [ˈɪnvɔɪs ɔːdɪtɪŋ]		
partial-load shipment [ˌpɑːʃl ləʊd ˈʃɪpmənt]	Teilladungssendung	
unbeatable [ʌnˈbiːtəbl]	unschlagbar	
firstly [ˈfɜːstli]	erstens	
to bundle sth together [ˈbʌndl təgeðə]	etw bündeln, etw zusammenfassen	
scale [skeɪl]	Umfang	
quality requirements pl [ˈkwɒləti rɪkwaɪəmənts]	Qualitätsanforderungen	
temperature level [ˈtemprətʃə levl]	Tempearturniveau, Temperaturbereich	
planning reliability [ˈplænɪŋ rɪlaɪəbɪləti]	Planungssicherheit	
collection [kəˈlekʃn]	Abholung	
departure [dɪˈpɑːtʃə]	Abfahrt, Start	
transparency [trænsˈpærənsi]	Nachvollziehbarkeit, Transparenz	
essential [ɪˈsenʃl]	wesentlich	
it's no wonder ... [ɪts ˌnəʊ ˈwɒndə]	kein Wunder, dass ...	
market leader [ˌmɑːkɪt ˈliːdə]	Marktführer	
recipient [rɪˈsɪpiənt]	Empfänger/in	
payment option [ˈpeɪmənt ɒpʃn]	Zahlungsweise, Zahlungsmöglichkeit	
positioned in the market [pəˌzɪʃnd ɪn ðə ˈmɑːkɪt]	im/am Markt aufgestellt	
billion [ˈbɪliən]	Milliarde	

T

editor [ˈedɪtə]	Herausgeber/in, Redakteur/in	
issue [ˈɪʃuː]	Ausgabe	
to publish sth [ˈpʌblɪʃ]	etw veröffentlichen	
comparison [kəmˈpærɪsn]	Vergleich	
surprising [səˈpraɪzɪŋ]	erstaunlich	
remarkable [rɪˈmɑːkəbl]	bemerkenswert	
sort [sɔːt]	Art	
to generate sth [ˈdʒenəreɪt]	etw (Umsatz usw.) erwirtschaften	
You make a good point. [juː ˌmeɪk ə ˌɡʊd ˈpɔɪnt]	Da haben Sie recht.	
competitive [kəmˈpetətɪv]	wettbewerbsorientiert, konkurrenzfähig	
particularly [pəˈtɪkjələli]	besonders	
innovative [ˈɪnəveɪtɪv]	innovativ	
reputation [ˌrepjuˈteɪʃn]	Ruf	
to set sb/sth apart from sb/sth [ˌset əˈpɑːt frəm]	jdn/etw von jdm/etw abheben, jdn/etw von jdm/etw unterscheiden	
to be proud of sth [bi ˈpraʊd əv]	auf etw stolz sein	
frozen logistics [ˈfrəʊzn lədʒɪstɪks]	Tiefkühllogistik	
refrigerator lorry [rɪˈfrɪdʒəreɪtə lɒri]	Kühllastwagen, Kühlfahrzeug	
season [ˈsiːzn]	Jahreszeit, Saison	

sustainable [səˈsteɪnəbl]	nachhaltig	
eco-friendly [ˈiːkəʊ frendli]	umweltfreundlich	

44

several [ˈsevrəl]	mehrere	
to clarify sth [ˈklærəfaɪ]	etw klären, etw abklären	
to review sth [rɪˈvjuː]	etw durchgehen, etw durcharbeiten	
currently [ˈkʌrəntli]	momentan, aktuell	
distillery [dɪˈstɪləri]	Brennerei	
palletized [ˈpælətaɪzd]	auf Paletten, palettiert	
distributor [dɪˈstrɪbjətə]	Händler, Vertragshändler	
on a regular basis [ɒn ə ˌreɡjələ ˈbeɪsɪs]	regelmäßig	
quotation [kwəʊˈteɪʃn]	Preisangebot, Angebot	
to hesitate [ˈhezɪteɪt]	zögern	

45

to follow up [ˌfɒləʊ ˈʌp]	nachfassen	
to enquire about sth [ɪnˈkwaɪər əbaʊt]	sich nach etw erkundigen	

T

first of all [ˌfɜːst əv ˈɔːl]	zunächst, als Erstes	
additional [əˈdɪʃənl]	zusätzlich	
detailed [ˈdiːteɪld]	detailliert, genau	
reliable [rɪˈlaɪəbl]	zuverlässig, seriös	
to go ahead [ˌɡəʊ əˈhed]	loslegen	
to pick sth up [ˌpɪk ˈʌp]	etw abholen	
to calculate sth [ˈkælkjuleɪt]	etw berechnen	
distance [ˈdɪstəns]	Strecke, Entfernung	
Westphalia [westˈfeɪliə]	Westfalen	
postcode [ˈpəʊstkəʊd]	Postleitzahl	
height [haɪt]	Höhe	
possibility [ˌpɒsəˈbɪləti]	Möglichkeit	
rough [rʌf]	grob	
estimate [ˈestɪmət]	Schätzung	
terms pl of payment [ˌtɜːmz əf ˈpeɪmənt]	Zahlungsbedingungen	
net [net]	netto	
within ... days of invoice [wɪðɪn ˌdeɪz əv ˈɪnvɔɪs]	innerhalb von ... Tagen ab/nach Rechnungsdatum	
acceptable [əkˈseptəbl]	akzeptabel	
liability [ˌlaɪəˈbɪləti]	Haftung	
to get back to sb [ˌɡet ˈbæk tə]	sich (wieder) bei jdm melden	
to leave sth blank [ˌliːv ˈblæŋk]	etw leerlassen	
incomplete [ˌɪnkəmˈpliːt]	unvollständig	
relationship [rɪˈleɪʃnʃɪp]	Beziehung	

insurance [ɪnˈʃʊərəns]	Versicherung	
form [fɔːm]	Formular	
pretzel [ˈpretsl]	Brezel	
crisps pl BE [krɪsps]	Chips	
freight exchange [ˈfreɪt ɪkstʃeɪndʒ]	Transportbörse, Frachtenbörse	
instead of [ɪnˈsted əv]	anstatt, statt	
common(ly) [ˈkɒmən]	üblich, verbreitet, häufig	
cargo [ˈkɑːɡəʊ]	Fracht	

P

Munich [ˈmjuːnɪk]	München	
to execute sth [ˈeksɪkjuːt]	etw ausführen	

46

exhibition [ˌeksɪˈbɪʃn]	Messe, Ausstellung	

213

to come up	[ˌkʌm ˈʌp]	bevorstehen
to respond to sth	[rɪˈspɒnd tə]	auf etw antworten
family-owned company	[ˌfæməli əʊnd ˈkʌmpəni]	Familienbetrieb
excellent	[ˈeksələnt]	hervorragend
as regards	[əz rɪˈɡɑːdz]	bezüglich, betreffend
total	[ˈtəʊtl]	gesamt, insgesamt
excluding	[ɪkˈskluːdɪŋ]	ohne
VAT	[ˌviː eɪ ˈtiː]	MwSt
loading	[ˈləʊdɪŋ]	Verladung
unloading	[ˌʌnˈləʊdɪŋ]	Entladung
exhibition centre	[ˌeksɪˈbɪʃn sentə]	Messegelände
insurance rate	[ɪnˈʃʊərəns reɪt]	Versicherungstarif, Versicherungsprämie
as well as	[əz ˈwel əz]	sowie, ebenso wie
introductory discount	[ˌɪntrəˌdʌktəri ˈdɪskaʊnt]	Einführungsrabatt
first-time customer	[ˌfɜːst taɪm ˈkʌstəmə]	Erstkunde/-kundin, Neukunde/-kundin
total	[ˈtəʊtl]	Gesamtbetrag, Summe
(general) terms and conditions pl	[ˌtɜːmz ənd kənˈdɪʃnz]	Allgemeine Geschäftsbedingungen
to assure sb that …	[əˈʃʊə ðət]	jdm zusichern, dass …; jdm versichern, dass …
attention	[əˈtenʃn]	Aufmerksamkeit
tax	[tæks]	Steuer(n)
reduction	[rɪˈdʌkʃn]	Ermäßigung, (Preis-)Nachlass
to deduct sth from sth	[dɪˈdʌkt frəm]	etw von etw abziehen
list price	[ˈlɪst praɪs]	Listenpreis
quantity discount	[ˈkwɒntəti dɪskaʊnt]	Mengenrabatt
special discount	[ˌspeʃl ˈdɪskaʊnt]	Sonderrabatt
(customer) loyalty	[ˈlɔɪəlti]	Kundentreue
to grant sb sth	[ɡrɑːnt]	jdm etw gewähren, jdm etw einräumen
rebate	[ˈriːbeɪt]	Rabatt
47 calculation	[ˌkælkjuˈleɪʃn]	Berechnung, Kalkulation
carriage	[ˈkærɪdʒ]	Beförderung, Transport
competitor	[kəmˈpetɪtə]	Wettbewerber/in, Konkurrent/in
rate	[reɪt]	Tarif, Satz, Preis
administration fee	[ədˌmɪnɪˈstreɪʃn fiː]	Regiekosten, Verwaltungsgebühr
reduced rate	[rɪˌdjuːst ˈreɪt]	ermäßigter Satz, Ermäßigung
T actual	[ˈæktʃuəl]	tatsächlich, eigentlich
to add to the cost	[ˌæd tə ðə ˈkɒst]	die Kosten erhöhen
labour-intensive	[ˌleɪbər ɪnˈtensɪv]	arbeitsaufwändig, arbeitsintensiv
in reverse	[ɪn rɪˈvɜːs]	umgekehrt
to make sense	[meɪk ˈsens]	einleuchten
though	[ðəʊ]	allerdings, aber
receipt of invoice	[rɪˌsiːt əv ˈɪnvɔɪs]	Rechnungseingang, Erhalt der Rechnung
time period	[ˈtaɪm pɪəriəd]	Zeitraum, Frist
to insist on sth	[ɪnˈsɪst ɒn]	auf etw bestehen
date of delivery	[ˌdeɪt əv dɪˈlɪvəri]	Lieferdatum
extra fee	[ˌekstrə ˈfiː]	Zuschlag, Zusatzgebühr
equivalent	[ɪˈkwɪvələnt]	Entsprechung, Übersetzung
owner	[ˈəʊnə]	Inhaber/in
48 layout	[ˈleɪaʊt]	Gestaltung, Aufbau, Layout
supplier	[səˈplaɪə]	Zulieferer, Lieferant, Anbieter
letter of enquiry	[ˌletər əv ɪnˈkwaɪəri]	(schriftliche) Anfrage
address	[əˈdres]	Anschrift
letterhead	[ˈletəhed]	Briefkopf
body	[ˈbɒdi]	(Brief:) Haupttext
copy	[ˈkɒpi]	Exemplar, Kopie
enclosure	[ɪnˈkləʊʒə]	(Brief:) Anlage
inside address	[ˌɪnsaɪd əˈdres]	Innenadresse
reference initials pl	[ˈrefərəns ɪnɪʃlz]	(Brief:) Zeichen
signature	[ˈsɪɡnətʃə]	Unterschrift
signature block	[ˈsɪɡnətʃə blɒk]	Signatur
attention line	[əˈtenʃn laɪn]	Zeile „zu Händen"
purchase	[ˈpɜːtʃəs]	Kauf
Cordially yours, AE	[ˌkɔːdiəli ˈjɔːz]	(Brief:) Mit herzlichen Grüßen
49 reference (ref.)	[ˈrefərəns]	(Brief:) Zeichen
for the attention of	[fə ði əˈtenʃn əv]	zu Händen
cheese wheel	[ˈtʃiːz wiːl]	Käselaib
trial shipment	[ˈtraɪəl ʃɪpmənt]	Probelieferung
company magazine	[ˌkʌmpəni mæɡəˈziːn]	Firmenzeitschrift, Hauszeitung

UNIT 6

50 road transport	[ˌrəʊd ˈtrænspɔːt]	Straßenverkehr, Straßentransport
rail transport	[ˈreɪl trænspɔːt]	Schienenverkehr, Eisenbahnverkehr
overland transport	[ˌəʊvəlænd ˈtrænspɔːt]	Landverkehr, Landtransport
manufacturing site	[ˌmænjuˈfæktʃərɪŋ saɪt]	Produktionsstätte, Produktionsstandort
border control	[ˈbɔːdə kəntrəʊl]	Grenzkontrolle
door-to-door delivery	[ˌdɔː tə ˌdɔː dɪˈlɪvəri]	Haus-zu-Haus-Lieferung, Tür-zu-Tür-Lieferung
express delivery	[ɪkˌspres dɪˈlɪvəri]	Expresslieferung, Eilzustellung
huge loads pl	[ˌhjuːdʒ ˈləʊdz]	große Tonnagen, große Lasten

Unit word list

	pollution [pəˈluːʃn]	Umweltverschmutzung	
	toll [təʊl]	Maut	
	charge [tʃɑːdʒ]	Gebühr	
	traffic jam [ˈtræfɪk dʒæm]	Stau	
	to take a closer look at sth [teɪk ə ˌkləʊsə ˈlʊk ət]	sich etw näher/genauer ansehen	
	on-board unit (OBU) [ˌɒnˌbɔːd ˈjuːnɪt]	Bordgerät, Transponder, OBU	
	vignette [vɪnˈjet]	Vignette	
	toll station [ˈtəʊl steɪʃn]	Mautstelle, Mautstation	
	Belgium [ˈbeldʒəm]	Belgien	
	Slovenia [sləʊˈviːniə]	Slowenien	
	Switzerland [ˈswɪtsələnd]	Schweiz	
	border [ˈbɔːdə]	(Landes-)Grenze	
	motorway [ˈməʊtəweɪ]	Autobahn	
	trip [trɪp]	Fahrt	
	light [laɪt]	leicht	
	van [væn]	Lieferwagen	
51	in preparation for sth [ɪn ˌprepəˈreɪʃn fə]	zur Vorbereitung auf etw	
	mixture [ˈmɪkstʃə]	Mischung, Vermischung, Gemisch	
	confusing [kənˈfjuːzɪŋ]	verwirrend	
	body [ˈbɒdi]	(Lkw:) Aufbau	
	box van BE [ˈbɒks væn]	Lkw mit Kastenaufbau	
	box truck AE [ˈbɒks trʌk]	LKW mit Kastenaufbau	
	Luton van BE [ˈluːtən væn]	Lkw mit Kastenaufbau und überbautem Führerhaus	
	heavy goods vehicle (HGV) BE [ˌhevi gʊdz ˈviːəkl]	Schwerlastwagen	
	articulated lorry BE [ɑːˌtɪkjuleɪtɪd ˈlɒri]	Sattelzug	
	artic [ˈɑːtɪk]	Sattelzug	
	cab [kæb]	Fahrerhaus, Führerhaus	
	trailer [ˈtreɪlə]	Auflieger	
	semi-trailer truck AE [ˌsemi treɪlə ˈtrʌk]	Sattelzug	
	standardized [ˈstændədaɪzd]	genormt	
	swap body [ˈswɒp bɒdi]	Wechselaufbau	
	curtainsider [ˈkɜːtnsaɪdə]	Gardinenplanenauflieger, Schiebeplanenauflieger, Curtainsider	
	curtain [ˈkɜːtn]	Vorhang, Gardine	
	taut [tɔːt]	straff	
	load [ləʊd]	Ladung, Fracht	
	recently [ˈriːsntli]	vor kurzem, in letzter Zeit	
52	dangerous goods pl [ˌdeɪndʒərəs ˈgʊdz]	Gefahrgüter	
	hazardous material [ˌhæzədəs məˈtɪəriəl]	Gefahrstoff, Gefahrgut	
	to brief sb [briːf]	jdn einweisen, jdn informieren	
	to classify sth [ˈklæsɪfaɪ]	etw klassifizieren, etw einordnen	
	placard [ˈplækɑːd]	Warntafel	
	warning sign [ˈwɔːnɪŋ saɪn]	Warnhinweis, Warnschild	
	arsenic [ˈɑːsnɪk]	Arsen	
	fireworks pl [ˈfaɪəwɜːks]	Feuerwerk	
	hydrogen [ˈhaɪdrədʒən]	Wasserstoff	
	sulphuric acid [sʌlˌfjʊərɪk ˈæsɪd]	Schwefelsäure	
	dangerous goods note (DGN) [ˌdeɪndʒərəs ˈgʊdz nəʊt]	brit. Gefahrguterklärung	
	to commission sb [kəˈmɪʃn]	jdn beauftragen	
	exporter [ɪkˈspɔːtə]	Exporteur, Ausführer	
	importer [ɪmˈpɔːtə]	Importeur, Einführer	
	volume [ˈvɒljuːm]	Volumen	
	shipping clerk [ˈʃɪpɪŋ clerk]	Expedient/in, Spediteur/in, Kaufmann/-frau für Spedition und Logistikdienstleistung	
53	shipper [ˈʃɪpə]	Absender	
	consignor [kənˈsaɪnə]	Absender, Konsignant	
	sender [ˈsendə]	Absender	
	reference [ˈrefərəns]	Kennziffer, Vorgangsnummer	
	consignee [ˌkɒnsaɪˈniː]	Empfänger/in, Konsignatar	
	carrier [ˈkæriə]	Frachtführer	
	declaration [ˌdekləˈreɪʃn]	Erklärung	
	hereby [ˌhɪəˈbaɪ]	hiermit, hierdurch	
	fully [ˈfʊli]	vollständig	
	accurate(ly) [ˈækjərət]	exakt, genau	
	below [bɪˈləʊ]	untengenannt	
	proper shipping name [ˌprɒpə ˈʃɪpɪŋ neɪm]	offizielle Versandbezeichnung	
	to placard sth [ˈplækɑːd]	etw mit einer Warntafel versehen	
	in all respects [ɪn ˌɔːl rɪˈspekts]	in jeder Hinsicht	
	applicable [əˈplɪkəbl]	(Recht usw.:) geltend	
	governmental regulations pl [gʌvənˌmentl regjuˈleɪʃnz]	gesetzliche/behördliche Vorschriften	
	to prescribe sth for sth [prɪˈskraɪb fə]	etw für etw vorsehen	
	to delete sth [dɪˈliːt]	etw streichen	
	non-applicable [ˌnɒn əˈplɪkəbl]	unzutreffend	
	aircraft [ˈeəkrɑːft]	Flugzeug	
	vessel [ˈvesl]	Schiff	
	port of discharge [ˌpɔːt əv ˈdɪstʃɑːdʒ]	Entladehafen, Löschungshafen	
	shipping marks pl [ˈʃɪpɪŋ mɑːks]	Versandzeichen	
	kind [kaɪnd]	Art	
	kerosene [ˈkerəsiːn]	Kerosin	
	environmentally hazardous [ɪnvaɪrənˌmentəli ˈhæzədəs]	umweltgefährdend	
	gross [grəʊs]	brutto	
	mass [mæs]	Masse	
	cube [kjuːb]	Würfel, Kubus, Kubik	
	identification (ID) [aɪˌdentɪfɪˈkeɪʃn]	Identifikation	
	seal [siːl]	Plombe, Siegel	
	tare [teə]	Leergewicht, Tara	

container packing certificate [kənˌteɪnə ˈpækɪŋ sətɪfɪkət]	Containerpackzertifikat	
vehicle packing certificate [ˌviːəkl ˈpækɪŋ sətɪfɪkət]	Fahrzeugpackzertifikat	
in accordance with [ɪn əˈkɔːdəns wɪð]	in Übereinstimmung mit, nach	
provisions pl [prəˈvɪʒnz]	Bestimmungen	
declarant [dɪˈkleərənt]	Anmelder/in	
in apparent good order and condition [ɪn əˌpærənt gʊd ˌɔːdər ənd kənˈdɪʃn]	in äußerlich gutem Zustand, ohne äußerlich erkennbare Schäden	
unless [ənˈles]	außer, außer wenn	
hereon [hɪərˈɒn]	nachfolgend	
haulier [ˈhɔːliə]	(Straßen-)Spediteur	
hazard class [ˈhæzəd klɑːs]	Gefahrenklasse	
packing group [ˈpækɪŋ gruːp]	Verpackungsgruppe	
to assign sth [əˈsaɪn]	etw zuweisen	
required [rɪˈkwaɪəd]	erforderlich, vorgeschrieben	

T

delayed [dɪˈleɪd]	verspätet, verzögert
error [ˈerə]	Fehler, Irrtum
intermediate bulk container (IBC) [ˌɪntəˌmiːdiət ˈbʌlk kənˈteɪnə]	Großpackmittel (IBC)
empty [ˈempti]	leer
query [ˈkwɪəri]	Rückfrage, Frage
figure [ˈfɪgə]	Ziffer, Zahl
apology [əˈpɒlədʒi]	Entschuldigung
to sort sth out [ˌsɔːt ˈaʊt]	etw klären, etw regeln
My pleasure. [maɪ ˈpleʒə]	Ganz meinerseits! Gern geschehen!

54

safety precautions pl [ˈseɪfti prɪkɔːʃnz]	Sicherheitsvorkehrungen, Sicherheitsmaßnahmen
to accompany sb/sth [əˈkʌmpəni]	jdn/etw begleiten
emergency [ɪˈmɜːdʒənsi]	Notfall
Transport Emergency Card [ˈtrænspɔːt ɪmɜːdʒənsi kɑːd]	Unfallmerkblatt
safety equipment [ˌseɪfti ɪˈkwɪpmənt]	Sicherheitsausrüstung
to carry sth [ˈkæri]	etw mitführen
division [dɪˈvɪʒn]	Unterklasse
subsidiary risk [səbˌsɪdiəri ˈrɪsk]	Nebengefahr(en)
protective equipment [prəˌtektɪv ɪˈkwɪpmənt]	Schutzausrüstung
face shield [ˈfeɪs ʃiːld]	Gesichtsschutz, Gesichtsschirm
protective clothing [prəˌtektɪv ˈkləʊðɪŋ]	Schutzkleidung
protective gloves pl [prəˌtektɪv ˈglʌvz]	Schutzhandschuhe
protective footwear [prəˌtektɪv ˈfʊtweə]	Sicherheitsschuhe

eyewash bottle [ˈaɪwɒʃ bɒtl]	Augenspülflasche
emergency equipment [ɪˈmɜːdʒənsi ɪkwɪpmənt]	Notfallausrüstung
spill kit [ˈspɪl kɪt]	Notfallset für Leckagen und Verschüttungen
non-sparking [ˌnɒn ˈspɑːkɪŋ]	funkenfrei
shovel [ˈʃʌvl]	Schaufel
broom [bruːm]	Besen
absorbent [əbˈsɔːbənt]	Absorptionsmittel
engine [ˈendʒɪn]	Motor
naked lights pl [ˌneɪkɪd ˈlaɪts]	offene Flammen
danger area [ˈdeɪndʒər eəriə]	Gefahrenbereich, Gefahrenzone
upwind [ʌpˈwɪnd]	windwärts
fire brigade [ˈfaɪə brɪgeɪd]	Feuerwehr

P

litre [ˈliːtə]	Liter
ADR emergency kit [eɪ diː ˌɑːr ɪˈmɜːdʒənsi kɪt]	Gefahrgut-Notfallset
Polish [ˈpəʊlɪʃ]	polnisch
goggles pl [ˈgɒglz]	Schutzbrille

55

to follow standard procedures [fɒləʊ ˌstændəd prəˈsiːdʒəz]	übliche Verfahren einhalten
to shadow sb [ˈʃædəʊ]	mit jdm mitlaufen
request [rɪˈkwest]	Anfrage
Croatia [krəʊˈeɪʃə]	Kroatien
arrangements pl [əˈreɪndʒmənts]	Modalitäten, Vereinbarungen, Abmachungen
turnaround time [ˈtɜːnəraʊnd taɪm]	Umschlagzeit
to speed sth up [ˌspiːd ˈʌp]	etw beschleunigen
trade [treɪd]	Handel
since [sɪns]	seit
introduction [ˌɪntrəˈdʌkʃn]	Einführung
exchange [ɪksˈtʃeɪndʒ]	Austausch
thereby [ˌðeəˈbaɪ]	dadurch
to save sth [seɪv]	etw sparen
sturdy [ˈstɜːdi]	stabil, robust
to pool sth [puːl]	etw zusammenlegen
to be designed to do sth [bi dɪˈzaɪnd tə]	dafür ausgelegt, etw zu tun
dimensions pl [dɪˈmenʃnz]	Abmessungen
width [wɪdθ]	Breite
measurement [ˈmeʒəmənt]	Maß
imperial measurements pl [ɪmˌpɪəriəl ˈmeʒəmənts]	angloamerikanisches Maßsystem
inch [ɪntʃ]	Zoll (ca. 2,54 cm)
board [bɔːd]	Brett
nail [neɪl]	Nagel
pound (lb) [paʊnd]	Pfund (ca. 454 g)
branded marking [ˌbrændɪd ˈmɑːkɪŋ]	Brandmarke
control staple [kənˈtrəʊl steɪpl]	Prüfklammer
fake [feɪk]	Fälschung, Plagiat

Unit word list

	measure ['meʒə]	Maßeinheit
	metric ['metrɪk]	metrisch
	unit ['juːnɪt]	Einheit
	domestic trade [dəˌmestɪk 'treɪd]	Binnenhandel
	foreign trade [ˌfɒrən 'treɪd]	Außenhandel
P	load [ləʊd]	Last
	sportswear ['spɔːtsweə]	Sportbekleidung
	parcel ['pɑːsl]	Paket, Karton
	weight training ['weɪt treɪnɪŋ]	Kraftsport
	instruction manual [ɪnˈstrʌkʃn ˈmænjuəl]	Lehrbuch
	mainland ['meɪnlænd]	Festland
	AC [ˌeɪ 'siː]	Wechselstrom
	DC [ˌdiː 'siː]	Gleichstrom
	point [pɔɪnt]	Komma
56	consignment note [kənˈsaɪnmənt nəʊt]	Frachtbrief
	opening hours pl ['əʊpənɪŋ aʊəz]	Öffnungszeiten
	method of packing [ˌmeθəd əf 'pækɪŋ]	Verpackungsmethode
	sealed [siːld]	verplombt
	permitted [pəˈmɪtɪd]	gestattet, erlaubt
	delivery note [dɪˈlɪvəri nəʊt]	Lieferschein
	certificate of origin [səˌtɪfɪkət əv 'ɒrɪdʒɪn]	Ursprungszeugnis, Herkunftszeugnis
	freight list ['freɪt lɪst]	Ladeliste
	carriage charges pl ['kærɪdʒ tʃɑːdʒɪz]	Frachtgebühr(en)
	supplementary charges pl [sʌplɪˌmentri 'tʃɑːdʒɪz]	Zusatzgebühren, zusätzliche Kosten
	customs duties pl ['kʌstəmz djuːtiz]	Zollgebühren
	particulars pl [pəˈtɪkjələz]	Einzelheiten, Angaben
	licence plate ['laɪsns pleɪt]	Nummernschild, Kfz-Kennzeichen
	cash on delivery [ˌkæʃ ɒn dɪˈlɪvəri]	(per) Nachnahme
	to be subject to sth [bi 'sʌbdʒekt tə]	einer Sache unterliegen
	notwithstanding any clause to the contrary [nɒtwɪθˌstændɪŋ eni ˌklɔːz tə ðə 'kɒntrəri]	ungeachtet etwaiger anderslautender Bestimmungen
	established in ... on ... [ɪˈstæblɪʃt ɪn ɒn]	ausgefertigt in ... am ...
57 T	to instruct sb to do sth [ɪnˈstrʌkt]	jdn anweisen, etw zu tun
	to steal [stiːl]	stehlen
	depot ['depəʊ]	Depot
	to transfer sth [trænsˈfɜː]	etw (Container usw.) umladen
	to disappoint sb [ˌdɪsəˈpɔɪnt]	jdn enttäuschen
	trailer ['treɪlə]	Anhänger

	pro-forma invoice [ˌprəʊ ˌfɔːmə 'ɪnvɔɪs]	Pro-forma-Rechnung
	to charge sth [tʃɑːdʒ]	etw (Preis usw.) verlangen, etw berechnen
	to exchange sth [ɪksˈtʃeɪndʒ]	etw austauschen
	written ['rɪtn]	schriftlich
	final ['faɪnl]	endgültig
	musical instrument [ˌmjuːzɪkl 'ɪnstrəmənt]	Musikinstrument
	terms pl of delivery [ˌtɜːmz əv dɪˈlɪvəri]	Lieferbedingungen
	to replace sth [rɪˈpleɪs]	etw ersetzen
	reference (to sth) ['refərəns]	Bezugnahme (auf etw), Erwähnung (von etw)
58	return load [rɪˈtɜːn ləʊd]	Rückladung
	freight agent ['freɪt eɪdʒənt]	Frachtvermittler/in
	tail lift ['teɪl lɪft]	Ladebordwand, Hebebühne
	rigid vehicle [ˌrɪdʒɪd 'viːɪkl]	Einzelfahrzeug, starres Fahrzeug
	articulated vehicle [ɑːˌtɪkjuleɪtɪd 'viːɪkl]	Gelenkfahrzeug
	payload ['peɪləʊd]	Zuladung, Nutzlast
T	to head out for ... [ˌhed 'aʊt fə]	sich nach ... aufmachen
	Russia ['rʌʃə]	Russland
	to process sth ['prəʊses]	etw bearbeiten, verarbeiten
	to be in a hurry [bi ɪn ə 'hʌri]	in Eile sein, es eilig haben
	mandatory box [ˌmændətri 'bɒks]	(Formular:) Pflichtfeld
	low-loader [ˌləʊ 'ləʊdə]	Tieflader
	enclosed body [ɪnˌkləʊzd 'bɒdi]	geschlossener Aufbau
	database ['deɪtəbeɪs]	Datenbank
	straight away [ˌstreɪt əˈweɪ]	sofort
	to tick sth [tɪk]	etw abhaken
59	bottling plant ['bɒtlɪŋ plɑːnt]	Abfüllanlage
	machinery [məˈʃiːnəri]	Maschinen
	to request sth [rɪˈkwest]	etw anfordern, um etw bitten, etw wünschen

UNIT 7

62	air transport ['eə trænspɔːt]	Luftfracht, Luftverkehr
	handling procedures pl ['hændlɪŋ prəsiːdʒəz]	Abfertigung, Abwicklung, Umschlag
	to report back to sb [rɪˌpɔːt 'bæk tə]	jdm Bericht erstatten
	fashion wear ['fæʃn weə]	Modekleidung
	aviation [ˌeɪviˈeɪʃn]	Luftverkehr, Luftfahrt
	time zone ['taɪm zəʊn]	Zeitzone
	local time ['ləʊkl taɪm]	Ortszeit
	airport code ['eəpɔːt kəʊd]	Flughafen-Code

East Asia [ˌiːst ˈeɪʃə]	Ostasien
overland [ˈəʊvəlænd]	auf dem Landweg, über Land
for this reason [fə ðɪs ˈriːzn]	deshalb, aus diesem Grund
passenger plane [ˈpæsɪndʒə pleɪn]	Passagierflugzeug
air freighter [ˈeə freɪtə]	Frachtflugzeug
time-sensitive [ˈtaɪm sensətɪv]	zeitkritisch
medicine [ˈmedsn]	Arzneimittel
part [pɑːt]	Teil, Bauteil, Ersatzteil
cash [kæʃ]	Bargeld
precious metal [ˌpreʃəs ˈmetl]	Edelmetall
work of art [ˌwɜːk əv ˈɑːt]	Kunstwerk
temperature-sensitive [ˈtemprətʃə sensətɪv]	temperaturempfindlich
wheat [wiːt]	Weizen
cherry [ˈtʃeri]	Kirsche
coal [kəʊl]	Kohle
painting [ˈpeɪntɪŋ]	Gemälde
Coordinated Universal Time [kəʊˌɔːdɪneɪtɪd juːnɪˌvɜːsl ˈtaɪm]	koordinierte Weltzeit
Greenwich Mean Time [ˌgrenɪtʃ ˈmiːn taɪm]	mittlere Greenwich-Zeit, Weltzeit
Moscow [ˈmɒskəʊ]	Moskau
Beijing [ˌbeɪ ˈdʒɪŋ]	Peking
63 return journey [rɪˈtɜːn dʒɜːni]	Rückfahrt, Rückflug, Rückreise
exception [ɪkˈsepʃn]	Ausnahme
to cover sth [ˈkʌvə]	etw bedecken, etw abdecken
standard time [ˌstændəd ˈtaɪm]	Normalzeit
daylight saving time [ˌdeɪlaɪt ˈseɪvɪŋ taɪm]	Sommerzeit
to maximize sth [ˈmæksɪmaɪz]	etw maximieren
Japanese [ˌdʒæpəˈniːz]	japanisch
poor quality [ˌpʊə ˈkwɒləti]	schlechte Qualität
to swap sth [swɒp]	etw tauschen
to finalize sth [ˈfaɪnəlaɪz]	etw zum Abschluss bringen, etw endgültig festlegen
rose [rəʊz]	Rose
Kenya [ˈkenjə]	Kenia
medical supplies pl [ˌmedɪkl səˈplaɪz]	medizinische Bedarfsartikel, Sanitätsartikel
jet engine [ˌdʒet ˈendʒɪn]	Düsentriebwerk
component [kəmˈpəʊnənt]	Bauteil
64 cargo agent [ˈkɑːgəʊ eɪdʒənt]	Frachtspediteur
to schedule sth [ˈʃedjuːl]	etw (Termin usw.) planen, etw festlegen, etw ansetzen
trade association [ˈtreɪd əsəʊsieɪʃn]	Branchenvereinigung, Wirtschaftsverband
carrier [ˈkæriə]	Fluggesellschaft
to support sth [səˈpɔːt]	etw finanzieren
trillion [ˈtrɪljən]	Billion
global economy [ˌgləʊbl ɪˈkɒnəmi]	Weltwirtschaft
airline [ˈeəlaɪn]	Fluggesellschaft
safety rating [ˈseɪfti reɪtɪŋ]	Sicherheitseinstufung
cabin [ˈkæbɪn]	Kabine
cargo screening [ˈkɑːgəʊ skriːnɪŋ]	Frachtkontrolle
live animals pl [ˌlaɪv ˈænɪmlz]	lebende Tiere
infectious substances pl [ɪnˌfekʃəs ˈsʌbstənsɪz]	infektiöse Stoffe
environment [ɪnˈvaɪrənmənt]	Umwelt
sustainability [səˌsteɪnəˈbɪləti]	Nachhaltigkeit
noise footprint [ˈnɔɪz fʊtprɪnt]	Lärmteppich, Lärmemission
simplified [ˈsɪmplɪfaɪd]	vereinfacht, einheitlich
clearance [ˈklɪərəns]	Abfertigung, Freigabe
currency [ˈkʌrənsi]	Währung
currency clearance [ˈkʌrənsi klɪərəns]	Devisenclearing
intelligence [ɪnˈtelɪdʒəns]	Informationen
trade publications pl [ˈtreɪd pʌblɪkeɪʃnz]	Fachzeitschriften, Fachpresse
to prevent sth [prɪˈvent]	etw verhindern
bomb [bɒm]	Bombe
to enable sb to do sth [ɪˈneɪbl]	jdm ermöglichen, etw zu tun; jdn in die Lage versetzen, etw zu tun
to monitor sth [ˈmɒnɪtə]	etw überwachen
pollution levels pl [pəˈluːʃn levlz]	Schadstoffwerte
to issue sth [ˈɪʃuː]	etw (Dokument usw.) ausstellen
65 cargo handling [ˈkɑːgəʊ hændlɪŋ]	Frachtumschlag, Warenumschlag
term [tɜːm]	Begriff, Fachbegriff
Unit Load Device (ULD) [ˈjuːnɪtləʊd dɪvaɪs]	Ladeeinheit (ULD)
long-haul [ˈlɒŋ hɔːl]	Langstrecken-
capacity [kəˈpæsəti]	Fassungsvermögen, Volumen
range [reɪndʒ]	Reichweite
swinging door [ˌswɪŋɪŋ ˈdɔː]	Schwenktür
scissor lift [ˈsɪzə lɪft]	Scherenlift
cargo hold [ˈkɑːgəʊ həʊld]	Frachtraum, Laderaum
roller floor [ˈrəʊlə flɔː]	Rollenboden
wingspan [ˈwɪŋspæn]	Spannweite
documentary requirements pl [dɒkjuˌmentri rɪˈkwaɪəmənts]	Dokumentationsanforderungen
to be required for/of sth [bi rɪˈkwaɪəd fə/ɒf]	für etw erforderlich sein
imprecise [ˌɪmprɪˈsaɪs]	ungenau
to be considered sth [bi kənˈsɪdəd]	als etw gelten
appliance [əˈplaɪəns]	Elektrogerät
carpet [ˈkɑːpɪt]	Teppichboden, Teppich
electric saw [ɪˌlektrɪk ˈsɔː]	Elektrosäge

Unit word list

	flooring ['flɔːrɪŋ]	Bodenbelag
	foodstuffs pl ['fuːdstʌfs]	Lebensmittel, Nahrungsmittel
	leather ['leðə]	Leder
	tumble dryer [ˌtʌmbl 'draɪə]	Wäschetrockner
	saddle ['sædl]	Sattel
	contoured ['kɒntʊəd]	konturiert, geformt
	manifest ['mænɪfest]	Ladungsverzeichnis
	10-digit [ˌten 'dɪdʒɪt]	zehnstellig
	garment ['gɑːmənt]	Kleidungsstück
	hanger ['hæŋə]	Kleiderbügel
66	costume ['kɒstjuːm]	(Theater-)Kostüm
T	to enter sth ['entə]	etw (Daten usw.) eingeben
	to log on [ˌlɒg 'ɒn]	sich einloggen
	origin ['ɒrɪdʒɪn]	Herkunftsort, Ursprungsort
	to type sth in [ˌtaɪp 'ɪn]	etw eintippen
	to leave sth blank [ˌliːv 'blæŋk]	etw frei lassen, etw offenlassen
	commodity [kə'mɒdəti]	Ware
	careful ['keəfl]	sorgfältig
	wearing apparel ['weərɪŋ əpærəl]	Bekleidung
	opera ['ɒprə]	Oper
	source [sɔːs]	Quelle
	to make sure [tə ˌmeɪk 'ʃʊə]	um sicherzugehen
	automatically [ˌɔːtə'mætɪkli]	automatisch
	volumetric [ˌvɒljuː'metrɪk]	volumetrisch
	chargeable weight [ˌtʃɑːdʒəbl 'weɪt]	frachtpflichtiges Gewicht
P	cargo agent ['kɑːgəʊ eɪdʒənt]	Spediteur/in, Kaufmann/-frau für Spedition und Logistikdienstleistung
	spelling ['spelɪŋ]	Schreibweise
	authorities pl [ɔː'θɒrətiz]	Behörden
	parquet flooring [ˌpɑːkɪ 'flɔːrɪŋ]	Parkett
	royal ['rɔɪəl]	königlich
	Dutch [dʌtʃ]	niederländisch, holländisch
	minimum charge [ˌmɪnɪməm 'tʃɑːdʒ]	Mindestgebühr
	hardwood ['hɑːdwʊd]	Hartholz
	Sweden ['swiːdn]	Schweden
	to consist of sth [kən'sɪst əv]	aus etw bestehen
	trial order [ˌtraɪəl 'ɔːdə]	Probebestellung
	total charges pl [ˌtəʊtl 'tʃɑːdʒɪz]	Gesamtbetrag (der Gebühren)
	available [ə'veɪləbl]	verfügbar, erhältlich
	to read sth back to sb [ˌriːd 'bæk]	etw jdm nochmals vorlesen
	to promise ['prɒmɪs]	versprechen
67	air waybill [ˌeə 'weɪbɪl]	Luftfrachtbrief
	unfinished [ʌn'fɪnɪʃt]	unerledigt, unfertig
	to call in sick [ˌkɔːl ɪn 'sɪk]	sich krankmelden
	further to … ['fɜːðə tu]	bezugnehmend auf …
	dispatch [dɪ'spætʃ]	Versand
	airport of departure [ˌeəpɔːt əv dɪ'pɑːtʃə]	Abgangsflughafen
68	to reserve sth [rɪ'zɜːv]	etw reservieren
	freight space ['freɪt speɪs]	Frachtraum
	nature ['neɪtʃə]	Beschaffenheit
	fee [fiː]	Gebühr
	to date sth [deɪt]	etw datieren
	to advise sb to do sth [əd'vaɪz]	jdm raten, etw zu tun
	to take out insurance [teɪk ˌaʊt ɪn'ʃʊərəns]	eine Versicherung abschließen
	fuel ['fjuːəl]	Treibstoff
	surcharge ['sɜːtʃɑːdʒ]	Zuschlag
T	to be off sick [bi ˌɒf 'sɪk]	krankgeschrieben sein
	to declare sth [dɪ'kleə]	etw anmelden, etw angeben, etw deklarieren
	value ['væljuː]	Wert
	amount [ə'maʊnt]	Betrag, Summe
	nil [nɪl]	null
	compensation [ˌkɒmpən'seɪʃn]	Schadenersatz, Entschädigung
	air cargo insurance ['eə kɑːgəʊ ɪnʃʊərəns]	Luftfrachtversicherung
	to cover sth ['kʌvə]	etw versichern, etw decken
	pre-carriage ['priː kærɪdʒ]	Vorlauf, Vortransport
	post-carriage ['pəʊst kærɪdʒ]	Nachlauf, Nachtransport
	insurer [ɪn'ʃʊərə]	Versicherer, Versicherungsunternehmen
	total weight [ˌtəʊtl 'weɪt]	Gesamtgewicht
	fixed rate [ˌfɪkst 'reɪt]	Pauschaltarif, Festpreis
	prepaid [priː'peɪd]	im Voraus bezahlt
	due [djuː]	zahlbar, fällig
	sick [sɪk]	krank
70	on-board courier [ˌɒnbɔːd 'kʊriə]	On-Board-Kurier
	DNA sample [ˌdiː en 'eɪ sɑːmpl]	DNA-Probe
	outward journey [ˌaʊtwəd 'dʒɜːni]	Anreise, Hinflug
	pick-up ['pɪkʌp]	Abholung
	lightweight ['laɪtweɪt]	leicht
	attaché case [ə'tæʃeɪ keɪs]	Aktentasche, Aktenkoffer
	flooding ['flʌdɪŋ]	Überschwemmung(en)
	four-wheel drive [ˌfɔːwiːl 'draɪv]	Vierradantrieb, Geländewagen
	advisable [əd'vaɪzəbl]	ratsam, geboten, zweckmäßig
	aerospace ['eərəʊspeɪs]	Raumfahrt-
	automotive [ˌɔːtə'məʊtɪv]	Automobil-
	pharmaceutical [ˌfɑːmə'suːtɪkl]	Pharma-, pharmazeutisch
	to check sth in [ˌtʃek 'ɪn]	etw (Gepäck usw.) aufgeben
	public transport [ˌpʌblɪk 'trænspɔːt]	öffentliche Verkehrsmittel, öffentlicher Nahverkehr
	section ['sekʃn]	Abteilung
	departure [dɪ'pɑːtʃə]	Abflug
	arrival [ə'raɪvl]	Ankunft
T	seat [siːt]	Platz, Sitzplatz

	hand-carry shipment ['hænd ˌkæri ˈʃɪpmənt]	Handcarry-Lieferung, persönlich begleiteter Transport	
	to get bumped from a flight [get ˌbʌmpt frəm ə ˈflaɪt]	aus einem Flug ausgebucht werden	
	overbooked [ˌəʊvəˈbʊkt]	überbucht, überbelegt	
	to depart [dɪˈpɑːt]	abfliegen	
	boarding card [ˈbɔːdɪŋ kɑːd]	Bordkarte	

71
- accommodation [əˌkɒməˈdeɪʃn] — Unterkunft
- check-in date [ˌtʃek ˈɪn deɪt] — Anreisedatum
- check-out date [ˌtʃek ˈaʊt deɪt] — Abreisedatum
- laundry [ˈlɔːndri] — Wäsche
- half board [ˌhɑːfˈbɔːd] — Halbpension
- full board [ˌfʊl ˈbɔːd] — Vollpension
- self-catering [ˌselfˈkeɪtərɪŋ] — Selbstversorger-
- coach [kəʊtʃ] — Reisebus
- hire car [ˌhaɪə ˈkɑː] — Mietwagen
- to submit sth [səbˈmɪt] — etw einreichen, etw vorlegen, etw abgeben

T
- delay [dɪˈleɪ] — Verzögerung, Verspätung, Verzug
- transport link [ˈtrænspɔːt lɪŋk] — Verkehrsverbindung
- to afford sth [əˈfɔːd] — sich etw leisten (können)
- air conditioning [ˈeə kəndɪʃnɪŋ] — Klimaanlage
- satnav [ˈsætnæv] — Navi
- bed and breakfast (B&B) [ˌbed ən ˈbrekfəst] — Frühstückspension, Übernachtung mit Frühstück
- dietary restrictions pl [ˌdaɪətri rɪˈstrɪkʃnz] — Nahrungsmittelunverträglichkeiten, besondere Kost
- in the countryside [ɪn ðə ˈkʌntrisaɪd] — auf dem Land

- rally [ˈræli] — Rallye

P
- racing team [ˈreɪsɪŋ tiːm] — Rennstall
- to take part in sth [ˌteɪk ˈpɑːt ɪn] — an etw teilnehmen
- via [ˈvaɪə] — über
- Nice [naɪs] — Nizza
- transfer [ˈtrænsfɜː] — Transfer, Transport
- apart from [əˈpɑːt frəm] — außer, abgesehen von

UNIT 8

72
- sea transport [ˈsiː trænspɔːt] — Seetransport, Seeverkehr
- freight planning [ˈfreɪt plænɪŋ] — Frachtplanung
- to categorize [ˈkætɪɡəraɪz] — klassifizieren, kategorisieren
- global trade [ˌɡləʊbl ˈtreɪd] — Welthandel
- to carry sth [ˈkæri] — etw befördern
- granular [ˈɡrænjələ] — körnig
- bulk [bʌlk] — Schüttgut, Massengut
- unpackaged [ʌnˈpækɪdʒd] — unverpackt
- gravel [ˈɡrævl] — Kies, Schotter
- infrastructure [ˈɪnfrəstrʌktʃə] — Infrastruktur, Verkehrsnetz
- cost-effective [ˌkɒstɪˈfektɪv] — wirtschaftlich, kostengünstig
- environmentally friendly [ɪnˌvaɪrənˌmentəli ˈfrendli] — umweltfreundlich
- low-sulphur [ˌləʊ ˈsʌlfə] — schwefelarm
- to estimate [ˈestɪmeɪt] — schätzen
- transit time [ˈtrænzɪt taɪm] — Laufzeit, Transitzeit
- in comparison (to sth) [ɪn kəmˈpærɪsn] — im Vergleich (zu/mit etw)
- mode of transport [ˌməʊd əv ˈtrænspɔːt] — Beförderungsart, Verkehrsmittel
- inflexible [ɪnˈfleksəbl] — unflexibel
- unsuitable [ʌnˈsuːtəbl] — ungeeignet
- piracy [ˈpaɪrəsi] — Piraterie, Piraten
- high-sulphur [ˌhaɪ ˈsʌlfə] — mit hohem Schwefelgehalt
- bunker fuel [ˈbʌŋkə fjuːəl] — Bunkeröl, Schweröl
- to break up [ˌbreɪk ˈʌp] — auseinanderbrechen
- oil spill [ˈɔɪl spɪl] — (auf See:) Ölteppich
- ocean liner [ˈəʊʃn laɪnə] — Ozeandampfer, Passagierschiff
- propeller [prəˈpelə] — Schiffsschraube
- emergency food aid [ɪˌmɜːdʒənsi ˈfuːd eɪd] — Nahrungsmittelsoforthilfe
- iron ore [ˈaɪən ɔː] — Eisenerz
- vegetable oil [ˈvedʒtəbl ɔɪl] — Pflanzenöl

73
- bulk carrier [ˈbʌlk kæriə] — Schüttgutfrachter, Massengutfrachter
- to drop sth [drɒp] — etw fallen lassen, etw (Ladung usw.) löschen
- to pour sth [pɔː] — etw schütten, etw gießen
- crude carrier [ˈkruːd kæriə] — Rohöltanker
- crude oil [ˌkruːd ˈɔɪl] — Rohöl
- oil rig [ˈɔɪl rɪɡ] — Bohrinsel
- refinery [rɪˈfaɪnəri] — Raffinerie
- liquefied gas carrier [ˌlɪkwɪfaɪd ˈɡæs kæriə] — Flüssiggastanker
- petroleum gas [pəˈtrəʊliəm ɡæs] — Propangas
- natural gas [ˌnætʃrəl ˈɡæs] — Erdgas
- pressurized tank [ˌpreʃəraɪzd ˈtæŋk] — Drucktank, Druckbehälter
- reefer vessel [ˈriːfə vesl] — Kühlschiff
- ro-ro vessel [ˈrəʊ rəʊ vesl] — RoRo-Schiff
- to close down [ˌkləʊz ˈdaʊn] — schließen, zumachen
- charity [ˈtʃærəti] — Hilfsorganisation
- to be preferable to sth [bi ˈprefərəbl tə] — einer Sache vorzuziehen sein
- cargo category [ˈkɑːɡəʊ kætəɡəri] — Ladungskategorie

Unit word list

step by step [ˌstep baɪ ˈstep]	Schritt für Schritt	
export [ˈekspɔːt]	Ausfuhr	
formalities pl [fɔːˈmælətiz]	Formalitäten	
import [ˈɪmpɔːt]	Einfuhr	
74 medical equipment [ˌmedɪkl ɪˈkwɪpmənt]	Medizingeräte	
Singapore [ˌsɪŋəˈpɔː]	Singapur	
handling [ˈhændlɪŋ]	Umschlag	
stowage [ˈstəʊɪdʒ]	Stauung	
to stow sth [stəʊ]	etw stauen, etw beladen	
to secure sth [sɪˈkjʊə]	etw sichern, etw befestigen, etw verriegeln	
automated [ˈɔːtəmeɪtɪd]	automatisiert, (voll)automatisch	
truck gate [ˈtrʌk geɪt]	Lkw-Gate	
to record sth [rɪˈkɔːd]	etw aufzeichnen	
to reverse [rɪˈvɜːs]	rückwärts fahren	
gantry crane [ˈgæntri kreɪn]	Portalkran	
to stack sth [stæk]	etw stapeln	
Automated Guided Vehicle (AGV) [ˌɔːtəmeɪtɪd ˌgaɪdɪd ˈviːəkl]	fahrerloses Transportfahrzeug (FTF)	
slippage [ˈslɪpɪdʒ]	Rutschen	
toppling [ˈtɒplɪŋ]	Kippen	
to lock sth [lɒk]	etw verriegeln, etw arretieren, etw sperren	
lock [lɒk]	Verriegelung, Riegel	
to twist sth [twɪst]	etw drehen, etw verdrehen	
to attach sth to sth [əˈtætʃ tə]	etw an etw befestigen	
lashing rod [ˈlæʃɪŋ rɒd]	Laschstange	
75 standard size [ˌstændəd ˈsaɪz]	Einheitsgröße, Normgröße	
dry load [ˈdraɪ ləʊd]	Trockenladung	
hard-top container [ˌhɑːd tɒp kənˈteɪnə]	Hardtop-Container	
dry container [ˌdraɪ kənˈteɪnə]	Trockencontainer	
tare weight [ˌteə ˈweɪt]	Eigengewicht, Leergewicht	
net weight [ˈnet weɪt]	Nettogewicht	
stuffing weight [ˈstʌfɪŋ weɪt]	Zuladung, Ladegewicht	
gross weight [ˌgrəʊs ˈweɪt]	Bruttogewicht	
unexact [ˌʌnɪgˈzækt]	ungenau	
unit of measurement [ˌjuːnɪt əv ˈmeʒəmənt]	Maßeinheit	
abbreviation [əˌbriːviˈeɪʃn]	Abkürzung	
cubic metre [ˈkjuːbɪk miːtə]	Kubikmeter	
cubic foot [ˌkjuːbɪk ˈfʊt]	Kubikfuß	
76 over-height [ˌəʊvə ˈheɪt]	zu hoch	
open-top container [ˌəʊpən tɒp kənˈteɪnə]	Opentop-Container, oben offener Container	
flat rack container [ˌflætræk kənˈteɪnə]	Flachcontainer, Flat-Rack-Container	
over-sized [ˌəʊvəsaɪzd]	übergroß	
weather-resistant [ˈweðə rɪzɪstənt]	wetterfest	
organic [ɔːˈgænɪk]	organisch	
to give off sth [ˌgɪv ˈɒf]	etw abgeben	
condensation [ˌkɒndenˈseɪʃn]	Kondensat, Kondenswasser, Schwitzwasser	
ventilated [ˈventɪleɪtɪd]	belüftet, ventiliert	
slat [slæt]	Lamelle	
cocoa bean [ˈkəʊkəʊ biːn]	Kakaobohne	
steel coil [ˈstiːl kɔɪl]	Stahlblechrolle	
saw [sɔː]	Säge	
measuring ... [ˈmeʒərɪŋ]	mit den Maßen ...	
coffee bean [ˈkɒfi biːn]	Kaffeebohne	
frozen meat [ˌfrəʊzn ˈmiːt]	Gefrierfleisch	
grain [greɪn]	Getreide	
steel piping [ˌstiːl ˈpaɪpɪŋ]	Stahlrohre, Stahlröhren	
patient monitor [ˈpeɪʃnt mɒnɪtə]	Patientenmonitor	
sterilizer [ˈsterɪlaɪzə]	Sterilisator	
ECG machine [ˌiː siː ˈdʒiː məʃiːn]	EKG-Gerät	
hospital supplies pl [ˈhɒspɪtl səplaɪz]	Krankenhausbedarf	
bedding [ˈbedɪŋ]	Bettwäsche, Bettzeug	
bandage [ˈbændɪdʒ]	Verband	
asap (as soon as possible) [ˌeɪ es eɪ ˈpiː]	baldmöglichst	
contact [ˈkɒntækt]	Ansprechpartner/in	
77 theft [θeft]	Diebstahl	
set of documents [ˌset əv ˈdɒkjumənts]	Dokumentensatz	
one-stop [ˈwʌn stɒp]	durchgehend, aus einer Hand, als Komplettlösung	
customs clearance [ˈkʌstəmz klɪərəns]	Zollabfertigung	
to lock sth [lɒk]	etw verschließen, etw abschließen	
to unlock sth [ˌʌnˈlɒk]	etw aufschließen, etw öffnen	
multiple [ˈmʌltɪpl]	mehrfache, wiederholte	
multiple times [ˌmʌltɪpl ˈtaɪmz]	mehrfach	
entire [ɪnˈtaɪə]	gesamte/r/s	
multi-stop [ˈmʌlti stɒp]	mit Zwischenstopps, Multistopp-	
78 transport documents pl [ˈtrænspɔːt dɒkjumənts]	Beförderungspapiere, Frachtdokumente	
bill of lading (B/L) [ˌbɪl əv ˈleɪdɪŋ]	Frachtbrief, Konnossement	
sea waybill (SWB) [ˈsiː weɪbɪl]	Seefrachtbrief	
contract of carriage [ˌkɒntrækt əv ˈkærɪdʒ]	Beförderungsvertrag, Frachtvertrag	
document of title [ˌdɒkjumənt əv ˈtaɪtl]	Inhaberpapier, Traditionspapier, Warenwertpapier	
in triplicate [ɪn ˈtrɪplɪkət]	in dreifacher Ausfertigung	
on receipt of sth [ɒn rɪˈsiːt əv]	bei Erhalt einer Sache	
seller [ˈselə]	Verkäufer/in	
on the terms agreed [ɒn ðə ˌtɜːmz əˈgriːd]	zu den vereinbarte Konditionen	

to **present** sth [prɪˈzent]	etw *(Dokument usw.)* vorlegen	**means** [miːnz]	Mittel, Art
void [vɔɪd]	ungültig	to **be obliged to do sth** [bi əˈblaɪdʒd]	(dazu) verpflichtet sein, etw zu tun
negotiable [nɪˈgəʊʃɪəbl]	begebbar, übertragbar	to **surrender sth** [səˈrendə]	etw aushändigen, etw übergeben
to **transfer sth** [trænsˈfɜː]	etw übertragen	**duly endorsed** [ˌdjuːli ɪnˈdɔːst]	ordnungsgemäß abgezeichnet
ownership [ˈəʊnəʃɪp]	Eigentum, Eigentumsrecht	**duty of care** [ˌdjuːti əv ˈkeə]	Sorgfaltspflicht
order bill of lading [ˌɔːdə ˌbɪl əv ˈleɪdɪŋ]	Orderkonnossement	**genuine** [ˈdʒenjuɪn]	echt
received for shipment bill of lading [rɪˌsiːvd fə ˈʃɪpmənt bɪl əv leɪdɪŋ]	Übernahmekonnossement	to **comply with sth** [kəmˈplaɪ wɪð]	einer Sache *(Vorschrift usw.)* nachkommen, einer Sache entsprechen
shipped on board bill of lading [ˌʃɪpt ɒn ˈbɔːd bɪl əv leɪdɪŋ]	Bordkonnossement	to **be entitled to sth** [bi ɪnˈtaɪtld tə]	einen Anspruch auf etw haben
to **convert sth into sth** [kənˈvɜːt ɪntə]	etw in etw umwandeln	to **discharge sb an obligation** [dɪsˈtʃɑːdʒ ən ɒblɪˈgeɪʃn]	jdn von einer Verpflichtung entbinden
port-to-port bill of lading [ˌpɔːt tə ˈpɔːt bɪl əv leɪdɪŋ]	Seefrachtbrief, Seekonnossement	**export sales manager** [ˌekspɔːt ˈseɪlz mænɪdʒə]	Exportleiter/in
ocean bill of lading [ˈəʊʃn bɪl əv leɪdɪŋ]	Seefrachtbrief, Seekonnossement	81 **T** to **stand in for sb** [ˌstænd ˈɪn fə]	jdn vertreten
port of shipment [ˌpɔːt əv ˈʃɪpmənt]	Verschiffungshafen	**Is everything in place?** [ɪz ˌevrɪθɪŋ ɪn ˈpleɪs]	Ist alles geregelt? Ist alles in Ordnung?
clean bill of lading [ˌkliːn ˌbɪl əv ˈleɪdɪŋ]	reines Konnossement	to **be set** [bi ˈset]	startklar sein
foul/claused bill of lading [faʊl/ˈklɔːzd ˌbɪl əv ˈleɪdɪŋ]	unreines Konnossement	to **be precise** [tə bi prɪˈsaɪs]	um genau zu sein
external [ɪkˈstɜːnl]	äußerlich	**anaesthesia machine** [ˌænɪsˈθiːzɪə məʃiːn]	Anästhesiegerät
sign (of sth) [saɪn]	Anzeichen (von etw)	**freight prepaid** [ˌfreɪt priːˈpeɪd]	frachtfrei
letter of credit (L/C) [ˌletər əv ˈkredɪt]	Akkreditiv	to **delete sth** [dɪˈliːt]	etw löschen, etw entfernen
non-negotiable [ˌnɒn nɪˈgəʊʃɪəbl]	nicht begebbar, nicht übertragbar	**on-carriage** [ˈɒnkærɪdʒ]	Weitertransport
proof of identity [ˌpruːf əv aɪˈdentəti]	Identitätsnachweis	to **seem** [siːm]	scheinen
to **obtain sth** [əbˈteɪn]	etw erhalten, etw bekommen	82 **lunchtime** [ˈlʌntʃtaɪm]	Mittag, Mittagszeit
to **trust sb** [trʌst]	jdm vertrauen	**above-mentioned** [əˌbʌv ˈmenʃnd]	obengenannt
buyer [ˈbaɪə]	Käufer/in	to **advise sb that/if ...** [ədˈvaɪz ðət/ɪf]	jdm mitteilen, dass/ob ...
party [ˈpɑːti]	(Vertrags-)Partei	**access** [ˈækses]	Zugang, Zutritt
in advance [ɪn ədˈvɑːns]	im Voraus	83 to **re-schedule sth** [ˌriːˈʃedjuːl]	etw *(Termin usw.)* verschieben
79 to **have sth in common** [həv ɪn ˈkɒmən]	etw gemeinsam haben	to **do sth about sth** [ˈduː əbaʊt]	etw gegen etw unternehmen
holder [ˈhəʊldə]	Inhaber/in, Besitzer/in	**no idea** [nəʊ aɪˈdɪə]	keine Ahnung
to **take possession of sth** [teɪk pəˈzeʃn əv]	etw in Besitz nehmen	**firm** [fɜːm]	fest
to **insure sth** [ɪnˈʃʊə]	etw versichern	**inconvenience** [ˌɪnkənˈviːnɪəns]	Unannehmlichkeiten, Umstände
to **prove sth** [pruːv]	etw nachweisen	**explanation** [ˌekspləˈneɪʃn]	Erklärung
80 **merchant** [ˈmɜːtʃənt]	Händler/in	**priority** [praɪˈɒrəti]	Vorrang
to **consign sth** [kənˈsaɪn]	etw verschicken, etw senden	to **be due to sth** [bi ˈdjuː tə]	an etw liegen
bearer [ˈbeərə]	Inhaber/in	**circumstances** *pl* [ˈsɜːkəmstənsɪz]	Umstände
to **furnish sth** [ˈfɜːnɪʃ]	etw zur Verfügung stellen, etw angeben	**circumstances beyond our control** [ˌsɜːkəmstənsɪz bɪjɒnd aʊə kənˈtrəʊl]	Umstände, auf die wir keinen Einfluss haben
without responsibility or representation [wɪðaʊt rɪspɒnsəˌbɪləti ɔː reprɪzenˈteɪʃn]	ohne Verantwortung oder Gewähr		
to **ascertain sth** [ˌæsəˈteɪn]	etw feststellen, etw sicherstellen		
reasonable(-bly) [ˈriːznəbl]	angemessen, hinreichend		

T	storm [stɔːm]	Unwetter, Sturm	
	estimated time of arrival (ETA) [ˌestɪmeɪtɪd ˌtaɪm əv əˈraɪvl]	voraussichtliche Ankunftszeit	
	to be/get in touch [bi/get ɪn ˈtʌtʃ]	sich melden	
P	wing [wɪŋ]	Flügel, Gebäudetrakt	
	catering equipment [ˈkeɪtərɪŋ ɪkwɪpmənt]	Großküchengeräte, Gastronomieausstattung	

UNIT 9

86	purchasing director [ˈpɜːtʃəsɪŋ dərektə]	Einkaufsleiter/in	
	terms pl [tɜːmz]	Konditionen	
	export sales department [ˈekspɔːt seɪlz dɪpɑːtmənt]	Exportabteilung	
	as specified [əz ˈspesɪfaɪd]	wie angegeben	
	telegraphic transfer [telɪˌɡræfɪk ˈtrænsfə]	telegrafische Überweisung	
	with order [wɪð ˈɔːdə]	bei Bestellung, bei Auftragserteilung	
	guarantee [ˌɡærənˈtiː]	Garantie	
	receipt of order [rɪˌsiːt əv ˈɔːdə]	Auftragseingang	
	to enter the EU [ˌentə ðə ˌiː ˈjuː]	(Waren usw.:) in die EU eingeführt werden	
	shipping charges pl [ˈʃɪpɪŋ tʃɑːdʒɪz]	Versandkosten	
	as per [əz ˈpɜː]	nach, gemäß	
	specifications pl [ˌspesɪfɪˈkeɪʃnz]	Angaben, Technische Daten, Spezifikationen	
	on delivery [ɒn dɪˈlɪvəri]	bei Lieferung	
	delivery period [dɪˈlɪvəri pɪəriəd]	Lieferzeit	
	cash with order (CWO) [ˌkæʃ wɪð ˈɔːdə]	Vorkasse	
87	exchange rate [ɪksˈtʃeɪndʒ reɪt]	Wechselkurs	
	rule [ruːl]	Regel, Vorschrift	
	main carriage [ˈmeɪn kærɪdʒ]	Hauptlauf, Haupttransport	
	at sb's own expense [ət ˌsʌmbədiz əʊn ɪkˈspens]	auf (jds) eigene Kosten	
	customary [ˈkʌstəməri]	üblich	
	cleared for export [ˌklɪəd fər ˈekspɔːt]	zur Ausfuhr freigemacht	
	unless otherwise agreed [ʌnles ˌʌðəwaɪz əˈɡriːd]	sofern nicht anders vereinbart	
	thereafter [ˌðeərˈɑːftə]	danach	
	transport insurance [ˈtrænspɔːt ɪnʃʊərəns]	Transportversicherung	
	import duties pl [ˈɪmpɔːt djuːtiz]	Einfuhrzölle	
	taxes pl [ˈtæksɪz]	Steuern	
	to nominate sb [ˈnɒmɪneɪt]	jdn benennen, jdn bestellen	
	to require sb to do sth [rɪˈkwaɪə tə duː]	von jdm verlangen, etw zu tun	
	final price [ˌfaɪnl ˈpraɪs]	Endpreis	
	to assume [əˈsjuːm]	davon ausgehen	
	insured value [ɪnˌʃʊəd ˈvæljuː]	Versicherungswert	
	despite [dɪˈspaɪt]	trotz	
	fluctuation [ˌflʌktʃuˈeɪʃn]	Schwankung(en)	
88	to evaluate sth [ɪˈvæljueɪt]	etw bewerten, etw beurteilen, etw einschätzen	
	counter-offer [ˈkaʊntə ɒfə]	Gegenangebot	
	favourable [ˈfeɪvərəbl]	günstig, vorteilhaft	
	satisfied [ˈsætɪsfaɪd]	zufrieden	
	range [reɪndʒ]	Sortiment	
	to be to sb's liking [bi tə sʌmbədiz ˈlaɪkɪŋ]	jdm zusagen	
	People's Republic of China [ˌpiːplz rɪˌpʌblɪk əv ˈtʃaɪnə]	Volksrepublik China	
89	information sheet [ˌɪnfəˈmeɪʃn ʃiːt]	Merkblatt	
	to pass to sb [ˈpɑːs tə]	auf jdn übergehen	
	to hand sth over to sb [ˌhænd ˈəʊvə tə]	jdm etw übergeben	
	import clearance [ˈɪmpɔːt klɪərəns]	Einfuhrabfertigung, Einfuhrfreigabe	
	export clearance [ˈekspɔːt klɪərəns]	Ausfuhrabfertigung, Ausfuhrfreigabe	
	export licence [ˈekspɔːt laɪsns]	Ausfuhrgenehmigung, Ausfuhrlizenz	
	import licence [ˈɪmpɔːt laɪsns]	Einfuhrgenehmigung, Einfuhrlizenz	
90	irrevocable and confirmed documentary letter of credit [ɪˌrevəkəbl ən kənˌfɜːmd dɒkjuˌmentri letər əv ˈkredɪt]	unwiderrufliches und bestätigtes Dokumentenakkreditiv	
	transaction [trænˈzækʃn]	(Geschäfts-)Vorgang	
	either … or [ˈaɪðə ˈɔː]	entweder … oder	
	to entitle sb to do sth [ɪnˈtaɪtl]	jdn berechtigen, etw zu tun	
	to recover sth [rɪˈkʌvə]	etw einfordern, etw zurückerlangen	
	irrevocable [ɪˈrevəkəbl]	unwiderruflich	
	consent [kənˈsent]	Zustimmung	
	stage [steɪdʒ]	Phase, Schritt, Etappe, Abschnitt	
	to inspect sth [ɪnˈspekt]	etw prüfen	
	documentary credit [dɒkjuˌmentri ˈkredɪt]	Dokumentenakkreditiv	
91	in view of sth [ɪn ˈvjuː əv]	angesichts von etw	
	to be willing to do sth [bi ˈwɪlɪŋ tə]	bereit sein, etw zu tun	
	quarterly settlement [ˌkwɔːtəli ˈsetlmənt]	vierteljährliche Abrechnung	
	to find sb's approval [ˌfaɪnd əˈpruːvl]	jds Zustimmung finden	
	significant(ly) [sɪɡˈnɪfɪkənt]	erheblich	
	competition [ˌkɒmpəˈtɪʃn]	Wettbewerb	

	minimum order quantity [ˌmɪnɪməm ˈɔːdə kwɒntəti]	Mindestbestellmenge		T	tricky [ˈtrɪki]	schwierig
	unit [ˈjuːnɪt]	Stück			to bear left/right [beə ˈleft, ˈraɪt]	sich links/rechts halten
	initial order [ɪˌnɪʃl ˈɔːdə]	Erstauftrag, Erstbestellung			complicated [ˈkɒmplɪkeɪtɪd]	kompliziert
	to draft sth [drɑːft]	etw *(Text)* entwerfen, etw verfassen			to slow down [ˌsləʊ ˈdaʊn]	langsamer fahren
	dated … [ˈdeɪtɪd]	vom …, mit Datum vom …			on foot [ɒn ˈfʊt]	zu Fuß
92	to proceed [prəˈsiːd]	vorgehen, verfahren		P	multi-storey car park [ˌmʌltɪstɔːri ˈkɑː pɑːk]	Parkhaus
	to negotiate sth [nɪˈɡəʊʃieɪt]	etw verhandeln			health food shop [ˈhelθ fuːd ʃɒp]	Reformhaus, Naturkostladen
	subtotal [ˈsʌbtəʊtl]	Zwischensumme			butcher's [ˈbʊtʃəz]	Metzgerei
	advice of dispatch [ədˌvaɪs əv dɪˈspætʃ]	Versandanzeige			greengrocer's [ˈɡriːnɡrəʊsəz]	Gemüseladen
	to trust [trʌst]	hoffen(, dass …)			baker's [ˈbeɪkəz]	Bäckerei
	punctually [ˈpʌŋktʃuəli]	pünktlich			toy [tɔɪ]	Spielzeug
93	sample [ˈsɑːmpl]	Muster, Probe			chemist's [ˈkemɪsts]	Drogerie
T	introductory offer [ˌɪntrəˈdʌktəri ɒfə]	Einführungsangebot			jeweller's [ˈdʒuːələz]	Schmuckgeschäft, Juwelierladen
	third party [ˌθɜːd ˈpɑːti]	Dritte/r			department store [dɪˈpɑːtmənt stɔː]	Kaufhaus
	inspection agency [ɪnˈspekʃn eɪdʒənsi]	Prüfstelle, Überwachungsstelle			optician [ɒpˈtɪʃn]	Optiker
	chamber of commerce [ˌtʃeɪmbər əv ˈkɒmɜːs]	Handelskammer			Indian [ˈɪndiən]	indisch
	packing list [ˈpækɪŋ lɪst]	Packliste			newsagent's [ˈnjuːzeɪdʒənts]	Zeitschriftenladen, Zeitungskiosk
	commercial invoice [kəˌmɜːʃl ˈɪnvɔɪs]	Handelsrechnung			police station [pəˈliːs steɪʃn]	Polizeiwache
	inspection report [ɪnˈspekʃn rɪpɔːt]	Prüfbericht			flat *BE* [flæt]	Wohnung
	standard practice [ˌstændəd ˈpræktɪs]	gängige Praxis, übliches Verfahren			DIY store [ˌdiː aɪ ˈwaɪ stɔː]	Heimwerkermarkt
	third-party inspection [θɜːd ˌpɑːti ɪnˈspekʃn]	Fremdprüfung			hypermarket [ˈhaɪpəmɑːkɪt]	großer Einkaufsmarkt
	deal [diːl]	Geschäft, Abschluss				
94	acknowledgement (of an order) [əkˈnɒlɪdʒmənt]	Auftragsbestätigung		**UNIT 10**		
	cash discount [ˈkæʃ dɪskaʊnt]	Skonto		98	quality management [ˈkwɒləti mænɪdʒmənt]	Qualitätssicherung
	trade discount [ˈtreɪd dɪskaʊnt]	Händlerrabatt, Handelsrabatt			committee [kəˈmɪti]	Arbeitsgemeinschaft, Ausschuss
	unit price [ˌjuːnɪt ˈpraɪs]	Stückpreis			to develop sth [dɪˈveləp]	etw erarbeiten, etw entwickeln
	carton [ˈkɑːtn]	Karton			guidelines *pl* [ˈɡaɪdlaɪnz]	Richtlinien, Vorgaben
96	instalment [ɪnˈstɔːlmənt]	Rate, Tranche			loyal [ˈlɔɪəl]	treu, loyal
	to transfer sth [trænsˈfɜː]	etw *(Geld)* überweisen			to keep sb loyal [ˌkiːp ˈlɔɪəl]	jdn *(Kunde/-in usw.)* an sich binden
	sb realizes sth [ˈrɪəlaɪzɪz]	jdm wird etw klar, jdm fällt etw auf			globalization [ˌɡləʊbəlaɪˈzeɪʃn]	Globalisierung
T	ferry [ˈferi]	Fähre			stressful [ˈstresfl]	anstrengend, stressig
	to be unsure about sth [bi ˌʌnˈʃʊə əbaʊt]	sich einer Sache nicht sicher sein			to represent sb/sth [ˌreprɪˈzent]	jdn/etw repräsentieren, jdn/etw vertreten
97	roadwork [ˈrəʊdwɜːk]	Straßenbauarbeiten			challenge [ˈtʃælɪndʒ]	Herausforderung, (schwierige) Aufgabe
	bend [bend]	Kurve			native speaker [ˌneɪtɪv ˈspiːkə]	Muttersprachler/in
	crossroads [ˈkrɒsrəʊdz]	Kreuzung			to be/feel uncomfortable [ˌbi/ˌfiːl ʌnˈkʌmftəbl]	sich unbehaglich fühlen
	roundabout [ˈraʊndəbaʊt]	Kreisverkehr			the basics *pl* [ðə ˈbeɪsɪks]	das Wesentliche, die Grundlagen
	T-junction [ˈtiː dʒʌŋkʃn]	Einmündung			politeness [pəˈlaɪtnəs]	Höflichkeit
	turning [ˈtɜːnɪŋ]	Abzweigung, Querstraße			tone [təʊn]	Tonfall, Ton
	fork [fɔːk]	Gabelung				
	traffic lights *pl* [ˈtræfɪk laɪts]	Ampel				
	exit [ˈeksɪt]	Ausfahrt				

	sympathetic [ˌsɪmpəˈθetɪk]	mitfühlend, wohlwollend, sympathisch			ritual [ˈrɪtʃuəl]	Ritual
	smile [smaɪl]	Lächeln			personal space [ˌpɜːsənl ˈspeɪs]	persönliche Distanzzone
	to soften sth [ˈsɒfn]	etw abmildern			to witness sth [ˈwɪtnəs]	etw beglaubigen
	rude [ruːd]	unhöflich, unverschämt			bribe [braɪb]	Bestechung(sversuch)
	to tend to do sth [ˈtend tə]	dazu neigen, etw zu tun			inexpensive [ˌɪnɪkˈspensɪv]	billig
	to value sth [ˈvæljuː]	etw schätzen, etw wertschätzen			insult [ˈɪnsʌlt]	Beleidigung
					to fool sb [fuːl]	jdn täuschen
	right away [raɪt əˈweɪ]	sogleich, sofort			flashy [ˈflæʃi]	protzig, großspurig
	to rush [rʌʃ]	sich beeilen, eilen, hetzen			Lisbon [ˈlɪzbən]	Lissabon
	to take sb/sth seriously [teɪk ˈsɪəriəsli]	jdn/etw ernst nehmen		T	giveaway [ˈɡɪvəweɪ]	Werbegeschenk
	to be afraid [bi əˈfreɪd]	sich fürchten, Angst haben			to remind sb of sb/sth [rɪˈmaɪnd əv]	jdn an jdn/etw erinnern
	clarification [ˌklærɪfɪˈkeɪʃn]	Klärung, Erläuterung			corner [ˈkɔːnə]	Ecke
					crowded [ˈkraʊdɪd]	voll (mit Leuten)
	impression [ɪmˈpreʃn]	Eindruck			to cancel sth [ˈkænsl]	etw absagen
99	quote [kwəʊt]	Zitat				
	lately [ˈleɪtli]	in letzter Zeit		102	to smile [smaɪl]	lächeln
	basic rate [ˌbeɪsɪk ˈreɪt]	Grundtarif, Basistarif		103	unacceptable [ˌʌnəkˈseptəbl]	inakzeptabel, unzumutbar
	to upset sb [ˌʌpˈset]	jdn verärgern			to scratch sth [skrætʃ]	etw verkratzen
	to bump into sb [ˈbʌmp ɪntə]	jdn anrempeln			to dent sth [dent]	etw verbeulen
	by accident [baɪ ˈæksɪdənt]	aus Versehen			mix-up [ˈmɪks ʌp]	Durcheinander, Verwechslung
	empathy [ˈempəθi]	Mitgefühl			to contrast sth [kənˈtrɑːst]	etw (einander) gegenüberstellen, etw (miteinander) vergleichen
	tough [tʌf]	schwierig				
	to be sb's fault [bi ˌsʌmbədiz ˈfɒlt]	jds Schuld sein				
					findings pl [ˈfaɪndɪŋz]	(Untersuchungs-)Ergebnisse
T	disruption [dɪsˈrʌpʃn]	Störung, Behinderung, Unterbrechung			pie chart [ˈpaɪ tʃɑːt]	Tortendiagramm
					majority [məˈdʒɒrəti]	Mehrheit, Großteil
	Hang on. [ˌhæŋ ˈɒn]	Einen Moment!			to relate to sth [rɪˈleɪt tə]	sich auf etw beziehen
	inconvenient [ˌɪnkənˈviːniənt]	ungünstig, unpraktisch		104	to skim [skɪm]	(Text) überfliegen
					to enclose [ɪnˈkləʊz]	(Brief:) beifügen
100	cultural [ˈkʌltʃərəl]	kulturell, Kultur-			whatever the case may be [wɒtevə ðə ˌkeɪs meɪ ˈbiː]	wie auch immer
	exhibitor [ɪɡˈzɪbɪtə]	Aussteller/in				
	to interact with sb [ˌɪntərˈækt wɪð]	mit jdm kommunizieren			to appreciate sth [əˈpriːʃieɪt]	etw verstehen, für etw Verständnis haben
	to encounter sth [ɪnˈkaʊntə]	einer Sache begegnen, auf etw stoßen			matter [ˈmætə]	Angelegenheit
					consequence [ˈkɒnsɪkwəns]	Folge, Konsequenz, Auswirkung
	behaviour [bɪˈheɪvjə]	Verhalten, Benehmen		105	subcontractor [ˌsʌbkənˈtræktə]	Subunternehmer/in
	to observe sth [əbˈzɜːv]	etw beobachten				
	gift [ɡɪft]	Geschenk			to meet with sb's approval [ˌmiːt wɪð əˈpruːvl]	jds Zustimmung finden
	close (to sb/sth) [ˈkləʊs tə]	dicht (bei jdm/etw), nahe (an jdm/etw)			to compensate sb for sth [ˈkɒmpənseɪt fə]	jdn für etw entschädigen, jdm etw erstatten
	to touch sth [tʌtʃ]	etw berühren, etw anfassen				
	characteristics pl [ˌkærəktəˈrɪstɪks]	(Charakter-)Eigenschaften, (charakteristische) Merkmale			patience [ˈpeɪʃns]	Geduld
					car manufacturer [ˌkɑː mænjuˈfæktʃərə]	Auto(mobil)hersteller
	to share sth [ʃeə]	etw gemeinsam haben			in time [ɪn ˈtaɪm]	rechtzeitig
	to lead to sth [ˈliːd tə]	zu etw führen			to be meant to do sth [bi ˈment tə duː]	etw (eigentlich/ ursprünglich) tun sollen
	misunderstanding [ˌmɪsʌndəˈstændɪŋ]	Missverständnis				
101	humour [ˈhjuːmə]	Humor			upset [ʌpˈset]	verärgert, ungehalten
	counterpart [ˈkaʊntəpɑːt]	Gegenüber, Ansprechpartner/in			memo [ˈmeməʊ]	Notiz, Vermerk
				106	action [ˈækʃn]	Maßnahme(n)
	etiquette [ˈetɪket]	Umgangsformen, Etikette			not at all [ˌnɒt ət ˈɔːl]	überhaupt nicht
	to refuse sth [rɪˈfjuːz]	etw ablehnen			reminder [rɪˈmaɪndə]	Mahnung
	offensive [əˈfensɪv]	beleidigend		T	match [mætʃ]	Streichholz
	obvious [ˈɒbviəs]	offensichtlich, deutlich			Warsaw [ˈwɔːsɔː]	Warschau

to **get sth sorted** [ˌget ˈsɔːtɪd]	etw klären, sich um etw kümmern	to **complete an order** [kəmˌpliːt ən ˈɔːdə]	eine Bestellung ausführen
to **look into sth** [ˌlʊk ˈɪntə]	einer Sache nachgehen	**quality control** [ˈkwɒləti kəntrəʊl]	Qualitätskontrolle
to **fulfil a contract** [fʊlˌfɪl ə kənˈtrækt]	einen Vertrag erfüllen	**cost savings** *pl* [ˈkɒst seɪvɪŋz]	Einsparungen, Kostenersparnis
107 **record** [ˈrekɔːd]	Datensatz	**job security** [ˌdʒɒb sɪˈkjʊərəti]	Arbeitsplatzsicherheit
I realize that. [aɪ ˈrɪəlaɪz ðæt]	Das ist mir bewusst.	to **implement sth** [ˈɪmplɪmənt]	etw (*Plan usw.*) umsetzen
to **show concern** [ˌʃəʊ kənˈsɜːn]	Bedenken äußern, sich besorgt zeigen	112 to **increase sth** [ɪnˈkriːs]	etw erhöhen, etw steigern
refund [ˈriːfʌnd]	Rückerstattung	to **accomplish sth** [əˈkʌmplɪʃ]	etw erreichen
P **supervision** [ˌsuːpəˈvɪʒn]	Überwachung, Kontrolle	to **rise** [raɪz]	steigen, ansteigen, zunehmen
to **refer to sth** [rɪˈfɜː tə]	sich auf etw beziehen, etw erwähnen	**chart** [tʃɑːt]	Diagramm
		the whole of … [ðə ˈhəʊl əv]	der/die/das gesamte/ganze …
UNIT 11		**worries** *pl* (**about sth**) [ˈwʌriz]	Sorge(n) (um etw)
110 **parcel service** [ˈpɑːsl sɜːvɪs]	Paketdienst	**although** [ɔːlˈðəʊ]	obwohl
smart [smɑːt]	intelligent	to **take action** [ˌteɪk ˈækʃn]	Maßnahmen ergreifen, handeln
to **affect sth** [əˈfekt]	sich auf etw auswirken, etw beeinflussen	**upper management** [ˌʌpə ˈmænɪdʒmənt]	obere Führungsebene, Chefetage
autonomous [ɔːˈtɒnəməs]	autonom	**diary** [ˈdaɪəri]	Terminkalender
to **mix sth up** [ˌmɪks ˈʌp]	etw durcheinander bringen	**ream** [riːm]	Ries (= 500 Blatt Papier)
fully automated [ˌfʊli ˈɔːtəmeɪtɪd]	vollautomatisch	**bar graph** [ˈbɑː grɑːf]	Säulendiagramm
driverless [ˈdraɪvələs]	fahrerlos	**increase** [ˈɪŋkriːs]	Zunahme, Anstieg
drone [drəʊn]	Drohne	**decrease** [ˈdiːkriːs]	Abnahme, Rückgang
robot [ˈrəʊbɒt]	Roboter	**distribution cost** [ˌdɪstrɪˈbjuːʃn kɒst]	Vertriebskosten
T **keyword** [ˈkiːwɜːd]	Schlagwort, Stichwort, Schlüsselwort	113 to **climb** [klaɪm]	ansteigen
automation [ɔːtəˈmeɪʃn]	Automatisierung	to **decrease** [dɪˈkriːs]	abnehmen, zurückgehen
last mile [ˌlɑːst ˈmaɪl]	letzte Meile	to **drop** [drɒp]	fallen, zurückgehen
111 **means of transport** [ˌmiːnz əv ˈtrænspɔːt]	Transportmittel	to **flatten out** [ˌflætn ˈaʊt]	auf gleichem Stand bleiben
capsule [ˈkæpsjuːl]	Kapsel	to **fluctuate** [ˈflʌktʃueɪt]	schwanken
tube [tjuːb]	Röhre	to **increase** [ɪnˈkriːs]	zunehmen, ansteigen
shipyard [ˈʃɪpjɑːd]	Werft	to **level off** [ˌlevl ˈɒf]	sich einpendeln
inland [ˈɪnlænd]	ins/im Landesinnere/n	to **remain constant** [rɪˌmeɪn ˈkɒnstənt]	gleich bleiben
solar energy [ˌsəʊlə ˈenədʒi]	Solarenergie	T to **look into sth** [ˌlʊk ˈɪntə]	etw prüfen, etw untersuchen
in turn [ɪn ˈtɜːn]	wiederum	to **lower sth** [ˈləʊə]	etw senken
elsewhere [ˌelsˈweə]	anderswo	**x-axis** [ˈeks æksɪs]	X-Achse
collaboration [kəˌlæbəˈreɪʃn]	Zusammenarbeit	**gradual** [ˈgrædʒuəl]	allmählich, langsam
interconnected [ˌɪntəkəˈnektɪd]	vernetzt	**jump** [dʒʌmp]	Sprung
to **recharge** [ˌriːˈtʃɑːdʒ]	sich (wieder)aufladen	**drop** [drɒp]	Rückgang, Abnahme
self-driving [ˌself ˈdraɪvɪŋ]	selbstfahrend	**volunteer** [ˌvɒlənˈtɪə]	Freiwillige/r
efficiency [ɪˈfɪʃnsi]	Wirtschaftlichkeit, Effizienz	to **make sth up** [ˌmeɪk ˈʌp]	etw ausmachen
overhead cable [ˌəʊvəˌhed ˈkeɪbl]	Oberleitung	**fleet** [fliːt]	Fuhrpark, Flotte
to **connect to sth** [kəˈnekt tə]	sich mit etw verbinden	**maintenance** [ˈmeɪntənəns]	Wartung, Instandhaltung
to **reduce sth** [rɪˈdjuːs]	etw verringern, etw senken	114 **at present** [ət ˈpreznt]	momentan, gegenwärtig
emissions *pl* [ɪˈmɪʃnz]	Ausstoß, Emissionen	to **pick sth** [pɪk]	etw nehmen
climate [ˈklaɪmət]	Klima	**glasses** *pl* [ˈglɑːsɪz]	Brille
		tachograph [ˈtækəgrɑːf]	Fahrtenschreiber
		wallet [ˈwɒlɪt]	Brieftasche, Portemonnaie
		locker [ˈlɒkə]	Schließfach, Spind

Unit word list

old-fashioned [ˌəʊldˈfæʃənd]	altmodisch	
time clock [ˈtaɪm klɒk]	Stechuhr	
robotic cleaning machine [rəʊˌbɒtɪk ˈkliːnɪŋ məʃiːn]	Reinigungsroboter	
to install sth [ɪnˈstɔːl]	etw installieren	
front door [ˌfrʌnt ˈdɔː]	Haustür	
temporary [ˈtemprəri]	befristet	
keyless access [ˌkiːləs ˈækses]	schlüsselloser Zugang	
boot [buːt]	Kofferraum	
to doubt sth [daʊt]	etw bezweifeln	
as [əz]	weil	
time-clock software [ˈtaɪm klɒk ˌsɒftweə]	Zeiterfassungssoftware	

115
popular [ˈpɒpjələ]	beliebt	
T to believe that … [bɪˈliːv ðət]	davon überzeugt sein, dass …	
the right way forward [ðə ˌraɪt weɪ ˈfɔːwəd]	der richtige Weg	
to innovate [ˈɪnəveɪt]	innovativ sein	
luckily [ˈlʌkɪli]	glücklicherweise	
to operate [ˈɒpəreɪt]	in Betrieb sein, tätig sein, laufen	
to introduce sth [ˌɪntrəˈdjuːs]	etw einführen	
shift [ʃɪft]	Schicht	
personal life [ˌpɜːsənl ˈlaɪf]	Privatleben	
flexibility [ˌfleksəˈbɪləti]	Flexibilität	
employment [ɪmˈplɔɪmənt]	Anstellung, Arbeitsplatz, Beschäftigung	
to affect sb [əˈfekt]	jdn betreffen	
to upgrade [ˌʌpˈgreɪd]	aufrüsten, hochrüsten	
self-maintaining [ˌself meɪnˈteɪnɪŋ]	selbstwartend	
self-correcting [ˌself kəˈrektɪŋ]	selbstkorrigierend	
to be a thing of the past [bi ə ˌθɪŋ əv ðə ˈpɑːst]	der Vergangenheit angehören	
to re-fit sth [riːˈfɪt]	etw umbauen, etw neu ausstatten	
high-rise shelving system [ˌhaɪ raɪz ˈʃelvɪŋ sɪstəm]	Hochregalsystem	
to accommodate sth [əˈkɒmədeɪt]	etw unterbringen	
turnaround [ˈtɜːnəraʊnd]	Umschlag	
turnover [ˈtɜːnəʊvə]	Umschlag	
health and safety [ˌhelθ ənd ˈseɪfti]	Arbeitsschutz, Arbeitssicherheit	
reliability [rɪˌlaɪəˈbɪləti]	Zuverlässigkeit	
outcome [ˈaʊtkʌm]	Ergebnis, Resultat, Auswirkung(en)	
announcement [əˈnaʊnsmənt]	Ankündigung	
serious change [ˌsɪəriəs ˈtʃeɪndʒ]	bedeutende Veränderung	
to operate sth [ˈɒpəreɪt]	etw bedienen, etw betreiben	

116
HR department [ˌeɪtʃ ˈɑː dɪpɑːtmənt]	Personalabteilung	
to keep sb up to date [kiːp ˌʌp tə ˈdeɪt]	jdm auf dem Laufenden halten	
HR director [ˌeɪtʃ ˌɑː dəˈrektə]	Personalchef/in, Personalleiter/in	
participant [pɑːˈtɪsɪpənt]	Teilnehmer/in	
to postpone [pəˈspəʊn]	(nach hinten) verschieben	
to be unable to do sth [bi ʌnˈeɪbl tə]	etw nicht tun können	
item (on the agenda) [ˈaɪtəm]	Tagesordnungspunkt	
any other business (AOB) [ˌeni ˌʌðə ˈbɪznəs]	(Tagesordnung:) Verschiedenes	
minutes pl [ˈmɪnɪts]	Protokoll	
T full-time [ˌfʊl ˈtaɪm]	Vollzeit(-)	
to pass an exam [ˌpɑːs ən ɪgˈzæm]	eine Prüfung bestehen	
to conclude [tə kənˈkluːd]	abschließend sich (dazu) äußern	
to comment [ˈkɒment]		
importance [ɪmˈpɔːtns]	Wichtigkeit, Bedeutung	
leftover holiday [ˌleftəʊvə ˈhɒlədeɪ]	Resturlaub	
reminder [rɪˈmaɪndə]	Erinnerung, Hinweis	
Easter [ˈiːstə]	Ostern	
thoroughly [ˈθʌrəli]	völlig, voll und ganz	
to come in on sth [ˌkʌm ˈɪn ɒn]	etwas zu etw sagen	
to wrap sth up [ˌræp ˈʌp]	etw abschließen, etw zum Abschluss bringen	
input [ˈɪnpʊt]	Beitrag, Beiträge	

117
changeover [ˈtʃeɪndʒəʊvə]	Umstellung	
to volunteer to do sth [ˌvɒlənˈtɪə tə duː]	sich bereit erklären, etw zu tun	
to be in favour of sth [bi ɪn ˈfeɪvər əv]	für etw sein	
General Manager [ˌdʒenrəl ˈmænɪdʒə]	Geschäftsführer/in	
P early shift [ˈɜːli ʃɪft]	Frühschicht	
day shift [ˈdeɪ ʃɪft]	Tagschicht	
staff member [ˈstɑːf membə]	Mitarbeiter/in, Angestellte/r	
neutral [ˈnjuːtrəl]	neutral	
to consult with sb [kənˈsʌlt wɪð]	mit jdm Rücksprache halten, sich mit jdm besprechen	
core time [ˈkɔː taɪm]	Kernzeit	
to invent sth [ɪnˈvent]	sich etw ausdenken	
married [ˈmærɪd]	verheiratet	
to make up for sth [ˌmeɪk ˈʌp fə]	etw nachholen	
in a row [ɪn ə ˈrəʊ]	nacheinander	

UNIT 12

118
(job) application [ˌæplɪˈkeɪʃn]	Bewerbung	
to near sth [nɪə]	sich einer Sache nähern	
to apply for a job [əˌplaɪ fər ə ˈdʒɒb]	sich um eine Stelle bewerben	
job agency [ˈdʒɒb eɪdʒənsi]	Arbeitsagentur, Arbeitsvermittlung	

newly-qualified [ˌnjuːli ˈkwɒlɪfaɪd]	jd, der gerade seinen Abschluss gemacht hat	
T coordinator [kəʊˈɔːdɪneɪtə]	Koordinator/in	
on one's own [ɒn wʌnz ˈəʊn]	alleine	
insurance policy [ɪnˈʃʊərəns pɒləsi]	Versicherungspolice	
varied [ˈveərɪd]	vielfältig	
experienced [ɪkˈspɪərɪənst]	erfahren	

119	to develop sth [dɪˈveləp]	etw ausbauen, etw entwickeln
	spreadsheet [ˈspredʃiːt]	Tabellenkalkulation, Tabelle
	job title [ˈdʒɒb taɪtl]	Stellenbezeichnung
	job opportunities pl [dʒɒb ˌɒpəˈtjuːnətiz]	Arbeitsmöglichkeiten
	career prospects pl [kəˈrɪə prɒspekts]	berufliche Perspektiven
	sector [ˈsektə]	Sektor, Bereich
	to pin sth to sth [pɪn]	etw an etw heften
	to rank sth [ræŋk]	etw einstufen, etw (in einer Rangliste) bewerten
	design [dɪˈzaɪn]	Gestaltung
	overall effect [ˌəʊvərˌɔːl ɪˈfekt]	Gesamteindruck, Gesamtwirkung
	to come across sth [ˌkʌm əˈkrɒs]	auf etw stoßen
	passport [ˈpɑːspɔːt]	Pass
	CV (curriculum vitae) [ˌsiː ˈviː]	Lebenslauf
	particular [pəˈtɪkjələ]	besondere/r/s
	self-assessment [ˌself əˈsesmənt]	Selbsteinstufung
	mobility [məʊˈbɪləti]	Freizügigkeit
	to acquire sth [əˈkwaɪə]	etw erlangen, etw erwerben
	vocational training certificate [vəʊˌkeɪʃənl ˈtreɪnɪŋ sətɪfɪkət]	Berufsabschluss
	supplement [ˈsʌplɪmənt]	Zusatz, Ergänzung
	agent [ˈeɪdʒənt]	zuständige/r Mitarbeiter/in
120	job advert(isement) [ˈdʒɒb ædvɜːt, ədvɜːtɪsmənt]	Stellenanzeige
	recruitment agency [rɪˈkruːtmənt eɪdʒənsi]	Personalvermittlung
121	freight forwarding company [ˈfreɪt fɔːwədɪŋ kʌmpəni]	Spedition
	export customs entry [ˈekspɔːt kʌstəmz entri]	Ausfuhranmeldung
	administrative work [ədˌmɪnɪstrətɪv ˈwɜːk]	Verwaltungstätigkeiten
	invoicing [ˈɪnvɔɪsɪŋ]	Fakturierung, Rechnungsstellung
	correspondence [ˌkɒrɪˈspɒndəns]	Schriftverkehr, Korrespondenz
	school leaving certificate [ˌskuːl liːvɪŋ səˈtɪfɪkət]	Schulabschluss

fluent [ˈfluːənt]	(Sprache:) fließend	
to take sb on [ˌteɪk ˈɒn]	jdn einstellen, jdn übernehmen	
reference number [ˈrefərəns nʌmbə]	Aktenzeichen, Kennziffer	
to optimise sth [ˈɒptɪmaɪz]	etw optimieren	
recognized [ˈrekəgnaɪzd]	anerkannt	
continuous [kənˈtɪnjuəs]	ständig, kontinuierlich	
support [səˈpɔːt]	Betreuung	
opportunity [ˌɒpəˈtjuːnəti]	Gelegenheit, Möglichkeit, Chance	
follow-up education [ˌfɒləʊ ʌp edʒuˈkeɪʃn]	Weiterbildung	
promotion [prəˈməʊʃn]	Beförderung, Aufstieg	
candidate [ˈkændɪdət]	Bewerber/in	
prospective [prəˈspektɪv]	potenziell	

122	(job) interview [ˈɪntəvjuː]	Vorstellungsgespräch
	to be shortlisted [bi ˈʃɔːtlɪstɪd]	in die engere Auswahl kommen
	face-to-face [ˌfeɪs tə ˈfeɪs]	persönlich
	to carry sth out [ˌkæri ˈaʊt]	etw durchführen

T	recruitment [rɪˈkruːtmənt]	Einstellung, Anwerbung (von Personal)
	strength [streŋθ]	Stärke
	weakness [ˈwiːknəs]	Schwäche
	reminder function [rɪˈmaɪndə fʌŋkʃn]	Erinnerungsfunktion
	independent(ly) [ˌɪndɪˈpendənt]	unabhängig
	battery [ˈbætəri]	Akku
	post [pəʊst]	Posten, Stelle
	permission [pəˈmɪʃn]	Erlaubnis
	honest(ly) [ˈɒnɪst]	ehrlich
	hard-working [ˌhɑːd ˈwɜːkɪŋ]	fleißig
	standards pl [ˈstændədz]	Ansprüche
	in particular [ɪn pəˈtɪkjələ]	ausgerechnet, gerade
	project managment [ˌprɒdʒekt ˈmænɪdʒmənt]	Projektleitung
	Norway [ˈnɔːweɪ]	Norwegen
	in a nutshell [ɪn ə ˈnʌtʃel]	kurz gesagt, mit einem Wort
	to take the initiative [ˌteɪk ði ɪˈnɪʃətɪv]	die Initative ergreifen
	lack (of sth) [læk]	Mangel (an etw)
	traineeship [treɪˈniːʃɪp]	Ausbildung, Lehre
	link [lɪŋk]	Zusammenhang, Verbindung
	to make a contribution [ˌmeɪk ə ˌkɒntrɪˈbjuːʃn]	einen Beitrag leisten
	to develop [dɪˈveləp]	sich (weiter)entwickeln
	to post sb to … [ˈpəʊst tə]	jdn nach … versetzen

present [ˈpreznt]	aktuell, gegenwärtig	
role model [ˈrəʊl mɒdl]	Vorbild	
to gather sth [ˈgæðə]	etw zusammenstellen	
reference [ˈrefərəns]	Referenz	
interviewer [ˈɪntəvjuːə]	jd, der ein Vorstellungsgespräch mit einem/einer Bewerber/in führt	

Unit word list

	to **flick through** sth ['flɪk θruː]	etw durchblättern		**chronological** [ˌkrɒnə'lɒdʒɪkl]	chronologisch
	pile [paɪl]	Stapel, Haufen		**achievement** [ə'tʃiːvmənt]	Leistung
	landline ['lændlaɪn]	Festnetz(telefon)		**driving licence** ['draɪvɪŋ laɪsns]	Führerschein
	to **charge** [tʃɑːdʒ]	(Akku) aufladen		**socializing** ['səʊʃəlaɪzɪŋ]	Ausgehen
	reception [rɪ'sepʃn]	Empfang		**date of birth** [ˌdeɪt əv 'bɜːθ]	Geburtsdatum
123 P	(job) **vacancy** ['veɪkənsi] **applicant** ['æplɪkənt] **expectations** pl [ˌekspek'teɪʃnz] **particular** [pə'tɪkjələ] **point of view** [ˌpɔɪnt əv 'vjuː] to **justify** ['dʒʌstɪfaɪ]	offene Stelle Bewerber/in Erwartungen bestimmte/r/s Sicht, Perspektive rechtfertigen, begründen		**nationality** [ˌnæʃə'næləti] **data protection** [ˌdeɪtə prətekʃn] **referee** [ˌrefə'riː] **on request** [ɒn rɪ'kwest]	Staatsangehörigkeit Datenschutz Referenz(geber) auf Wunsch, auf Anfrage
			125	**mobile** ['məʊbaɪl] to **seek** sth [siːk] **accountancy** [ə'kaʊntənsi] **economics** [ˌiːkə'nɒmɪks] **Polish** ['pəʊlɪʃ] **computer studies** pl [kəm'pjuːtə stʌdiz] **primary education** [ˌpraɪməri edʒu'keɪʃn] **secondary education** [ˌsekəndri edʒu'keɪʃn] **first aid** [ˌfɜːst 'eɪd] **athletics** [æθ'letɪks]	mobil etw suchen Buchführung Wirtschaft Polnisch Informatik Grundschule, Grundschulbildung Sekundarschule, Sekundarschulbildung Erste Hilfe Leichtathletik
	not quite [nɒt 'kwaɪt]	nicht ganz			
T	to **relax** [rɪ'læks] to **calm down** [ˌkɑːm 'daʊn] to **advise** sb sth [əd'vaɪz] **Not particularly.** [nɒt pə'tɪkjələli] **confident(ly)** ['kɒnfɪdənt] to **shake hands with** sb [ˌʃeɪk 'hændz wɪð] **shy** [ʃaɪ] **habit** ['hæbɪt] to **get into the habit of doing** sth [ˌget ɪntə ðə 'hæbɪt əv] **panel** ['pænl] to **relate** sth **to** sth [rɪ'leɪt tə] to **clarify** sth ['klærəfaɪ] **future prospects** pl [ˌfjuːtʃə 'prɒspekts] to **occur to** sb [ə'kɜː tə] **concerning** sth [kən'sɜːnɪŋ] **firm handshake** [ˌfɜːm 'hændʃeɪk] to **put** sth **to good use** [pʊt tə ˌgʊd 'juːs]	sich entspannen sich beruhigen jdm (zu) etw raten Eigentlich nicht. Nicht unbedingt. selbstbewusst jdm die Hand geben schüchtern Gewohnheit sich zu Gewohnheit machen, etw zu tun Gremium etw auf etw beziehen etw erläutern Zukunftsperspektiven jdm einfallen etw betreffend fester Händedruck etw sinnvoll nutzen	126	to **procure** sth [prə'kjʊə] **relevant** ['reləvənt] **basic knowledge** [ˌbeɪsɪk 'nɒlɪdʒ] **personable** ['pɜːsnəbl] to **be keen to do** sth [bɪ 'kiːn tə] **atmosphere** ['ætməsfɪə]	etw beschaffen einschlägig, entsprechend Grundkenntnisse umgänglich, sympathisch jdm liegt sehr daran, etw zu tun Atmosphäre
			127	**with reference to** [wɪð 'refrəns tə] to **apply** sth [ə'plaɪ] **on a daily basis** [ɒn ə ˌdeɪli 'beɪsɪs] to **benefit** sb/sth ['benɪfɪt] **at short notice** [ət ˌʃɔːt 'nəʊtɪs] to **appreciate** sth [ə'priːʃieɪt]	mit Bezug auf, bezugnehmend auf etw anwenden täglich, jeden Tag jdm/einer Sache nützen, jdm/einer Sache Nutzen bringen kurzfristig etw zu schätzen wissen
P	to **be familiar with** sth [bɪ fə'mɪliə wɪð] to **achieve** sth [ə'tʃiːv] to **stress** sth [stres] to **progress** [prə'gres]	mit etw vertraut sein, etw kennen etw erreichen etw betonen, etw hervorheben vorankommen			
124	**ability** [ə'bɪləti] **set** [set] to **grab** sb's **attention** [ˌgræb sʌmbədiz ə'tenʃn] **motivated** ['məʊtɪveɪtɪd] **relevant (to** sth**)** ['reləvənt] **reverse order** [rɪˌvɜːs 'ɔːdə]	Fähigkeit vorgegeben, starr, fest jds Aufmerksamkeit fesseln motiviert wichtig, relevant (für etw) umgekehrte Reihenfolge			

A–Z word list

Dieses Wörterverzeichnis enthält alle neuen Wörter aus *Logistics Matters 3rd Edition* in alphabetischer Reihenfolge. Nicht angeführt sind Wörter, die zum Grundwortschatz gehören. Die Zahl nach dem Stichwort bezieht sich auf die Seite, auf der das Wort zum ersten Mal erscheint. Wörter aus den Hörverständnisübungen sind zusätzlich mit einem **T** (Transkript) und Wörter aus den *Partner files* mit einem **P** gekennzeichnet.

A

A levels *pl* *6* Abitur, Abiturfächer
abbreviation *75* Abkürzung
ability *124* Fähigkeit
above-mentioned *82* obengenannt
abroad *7* im/ins Ausland
absorbent *54* Absorptionsmittel
AC *55P* Wechselstrom
academic *11* akademisch, schulisch, Schul-, universitär, Universitäts-
acceptable *45T* akzeptabel
access *82* Zugang, Zutritt; **keyless ~** *114* schlüsselloser Zugang
accident, by ~ *99* aus Versehen
accidentally *33* versehentlich
to **accommodate sth** *115T* etw unterbringen
accommodation *71* Unterkunft
to **accompany sb/sth** *54* jdn/etw begleiten
to **accomplish sth** *112* etw erreichen
accordance, in ~ with *53* in Übereinstimmung mit, nach
according to *15* gemäß, entsprechend, zufolge
accountancy *125* Buchführung
accounting manager *19* Buchhaltungsleiter/in
accounts (department) *16* Buchhaltung
accurate(ly) *53* exakt, genau
to **achieve sth** *123P* etw erreichen
achievement *124* Leistung
acid, sulphuric ~ *52* Schwefelsäure
acknowledgement (of an order) *94* Auftragsbestätigung
to **acquire: ~ sb** *18* jdn akquirieren; **~ sth** *119* etw erlangen, etw erwerben
action *106* Maßnahme(n); to **take ~** *112* Maßnahmen ergreifen, handeln
actual *47T* tatsächlich, eigentlich
to **add to the cost** *47T* die Kosten erhöhen
addition, in ~ to sth *33* zusätzlich zu etw; **perfect ~** *24* optimale Ergänzung
additional *45T* zusätzlich
address *48* Anschrift; **inside ~** *48* Innenadresse
administration *8T* Verwaltung; **business ~** *11* Betriebswirtschaft; **~ fee** *47* Regiekosten, Verwaltungsgebühr
administrative work *121* Verwaltungstätigkeiten

administrator *11* Leiter/in, Manager/in
ADR emergency kit *54P* Gefahrgut-Notfallset
advance, in ~ *78* im Voraus
advanced *11* fortgeschritten, weiterführend
advantage *10* Vorteil
advert(isement), job ~ *120* Stellenanzeige
to **advertise sth** *33* etw bewerben, für etw Werbung machen
advertising *17* Werbung; to **run ~** *17T* Werbung schalten
advice *35* Rat, Ratschlag, Ratschläge, Empfehlung(en); **~ of dispatch** *92* Versandanzeige
advisable *70* ratsam, geboten, zweckmäßig
to **advise: ~ sb** *35T* jdn beraten; **~ sb to do sth** *68* jdm raten, etw zu tun; **~ sb that/if …** *82* jdm mitteilen, dass/ob …; **~ sb sth** *123T* jdm (zu) etw raten
aeroplane *17* Flugzeug
aerospace *70* Raumfahrt-
to **affect: ~ sth** *37* etw beeinträchtigen; *110* sich auf etw auswirken, etw beeinflussen; **~ sb** *115T* jdn betreffen
to **afford sth** *71T* sich etw leisten (können)
affordable *33* erschwinglich
afraid, to be ~ *98* sich fürchten, Angst haben; **I'm ~ …** *10T* leider
agency *24* Agentur; **inspection ~** *93T* Prüfstelle, Überwachungsstelle; **job ~** *118* Arbeitsagentur, Arbeitsvermittlung; **recruitment ~** *120* Personalvermittlung
agenda *28T* Programm, Tagesordnung; **item on the ~** *116* Tagesordnungspunkt
agent *119* zuständige/r Mitarbeiter/in; **cargo ~** *64* Frachtspediteur; *66P* Spediteur/in, Kaufmann/-frau für Spedition und Logistikdienstleistung; **drying ~** *35T* Trockenmittel, Trocknungsmittel; **forwarding ~** *6T* Spediteur/in, Kaufmann/-frau für Spedition und Logistikdienstleistung; **freight ~** *58* Frachtvermittler/in
agreed, on the terms ~ *78* zu den vereinbarte Konditionen; **unless**

otherwise ~ *87* sofern nicht anders vereinbart
agreement, to come to an ~ *24* handelseinig werden
ahead, straight ~ *26T* geradeaus; to **lie ~ (of sb)** *24* vor jdm liegen, (jdm) bevorstehen
aid *29* Hilfsmittel; **emergency food ~** *72* Nahrungsmittelsoforthilfe; **first ~** *125* Erste Hilfe; **visual ~s** *pl* *31* visuelle Hilfsmittel
air: ~ cargo insurance *68T* Luftfrachtversicherung; **~ conditioning** *71T* Klimaanlage; **~ freight** *16* Luftfracht; **~ freighter** *62* Frachtflugzeug; **~ transport** *62* Luftfracht, Luftverkehr; **~ waybill** *64* Luftfrachtbrief
aircraft *53* Flugzeug
airline *64* Fluggesellschaft
airport: ~ of departure *67* Abgangsflughafen; **~ code** *62* Flughafen-Code
airy *15* luftig
aisle *36* Gang
alert, medical ~ badge *9* Notfallanhänger
all, first of ~ *45T* zunächst, als Erstes; **not at ~** *106* überhaupt nicht
allowed *9* zulässig, erlaubt; to **be ~ to do sth** *37T* etw tun dürfen
alongside, to work ~ sb *26T* mit jdm arbeiten
although *112* obwohl
amount *68T* Betrag, Summe; **~ (of sth)** *33* Menge (an etw)
anaesthesia machine *81T* Anästhesiegerät
to **analyze** *17T* analysieren
to **announce** *38* ankündigen
announcement *115* Ankündigung
annual leave *10* Jahresurlaub
antistatic bag *34* Antistatik-Beutel
any other business (AOB) *116* (Tagesordnung:) Verschiedenes
apart from *71P* außer, abgesehen von
to **apologize** *39* sich entschuldigen
apology *53T* Entschuldigung
apparel, wearing ~ *66T* Bekleidung
apparent, in ~ good order and condition *53* in äußerlich gutem Zustand, ohne äußerlich erkennbare Schäden
appealing *25* ansprechend
to **appear** *38* vorkommen, auftauchen

A–Z word list

appliance *65* Elektrogerät
applicable *53* (Recht usw.:) geltend; **non-~** *53* unzutreffend
applicant *123P* Bewerber/in
application: ~ (for sth) *38* Antrag (auf/für etw); **(job) ~** *118* Bewerbung
to **apply for a job** *118* sich um eine Stelle bewerben
to **apply sth** *127* etw anwenden
to **appreciate sth** *104* etw verstehen, für etw Verständnis haben; *127* etw zu schätzen wissen
apprentice *6* Auszubildende/r, Lehrling
apprenticeship *6* Lehre, Ausbildung
approach (to sth) *33* Herangehensweise (an etw), Konzept (für etw)
to **approach sb** *24* an jdn herantreten, auf jdn zukommen
appropriate(ly) *17T* angemessen, passend
approval, to find sb's ~ *91* jds Zustimmung finden; to **meet with sb's ~** *105* jds Zustimmung finden
approximately (approx.) *28* ungefähr, zirka
area *17T* Bereich, Gebiet
to **arrange: ~ (for) sth** *16* etw veranlassen, etw organisieren, etw planen; **~ sth** *38* etw (Termin usw.) vereinbaren
arrangements *pl 55* Modalitäten, Vereinbarungen, Abmachungen
arrival *70* Ankunft; **estimated time of ~ (ETA)** *83T* voraussichtliche Ankunftszeit
arsenic *52* Arsen
art, work of ~ *62* Kunstwerk
artic *51* Sattelzug
articulated: ~ lorry *BE 51* Sattelzug; **~ vehicle** *58* Gelenkfahrzeug
artificial *35* künstlich, Kunst-
as *114* weil; **~ follows** *20* wie folgt; **~ per** *86* nach, gemäß; **~ regards** *46* bezüglich, betreffend; **~ specified** *86* wie angegeben; **~ well as** *46* sowie, ebenso wie
asap (as soon as possible) *76* baldmöglichst
to **ascertain sth** *80* etw feststellen, etw sicherstellen
aspect *32* Seite, Gesichtspunkt, Aspekt
assembly *33* Montage; **~ line** *33* Montagelinie, -kette, -band
assessment *11* Beurteilung, Bewertung, Einschätzung, Urteil
assessor *11* Betreuer/in, Gutachter/in
to **assign sth** *53* etw zuweisen
assistance *38* Hilfe, Unterstützung
assistant, personal ~ *20T* persönliche/r Assistent/in; **management ~ for**
freight forwarding and logistics *6* Kaufmann/-frau für Spedition und Logistikdienstleistung; **management ~ for office communications** *12T* Kaufmann/-frau für Bürokommunikation
associate's degree *11* US-Berufsschulabschluss
association, trade ~ *64* Branchenvereinigung, Wirtschaftsverband
assortment *35* Auswahl, Zusammenstellung
to **assume** *87* davon ausgehen
to **assure sb that …** *46* jdm zusichern, dass …; jdm versichern, dass …
athletics *125* Leichtathletik
atmosphere *126* Atmosphäre
to **attach** *38* (E-Mail:) anhängen; **~ sth to sth** *74* etw an etw befestigen
attaché case *70* Aktentasche, Aktenkoffer
attached, to be ~ to sth *15T* mit etw verbunden sein
to **attend sth** *10* an etw teilnehmen, etw besuchen
attention *46* Aufmerksamkeit; to **pay ~ to sth** *19* auf etw achten; **for the ~ of** *49* zu Händen; to **grab sb's ~** *124* jds Aufmerksamkeit fesseln; **~ line** *48* Zeile „zu Händen"
attire *31* Kleidung
to **attract sb** *42* jdn anlocken, jdn ansprechen, jdn anziehen
attractive *10* reizvoll, attraktiv
audience *29* Publikum
auditing, invoice ~ *43* Rechnungsprüfung
Austria *10* Österreich
authorities *pl 66P* Behörden
automated *74* automatisiert, (voll) automatisch; **fully ~** *110* vollautomatisch; **A~ Guided Vehicle (AGV)** *74* fahrerloses Transportfahrzeug (FTF)
automatic, fully ~ *28T* vollautomatisch
automatically *66T* automatisch
automation *110T* Automatisierung
automotive *70* Automobil-
autonomous *110* autonom
availability *8* Verfügbarkeit
available *66P* verfügbar, erhältlich; to **be ~** *21* (Telefon:) zu sprechen sein
average *35* Durchschnitt
aviation *62* Luftverkehr, Luftfahrt
to **avoid sth** *13* etw vermeiden, etw umgehen
away, right ~ *98* sogleich, sofort; **straight ~** *58T* sofort

B

back, to turn one's ~ on sb *31* jdm den Rücken zuwenden
background *28T* Hintergrund
badge, medical alert ~ *9* Notfallanhänger
baker's *97P* Bäckerei
bakery *32* Bäckerei
bale *24* Ballen
bandage *76* Verband
bankrupt, to go ~ *25* Pleite gehen
bankruptcy *25* Konkurs
bar graph *112* Säulendiagramm
barge *26T* Lastkahn
base *35T* Fuß, Sockel; to **grow the customer ~** *32* den Kundenstamm ausbauen/erweitern
based, to be ~ in … *13* seinen Sitz in … haben, in … sein
basic: ~ knowledge *126* Grundkenntnisse; **~ rate** *99* Grundtarif, Basistarif
the basics *pl 98* das Wesentliche, die Grundlagen
basis, on a daily ~ *127* täglich, jeden Tag; **on a regular ~** *44* regelmäßig
battery *122T* Akku
bay, lorry ~ *BE 26T* Ladebucht; **high-~ shelving** *36* Hochregallager
to **be: if I were you** *35T* an Ihrer Stelle
bean, cocoa ~ *76* Kakaobohne; **coffee ~** *76* Kaffeebohne
to **bear: ~ sth** *25* etw (Risiko, Kosten) tragen; **~ left/right** *97T* sich links/rechts halten
bearer *80* Inhaber/in
bed and breakfast (B&B) *71T* Frühstückspension, Übernachtung mit Frühstück
bedding *76* Bettwäsche, Bettzeug
behalf, on ~ of sb *20* für jdn, in jds Namen
behaviour *100* Verhalten, Benehmen
Beijing *62* Peking
Belgium *50* Belgien
to **believe that …** *115T* davon überzeugt sein, dass …
to **belong to sb** *25* jdm gehören
below *53* untengenannt
belt, conveyor ~ *36* Förderband
bend *97* Kurve
to **benefit sb/sth** *127* jdm/einer Sache nützen, jdm/einer Sache Nutzen bringen
benefit *15T* Vorteil, Nutzen
benefits *pl 8* Zusatzleistungen, Sozialleistungen
bill of lading (B/L) *78* Frachtbrief, Konnossement; **claused ~** *78* unreines Konnossement; **clean ~** *78* reines

Konnossement; **foul ~** *78* unreines Konnossement; **ocean ~** *78* Seefrachtbrief, Seekonnossement; **order ~** *78* Orderkonnossement; **port-to-port ~** *78* Seefrachtbrief, Seekonnossement; **received for shipment ~** *78* Übernahmekonnossement; **shipped on board ~** *78* Bordkonnossement
billion *43* Milliarde
birth, date of ~ *124* Geburtsdatum; **place of ~** *12* Geburtsort
blackboard *19* Wandtafel
blank, to leave sth ~ *45T* etw leerlassen; *66T* etw frei lassen, etw offenlassen
block release *6* Blockunterricht *(an der Berufsschule)*
blouse *9* Bluse
board *11* (Wand-)Tafel; *55* Brett; **full ~** *71* Vollpension; **half ~** *71* Halbpension; **shipped on ~ bill of lading** *78* Bordkonnossement
boarding card *70T* Bordkarte
body *48* *(Brief:)* Haupttext; *51* *(Lkw:)* Aufbau; **enclosed ~** *58T* geschlossener Aufbau; **swap ~** *51* Wechselaufbau; **~ language** *31* Körpersprache
bomb *64* Bombe
bonus *33* zusätzlicher Vorteil
bookkeeping *16* Buchhaltung, Buchführung
boot *114* Kofferraum
boots *pl 9* Stiefel
border *50* (Landes-)Grenze; **cross-~** *43* grenzübergreifend; **~ control** *50* Grenzkontrolle
both … and *26T* sowohl … als auch
bottled *35* in Flaschen
bottling plant *59* Abfüllanlage
box, mandatory ~ *58T (Formular:)* Pflichtfeld; **to double ~ sth** *35T* etw zweifach in einer Kiste verpacken; **~ truck** *AE 51* Lkw mit Kastenaufbau; **~ van** *BE 51* Lkw mit Kastenaufbau
to brainstorm *8* Ideen sammeln
branch *6* Niederlassung, Filiale
branded marking *55* Brandmarke
break *8* Pause; **to take a ~** *10T* eine Pause machen; **lunch ~** *8T* Mittagspause; **morning ~** *8T* Frühstückspause
to break up *72* auseinanderbrechen
bribe *101* Bestechung(sversuch)
brief *26T* kurz, knapp
to brief sb *52* jdn einweisen, jdn informieren
brochure *38* Prospekt
broom *54* Besen
bubble *34* Blase; **~ wrap** *34* Luftpolsterfolie

bud, ear ~s *pl 9* In-Ear-Kopfhörer
budget *17T* Etat, Budget
building *15T* Gebäude; **~ materials** *pl 36* Baustoffe, Baumaterial; **~ site** *37* Baustelle
bulb, light ~ *34* Glühbirne
bulk *72* Schüttgut, Massengut; **intermediate ~ container (IBC)** *53T* Großpackmittel (IBC); **~ carrier** *73* Schüttgutfrachter, Massengutfrachter; **~ sale** *37* Massenverkauf, Großhandelsverkauf
bulky *37T* sperrig
to bump: ~ into sb *99* jdn anrempeln; **to get ~ed from a flight** *70T* aus einem Flug ausgebucht werden
to bundle sth together *43* etw bündeln, etw zusammenfassen
bunker fuel *72* Bunkeröl, Schweröl
business, to go out of ~ *24* das Geschäft aufgeben, zumachen; **family ~** *8T* Familienunternehmen; **any other ~ (AOB)** *116* (Tagesordnung:) Verschiedenes; **~ administration** *11* Betriebswirtschaft; **~ card** *31* (geschäftliche) Visitenkarte; **~ partner** *24* Geschäftspartner/in; **~ trip** *8* Geschäftsreise
butcher's *97P* Metzgerei
buyer *78* Käufer/in
by *35* mal; **~ accident** *99* aus Versehen; **~ hand** *37T* von Hand; **~ the way** *10T* übrigens

C

cab *51* Fahrerhaus, Führerhaus
cabin *64* Kabine
cable, overhead ~ *111* Oberleitung; **~ drum** *35* Kabeltrommel
cage, pallet ~ *34* Gitterboxpalette
to calculate sth *45T* etw berechnen
calculation *47* Berechnung, Kalkulation
to call: ~ back *20* zurückrufen; **~ in sick** *67* sich krankmelden; **to be ~ed** *13* heißen
call, to take a (phone) ~ *20* ein Gespräch entgegennehmen
caller *20* Anrufer/in
to calm down *123T* sich beruhigen
campaign *18* (Werbe-)Kampagne
to cancel sth *101T* etw absagen
candidate *121* Bewerber/in
canister *34* Kanister
canteen *8T* Kantine
capable, to be ~ of sth *28T* zu etw in der Lage sein
capacity *65* Fassungsvermögen, Volumen; **freight ~** *42* Frachtkapazität, Laderaum

capsule *111* Kapsel
car, company ~ *8* Firmenwagen; **hire ~** *71* Mietwagen; **~ manufacturer** *105* Auto(mobil)hersteller; **multi-storey ~ park** *97P* Parkhaus
carbon footprint *43* CO_2-Fußabdruck
card, boarding ~ *70T* Bordkarte; **business ~** *31* (geschäftliche) Visitenkarte; **index ~** *30* Karteikarte; **prompt ~** *30* Moderationskarte; **Transport Emergency C~** *54* Unfallmerkblatt
cardboard *34* Pappe
care, duty of ~ *80* Sorgfaltspflicht; **take ~ of sth** *16* sich um etw kümmern, etw bearbeiten, etw erledigen; **to handle sth with ~** *15* etw mit Vorsicht behandeln; **Handle with ~.** *35* Vorsicht, zerbrechlich! Zerbrechliches Packgut!
career *11* (berufliche) Laufbahn, Karriere; **~ prospects** *pl 119* berufliche Perspektiven
careful *66T* sorgfältig
cargo *45* Fracht; **~ agent** *64* Frachtspediteur; *66P* Spediteur/in, Kaufmann/-frau für Spedition und Logistikdienstleistung; **~ category** *73* Ladungskategorie; **~ handling** *65* Frachtumschlag, Warenumschlag; **~ hold** *65* Frachtraum, Laderaum; **~ screening** *64* Frachtkontrolle; **air ~ insurance** *68T* Luftfrachtversicherung
carpet *65* Teppichboden, Teppich
carriage *47* Beförderung, Transport; **main ~** *87* Hauptlauf, Haupttransport; **on-~** *81T* Weitertransport; **post-~** *68T* Nachlauf, Nachtransport; **pre-~** *68T* Vorlauf, Vortransport; **contract of ~** *78* Beförderungsvertrag, Frachtvertrag; **~ charges** *pl 56* Frachtgebühr(en)
carrier *53* Frachtführer; *64* Fluggesellschaft; **bulk ~** *73* Schüttgutfrachter, Massengutfrachter; **crude ~** *73* Rohöltanker; **liquefied gas ~** *73* Flüssiggastanker
to carry: ~ sth *54* etw mitführen; *72* etw befördern; **~ sth out** *122* etw durchführen; **hand-~ shipment** *70T* Handcarry-Lieferung, persönlich begleiteter Transport
carton *94* Karton
case *20T* Fall; *35* Kasten, Kiste; **attaché ~** *70* Aktentasche, Aktenkoffer; **whatever the ~ may be** *104* wie auch immer
cash *62* Bargeld; **~ discount** *94* Skonto; **~ on delivery** *56* (per) Nachnahme; **~ with order (CWO)** *86* Vorkasse

casual 9 (Kleidung:) leger
to catch sth 20T etw verstehen, etw mitbekommen
to categorize 72 klassifizieren, kategorisieren
category, cargo ~ 73 Ladungskategorie
catering equipment 83P Großküchengeräte, Gastrononmieausstattung
centre of gravity 35 Schwerpunkt
CEO (Chief Executive Officer) 16 Vorstandsvorsitzende/r, Geschäftsführer/in
certificate: ~ of origin 56 Ursprungszeugnis, Herkunftszeugnis; container packing ~ 53 Containerpackzertifikat; school leaving ~ 121 Schulabschluss; vehicle packing ~ 53 Fahrzeugpackzertifikat; vocational training ~ 119 Berufsabschluss
challenge 98 Herausforderung, (schwierige) Aufgabe
chamber of commerce 93T Handelskammer
chain, cold ~ 34 Kühlkette; supply ~ 24 Lieferkette, Versorgungskette
change, serious ~ 115 bedeutende Veränderung; ~ of plan 38 Planänderung
changeover 117 Umstellung
characteristics pl 100 (Charakter-)Eigenschaften, (charakteristische) Merkmale
charge 50 Gebühr; total ~s pl 66P Gesamtbetrag (der Gebühren); minimum ~ 66P Mindestgebühr; supplementary ~s pl 56 Zusatzgebühren, zusätzliche Kosten; carriage ~s pl 56 Frachtgebühr(en); shipping ~s pl 86 Versandkosten; to be in ~ of sth 17 für etw zuständig sein, für etw verantwortlich sein
to charge 122 (Akku) aufladen; ~ sth 57T etw (Preis usw.) verlangen, etw berechnen
chargeable weight 66T frachtpflichtiges Gewicht
charity 73 Hilfsorganisation
chart 112 Diagramm; flow ~ 19 Flussdiagramm; organization ~ 16 Organigramm; pie ~ 103 Tortendiagramm
to check sth in 70 etw (Gepäck usw.) aufgeben
check-in date 71 Anreisedatum
check-out date 71 Abreisedatum
cheese wheel 49 Käselaib
chemist's 97P Drogerie
cherry 62 Kirsche

China, People's Republic of ~ 88 Volksrepublik China
chronological 124 chronologisch
circle 25 Kreis
circuit 37 Schaltkreis
circumstances pl 83 Umstände; ~ beyond our control 83 Umstände, auf die wir keinen Einfluss haben
clarification 98 Klärung, Erläuterung
to clarify sth 44 etw klären, etw abklären; 123T etw erläutern
clarity 25 Klarheit, Deutlichkeit
class, hazard ~ 53 Gefahrenklasse
to classify sth 52 etw klassifizieren, etw einordnen
clause, notwithstanding any ~ to the contrary 56 ungeachtet etwaiger anderslautender Bestimmungen
claused bill of lading 78 unreines Konnossement
clean bill of lading 78 reines Konnossement
to clear: ~ up 8T aufräumen; ~ a space 15T einen Platz räumen; ~ a payment 28T eine Zahlung freigeben, eine Zahlung abrechnen
clearance 64 Abfertigung, Freigabe; currency ~ 64 Devisenclearing; customs ~ 77 Zollabfertigung; export ~ 89 Ausfuhrabfertigung, Ausfuhrfreigabe; import ~ 89 Einfuhrabfertigung, Einfuhrfreigabe
cleared for export 87 zur Ausfuhr freigemacht
clerk, export ~ 38 Außenhandelskaufmann/-frau; shipping ~ 52 Expedient/in, Spediteur/in, Kaufmann/-frau für Spedition und Logistikdienstleistung
client 16 Kunde/Kundin
climate 111 Klima
to climb 113 ansteigen
to clock in/out 8T ein-/ausstempeln
to close down 73 schließen, zumachen
close: ~ (to sb/sth) 100 dicht (bei jdm/etw), nahe (an jdm/etw); to take a ~er look at sth 50 sich etw näher/genauer ansehen; complimentary ~ 39 (Brief:) Schlussformel
closed 25 geschlossen; ~-toe 9 (Schuh:) geschlossen
closely, to work ~ with sb 19 eng mit jdm zusammenarbeiten
clothing 9 Kleidung; protective ~ 54 Schutzkleidung
coach 71 Reisebus
coal 62 Kohle
coat 13 Jacke, Mantel
cocoa bean 76 Kakaobohne

code, airport ~ 62 Flughafen-Code; dress ~ 8 Kleiderordnung
coffee bean 76 Kaffeebohne
coil 34 Rolle, Spule; steel ~ 76 Stahlblechrolle
cold: ~ chain 34 Kühlkette; ~ storage 36 Kühllager, Kühlhaus
collaboration 111 Zusammenarbeit
colleague 6 Kollege/-in
to collect sth 24 etw abholen; 25 etw sammeln
collection 43 Abholung
colourful 29 bunt, farbenfroh
to come: ~ across 30 wirken; ~ across sth 119 auf etw stoßen; ~ up 46 bevorstehen; ~ in on sth 116T etwas zu etw sagen; ~ to an agreement 24 handelseinig werden; C~ to think of it … 8T Wenn ich es mir recht/genau überlege …
comfortable, to feel ~ 15T sich wohlfühlen
to comment 116T sich (dazu) äußern
commerce 7 Handel, Wirtschaft; chamber of ~ 93T Handelskammer
commercial invoice 93T Handelsrechnung
to commission sb 52 jdn beauftragen
committee 98 Arbeitsgemeinschaft, Ausschuss
commodity 66T Ware
common, to have sth in ~ 79 etw gemeinsam haben; ~(ly) 45 üblich, verbreitet, häufig
to communicate 15T kommunizieren
community, sense of ~ 15T Gemeinschaftssinn
company, family-owned ~ 46 Familienbetrieb; freight forwarding ~ 121 Spedition; age ~ 24 (Straßen-)Spedition(sfirma), Frachtfuhrunternehmen; limited liability ~ (LLC) AE 25 Gesellschaft mit beschränkter Haftung (GmbH); private limited ~ (Ltd) 24 Gesellschaft mit beschränkter Haftung (GmbH); public limited ~ (plc) 24 Aktiengesellschaft (AG); training ~ 6 Ausbildungsbetrieb; in-~ 7 betriebsintern; to join a ~ 24 in ein Unternehmen eintreten, zu einem Unternehmen kommen; ~ car 8 Firmenwagen; ~ magazine 49 Firmenzeitschrift, Hauszeitung
to compare sth (to sth) 8 etw (mit etw) vergleichen
comparison 43T Vergleich; in ~ (to sth) 72 im Vergleich (zu/mit etw)
to compensate sb for sth 105 jdn für etw entschädigen, jdm etw erstatten

compensation 68T Schadenersatz, Entschädigung
competition 42 Konkurrenz; 91 Wettbewerb
competitive 43T wettbewerbsorientiert, konkurrenzfähig; ~ **price** 42 günstiger Preis
competitor 47 Wettbewerber/in, Konkurrent/in
to **complain** 37T sich beschweren, sich beklagen
complaint 16 Reklamation, Beschwerde
to **complete an order** 111 eine Bestellung ausführen
complicated 97T kompliziert
complimentary close 39 (Brief:) Schlussformel
to **comply with sth** 80 einer Sache (Vorschrift usw.) nachkommen, einer Sache entsprechen
component 63 Bauteil
computer studies pl 125 Informatik
computerized 12 elektronisch, Computer-
to **concentrate (on sth)** 15T sich (auf etw) konzentrieren
concern, to show ~ 107 Bedenken äußern, sich besorgt zeigen
concerning sth 123T etw betreffend
to **conclude:** ~ **sth** 26T etw beschließen, etw beenden; **to** ~ 116T abschließend
conclusion 29 Schluss
condensation 76 Kondensat, Kondenswasser, Schwitzwasser
to **condense** 35T sich niederschlagen, kondensieren
condition 6 Bedingung; 33 Zustand; **in apparent good order and** ~ 53 in äußerlich gutem Zustand, ohne äußerlich erkennbare Schäden; **working ~s** pl 6 Arbeitsbedingungen; **(general) terms and ~s** pl 46 Allgemeine Geschäftsbedingungen
to **conduct sth** 8 etw durchführen
conference room 26 Besprechungsraum
confident(ly) 123T selbstbewusst
to **confirm sth** 20 etw bestätigen
confirmation 39 Bestätigung
confusing 51 verwirrend
to **connect** 20T verbinden; ~ **to sth** 111 sich mit etw verbinden
connection 26T Kontakt, Verbindung
consent 90 Zustimmung
consequence 104 Folge, Konsequenz, Auswirkung
to **consider:** ~ **sth** 42 etw in Betracht ziehen, über etw nachdenken, etw berücksichtigen; **to be ~ed sth** 65 als etw gelten

to **consign sth** 80 etw verschicken, etw senden
consignee 53 Empfänger/in, Konsignatar
consignment 17 Sendung, Lieferung; ~ **note** 56 Frachtbrief
consignor 53 Absender, Konsignant
to **consist of sth** 66P aus etw bestehen
to **consolidate sth** 17T etw zusammenfassen, etw konsolidieren
consolidated freight 16 Sammelgut
constant, to remain ~ 113 gleich bleiben
constantly 37 ständig
construction contractor 37 Bauunternehmen, Bauunternehmer/in
to **consult with sb** 117P mit jdm Rücksprache halten, sich mit jdm besprechen
consultant 15 Berater/in
contact 76 Ansprechpartner/in; **eye** ~ 31 Blickkontakt; ~ **details** pl 31 Kontaktdaten
to **contain sth** 28T etw enthalten
container 34 Behälter; **dry** ~ 75 Trockencontainer; **flat rack** ~ 76 Flachcontainer, Flat-Rack-Container; **hard-top** ~ 75 Hardtop-Container; **intermediate bulk** ~ **(IBC)** 53T Großpackmittel (IBC); **open-top** ~ 76 Opentop-Container, oben offener Container; ~ **packing certificate** 53 Containerpackzertifikat
contents 30 Inhalt
continuous 34 endlos; 121 ständig, kontinuierlich
contoured 65 konturiert, geformt
contract 7 Vertrag; **to fulfil a** ~ 106 einen Vertrag erfüllen; ~ **of carriage** 78 Beförderungsvertrag, Frachtvertrag
contractor, construction ~ 37 Bauunternehmen, Bauunternehmer/in; **plumbing** ~ 37 Klempnereibetrieb; **sub~** 105 Subunternehmer/in
contrary, notwithstanding any clause to the ~ 56 ungeachtet etwaiger anderslautender Bestimmungen
to **contrast sth** 103 etw (einander) gegenüberstellen, etw (miteinander) vergleichen
contrast, in ~ **(to sth)** 15T im Gegensatz (dazu/zu etw)
contribution, to make a ~ 122T einen Beitrag leisten
control, border ~ 50 Grenzkontrolle; **quality** ~ 111 Qualitätskontrolle; **circumstances beyond our** ~ 83 Umstände, auf die wir keinen Einfluss haben; ~ **staple** 55 Prüfklammer

convenience 42 günstige Lage; ~ **store** AE 11 lang geöffneter Laden (oft mit Tankstelle), Mini-Markt
convenient(ly) 33 praktisch, (verkehrs)günstig
to **convert sth into sth** 78 etw in etw umwandeln
conveyor belt 36 Förderband
to **coordinate:** ~ **with sb** 8T sich mit jdm abstimmen; ~ **sth** 17 etw miteinander abstimmen, etw koordinieren;
coordinated: C~ Universal Time 62 koordinierte Weltzeit
coordinator 118T Koordinator/in
copy 48 Exemplar, Kopie
cordially: C~ yours, AE 48 Mit herzlichen Grüßen
core time 117P Kernzeit
corner 101T Ecke
Corporation (Corp/Inc) AE 25 Aktiengesellschaft (AG)
correctness 30 Richtigkeit
correspondence 121 Schriftverkehr, Korrespondenz
corridor 15T Flur, Gang
cost, to add to the ~ 47T die Kosten erhöhen; **at** ~ **price** 8T zum Selbstkostenpreis; **distribution** ~ 112 Vertriebskosten; ~ **savings** pl 111 Einsparungen, Kostenersparnis
cost-effective 72 wirtschaftlich, kostengünstig
costume 66 (Theater-)Kostüm
council, works ~ 26 Betriebsrat
counter-offer 88 Gegenangebot
counterpart 101 Gegenüber, Ansprechpartner/in
countryside, in the ~ 71T auf dem Land
courier, on-board ~ 70 On-Board-Kurier
course 11 Studiengang; **(training)** ~ 6T Ausbildung
coursework 11 schriftliche Arbeit(en)
to **cover sth** 27 etw (Thema) behandeln; 63 etw bedecken, etw abdecken; 68T etw versichern, etw decken
covering letter 38 Anschreiben, Begleitschreiben
crane 36 Kran; **gantry** ~ 74 Portalkran; **quay** ~ 74 Kaikran
crate 34 Transportkiste
to **create sth** 8 etw entwerfen, etw erstellen
credit, documentary ~ 90 Dokumentenakkreditiv; → **letter of credit (L/C)**
crisis, fuel ~ 24 Ölkrise
crisps pl BE 45 Chips
Croatia 55 Kroatien
cross-border 43 grenzübergreifend

crossroads *97* Kreuzung
crowded *101T* voll (mit Leuten)
crude: ~ oil *73* Rohöl; **~ carrier** *73* Rohöltanker
cube *53* Würfel, Kubus, Kubik
cubic: ~ foot *75* Kubikfuß; **~ metre** *75* Kubikmeter
cubicle *15T* Kabuff, Arbeitsplatz *(im Großraumbüro)*
cultural *100* kulturell, Kultur-
currency *64* Währung; **~ clearance** *64* Devisenclearing
current *8* aktuell, momentan
currently *44* momentan, aktuell
curtain *51* Vorhang, Gardine
curtainsider *51* Gardinenplanenauflieger, Schiebeplanenauflieger, Curtainsider
customary *87* üblich
customer *16* Kunde/Kundin;
customer, first-time ~ *46* Erstkunde/-kundin, Neukunde/-kundin; **~ loyalty** *46* Kundentreue; **~ service** *8T* Kundenbetreuung, Kundendienst; **~ service representative** *19* Kundenberater/in, Kundenbetreuer/in; to **grow the ~ base** *32* den Kundenstamm ausbauen/erweitern
customs *16* Zoll; **~ clearance** *77* Zollabfertigung; **~ duties** *pl* *56* Zollgebühren; **~ office** *17T* Zollamt, Zollstelle; **export ~ entry** *121* Ausfuhranmeldung
cut-out *35T* Aussparung
CV (curriculum vitae) *119* Lebenslauf
Czech Republic *8T* Tschechische Republik

D

daily, on a ~ basis *127* täglich, jeden Tag; **~ operations** *pl* *19* Tagesgeschäft
dairy products *pl* *37* Milchprodukte
damage *33* Beschädigung(en), Schaden, Schäden
damaged *33* beschädigt
danger area *54* Gefahrenbereich, Gefahrenzone
dangerous goods *pl* *52* Gefahrgüter; **~ note (DGN)** *52* brit. Gefahrguterklärung
dangling *9* herabhängend, baumelnd
data *pl* *14* Daten; **financial ~** *19* Finanzdaten; **~ protection** *124* Datenschutz
database *58T* Datenbank
date, to keep sb up to ~ *116* jdm auf dem Laufenden halten
to **date sth** *68* etw datieren
dated ... *91* vom ..., mit Datum vom ...

day: ~ release *6T* tagweise Freistellung zur beruflichen Weiterbildung; **~ shift** *117P* Tagschicht
daylight saving time *63* Sommerzeit
DC *55P* Gleichstrom
deadline *8T* Frist, Fertigstellungstermin; to **meet a ~** *8T* eine Frist einhalten
deal *93* Geschäft, Abschluss
to **deal with sb/sth** *16* sich um jdn/etw kümmern, sich mit jdm/etw befassen; *24* mit jdm/etw zu tun haben; *29* mit jdm/etw umgehen, sich mit jdm/etw befassen
debt, to be in ~ *11* Schulden haben, verschuldet sein; to **get into ~** *11* sich verschulden
declarant *53* Anmelder/in
declaration *53* Erklärung
to **declare sth** *68T* etw anmelden, etw angeben, etw deklarieren
decrease *112* Abnahme, Rückgang
to **decrease** *113* abnehmen, zurückgehen
to **deduct sth from sth** *46* etw von etw abziehen
deep sea transport *24* Hochseeschifffahrt
degree *7* Abschluss
delay *71T* Verzögerung, Verspätung, Verzug
delayed *53T* verspätet, verzögert
to **delete sth** *53* etw streichen; *81T* etw löschen, etw entfernen
delicate *34* empfindlich
delighted, to be ~ *26T* sich sehr freuen, (hoch)erfreut sein
to **deliver sth** *16* etw zustellen, etw liefern
delivery *8T* Lieferung, Zustellung; **on ~** *86* bei Lieferung; **door-to-door ~** *50* Haus-zu-Haus-Lieferung, Tür-zu-Tür-Lieferung; **express ~** *50* Expresslieferung, Eilzustellung; **on-demand ~** *33* bedarfsgerechte Lieferung, Lieferung auf Abruf; **parcel ~** *24* Paketzustellung; **date of ~** *47T* Lieferdatum; **terms** *pl* **of ~** *57* Lieferbedingungen; **cash on ~** *56* (per) Nachnahme; to **be scheduled for ~** *33* (zu einem bestimmten Zeitpunkt) geliefert werden (sollen); to **take ~ of sth** *20* etw in Empfang nehmen; **~ note** *56* Lieferschein; **~ period** *86* Lieferzeit
demand, on-~ delivery *33* bedarfsgerechte Lieferung, Lieferung auf Abruf
to **dent sth** *103* etw verbeulen
to **depart** *70T* abfliegen
department *8* Abteilung; **legal ~** *16* Rechtsabteilung; **sub-~** *16* Unter-

abteilung; **head of ~** *16* Abteilungsleiter/in; **~ store** *97P* Kaufhaus
departure *43* Abfahrt, Start; *70* Abflug; **airport of ~** *67* Abgangsflughafen
to **depend on sth** *15T* von etw abhängen, auf etw ankommen
depending on *7* je nach
depot *57T* Depot
deputy *26T* Stellvertreter/in
description *6* Beschreibung, Darstellung; **job ~** *12* Stellenbeschreibung
design *119* Gestaltung
designed, to be ~ to do sth *55* dafür ausgelegt, etw zu tun
despite *87* trotz
destination *26T* Zielort, Bestimmungsort
detailed *45T* detailliert, genau
details *pl* *6* Einzelheiten, Angaben; **contact ~** *31* Kontaktdaten
to **determine sth** *18* etw festlegen, etw bestimmen
to **develop** *122T* sich (weiter)entwickeln; **~ sth** *98* etw erarbeiten, etw entwickeln; *119* etw ausbauen
developer, software ~ *12T* Software-Entwickler/in
device *9* (elektronisches) Gerät; **Unit Load D~ (ULD)** *65* Ladeeinheit (ULD)
diagram *10* Grafik, Diagramm
diary *112* Terminkalender
to **dictate** *38* diktieren
dietary restrictions *pl* *71T* Nahrungsmittelunverträglichkeiten, besondere Kost
digit *21* Ziffer; **10-~** *65* zehnstellig
dimensions *pl* *55* Abmessungen
diploma *11* Abschlusszeugnis
directions *pl*, to **give ~** *27* den Weg beschreiben, den Weg erklären
director *25* Vorstand; **HR ~** *116* Personalchef/in, Personalleiter/in; **managing ~** *26T* Geschäftsführer/in; **purchasing ~** *86* Einkaufsleiter/in
disadvantage *10* Nachteil
to **disappoint sb** *57T* jdn enttäuschen
discharge, port of ~ *53* Entladehafen, Löschungshafen
to **discharge sb an obligation** *80* jdn von einer Verpflichtung entbinden
discount *8T* Rabatt, Skonto; **cash ~** *94* Skonto; **introductory ~** *46* Einführungsrabatt; **quantity ~** *46* Mengenrabatt; **special ~** *46* Sonderrabatt; **trade ~** *94* Händlerrabatt, Handelsrabatt
to **discover sth** *11* etw entdecken, etw feststellen

dislike, likes and ~s *pl 14* Vorlieben und Abneigungen
to **dislike sth** *15* etw nicht mögen, etw nicht leiden können
dispatch *67* Versand; **advice of** *~ 92* Versandanzeige
disruption *99T* Störung, Behinderung, Unterbrechung
distance *45T* Strecke, Entfernung
distillery *44* Brennerei
to **distribute sth** *26T* etw vertreiben, etw versenden; *37T* etw verteilen
distribution *8T* Vertrieb, Versand, Distribution; **weight** *~ 37* Gewichtsverteilung; **~ centre** *26T* Vertriebszentrale, Distributionszentrum; **~ cost** *112* Vertriebskosten
distributor *44* Händler, Vertragshändler
to **diversify** *24* sich diversifizieren
to **divide: ~ sth** *6* etw aufteilen; **~ sth into sth** *31* etw in etw unterteilen, etw in etw aufteilen
division *54* Unterklasse
DIY store *97P* Heimwerkermarkt
DNA sample *70* DNA-Probe
to **do sth about sth** *83* etw gegen etw unternehmen
document: ~ of title *78* Inhaberpapier, Traditionspapier, Warenwertpapier; **set of ~s** *77* Dokumentensatz; **transport ~s** *pl 78* Beförderungspapiere, Frachtdokumente
documentary: ~ credit *90* Dokumentenakkreditiv; **irrevocable and confirmed ~ letter of credit** *90* unwiderrufliches und bestätigtes Dokumentenakkreditiv; **~ requirements** *pl 65* Dokumentationsanforderungen
documentation *18* Papiere, Unterlagen, Dokumente, Dokumentation
domestic trade *55* Binnenhandeln
door, front ~ *114* Haustür; **swinging ~** *65* Schwenktür; **~-to-door delivery** *50* Haus-zu-Haus-Lieferung, Tür-zu-Tür-Lieferung
dot *38* Punkt
to **double box sth** *35T* etw zweifach in einer Kiste verpacken
to **doubt sth** *114* etw bezweifeln
downside *15T* Nachteil, Schattenseite
downstairs *26T* (nach) unten
to **draft sth** *91* etw *(Text)* entwerfen, etw verfassen
to **draw** *16* zeichnen
dress code *8* Kleiderordnung
drinks machine *8T* Getränkeautomat
drive, four-wheel ~ *70* Vierradantrieb, Geländewagen

drive-through pallet rack *36* Durchfahrregal
driverless *110* fahrerlos
driving licence *124* Führerschein
drone *110* Drohne
drop *113T* Rückgang, Abnahme
to **drop** *113* fallen, zurückgehen; **~ sth** *73* etw fallen lassen, etw *(Ladung usw.)* löschen
drum *34* Trommel; **cable ~** *35* Kabeltrommel
dry: Keep ~. *35* Vor Nässe schützen! **~ container** *75* Trockencontainer; **~ goods** *pl 34* Trockengüter, Trockenware(n); **~ load** *75* Trockenladung
drying agent *35T* Trockenmittel, Trocknungsmittel
dual education system *7* duale Ausbildung
due *68T* zahlbar, fällig; **~ to** *24* aufgrund von, wegen; **to be ~ to sth** *83* an etw liegen
duly endorsed *80* ordnungsgemäß abgezeichnet
Dutch *66P* niederländisch, holländisch
duties *pl*, **customs ~** *56* Zollgebühren; **import ~** *87* Einfuhrzölle
duty of care *80* Sorgfaltspflicht

E
e.g. *11* z.B.
ear buds *pl 9* In-Ear-Kopfhörer
early shift *117P* Frühschicht
to **earn sth** *11* etw verdienen
earring *9* Ohrring
East Asia *62* Ostasien
Easter *116T* Ostern
ECG machine *76* EKG-Gerät
eco-friendly *43T* umweltfreundlich
economics *125* Wirtschaft
economy, global ~ *64* Weltwirtschaft
editor *43T* Herausgeber/in, Redakteur/in
education, follow-up ~ *121* Weiterbildung; **primary ~** *125* Grundschule, Grundschulbildung; **secondary ~** *125* Sekundarschule, Sekundarschulbildung; **dual ~ system** *7* duale Ausbildung
effect, overall ~ *119* Gesamteindruck, Gesamtwirkung
effective, cost-~ *72* wirtschaftlich, kostengünstig
efficiency *111* Wirtschaftlichkeit, Effizienz
efficient(ly) *15T* effizient
either *30* beide/s, eine/r/s *(von zweien)*; **~ ... or** *90* entweder ... oder
electric saw *65* Elektrosäge
electricity *36* Strom, Elektrizität

electronics *pl 34* elektronische Geräte
element *25* Bestandteil, Element
elevator *AE 26* Aufzug, Fahrstuhl; **freight ~** *36* Lastenaufzug, Warenaufzug
elsewhere *111* anderswo
emergency *54* Notfall; **~ equipment** *54* Notfallausrüstung; **~ food aid** *72* Nahrungsmittelsoforthilfe; **ADR ~ kit** *54P* Gefahrgut-Notfallset; **Transport E~ Card** *54* Unfallmerkblatt
emissions *pl 111* Ausstoß, Emissionen
empathy *99* Mitgefühl
to **emphasize sth** *32* etw betonen, etw herausstellen
to **employ sb** *16* jdn einstellen, jdn beschäftigen
employment *115T* Anstellung, Arbeitsplatz, Beschäftigung
empty *53T* leer
to **enable sb to do sth** *64* jdm ermöglichen, etw zu tun; jdn in die Lage versetzen, etw zu tun
to **enclose** *104 (Brief:)* beifügen
enclosed body *58T* geschlossener Aufbau
enclosure *48 (Brief:)* Anlage
to **encounter sth** *100* einer Sache begegnen, auf etw stoßen
endorsed, duly ~ *80* ordnungsgemäß abgezeichnet
engaged *20T (Telefon:)* besetzt
engine *54* Motor; **jet ~** *63* Düsentriebwerk
engineering *20* Technik, Maschinenbau
to **enjoy: ~ doing sth** *14* etw gern tun; **sb ~s sth** *26T* jdm gefällt etw, jd genießt etw
to **enquire about sth** *45* sich nach etw erkundigen
enquiry *18* Anfrage; **letter of ~** *48* (schriftliche) Anfrage
to **ensure sth** *33* etw sicherstellen, etw gewährleisten
to **entail sth** *17T* etw mit sich bringen
to **enter: ~ sth** *66T* etw *(Daten usw.)* eingeben; **~ a scheme** *7* an einem Programm teilnehmen; **~ the EU** *86 (Waren usw.:)* in die EU eingeführt werden
entire *77* gesamte/r/s
to **entitle sb to do sth** *90* jdn berechtigen, etw zu tun
entitled, to be ~ to sth *80* einen Anspruch auf etw haben
entrance *26* Eingang
entry *12* Eintrag; **export customs ~** *121* Ausfuhranmeldung

environment *15T* Umgebung, Umfeld; *64* Umwelt
environmentally: ~ **friendly** *72* umweltfreundlich; ~ **hazardous** *53* umweltgefährdend
to **equip sth with sth** *37* etw mit etw ausstatten
equipment *14* Geräte, Ausstattung, Ausrüstung; **catering** ~ *83P* Großküchengeräte, Gastronomieausstattung; **emergency** ~ *54* Notfallausrüstung; **medical** ~ *74* Medizingeräte; **protective** ~ *54* Schutzausrüstung; **safety** ~ *54* Sicherheitsausrüstung
equivalent *47* Entsprechung, Übersetzung
error *53T* Fehler, Irrtum
escalator *27* Rolltreppe
especially *42* besonders
essential *43* wesentlich
established in … on … *56* ausgefertigt in … am …
estimate *45T* Schätzung
to **estimate** *72* schätzen; ~ed **time of arrival (ETA)** *83T* voraussichtliche Ankunftszeit
etiquette *101* Umgangsformen, Etikette
EU, to **be regulated under** ~ **laws** *25* EU-Recht unterliegen; to **enter the** ~ *86* (Waren usw.:) in die EU eingeführt werden
to **evaluate sth** *88* etw bewerten, etw beurteilen, etw einschätzen
even *19T* sogar; ~ **though** *7* auch wenn
event *8T* Veranstaltung
exam, to **pass an** ~ *116T* eine Prüfung bestehen
examination, final ~ *11* Abschlussprüfung
excellence *33* Spitzenleistungen
excellent *46* hervorragend
excelsior *AE 34* Holzwolle
except for *21* außer
exception *63* Ausnahme
excerpt *33* Auszug, Ausschnitt
exchange *55* Austausch; **freight** ~ *45* Transportbörse, Frachtenbörse; ~ **rate** *87* Wechselkurs
to **exchange sth** *57T* etw austauschen
excluding *46* ohne
to **excuse: E~ me.** *13* Verzeihung. Entschuldigung.
to **execute sth** *45P* etw ausführen
exhibition *46* Messe, Ausstellung; ~ **centre** *46* Messegelände
exhibitor *100* Aussteller/in
exit *97* Ausfahrt

to **expand** *24* expandieren; ~ **sth** *19* etw ausweiten, etw erweitern
expectations *pl 123P* Erwartungen
expense, at sb's own ~ *87* auf (jds) eigene Kosten
expenses *pl 6* Kosten, Auslagen; **living** ~ *6* Lebenshaltungskosten
experience, job ~ *7* Berufserfahrung, praktische Erfahrung; **work** ~ *18* Praktikum
experienced *118T* erfahren
explanation *7* Erläuterung; *83* Erklärung
to **export sth** *17* etw ausführen, etw exportieren
export *73* Ausfuhr; **cleared for** ~ *87* zur Ausfuhr freigemacht; ~ **clearance** *89* Ausfuhrabfertigung, Ausfuhrfreigabe; ~ **clerk** *38* Außenhandelskaufmann/-frau; ~ **customs entry** *121* Ausfuhranmeldung; ~ **licence** *89* Ausfuhrgenehmigung, Ausfuhrlizenz; ~ **sales department** *86* Exportabteilung; ~ **sales manager** *80* Exportleiter/in
exporter *52* Exporteur, Ausführer
express delivery *50* Expresslieferung, Eilzustellung
to **express sth** *10* etw äußern, etw ausdrücken
expression *20* Ausdruck
external *78* äußerlich; ~ **packaging** *34* Außenverpackung
extra *35* zusätzlich; ~ **fee** *47T* Zuschlag, Zusatzgebühr
extract *19* Auszug, Ausschnitt
eye contact *31* Blickkontakt
eyewash bottle *54* Augenspülflasche

F
face: ~ **shield** *54* Gesichtsschutz, Gesichtsschirm; ~-**to-face** *122* persönlich
to **face sb** *31* sich jdm zuwenden, jdn anschauen
facilities *pl 8* Einrichtungen, Anlage(n), Ausstattung
fact, in ~ *13* genau genommen, tatsächlich, eigentlich
factory *20* Fabrik, Werk; ~ **manager** *20* Betriebsleiter/in, Werksleiter/in
fair *38* Messe; **trade** ~ *17T* Fachmesse, Branchenmesse
faithfully: Yours ~ *39* (Brief:) … und verbleiben mit freundlichen Grüßen
fake *55* Fälschung, Plagiat
false *17* unzutreffend, falsch
familiar, to be ~ **with sth** *123P* mit etw vertraut sein, etw kennen

to **familiarize onself with sth** *34* sich mit etw vertraut machen, sich in etw einarbeiten
family: ~ **business** *8T* Familienunternehmen; ~-**owned company** *46* Familienbetrieb
fantastic *13* phantastisch, toll
fashion wear *62* Modekleidung
fault, to **be sb's** ~ *99* jds Schuld sein
favour, to **be in** ~ **of sth** *117* für etw sein
favourable *88* günstig, vorteilhaft
feature *37* Merkmal, Eigenschaft, Besonderheit
federal laws *pl 19T* Bundesgesetze
fee *11* Gebühr; **administration** ~ *47* Regiekosten, Verwaltungsgebühr; **extra** ~ *47T* Zuschlag, Zusatzgebühr; **tuition** ~**s** *pl 11* Studiengebühren
feedback *31* Reaktion(en), Rückmeldung(en)
to **feel: ~ comfortable** *15T* sich wohlfühlen; ~ **free to do sth** *26T* etw ruhig tun, gern etw tun können; ~ **like sth** *8T* Lust auf etw haben
ferry *96T* Fähre
figure *53T* Ziffer, Zahl; **sales** ~**s** *pl 17T* Umsatzzahlen, Verkaufszahlen
file *18* Akte; **personnel** ~ *12* Personalakte
film, plastic ~ *34* Plastikfolie; ~ **set** *35* Filmkulisse
final *57T* endgültig; ~ **examination** *11* Abschlussprüfung; ~ **grade** *11* Abschlussnote; ~ **price** *87* Endpreis
to **finalize sth** *63* etw zum Abschluss bringen, etw endgültig festlegen
finance *11* Finanz(en)
financial: ~ **data** *pl 19* Finanzdaten; ~ **report** *18* Finanzbericht
findings *pl 103* (Untersuchungs-) Ergebnisse
finishing point *26* Endpunkt
fire brigade *54* Feuerwehr
to **fire sb** *7* jdn entlassen
fireworks *pl 52* Feuerwerk
firm *38* Firma; *83* fest; ~ **handshake** *123T* fester Händedruck
first: ~ **aid** *125* Erste Hilfe; ~ **name** *20T* Vorname; ~ **of all** *45T* zunächst, als Erstes; ~-**time customer** *46* Erstkunde/-kundin, Neukunde/-kundin
firstly *43* erstens
to **fit** *35T* passen; **sth** ~ **sth** *35T* etw passt ein etw hinein
fixed rate *68T* Pauschaltarif, Festpreis
fixtures *pl 37* Armaturen
flashy *101* protzig, großspurig

flat BE 97P Wohnung; **~ rack container** 76 Flachcontainer, Flat-Rack-Container
to flatten out 113 auf gleichem Stand bleiben
fleet 113T Fuhrpark, Flotte
flexibility 115T Flexibilität
flexitime 8 Gleitzeit
to flick through sth 122 etw durchblättern
flight, to get bumped from a ~ 70T aus einem Flug ausgebucht werden
flooding 70 Überschwemmung(en)
floor, ground ~ 8T Erdgeschoss; **roller ~** 65 Rollenboden; **~ storage** 36 Bodenlager
flooring 65 Bodenbelag; **parquet ~** 66P Parkett
flour 34 Mehl
flow: ~ chart 19 Flussdiagramm; **~ of goods** 33 Warenfluss; **~ of information** 33 Informationsfluss
to fluctuate 113 schwanken
fluctuation 87 Schwankung(en)
fluent 121 (Sprache:) fließend
flyer 38 Faltblatt
foam 34 Schaum; **~ rubber** 34 Schaumgummi, Moosgummi
to focus on sth 15T sich auf etw konzentrieren
fog 35 Nebel
folder 28T Mappe, Ordner
folks 11 Leute; (AE) Eltern
to follow: ~ up 45 nachfassen; **~ a procedure** 26T sich an eine Vorgehensweise halten; **~ standard procedures** 55 übliche Verfahren einhalten; **as ~s** 20 wie folgt
follow-up education 121 Weiterbildung
food: ~ logistics 32 Lebensmittellogistik; **health ~ shop** 97P Reformhaus, Naturkostladen
foodstuffs pl 65 Lebensmittel, Nahrungsmittel
to fool sb 101 jdn täuschen
foot, on ~ 97 zu Fuß
footprint, carbon ~ 43 CO_2-Fußabdruck; **noise ~** 64 Lärmteppich, Lärmemission
footwear, protective ~ 54 Sicherheitsschuhe
foreign trade 55 Außenhandel
fork 97 Gabelung
forklift: ~ (truck) 28T Gabelstapler; **~ operator** 37 Gabelstaplerfahrer/in
form 45 Formular; **~ of transport** 17T Transportart
formal(ly) 13 formell, förmlich
formalities pl 73 Formalitäten

forward, the right way ~ 115T der richtige Weg
forwarder 18 Spediteur, Spedition
forwarding, freight ~ 6 Spedition(swesen); **freight ~ company** 121 Spedition; **~ agent** 6T Spediteur/in, Kaufmann/-frau für Spedition und Logistikdienstleistung
foul bill of lading 78 unreines Konnossement
to found sth 24 etw gründen
founder 24 Gründer/in
four-wheel drive 70 Vierradantrieb, Geländewagen
fragile 34 zerbrechlich
frayed 9 zerfranst
free, for ~ 11 umsonst; **to feel ~ to do sth** 26T etw ruhig tun, gern etw tun können
freight 9 Fracht, Frachtgut; **air ~** 16 Luftfracht; **consolidated ~** 16 Sammelgut; **groupage ~** 16 Sammelgut; **rail ~** 16 Bahnfracht; **road ~** 16 Straßenfracht; **sea ~** 16 Seefracht; **~ agent** 58 Frachtvermittler/in; **~ capacity** 42 Frachtkapazität, Laderaum; **~ elevator** 36 Lastenaufzug, Warenaufzug; **~ exchange** 45 Transportbörse, Frachtenbörse; **~ forwarder** 18 Spediteur, Spedition; **~ list** 56 Ladeliste; **~ movement** 19T Güterbewegung, Transport; **~ planning** 72 Frachtplanung; **~ space** 68 Frachtraum; **~ forwarding** 6 Spedition(swesen); **~ forwarding company** 121 Spedition; **management assistant for ~ forwarding and logistics** 6 Kaufmann/-frau für Spedition und Logistikdienstleistung; **~ prepaid** 81T frachtfrei
freighter, air ~ 62 Frachtflugzeug
frequency 37 Frequency; **radio-~ identification (RFID)** 37 Funkerkennung
frequent(ly) 20 häufig
fresh 34 frisch
front door 114 Haustür
frozen: ~ logistics 43T Tiefkühllogistik; **~ meat** 76 Gefrierfleisch
fuel 68 Treibstoff; **bunker ~** 72 Bunkeröl, Schweröl; **~ crisis** 24 Ölkrise
to fulfil a contract 106 einen Vertrag erfüllen
full: ~ board 71 Vollpension; **~ truckload** 42 Komplettladung (Lkw); **~-time** 116T Vollzeit(-)
fully 53 vollständig; **~ automated** 110 vollautomatisch; **~ automatic** 28T vollautomatisch

to furnish sth 80 etw zur Verfügung stellen, etw angeben
furniture 8T Möbel
further to … 67 bezugnehmend auf …
fuss 42 Heckmeck, Gedöns, Theater
future prospects pl 123T Zukunftsperspektiven

G

to gain sth 7 etw erlangen, etw erwerben, etw gewinnen
gallery walk 25 Galerierundgang
gantry crane 74 Portalkran
garage 24 Autowerkstatt
garment 65 Kleidungsstück
gas, natural ~ 73 Erdgas; **petroleum ~** 73 Propangas; **liquefied ~ carrier** 73 Flüssiggastanker
gate, truck ~ 74 Lkw-Gate
to gather sth 122 etw zusammenstellen
general: ~ terms and conditions pl 46 Allgemeine Geschäftsbedingungen; **G~ Manager** 117 Geschäftsführer/in
generally 15T normalerweise, im Allgemeinen
to generate sth 43T etw (Umsatz usw.) erwirtschaften
generator 20 Generator
gentleman 26T Herr
genuine 80 echt
gesture 31 Geste
to get: ~ back to sb 45T sich (wieder) bei jdm melden; **~ through to sb** 20T zum jdm durchkommen; **~ a message across** 25 eine Botschaft vermitteln; **~ on with one's work** 15T seine Arbeit machen; **~ sth sorted** 106T etw klären, sich um etw kümmern; **~ into the habit of doing sth** 123T sich zu Gewohnheit machen, etw zu tun
gift 100 Geschenk
to give: ~ off sth 76 etw abgeben; **~ reasons for sth** 8 etw begründen
giveaway 101T Werbegeschenk
glad, to be ~ (to do sth) 26T sich freuen(, etw zu tun)
glasses pl 114 Brille
global: ~ economy 64 Weltwirtschaft; **~ trade** 72 Welthandel
globalization 98 Globalisierung
gloves pl, **protective ~** 54 Schutzhandschuhe
gluten-free 32 glutenfrei
glycerine 35 Glyzerin
to go: ~ ahead 45T loslegen; **~ out of business** 24 das Geschäft aufgeben, zumachen; **~ bankrupt** 25 Pleite gehen
goal 11 Ziel

A–Z word list

goggles *pl 54P* Schutzbrille
goods *pl 16* Ware(n), Güter; **~ on hold** *28* Sperrlager; **dangerous ~** *52* Gefahrgüter; **dry ~** *34* Trockengüter, Trockenware(n); **inbound ~** *36* Wareneingang, eingehende Ware; **outbound ~** *36* Warenausgang, ausgehende Ware; **flow of ~** *33* Warenfluss; **type of ~** *35* Warenart; **heavy ~ vehicle (HGV) BE** *51* Schwerlastwagen
governmental regulations *pl 53* gesetzliche/behördliche Vorschriften
to **grab sb's attention** *124* jds Aufmerksamkeit fesseln
grade *11* Note; **final ~** *11* Abschlussnote
gradual *113T* allmählich, langsam
to **graduate** *11* den Abschluss machen
grain *76* Getreide
to **grant sb sth** *46* jdm etw gewähren, jdm etw einräumen
granular *72* körnig
graph, bar ~ *112* Säulendiagramm
graphic *25* Grafik
gravel *72* Kies, Schotter
gravity, centre of ~ *35* Schwerpunkt
Greece *10* Griechenland
greengrocer's *97P* Gemüseladen
Greenwich Mean Time *62* mittlere Greenwich-Zeit, Weltzeit
greeting *39* *(Brief:)* Anrede
gross *53* brutto; **~ weight** *75* Bruttogewicht
ground floor *8T* Erdgeschoss
group, packing ~ *53* Verpackungsgruppe
groupage freight *16* Sammelgut
to **grow the customer base** *32* den Kundenstamm ausbauen/erweitern
guarantee *86* Garantie
to **guarantee sth** *24* etw garantieren
to **guess sth** *10* etw erraten
to **guide** *29* leiten, führen
guide *26T* Führer/in
guided tour *26* Führung
guidelines *pl 98* Richtlinien, Vorgaben

H

habit *123T* Gewohnheit; to **get into the ~ of doing sth** *123T* sich zu Gewohnheit machen, etw zu tun
half board *71* Halbpension
to **hand: ~ over to sb** *31* an jdn übergeben; **~ sth over to sb** *89* jdm etw übergeben
hand, by ~ *37T* von Hand; **on the other ~** *28T* andererseits; to **shake ~s with sb** *123T* jdm die Hand geben

hand-carry shipment *70T* Hand-carry-Lieferung, persönlich begleiteter Transport
to **handle sth** *18* etw bearbeiten, etw erledigen; *35* etw handhaben, etw behandeln; **~ sth with care** *15* etw mit Vorsicht behandeln; **H~ with care.** *35* Vorsicht, zerbrechlich! Zerbrechliches Packgut!
handling *74* Umschlag; **cargo ~** *65* Frachtumschlag, Warenumschlag; **package ~** *9* Stückguthandhabung, Pakethandling; **~ marks** *pl 35* Handhabungskennzeichen, Versandzeichen; **~ procedures** *pl 62* Abfertigung, Abwicklung, Umschlag
handout *29* Arbeitsblatt, Broschüre
handshake, firm ~ *123T* fester Händedruck
to **hang: H~ on.** *99T* Einen Moment!
hanger *65* Kleiderbügel
happy, to be ~ to do sth *28T* etw gern tun
hard: ~ hat *8T* Schutzhelm; **~-top container** *75* Hardtop-Container; **~-working** *122T* fleißig
hardwood *66P* Hartholz
hat, hard ~ *8T* Schutzhelm
haul, long-~ *65* Langstrecken-; **short~** *43* Kurzstrecken-
haulage, road ~ *24* Güterkraftverkehr, Straßentransport; **~ company** *24* (Straßen-)Spedition(sfirma), Frachtfuhrunternehmen
haulier *53* (Straßen-)Spediteur
hazard class *53* Gefahrenklasse
hazardous, environmentally ~ *53* umweltgefährdend; **~ material** *52* Gefahrstoff, Gefahrgut
head of department *16* Abteilungsleiter/in
to **head out for …** *58T* sich nach … aufmachen
heading *28* Überschrift, Rubrik
health: ~ and safety *115T* Arbeitsschutz, Arbeitssicherheit; **~ food shop** *97P* Reformhaus, Naturkostladen
heat: Keep away from ~. *35* Vor Hitze schützen!
heavy goods vehicle (HGV) BE *51* Schwerlastwagen
heel, high ~s *pl 9* hochhackige Schuhe
height *45T* Höhe
hereby *53* hiermit, hierdurch
hereon *53* nachfolgend
to **hesitate** *44* zögern
to **hide sth** *15T* etw verbergen
high: ~ heels *pl 9* hochhackige Schuhe; **~-bay shelving** *36* Hochregallager;

~-rise shelving system *115T* Hochregalsystem; **~-rise warehouse** *28* Hochregallager; **~-sulphur** *72* mit hohem Schwefelgehalt
to **highlight** *30* hervorheben
hire car *71* Mietwagen
to **hire sb** *32* jdn beauftragen, jdn engagieren
to **hit sth** *24* etw (schwer) treffen
to **hold: ~ sb up** *13* jdn aufhalten; **~ sth in place** *35* etw halten, etw fixieren; **~ the line** *20T* *(Telefon:)* am Apparat bleiben
hold, goods on ~ *28* Sperrlager; **cargo ~** *65* Frachtraum, Laderaum
holder *79* Inhaber/in, Besitzer/in
holiday, leftover ~ *116T* Resturlaub; **national ~** *10* landesweiter Feiertag
honest(ly) *122T* ehrlich
hope *6* Hoffnung
hospital supplies *pl 76* Krankenhausbedarf
host *8T* (Talkshow-)Moderator/in
hour, working ~ *10T* Arbeitsstunde
hours *pl*, **opening ~** *56* Öffnungszeiten; **working ~** *8* Arbeitszeit(en)
house, open ~ *8T* Tag der Offenen Tür; **in-~** *19T* betriebsintern
How so? *33* Inwiefern?
hub *42* Knotenpunkt, Drehkreuz
huge loads *pl 50* große Tonnagen, große Lasten
Human Resources (HR) *12* Personal-(abteilung); **~ director** *116* Personalchef/in, Personalleiter/in
humidity *33* Feuchtigkeit
humour *101* Humor
hurry, to be in a ~ *58T* in Eile sein, es eilig haben
hydrogen *52* Wasserstoff
hypermarket *97P* großer Einkaufsmarkt
hyphen *38* Bindestrich, Minus

I

idea, no ~ *83* keine Ahnung
identification (ID) *53* Identifikation; **radio-frequency ~ (RFID)** *37* Funkerkennung
to **identify** *15* identifzieren, bestimmen
identity, proof of ~ *78* Identitätsnachweis
if I were you *35T* an Ihrer Stelle
illness *13* Krankheit
illustrated *29* bebildert, illustriert
immediately *37T* sofort, unverzüglich
imperial measurements *pl 55* anglo-amerikanisches Maßsystem
to **implement sth** *111* etw *(Plan usw.)* umsetzen

import *73* Einfuhr; **~ clearance** *89* Einfuhrabfertigung, Einfuhrfreigabe; **~ duties** *pl 87* Einfuhrzölle; **~ licence** *89* Einfuhrgenehmigung, Einfuhrlizenz
to **import sth** *17* etw einführen, etw importieren
importance *116T* Wichtigkeit, Bedeutung
importer *52* Importeur, Einführer
imprecise *65* ungenau
impression *98* Eindruck
improper *33* unsachgemäß
to **improve sth** *11* etw verbessern
improvement (to sth) *31* Verbesserung (von/an etw)
to **improvise** *21* improvisieren
inappropriate *9* unangemessen
inbound goods *pl 36* Wareneingang, eingehende Ware
inch *55* Zoll *(ca. 2,54 cm)*
to **include**: **~ sth** *17T* etw umfassen, etw einschließen, etw beinhalten; **~ sth (in sth)** *21* etw (in etw) aufnehmen
including *27* mit, einschließlich
inclusive *38* einschließlich
incoming *17T* eingehend
in-company *7* betriebsintern
incomplete *45T* unvollständig
inconvenience *83* Unannehmlichkeiten, Umstände
inconvenient *99T* ungünstig, unpraktisch
increase *112* Zunahme, Anstieg
to **increase** *113* zunehmen, ansteigen; **~ sth** *112* etw erhöhen, etw steigern
independent(ly) *122T* unabhängig
index card *30* Karteikarte
Indian *97P* indisch
individual *8* persönlich, individuell
industrialized country *11* Industrieland, -staat
inexpensive *34* preiswert, kostengünstig, billig
inexpensive *101* billig
infectious substances *pl 64* infektiöse Stoffe
inflexible *72* unflexibel
information sheet *89* Merkblatt
infrastructure *72* Infrastruktur, Verkehrsnetz
in-house *19T* betriebsintern
initial: **~ ideas** *pl 39* erste Ideen; **~ order** *91* Erstauftrag, Erstbestellung
initials *pl*, **reference ~** *48* (Brief:) Zeichen
initiative, to take the ~ *122T* die Initative ergreifen

inland *111* ins/im Landesinnere/n; **~ waterway transport** *24* Binnenschifffahrt
to **innovate** *115T* innovativ sein
innovative *43T* innovativ
input *116T* Beitrag, Beiträge
inside address *48* Innenadresse
to **insist on sth** *47T* auf etw bestehen
to **inspect sth** *90* etw prüfen
inspection, third-party ~ *93* Fremdprüfung; **~ agency** *93T* Prüfstelle, Überwachungsstelle; **~ report** *93T* Prüfbericht
to **install sth** *114* etw installieren
instalment *96* Rate, Tranche
instead of *45* anstatt, statt
to **instruct sb to do sth** *57T* jdn anweisen, etw zu tun
instruction *21* Anweisung; **~ manual** *55P* Lehrbuch
insult *101* Beleidigung
insurance *45* Versicherung; to **take out ~** *68* eine Versicherung abschließen; **air cargo ~** *68T* Luftfrachtversicherung; **transport ~** *87* Transportversicherung; **~ policy** *118T* Versicherungspolice; **~ rate** *46* Versicherungstarif, Versicherungsprämie
to **insure sth** *79* etw versichern
insured value *87* Versicherungswert
insurer *68T* Versicherer, Versicherungsunternehmen
intelligence *64* Informationen
to **interact with sb** *100* mit jdm kommunizieren
interconnected *111* vernetzt
intermediate *11* mittlere/r/s; **~ bulk container (IBC)** *53T* Großpackmittel (IBC)
intermodal transport *43* kombinierter Verkehr, intermodaler Transport
internal packaging *34* Innenverpackung
internship *11* Praktikum
to **interrupt** *15T* unterbrechen, stören
interview, (job) ~ *122* Vorstellungsgespräch
to **interview sb** *38* mit jdm ein Vorstellungsgespräch führen
interviewer *122* jd, der ein Vorstellungsgespräch mit einem/einer Bewerber/in führt
to **introduce**: **~ sb/oneself to sb** *12* jdn/sich jdm vorstellen; **~ sth** *115T* etw einführen
introduction *30* Einleitung; *55* Einführung
introductions *pl 11* Bekanntmachen, Vorstellen

introductory: **~ discount** *46* Einführungsrabatt; **~ offer** *93T* Einführungsangebot
to **invent sth** *117P* sich etw ausdenken
inventory *14* Bestandsliste
to **invest** *25* investieren
invitation *26T* Einladung
to **invite**: **~ sb** *39* jdn einladen; **~ sth** *30* zu etw auffordern, um etw bitten
invoice *16* Rechnung; **commercial ~** *93T* Handelsrechnung; **pro-forma ~** *57T* Pro-forma-Rechnung; **receipt of ~** *47T* Rechnungseingang, Erhalt der Rechnung; **within … days of ~** *45T* innerhalb von … Tagen ab/nach Rechnungsdatum; **~ auditing** *43* Rechnungsprüfung
invoicing *121* Fakturierung, Rechnungsstellung
to **involve sth** *17T* etw beinhalten, etw umfassen
involved, to be ~ in sth *17* mit etw zu tun haben
involving sb *19* mit jdm
iron ore *72* Eisenerz
irrevocable *90* unwiderruflich; **~ and confirmed documentary letter of credit** *90* unwiderrufliches und bestätigtes Dokumentenakkreditiv
issue *43T* Ausgabe
to **issue sth** *64* etw *(Dokument usw.)* ausstellen
it: **That's ~.** *8T* Das war's.
item *18* Artikel; **~ on the agenda** *116* Tagesordnungspunkt; **outsize ~s** *pl 37T* Sperrgut, überdimensionierte Ware(n); **perishable ~s** *pl 33* verderbliche Waren

J

jam, traffic ~ *50* Stau
Japanese *63* japanisch
jet engine *63* Düsentriebwerk
jeweller's *97P* Schmuckgeschäft, Juwelierladen
jewellery *9* Schmuck
job: **~ advert(isement)** *120* Stellenanzeige; **~ agency** *118* Arbeitsagentur, Arbeitsvermittlung; **~ application** *118* Bewerbung; **~ description** *12* Stellenbeschreibung; **~ experience** *7* Berufserfahrung, praktische Erfahrung; **~ interview** *122* Vorstellungsgespräch; **~ offer** *8T* Stellenangebot; **~ opportunities** *pl 119* Arbeitsmöglichkeiten; **~ profile** *18* Stellenprofil; **~ prospects** *pl 8* berufliche Perspektiven; **~ security** *111* Arbeitsplatzsicherheit; **~ title** *119*

A–Z word list

Stellenbezeichnung; ~ **vacancy** *123P* offene Stelle

to **join**: ~ **sb** *8T* *(Radio-/TV-Sendung:)* bei jdm zu Gast sein; ~ **sth** *26* sich einer Sache anschließen, bei etw mitmachen; ~ **a company** *24* in ein Unternehmen eintreten, zu einem Unternehmen kommen

journey *13* Fahrt, Anreise; **outward** ~ *70* Anreise, Hinflug; **return** ~ *63* Rückfahrt, Rückflug, Rückreise

juice *35* Saft

jump *113T* Sprung

to **justify** *123P* rechtfertigen, begründen

K

keen, to be ~ **to do sth** *126* jdm liegt sehr daran, etw zu tun

to **keep**: ~ **sb loyal** *98* jdn *(Kunde/-in usw.)* an sich binden; ~ **sb waiting** *13* jdn warten lassen; ~ **sb up to date** *116* jdm auf dem Laufenden halten; ~ **track of sth** *16* den Überblick über etw behalten; K~ **away from heat.** *35* Vor Hitze schützen! K~ **dry.** *35* Vor Nässe schützen!

Kenya *63* Kenia

kerosene *53* Kerosin

to **key sth in** *14* etw *(am Computer)* eingeben

key word *31* Stichwort

keyless access *114* schlüsselloser Zugang

keyword *110T* Schlagwort, Stichwort, Schlüsselwort

kind *26T* freundlich, nett

kind *53* Art

kit, ADR emergency ~ *54P* Gefahrgut-Notfallset; **spill** ~ *54* Notfallset für Leckagen und Verschüttungen

knowledge *7* Wissen, Kenntnisse; **basic** ~ *126* Grundkenntnisse

L

label printer *37* Etikettendrucker

to **label sth** *27* etw bezeichnen, etw etikettieren

labelling *26* Bezeichnung, Etikettierung; *34* Etikettieren

labour-intensive *47T* arbeitsaufwändig, arbeitsintensiv

lack (of sth) *122T* Mangel (an etw)

to **lack sth** *15T* etw nicht haben

lading → **bill of lading (B/L)**

lady *26T* Dame

landline *122* Festnetz(telefon)

lashing rod *74* Laschstange

last, second to ~ *10T* vorletze/r/s; ~ **mile** *110T* letzte Meile

to **last (for …)** *6* dauern

lately *99* in letzter Zeit

laundry *71* Wäsche

laws *pl*, **federal** ~ *19T* Bundesgesetze; **state** ~ *19T* Landesgesetze; to **be regulated under EU** ~ *25* EU-Recht unterliegen

layout *26* Grundriss, Anordnung, Plan; *48* Gestaltung, Aufbau, Layout

to **lead to sth** *100* zu etw führen

leader, market ~ *43* Marktführer

least, at ~ *8T* mindestens, zumindest

leather *65* Leder

leave, annual ~ *10* Jahresurlaub

to **leave**: ~ **sth blank** *45T* etw leer lassen; *66T* etw frei lassen, etw offen lassen; ~ **a message** *20* eine Nachricht hinterlassen

left, to take a ~ *26T* links abbiegen

leftover holiday *116T* Resturlaub

legal: ~ **department** *16* Rechtsabteilung; ~ **requirements** *pl 19T* gesetzliche Bestimmungen, rechtliche Vorgaben

less than truckload *42* Teilladung (Lkw)

to **let sb know sth** *38* jdm etw mitteilen, jdm Bescheid sagen

letter of credit (L/C) *78* Akkreditiv, **irrevocable and confirmed documentary** ~ *90* unwiderrufliches und bestätigtes Dokumentenakkreditiv

letterhead *48* Briefkopf

level *36* *(Gebäude:)* Ebene, Etage; **pollution** ~**s** *pl 64* Schadstoffwerte; **temperature** ~ *43* Tempearturniveau, Temperaturbereich

to **level off** *113* sich einpendeln

liability *45T* Haftung; **limited** ~ **company (LLC)** *AE 25* Gesellschaft mit beschränkter Haftung (GmbH)

licence, driving ~ *124* Führerschein; **export** ~ *89* Ausfuhrgenehmigung, Ausfuhrlizenz; **import** ~ *89* Einfuhrgenehmigung, Einfuhrlizenz; ~ **plate** *56* Nummernschild, Kfz-Kennzeichen

license *37T* Genehmigung, Führerschein

to **lie ahead (of sb)** *24* vor jdm liegen, (jdm) bevorstehen

life, personal ~ *115T* Privatleben

lift *BE 26T* Aufzug, Fahrstuhl; **scissor** ~ *65* Scherenlift; **tail** ~ *58* Ladebordwand, Hebebühne

to **lift sth** *36* etw anheben, etw hochheben

lifting platform *36* Hebebühne

light *50* leicht; ~ **bulb** *34* Glühbirne

lights *pl*, **naked** ~ *54* offene Flammen; **traffic** ~**s** *pl 97* Ampel

lighting stand *35* Leuchtenstativ

lightweight *70* leicht

like, to feel ~ **sth** *8T* Lust auf etw haben

likes and dislikes *pl 14* Vorlieben und Abneigungen

liking, to be to sb's ~ *88* jdm zusagen

limit *11* Beschränkung, Begrenzung

limitation *35* Begrenzung, Beschränkung, Unter-/Obergrenze; **temperature** ~**s** *pl 35* zulässiger Temperaturbereich

limited, private ~ **company (Ltd)** *24* Gesellschaft mit beschränkter Haftung (GmbH); ~ **liability company (LLC)** *AE 25* Gesellschaft mit beschränkter Haftung (GmbH); **public** ~ **company (plc)** *24* Aktiengesellschaft (AG)

line *20T* Leitung; to **hold the** ~ *20T* *(Telefon:)* am Apparat bleiben; **assembly** ~ *33* Montagelinie, -kette, -band; **attention** ~ *48* Zeile „zu Händen"; **subject** ~ *38* Betreffzeile; ~ **manager** *6* (direkte/r) Vorgesetzte/r

liner, ocean ~ *72* Ozeandampfer, Passagierschiff

link *122T* Zusammenhang, Verbindung; **transport** ~ *71T* Verkehrsverbindung

liquefied gas carrier *73* Flüssiggastanker

liquid *35* Flüssigkeit

Lisbon *101* Lissabon

list, freight ~ *56* Ladeliste; **packing** ~ *93T* Packliste; **tally** ~ *15* Abhakliste, Strichliste; ~ **price** *46* Listenpreis

litre *54P* Liter

live animals *pl 64* lebende Tiere

living expenses *pl 6* Lebenshaltungskosten

load *51* Ladung, Fracht; *55P* Last; **dry** ~ *75* Trockenladung; **return** ~ *58* Rückladung; **huge** ~**s** *pl 50* große Tonnagen, große Lasten; **partial-~ shipment** *43* Teilladungssendung; **Unit L~ Device (ULD)** *65* Ladeeinheit (ULD); ~ **planning** *37T* Ladeplanung, Verladeplanung

to **load sth** *26T* etw verladen

loader *37* Belader/in

loading *46* Verladung; ~ **area** *36* Ladefläche, Ladezone; ~ **station** *37T* Ladestation, Verladestation

local time *62* Ortzeit

located, to be ~ **in …** *7* in … sein/liegen

lock *74* Verriegelung, Riegel

to **lock sth** *74* etw verriegeln, etw arretieren, etw sperren; *77* etw verschließen, etw abschließen

locker *114* Schließfach, Spind

to **log**: ~ **in** *8T* sich einloggen; ~ **on** *66T* sich einloggen
logistics *6* Logistik; **food** ~ *32* Lebensmittellogistik; **frozen** ~ *43T* Tiefkühllogistik; **reverse** ~ *33* Rücknahmelogistik; **management assistant for freight forwarding and** ~ *6* Kaufmann/-frau für Spedition und Logistikdienstleistung
long-haul *65* Langstrecken-
long-term *11* langfristig
to **look**: ~ **after sb/sth** *12* sich um jdn/etw kümmern; ~ **into sth** *106T* einer Sache nachgehen; *113T* etw prüfen, etw untersuchen; ~ **the part** *9* entsprechend (rollengerecht) aussehen
look, to take a closer ~ **at sth** *50* sich etw näher/genauer ansehen
loop *36* Schleife, Schlaufe
loose *9* (Kleidung:) weit
lorry BE *16* Lastwagen; **articulated** ~ BE *51* Sattelzug; **refrigerator** ~ *43T* Kühllastwagen, Kühlfahrzeug; ~ **bay** BE *26T* Ladebucht
low: **~-loader** *58T* Tieflader; **~-sulphur** *72* schwefelarm
to **lower sth** *113T* etw senken
loyal *98* treu, loyal; to **keep sb** ~ *98* jdn (Kunde/-in usw.) an sich binden
loyalty, customer ~ *46* Kundentreue
luck, to be out of ~ *20T* kein Glück (mehr) haben
luckily *115T* glücklicherweise
lucky, to be ~ *13* Glück haben
lunch break *8T* Mittagspause
lunchtime *82* Mittag, Mittagszeit
Luton van BE *51* Lkw mit Kastenaufbau und überbautem Führerhaus

M

machine, anaesthesia ~ *81T* Anästhesiegerät; **drinks** ~ *8T* Getränkeautomat; **ECG** ~ *76* EKG-Gerät; **robotic cleaning** ~ *114* Reinigungsroboter
machinery *59* Maschinen
madam, Dear Sir or M~ *39* (Brief:) Sehr geehrte Damen und Herren,
magazine, company ~ *49* Firmenzeitschrift, Hauszeitung; **trade** ~ *19T* Fachzeitschrift
main carriage *87* Hauptlauf, Haupttransport
mainland *55P* Festland
maintenance *113T* Wartung, Instandhaltung
major *24* groß, bedeutend, wichtig
majority *103* Mehrheit, Großteil
to **make**: ~ **sth up** *113T* etw ausmachen; ~ **up for sth** *117P* etw nachholen;

~ **sense** *47T* einleuchten; ~ **sure** *17T* sicherstellen, gewährleisten, dafür sorgen; to ~ **sure** *66T* um sicherzugehen
management *16* Geschäftsleitung, Geschäftsführung; **quality** ~ *98* Qualitätssicherung; **stock** ~ *16* Bestandsführung, Lagerverwaltung; **upper** ~ *112* obere Führungsebene, Chefetage; ~ **assistant for freight forwarding and logistics** *6* Kaufmann/-frau für Spedition und Logistikdienstleistung; ~ **assistant for office communications** *12T* Kaufmann/-frau für Bürokommunikation
manager, accounting ~ *19* Buchhaltungsleiter/in; **export sales** ~ *80* Exportleiter/in; **factory** ~ *20* Betriebsleiter/in, Werksleiter/in; **General M**~ *117* Geschäftsführer/in; **line** ~ *6* (direkte/r) Vorgesetzte/r; **product** ~ *12T* Produktmanger/in
managing director *26T* Geschäftsführer/in
mandatory box *58T* (Formular:) Pflichtfeld
manifest *65* Ladungsverzeichnis
manner *31* Art (und Weise)
manpower *19* Arbeitskräfte
manual *28T* händisch, von Hand bedient; **instruction** ~ *55P* Lehrbuch
manufacturer *32* Hersteller/in, Produzent/in; **car** ~ *105* Auto(mobil)hersteller
manufacturing site *50* Produktionsstätte, Produktionsstandort
margin, profit ~ *17T* Gewinnspanne
to **mark sth** *35* etw kennzeichnen
mark, to put your personal ~ **on sth** *15T* einer Sache seinen persönlichen Stempel aufdrücken; **handling ~s** pl *35* Handhabungskennzeichen, Versandzeichen; **shipping ~s** pl *53* Versandzeichen
market *19T* Markt; **positioned in the** ~ *43* im/am Markt aufgestellt; **stock** ~ *24* Aktienmarkt; ~ **leader** *43* Marktführer; ~ **research** *18* Marktforschung; ~ **share** *28* Marktanteil
marking, branded ~ *55* Brandmarke
married *117P* verheiratet
mass *53* Masse
match *106T* Streichholz
to **match sth to sth** *9* etw einer Sache zuordnen
material, hazardous ~ *52* Gefahrstoff, Gefahrgut; **packing** ~ *35T* Verpackungsmaterial; **building ~s** pl *36* Baustoffe, Baumaterial; **raw ~s** pl *32* Rohstoffe, Rohmaterial(ien)

maths *37T* Mathematik
matter *104* Angelegenheit
to **maximize sth** *63* etw maximieren
mean, Greenwich M~ Time *62* mittlere Greenwich-Zeit, Weltzeit
means *80* Mittel, Art; ~ **of transport** *111* Transportmittel
meant, to be ~ **to do sth** *105* etw (eigentlich/ursprünglich) tun sollen
measure *55* Maßeinheit
measurement *55* Maß; **unit of** ~ *75* Maßeinheit; **imperial ~s** pl *55* anglo-amerikanisches Maßsystem
measuring … *76* mit den Maßen …
meat *34* Fleisch; **frozen** ~ *76* Gefrierfleisch
medical: ~ **alert badge** *9* Notfallanhänger; ~ **equipment** *74* Medizingeräte; ~ **supplies** pl *63* medizinische Bedarfsartikel, Sanitätsartikel
medicine *62* Arzneimittel
medium-sized *8* mittelgroß, mittelständisch
to **meet**: ~ **a deadline** *8T* eine Frist einhalten; ~ **sb's needs** *19* jds Anforderungen erfüllen, jds Bedürfnissen entsprechen; ~ **with sb's approval** *105* jds Zustimmung finden
meeting place *13* Treffpunkt
member, staff ~ *117P* Mitarbeiter/in, Angestellte/r; ~ **of the public** *25* Privatperson, Einzelperson
memo *105* Notiz, Vermerk
to **mention sth** *25* etw erwähnen, etw nennen
mentioned, above-~ *82* obengenannt
merchant *80* Händler/in
to **merge** *24* fusionieren
merger *24* Fusion
message, to leave a ~ *20* eine Nachricht hinterlassen; to **get a** ~ **across** *25* eine Botschaft vermitteln
metal, precious ~ *62* Edelmetall
method of packing *56* Verpackungsmethode
metric *55* metrisch
mile, last ~ *110T* letzte Meile
mill *24* Fabrik, Werk; **soya** ~ *32* Sojamühle
to **mind: I don't** ~. *8T* Ich habe nichts dagegen.
to **minimize sth** *33* etw minimieren
minimum: ~ **charge** *66P* Mindestgebühr; ~ **order quantity** *91* Mindestbestellmenge
minutes pl *116* Protokoll
to **miss sth** *19* etw übersehen
missing, to be ~ *20* fehlen

misunderstanding *100* Missverständnis
to **mix sth up** *110* etw durcheinander bringen
mix-up *103* Durcheinander, Verwechslung
mixture *51* Mischung, Vermischung, Gemisch
mobile *125* mobil; **BE** *20* Handy, Mobiltelefon
mobility *119* Freizügigkeit
mode of transport *72* Beförderungsart, Verkehrsmittel
model, role ~ *122* Vorbild
to **monitor sth** *64* etw überwachen
monthly *8T* monatlich
morning break *8T* Frühstückspause
Moscow *62* Moskau
motivated *124* motiviert
motorized *36* motorisiert
motorway *50* Autobahn
move *15* Umzug
movement, freight ~ *19T* Güterbewegung, Transport
multi: ~-stop *77* mit Zwischenstopps, Multistopp-; **~-storey car park** *97P* Parkhaus
multimodal *24* multimodal
multiple *77* mehrfache, wiederholte; **~ times** *77* mehrfach
Munich *45P* München
musical instrument *57* Musikinstrument

N

nail *55* Nagel
naked lights *pl 54* offene Flammen
name, first ~ *20T* Vorname; **proper shipping ~** *53* offizielle Versandbezeichnung
to **name sth** *19* etw nennen, etw benennen
national holiday *10* landesweiter Feiertag
nationality *124* Staatsangehörigkeit
native speaker *98* Muttersprachler/in
natural gas *73* Erdgas
nature *68* Beschaffenheit
to **near sth** *118* sich einer Sache nähern
nearby *8T* in der Nähe, nahegelegen
neat and tidy *15T* sauber und ordentlich
needs *pl*, to **meet sb's ~** *19* jds Anforderungen erfüllen, jds Bedürfnissen entsprechen
negotiable *78* begebarm, übertragbar; **non-~** *78* nicht begebbar, nicht übertragbar
to **negotiate sth** *92* etw verhandeln
net *45T* netto; **~ weight** *75* Nettogewicht
Netherlands *24* Niederlande

neutral *117P* neutral
newly-qualified *118* jd, der gerade seinen Abschluss gemacht hat
newsagent's *97P* Zeitschriftenladen, Zeitungskiosk
Nice *71P* Nizza
nil *68T* null
noise footprint *64* Lärmteppich, Lärmemission
noisy *15T* laut
to **nominate sb** *87* jdn benennen, jdn bestellen
non-applicable *53* unzutreffend
non-negotiable *78* nicht begebbar, nicht übertragbar
non-sparking *54* funkenfrei
Norway *122T* Norwegen
Norwegian *19* norwegisch
not ... yet *28T* noch nicht; **~ at all** *106* überhaupt nicht
note, consignment ~ *56* Frachtbrief; **dangerous goods ~ (DGN)** *52* brit. Gefahrguterklärung; **delivery ~** *56* Lieferschein
notice, at short ~ *127* kurzfristig
notwithstanding any clause to the contrary *56* ungeachtet etwaiger anderslautender Bestimmungen
now, for ~ *20T* einstweilen
nutshell, in a ~ *122T* kurz gesagt, mit einem Wort

O

obligation *10* Verpflichtung; to **discharge sb an ~** *80* jdn von einer Verpflichtung entbinden
obliged, to be ~ to do sth *80* (dazu) verpflichtet sein, etw zu tun
to **observe sth** *100* etw beobachten
to **obtain sth** *78* etw erhalten, etw bekommen
obvious *101* offensichtlich, deutlich
to **occur to sb** *123T* jdm einfallen
ocean: ~ bill of lading *78* Seefrachtbrief, Seekonnossement; **~ liner** *72* Ozeandampfer, Passagierschiff
off: to take time ~ (work) *10T* sich frei nehmen; to **be ~ sick** *68T* krankgeschrieben sein
offensive *101* beleidigend
offer *8T* Angebot; **counter-~** *88* Gegenangebot; **introductory ~** *93T* Einführungsangebot; **job ~** *8T* Stellenangebot
office, customs ~ *17T* Zollamt, Zollstelle; **open-plan ~** *8* Großraumbüro; **management assistant for ~ communications** *12T* Kaufmann/-frau für Bürokommunikation

official(ly) *8T* offiziell
oil, crude ~ *73* Rohöl; **vegetable ~** *72* Pflanzenöl; **~ rig** *73* Bohrinsel; **~ spill** *72* (auf See:) Ölteppich
old-fashioned *114* altmodisch
on-board: ~ courier *70* On-Board-Kurier; **~ unit (OBU)** *50* Bordgerät, Transponder, OBU
on-carriage *81T* Weitertransport
once *37* einmal; **~ again** *10T* erneut
on-demand delivery *33* bedarfsgerechte Lieferung, Lieferung auf Abruf
one-stop *77* durchgehend, aus einer Hand, als Komplettlösung
open: ~ house *8T* Tag der Offenen Tür; **~-plan office** *8* Großraumbüro; **~-toe** *9* zehenfrei; **~-top container** *76* Opentop-Container, oben offener Container
opening hours *pl 56* Öffnungszeiten
opera *66T* Oper
to **operate** *25* geschäftlich tätig sein; *115T* in Betrieb sein, tätig sein, laufen; **~ sth** *115* etw bedienen, etw betreiben
operation, daily ~s *pl 19* Tagesgeschäft
operations (department) *16* Betrieb (-sabteilung)
operator, forklift ~ *37* Gabelstaplerfahrer/in
opinion, in my ~ *8* meiner Meinung nach
opportunity *121* Gelegenheit, Möglichkeit, Chance; to **take an ~** *24* eine Chance nutzen; **job ~ies** *pl 119* Arbeitsmöglichkeiten
opposite *24* gegenüber
optician *97P* Optiker
to **optimise sth** *121* etw optimieren
option, payment ~ *43* Zahlungsweise, Zahlungsmöglichkeit
order *10* Reihenfolge; *16* Auftrag, Bestellung; ; to **be in ~** *15* in Ordnung sein; to **complete an ~** *111* eine Bestellung ausführen; to **place an ~** *42* einen Auftrag erteilen, eine Bestellung aufgeben; **initial ~** *91* Erstauftrag, Erstbestellung; **reverse ~** *124* umgekehrte Reihenfolge; **trial ~** *66P* Probebestellung; **acknowledgement of an ~** *94* Auftragsbestätigung; **receipt of ~** *86* Auftragseingang; **with ~** *86* bei Bestellung, bei Auftragserteilung; **cash with ~ (CWO)** *86* Vorkasse; **minimum ~ quantity** *91* Mindestbestellmenge; **in apparent good ~ and condition** *53* in äußerlich gutem Zustand, ohne äußerlich erkennbare Schäden; **in ~ to** *32* um ... zu; **~ bill of lading** *78* Orderkonnossement

ore, iron ~ 72 Eisenerz
organic 32 Bio-; 76 organisch
organization chart 16 Organigramm
origin 66T Herkunftsort, Ursprungsort; **certificate of ~** 56 Ursprungszeugnis, Herkunftszeugnis
otherwise, unless ~ agreed 87 sofern nicht anders vereinbart
outbound goods pl 36 Warenausgang, ausgehende Ware
outcome 115 Ergebnis, Resultat, Auswirkung(en)
outgoing 17T ausgehend
outlet, (retail) ~ 8T (Einzelhandels-) Geschäft
outsize items pl 37T Sperrgut, überdimensionierte Ware(n)
to outsource sth 32 etw auslagern
outward journey 70 Anreise, Hinflug
overall 19 Gesamt-; **~ effect** 119 Gesamteindruck, Gesamtwirkung; **~ score** 31 Gesamtpunktzahl
overbooked 70T überbucht, überbelegt
overhead cable 111 Oberleitung
over-height 76 zu hoch
overland 62 auf dem Landweg, über Land; **~ transport** 50 Landverkehr, Landtransport
to overload sth 31 etw überladen
overnight 24 über Nacht
to oversee sth 19T etw überwachen, etw beaufsichtigen
over-sized 76 übergroß
overtime 8 Überstunden
overview 26T Überblick
to own sth 24 etw besitzen
own, on one's ~ 118T alleine
owner 47 Inhaber/in
ownership 78 Eigentum, Eigentumsrecht

P

package 9 Paket; **~ handling** 9 Stückguthandhabung, Pakethandling
to package sth 34 etw verpacken
packaging 16 Verpackung; **external ~** 34 Außenverpackung; **internal ~** 34 Innenverpackung
packing: ~ group 53 Verpackungsgruppe; **~ list** 93T Packliste; **~ material** 35T Verpackungsmaterial; **method of ~** 56 Verpackungsmethode; **~ peanuts** pl 34 Verpackungschips, Füllchips; **container ~ certificate** 53 Containerpackzertifikat; **vehicle ~ certificate** 53 Fahrzeugpackzertifikat
to paint sth 24 etw lackieren
painting 62 Gemälde

pallet 16 Palette; **~ cage** 34 Gitterboxpalette; **~ rack shelving** 36 Palettenregal; **drive-through ~ rack** 36 Durchfahrregal; **~ truck** 36 Palettenhubwagen
palletized 44 auf Paletten, palettiert
panel 123T Gremium
paperless picking 37T beleglose Kommissionierung
papermill 24 Papierfabrik
paperwork 17 Formalitäten, Unterlagen, Papierkram
parcel 55P Paket, Karton; **~ delivery** 24 Paketzustellung; **~ service** 110 Paketdienst
parquet flooring 66P Parkett
part 62 Teil, Bauteil, Ersatzteil; **to take ~ in sth** 71P an etw teilnehmen; **~-time** 11 Teilzeit; **to look the ~** 9 entsprechend *(rollengerecht)* aussehen
partial-load shipment 43 Teilladungssendung
participant 116 Teilnehmer/in
particular 119 besondere/r/s; 123P bestimmte/r/s; **in ~** 122T ausgerechnet, gerade
particularly 43T besonders; **Not ~.** 123T Eigentlich nicht. Nicht unbedingt.
particulars pl 56 Einzelheiten, Angaben
partition 15T Trennwand
party 78 (Vertrags-)Partei; **third ~** 93T Dritte/r; **third-~ inspection** 93 Fremdprüfung
to pass: ~ to sb 89 auf jdn übergehen; **~ sth on** 20 etw weiterleiten; **~ an exam** 116T eine Prüfung bestehen
passenger plane 62 Passagierflugzeug
passport 119 Pass
past, to be a thing of the ~ 115T der Vergangenheit angehören
patience 105 Geduld
patient monitor 76 Patientenmonitor
pay 13 Bezahlung, Gehalt
to pay attention to sth 19 auf etw achten
payload 58 Zuladung, Nutzlast
payment 18 Zahlung; **to clear a ~** 28T eine Zahlung freigeben, eine Zahlung abrechnen; **terms** pl **of ~** 45T Zahlungsbedingungen; **~ option** 43 Zahlungsweise, Zahlungsmöglichkeit
peanuts pl, **packing ~** 34 Verpackungschips, Füllchips
People's Republic of China 88 Volksrepublik China
per 10T pro; **as ~** 86 nach, gemäß
perfect addition 24 optimale Ergänzung
period, delivery ~ 86 Lieferzeit; **time ~** 47T Zeitraum, Frist

perishable items pl 33 verderbliche Waren
perishables pl 19 verderbliche Güter
permanent 6T unbefristet
permission 122T Erlaubnis
permitted 56 gestattet, erlaubt
personable 126 umgänglich, sympathisch
personal: ~ assistant 20T persönliche/r Assistent/in; **~ life** 115T Privatleben; **~ space** 101 persönliche Distanzzone; **~ touch** 28T persönliche Note; **to put your ~ mark on sth** 15T einer Sache seinen persönlichen Stempel aufdrücken
personality 15T Persönlichkeit
personnel 12 Personal, Mitarbeiter/innen; **~ file** 12 Personalakte
petrol BE 36 Benzin
petroleum gas 73 Propangas
pharmaceutical 70 Pharma-, pharmazeutisch
photocopy 14 Fotokopie
to pick 36 kommissionieren; **~ sth** 114 etw nehmen; **~ sth up** 45T etw abholen
pick-up 70 Abholung
picker 37 Kommissionierer/in
picking, paperless ~ 37T beleglose Kommissionierung; **~ area** 36 Kommissionierzone; **~ station** 37T Kommissionierplatz
pie chart 103 Tortendiagramm
pile 122 Stapel, Haufen
to pin sth to sth 119 etw an etw heften
piping, steel ~ 76 Stahlrohre, Stahlröhren
piracy 72 Piraterie, Piraten
placard 52 Warntafel
to placard sth 53 etw mit einer Warntafel versehen
place, to hold sth in ~ 35 etw halten, etw fixieren; **Is everything in ~?** 81T Ist alles geregelt? Ist alles in Ordnung?
to place: ~ sth 28T etw platzieren, etw setzen; **~ an order** 42 einen Auftrag erteilen, eine Bestellung aufgeben
placement, work ~ BE 20 Praktikum
plan, change of ~ 38 Planänderung
planning, freight ~ 72 Frachtplanung; **load ~** 37T Ladeplanung, Verladeplanung; **route ~** 16 Routenplanung; **~ reliability** 43 Planungssicherheit
plant 34 Pflanze; **bottling ~** 59 Abfüllanlage; **processing ~** 32 Aufbereitungsanlage, Verarbeitungsanlage
plastic film 34 Plastikfolie
plate, licence ~ 56 Nummernschild, Kfz-Kennzeichen
platform, lifting ~ 36 Hebebühne

A–Z word list

pleased, to be ~ to do sth *10T* sich freuen, etw zu tun, etw gern tun
pleasure: It was my ~. *8T* Es war mit ein Vergnügen. Gern geschehen. **My ~.** *53T* Ganz meinerseits! Gern geschehen!
plumbing contractor *37* Klempnereibetrieb
point *55* Komma; **~ of view** *123P* Sicht, Perspektive; **finishing ~** *26* Endpunkt; **starting ~** *26* Ausgangspunkt; **You make a good ~.** *43T* Da haben Sie recht.
to **point to sth** *31* auf etw deuten, auf etw zeigen
Poland *12T* Polen
police station *97P* Polizeiwache
policy, insurance ~ *118T* Versicherungspolice
Polish *54P* polnisch; *125* Polnisch
polite(ly) *27* höflich
politeness *98* Höflichkeit
politics *13* Politik
pollution *50* Umweltverschmutzung; **~ levels** pl *64* Schadstoffwerte
polystyrene *34* Styropor
to **pool sth** *55* etw zusammenlegen
poor quality *63* schlechte Qualität
popular *115T* beliebt
port *26T* Hafen; **~ of discharge** *53* Entladehafen, Löschungshafen; **~ of shipment** *78* Verschiffungshafen; **~-to-port bill of lading** *78* Seefrachtbrief, Seekonnossement
portfolio *11* Arbeitsmappe
position *7* Stelle, Stellung
positioned in the market *43* im/am Markt aufgestellt
possibility *45T* Möglichkeit
to **post sb to ...** *122T* jdn nach ... versetzen
post *122T* Posten, Stelle
post-carriage *68T* Nachlauf, Nachtransport
postcode *45T* Postleitzahl
to **postpone** *116* (nach hinten) verschieben
potential *17T* möglich, potenziell
pound (lb) *55* Pfund (ca. 454 g)
to **pour sth** *73* etw schütten, etw gießen
to **power sth** *36* etw antreiben, etw mit Energie versorgen
practical *11* praktisch, Praxis-
practice, standard ~ *93T* gängige Praxis, übliches Verfahren
pre-carriage *68T* Vorlauf, Vortransport
precautions pl, **safety ~** *54* Sicherheitsvorkehrungen, Sicherheitsmaßnahmen
precious metal *62* Edelmetall

precise *33* genau; **to be ~** *81T* um genau zu sein
preferable, to be ~ to sth *73* einer Sache vorzuziehen sein
premises pl *15* Geschäftsräume, Betriebsgelände
prepaid *68T* im Voraus bezahlt; **freight ~** *81T* frachtfrei
preparation, in ~ for sth *51* zur Vorbereitung auf etw
to **prepare: ~ sth** *19* etw ausarbeiten, etw erstellen; *19T* etw vorbereiten; **~ for sth** *11* sich auf etw vorbereiten
to **prescribe sth for sth** *53* etw für etw vorsehen
present *122* aktuell, gegenwärtig; **at ~** *114* momentan, gegenwärtig
to **present sth** *78* etw (Dokument usw.) vorlegen
presenter *10* Redner/in, Vortragende/r, Moderator/in
pressurized tank *73* Drucktank, Druckbehälter
pretty *8T* ziemlich
pretzel *45* Brezel
to **prevent sth** *64* etw verhindern
price, competitive ~ *42* günstiger Preis; **final ~** *87* Endpreis; **list ~** *46* Listenpreis; **unit ~** *94* Stückpreis; **at cost ~** *8T* zum Selbstkostenpreis
to **pride onself on sth** *28T* auf etw (besonders) stolz sein
primary education *125* Grundschule, Grundschulbildung
priority *83* Vorrang
private limited company (Ltd) *24* Gesellschaft mit beschränkter Haftung (GmbH)
procedure, to follow a ~ *26T* sich an eine Vorgehensweise halten; to **follow standard ~s** *55* übliche Verfahren einhalten; **handling ~s** pl *62* Abfertigung, Abwicklung, Umschlag
to **proceed** *92* vorgehen, verfahren
process *19* Verfahren, Ablauf, Prozess
to **process sth** *58T* etw bearbeiten, verarbeiten
processing plant *32* Aufbereitungsanlage, Verarbeitungsanlage
to **procure sth** *126* etw beschaffen
procurement *11* Beschaffung, Einkauf
product manager *12T* Produktmanger/in
productivity *10* Produktivität
profession *7* Beruf
profile *11* Porträt, Profil; **job ~** *18* Stellenprofil
profit *24* Gewinn, Profit; **~ margin** *17T* Gewinspanne

profitable *32* rentabel, wirtschaftlich, gewinnbringend
pro-forma invoice *57T* Pro-forma-Rechnung
to **progress** *123P* vorankommen
project managment *122T* Projektleitung
to **promise** *66P* versprechen
to **promote sb** *18* jdn befördern
promotion *121* Beförderung, Aufstieg
prompt card *30* Moderationskarte
proof of identity *78* Identitätsnachweis
propeller *72* Schiffsschraube
proper(ly) *35* sachgemäß, richtig; **~ shipping name** *53* offizielle Versandbezeichnung
proposition, unique selling ~ (USP) *42* Alleinstellungsmerkmal
props pl *35* Requisiten
pros and cons pl *11* Argumente dafür und dagegen, Vor- und Nachteile
prospective *121* potenziell
prospects pl, **career ~** *119* berufliche Perspektiven; **future ~** *123T* Zukunftsperspektiven; **job ~** *8* berufliche Perspektiven
to **protect sb/sth from sth** *7* jdn/etw vor etw schützen
protection *35T* Schutz; **data ~** *124* Datenschutz
protective: ~ clothing *54* Schutzkleidung; **~ equipment** *54* Schutzausrüstung; **~ footwear** *54* Sicherheitsschuhe; **~ gloves** pl *54* Schutzhandschuhe
proud *24* stolz; to be ~ of sth *43T* auf etw stolz sein
to **prove sth** *79* etw nachweisen
to **provide sb with sth** *26T* jdm etw bieten, jdn mit etw versorgen
provisions pl *53* Bestimmungen
public *15T* öffentlich; *25* Öffentlichkeit; **~ limited company (plc)** *24* Aktiengesellschaft (AG); **~ transport** *70* öffentliche Verkehrsmittel, öffentlicher Nahverkehr; **member of the ~** *25* Privatperson, Einzelperson
publication, trade ~s pl *64* Fachzeitschriften, Fachpresse
to **publish sth** *43T* etw veröffentlichen
to **pull in** *26T* einfahren, heranfahren
punctually *92* pünktlich
purchase *48* Kauf
purchasing director *86* Einkaufsleiter/in
purpose *15T* Zweck, Absicht
to **put** *17T* formulieren, sagen; **to ~ it simply** *17T* vereinfacht gesagt; **~ sb through** *20T* (Telefon:) jdn

245

durchstellen; **~ sth to good use** *123T* etw sinnvoll nutzen; **~ your personal mark on sth** *15T* einer Sache seinen persönlichen Stempel aufdrücken

Q

qualification *11* Abschluss, Qualifikation; **school ~** *6* Schulabschluss
qualified, newly-~ *118* jd, der gerade seinen Abschluss gemacht hat
to **qualify** *6* einen/den Abschluss machen
quality, poor ~ *63* schlechte Qualität; **~ control** *111* Qualitätskontrolle; **~ management** *98* Qualitätssicherung; **~ requirements** *pl 43* Qualitätsanforderungen
quantity *33* Menge; **minimum order ~** *91* Mindestbestellmenge; **~ discount** *46* Mengenrabatt
quarterly settlement *91* vierteljährliche Abrechnung
query *53T* Rückfrage, Frage
quite *8T* ziemlich; **not ~** *123* nicht ganz
quotation *44* Preisangebot, Angebot
quote *99* Zitat

R

racing team *71P* Rennstall
rack, drive-through pallet ~ *36* Durchfahrregal; **flat ~ container** *76* Flach-container, Flat-Rack-Container; **pallet ~ shelving** *36* Palettenregal
radio: ~ signal *37* Funksignal; **~-frequency identification (RFID)** *37* Funkerkennung
rail: ~ freight *16* Bahnfracht; **~ transport** *50* Schienenverkehr, Eisenbahnverkehr
rally *71* Rallye
range *65* Reichweite; *88* Sortiment; **~ of services** *32* Dienstleistungsangebot
to **rank sth** *119* etw einstufen, etw (in einer Rangliste) bewerten
ranking *10* Einstufung, Bewertung
rate *47* Tarif, Satz, Preis; **basic ~** *99* Grundtarif, Basistarif; **exchange ~** *87* Wechselkurs; **fixed ~** *68T* Pauschaltarif, Festpreis; **insurance ~** *46* Versicherungstarif, Versicherungsprämie; **reduced ~** *47* ermäßigter Satz, Ermäßigung
rating, safety ~ *64* Sicherheitseinstufung
raw materials *pl 32* Rohstoffe, Rohmaterial(ien)

to **read sth back to sb** *66P* etw jdm nochmals vorlesen
reader *37* Lesegerät
to **realize: sb ~s sth** *96* jdm wird etw klar, jdm fällt etw auf; **I ~ that.** *107* Das ist mir bewusst.
ream *112* Ries (= 500 Blatt Papier)
reason, for this ~ *62* deshalb, aus diesem Grund; to **give ~s for sth** *8* etw begründen
reasonable(-bly) *80* angemessen, hinreichend
rebate *46* Rabatt
recall *33* Rücknahme, Rückruf
to **recall sth** *33* etw (Produkt) zurückrufen
receipt *18* Beleg, Quittung, Empfangsbestätigung; **~ of invoice** *47T* Rechnungseingang, Erhalt der Rechnung; **~ of order** *86* Auftragseingang; **on ~ of sth** *78* bei Erhalt einer Sache
to **receive sth** *29* etw bekommen, etw erhalten; *37T* etw in Empfang nehmen
received for shipment bill of lading *78* Übernahmekonnossement
receiver, (warehouse) ~ *37* Warenannehmer/in
recent, in ~ years *24* in den letzten Jahren
recently *51* vor kurzem, in letzter Zeit
reception *122* Empfang
to **recharge** *111* sich (wieder)aufladen
recipient *43* Empfänger/in
to **recognize sth** *7* etw anerkennen
recognized *121* anerkannt
recommended *9* empfohlen
to **record sth** *74* etw aufzeichnen
record *107* Datensatz
recording *19* Aufzeichnung, Aufnahme
to **recover sth** *90* etw einfordern, etw zurückerlangen
to **recruit** *18* (Personal) einstellen
recruitment *122T* Einstellung, Anwerbung (von Personal); **~ agency** *120* Personalvermittlung
to **reduce sth** *111* etw verringern, etw senken
reduced rate *47* ermäßigter Satz, Ermäßigung
reduction *46* Ermäßigung, (Preis-)Nachlass
reefer vessel *73* Kühlschiff
to **reenter the supply chain** *33* wieder in die Lieferkette gelangen
to **refer to sth** *107P* sich auf etw beziehen, etw erwähnen
referee *124* Referenz(geber)
reference *49* (Brief:) Zeichen; *53* Kennziffer, Vorgangsnummer; *122*

Referenz; **~ (to sth)** *57* Bezugnahme (auf etw), Erwähnung (von etw); **with ~ to** *127* mit Bezug auf, bezugnehmend auf; **~ initials** *pl 48* (Brief:) Zeichen; **~ number** *121* Aktenzeichen, Kennziffer
refinery *73* Raffinerie
to **re-fit sth** *115T* etw umbauen, etw neu ausstatten
refreshment *13* Erfrischung(sgetränk)
refrigerated transport *43* Kühltransport
refrigerator lorry *43T* Kühllastwagen, Kühlfahrzeug
refund *107* Rückerstattung
to **refuse sth** *101* etw ablehnen
to **regard, as ~s** *46* bezüglich, betreffend
regard: Best ~s *39* (Brief:) Viele Grüße, Mit freundlichen Grüßen
regular, on a ~ basis *44* regelmäßig
regulated, to be ~ under EU laws *25* EU-Recht unterliegen
regulations *pl 19* Vorschriften; **governmental ~** *53* gesetzliche/behördliche Vorschriften
reinforcement *8T* Verstärkung
to **relate: ~ to sth** *103* sich auf etw beziehen; **~ sth to sth** *123T* etw auf etw beziehen
relationship *45T* Beziehung
to **relax** *123T* sich entspannen
relaxed *8T* locker, entspannt
release, block ~ *6* Blockunterricht (an der Berufsschule); **day ~** *6T* tagweise Freistellung zur beruflichen Weiterbildung
to **release sth** *28T* etw freigeben
relevant *126* einschlägig, entsprechend; **~ (to sth)** *124* wichtig, relevant (für etw)
reliability *115T* Zuverlässigkeit; **planning ~** *43* Planungssicherheit
reliable *45T* zuverlässig, seriös
to **remain constant** *113* gleich bleiben
remaining *10T* übrige/r/s
remarkable *43T* bemerkenswert
to **remind sb of sb/sth** *101T* jdn an jdn/etw erinnern
reminder *106* Mahnung; *116T* Erinnerung, Hinweis; **~ function** *122T* Erinnerungsfunktion
rent *6* Miete
repeated *28* wiederholt
to **replace sth** *57* etw ersetzen
replacement *35* Ersatz
reply (to sth) *39* Antwort (auf etw)
to **reply (to sth)** *39* (auf etw) antworten, (etw) beantworten

report *11* Gutachten, Bericht; **financial ~** *18* Finanzbericht; **inspection ~** *93T* Prüfbericht
to report: ~ to sb *17* jdm unterstehen; **~ sth to sb** *17T* jdm etw melden; **~ back to sb** *62* jdm Bericht erstatten
to represent sb/sth *98* jdn/etw repräsentieren, jdn/etw vertreten
representation, without responsibility or ~ *80* ohne Verantwortung oder Gewähr
representative *27* Vertreter/in; **customer service ~** *19* Kundenberater/in, Kundenbetreuer/in
republic, Czech R~ *8T* Tschechische Republik; **People's R~ of China** *88* Volksrepublik China
reputation *43T* Ruf
request *55* Anfrage; **~ (for sth)** *38* Bitte (um etw); **special ~** *18* Sonderwunsch; **on ~** *124* auf Wunsch, auf Anfrage
to request: ~ sth *59* etw anfordern, um etw bitten, etw wünschen; **~ sb to do sth** *87* von jdm verlangen, etw zu tun
to require sth *37* etw erfordern, etw verlangen
required *53* erforderlich, vorgeschrieben; **to be ~ for/of sth** *65* für etw erforderlich sein
requirements *pl*, **documentary ~** *65* Dokumentationsanforderungen; **legal ~** *19T* gesetzliche Bestimmungen, rechtliche Vorgaben; **quality ~** *43* Qualitätsanforderungen
to re-schedule sth *83* etw *(Termin usw.)* verschieben
research, market ~ *18* Marktforschung
to research sth *10* etw recherchieren
to reserve sth *68* etw reservieren
respect, in all ~s *53* in jeder Hinsicht
to respond to sth *46* auf etw antworten
response *13* Antwort, Reaktion
responsibility *17T* Aufgabe, Zuständigkeit, Verantwortlichkeit, Verantwortung; **without ~ or representation** *80* ohne Verantwortung oder Gewähr
responsible, to be ~ for sth *7* für etw zuständig sein, für etw verantwortlich sein
restrictions *pl*, **dietary ~** *71T* Nahrungsmittelunverträglichkeiten, besondere Kost
to result in sth *15T* zu etw führen, etw ergeben
retail outlet *8T* (Einzelhandels-)Geschäft
retailer *32* Einzelhändler/in

return: ~ journey *63* Rückfahrt, Rückflug, Rückreise; **~ load** *58* Rückladung
to reverse *74* rückwärts fahren
reverse: ~ logistics *33* Rücknahmelogistik; **~ order** *124* umgekehrte Reihenfolge; **in ~** *47T* umgekehrt
to review sth *44* etw durchgehen, etw durcharbeiten
RFID tag *37T* RFID-Etikett
rig, oil ~ *73* Bohrinsel
right, to take a ~ *26T* rechts abbiegen; **~ away** *98* sogleich, sofort
rigid vehicle *58* Einzelfahrzeug, starres Fahrzeug
to rise *112* steigen, ansteigen, zunehmen
risk *25* Gefahr, Risiko; **subsidiary ~** *54* Nebengefahr(en)
ritual *101* Ritual
ro-ro vessel *73* RoRo-Schiff
road: ~ freight *16* Straßenfracht; **~ haulage** *24* Güterkraftverkehr, Straßentransport; **~ transport** *50* Straßenverkehr, Straßentransport; **the ~ to success** *24* der Weg zum Erfolg
roadwork *97T* Straßenbauarbeiten
robot *110* Roboter
robotic cleaning machine *114* Reinigungsroboter
rod, lashing ~ *74* Laschstange
role model *122* Vorbild
roller floor *65* Rollenboden
roof tile *37* Dachziegel
rough *45T* grob
roundabout *97* Kreisverkehr
route planning *16* Routenplanung
row, in a ~ *117P* nacheinander
royal *66P* königlich
rubber *34* Gummi; **foam ~** *34* Schaumgummi, Moosgummi
rude *98* unhöflich, unverschämt
rule *87* Regel, Vorschrift
to run: ~ sth *17* etw leiten; **~ into problems** *24* Probleme bekommen; **~ advertising** *17T* Werbung schalten
to rush *98* sich beeilen, eilen, hetzen
Russia *58T* Russland

S

saddle *65* Sattel
safety *19T* Sicherheit; **health and ~** *115T* Arbeitsschutz, Arbeitssicherheit; **~ equipment** *54* Sicherheitsausrüstung; **~ precautions** *pl* *54* Sicherheitsvorkehrungen, Sicherheitsmaßnahmen; **~ rating** *64* Sicherheitseinstufung; **~ vest** *8T* Sicherheitsweste
salary *6* Gehalt

sale, bulk ~ *37* Massenverkauf, Großhandelsverkauf
sales: ~ (department) *16* Verkauf(sabteilung); **~ figures** *pl* *17T* Umsatzzahlen, Verkaufszahlen; **export ~ department** *86* Exportabteilung; **sales, export ~ manager** *80* Exportleiter/in
salutation *39* *(Brief:)* Anrede
sample *93* Muster, Probe; **DNA ~** *70* DNA-Probe
satisfied *88* zufrieden
satnav *71T* Navi
sausage *35* (Brat-)Wurst, Würstchen
to save sth *55* etw sparen
savings *pl*, **cost ~** *111* Einsparungen, Kostenersparnis
saw *76* Säge; **electric ~** *65* Elektrosäge
scale *43* Umfang
scales *pl* *37* Waage
Scandinavia *17* Skandinavien
schedule *17T* Zeitplan; **on ~** *17T* planmäßig, termingerecht, pünktlich
to schedule sth *64* etw *(Termin usw.)* planen, etw festlegen, etw ansetzen
scheduled, to be ~ for delivery *33* (zu einem bestimmten Zeitpunkt) geliefert werden (sollen)
scheduling *19T* Disposition, Terminplanung
scheme, to enter a ~ *7* an einem Programm teilnehmen
school: ~ leaving certificate *121* Schulabschluss; **~ qualification** *6* Schulabschluss
scissor lift *65* Scherenlift
score, overall ~ *31* Gesamtpunktzahl
to scratch sth *103* etw verkratzen
screen *10* Leinwand, Bildschirm
screening, cargo ~ *64* Frachtkontrolle
sculpture *35* Skulptur
sea: ~ freight *16* Seefracht; **~ transport** *72* Seetransport, Seeverkehr; **deep ~ transport** *24* Hochseeschifffahrt; **~ waybill (SWB)** *78* Seefrachtbrief
seal *53* Plombe, Siegel
sealed *56* verplombt
season *43T* Jahreszeit, Saison
seat *70T* Platz, Sitzplatz
second to last *10T* vorletze/r/s
secondary education *125* Sekundarschule, Sekundarschulbildung
secretary *16* Sekretär/in
section *6* Bereich, Abschnitt; *70* Abteilung
sector *119* Sektor, Bereich
to secure sth *37T* etw sichern; *74* etw befestigen, etw verriegeln
secure(ly) *34* sicher, fest

security *35T* Sicherheit; **job ~** *111* Arbeitsplatzsicherheit
to see sth through *261* etw *(Projekt)* durchgehend betreuen
to seek sth *125* etw suchen
to seem *81T* scheinen
to select sth *37T* etw auswählen
self-assessment *119* Selbsteinstufung
self-catering *71* Selbstversorger-
self-correcting *115T* selbstkorrigierend
self-driving *111* selbstfahrend
self-maintaining *115T* selbstwartend
seller *78* Verkäufer/in
semi-trailer truck *AE* *51* Sattelzug
sender *53* Absender
sense, to make ~ *47T* einleuchten; **~ of community** *15T* Gemeinschaftssinn
sensitive, temperature-~ *62* temperaturempfindlich; **time-~** *62* zeitkritisch
separate(ly) *21* einzeln, separat
sequence *33* Folge, Abfolge, Reihenfolge
serious *25* ernst, schwer, groß, erheblich; **~ change** *115* bedeutende Veränderung
seriously, to take sb/sth ~ *98* jdn/etw ernst nehmen
service *24* Dienst, Dienstleistung; **customer ~** *8T* Kundenbetreuung, Kundendienst; **parcel ~** *110* Paketdienst; **range of ~s** *32* Dienstleistungsangebot
session *10T* Unterrichtseinheit
to set: ~ sb/sth apart from sb/sth *43T* jdn/etw von jdm/etw abheben, jdn/etw von jdm/etw unterscheiden; **~ sth up** *15T* etw einrichten, etw planen, etw aufbauen
set *124* vorgegeben, starr, fest; **to be ~** *81T* startklar sein; **~ of documents** *77* Dokumentensatz; **film ~** *35* Filmkulisse
settlement, quarterly ~ *91* vierteljährliche Abrechnung
set-up *15T* Anordnung, Einrichtung, System
several *44* mehrere
to shadow sb *55* mit jdm mitlaufen
to shake hands with sb *123T* jdm die Hand geben
share *24* Aktie; **market ~** *28* Marktanteil
to share sth *15T* sich etw teilen, etw gemeinsam nutzen; *100* etw gemeinsam haben
shared *15T* gemeinsam
shareholder *25* Aktionär/in
sheet: ~ (of paper) *15* Blatt (Papier); **information ~** *89* Merkblatt

shelving *37* Regallager; **high-bay ~** *36* Hochregallager; **high-rise ~ system** *115T* Hochregalsystem; **pallet rack ~** *36* Palettenregal
shield, face ~ *54* Gesichtsschutz, Gesichtsschirm
shift *115T* Schicht; **day ~** *117P* Tagschicht; **early ~** *117P* Frühschicht; **~ work** *8* Schichtarbeit
to ship sth *16* etw versenden, etw verschicken
shipment *17T* Sendung; **hand-carry ~** *70T* Handcarry-Lieferung, persönlich begleiteter Transport; **partial-load ~** *43* Teilladungssendung; **trial ~** *49* Probelieferung; **port of ~** *78* Verschiffungshafen; **~ status** *43* Sendungsstatus, Versandstatus; **received for ~ bill of lading** *78* Übernahmekonnossement
shipped on board bill of lading *78* Bordkonnossement
shipper *53* Absender
shipping: ~ charges *pl 86* Versandkosten; **~ clerk** *52* Expedient/in, Spediteur/in, Kaufmann/-frau für Spedition und Logistikdienstleistung; **~ marks** *pl 53* Versandzeichen; **proper ~ name** *53* offizielle Versandbezeichnung
shipyard *111* Werft
shorthaul *43* Kurzstrecken-
shortlisted, to be ~ *122* in die engere Auswahl kommen
shovel *54* Schaufel
to show sb around *26* jdn herumführen, jdm (etw) zeigen
showroom *26T* Ausstellungsraum, Verkaufsraum
shy *123T* schüchtern
sick *68T* krank; **to be off ~** *68T* krankgeschrieben sein; **to call in ~** *67* sich krankmelden
sign: ~ (of sth) *78* Anzeichen (von etw); **street ~** *35* Straßenschild; **warning ~** *52* Warnhinweis, Warnschild
to sign *24* unterzeichnen; **~ for sth** *37T* etw quittieren
signal, radio ~ *37* Funksignal
signature *48* Unterschrift; **~ block** *48* Signatur
significant(ly) *91* erheblich
signpost *30* orientierender Hinweis in einer Präsentation
similar (to sth) *6* (einer Sache) ähnlich
simplified *64* vereinfacht, einheitlich
simply, to put it ~ *17T* vereinfacht gesagt
since *55* seit

sincerely: Yours ~ *39* *(Brief:)* Mit freundlichen Grüßen
Singapore *74* Singapur
sir, Dear S~ or Madam *39* *(Brief:)* Sehr geehrte Damen und Herren,
site, building ~ *37* Baustelle; **manufacturing ~** *50* Produktionsstätte, Produktionsstandort
size *8T* Größe; **standard ~** *75* Einheitsgröße, Normgröße
to sketch sth out *25* etw (vor)zeichnen
to skim *104* *(Text)* überfliegen
slat *76* Lamelle
slide *28* *(Präsentation:)* Folie
slight(ly) *24* geringfügig, etwas
slippage *74* Rutschen
Slovenia *50* Slowenien
to slow down *97T* langsamer fahren
smart *8* *(Kleidung:)* elegant, schick; *110* intelligent
smile *98* Lächeln
to smile *102P* lächeln
smooth(ly) *17T* reibungslos
so: How ~? *33* Inwiefern?
socializing *124* Ausgehen
to soften sth *98* etw abmildern
software developer *12T* Software-Entwickler/in
solar energy *111* Solarenergie
solution *35* Lösung
sort *43T* Art
to sort sth out *53T* etw klären, etw regeln
sorted, to get sth ~ *106T* etw klären, sich um etw kümmern
source *66T* Quelle
soya mill *32* Sojamühle
space, freight ~ *68* Frachtraum; **personal ~** *101* persönliche Distanzzone; **to clear a ~** *15T* einen Platz räumen
spacious *15* geräumig
sparking, non-~ *54* funkenfrei
to speak: S~ing. *20T* *(Telefon:)* Am Apparat.
special: ~ discount *46* Sonderrabatt; **~ request** *18* Sonderwunsch
specialist *11* Fachmann/-frau, Experte/-in
to specialize in sth *32* sich auf etw spezialisieren
specifications *pl 86* Angaben, Technische Daten, Spezifikationen
specified: as ~ *86* wie angegeben
to specify sth *33* etw (genau) angeben
to speed sth up *55* etw beschleunigen
speedy *33* schnell, zügig
to spell *20T* buchstabieren
spelling *30* Rechtschreibung; *66P* Schreibweise

A–Z word list

spill, oil ~ *72* *(auf See:)* Ölteppich; **~ kit** *54* Notfallset für Leckagen und Verschüttungen
to split sth *7* etw aufteilen
sportswear *55P* Sportbekleidung
spreadsheet *119* Tabellenkalkulation, Tabelle
to stack: ~ sth *74* etw stapeln; **Do not ~.** *35* Nicht belasten! Nicht stapeln!
staff *8T* Mitarbeiter/innen, Personal; **~ member** *117P* Mitarbeiter/in, Angestellte/r
stage *90* Phase, Schritt, Etappe, Abschnitt
stairs *pl 26* Treppe, Treppenhaus
stand *17T* (Messe-)Stand; **lighting ~** *35* Leuchtenstativ
to stand in for sb *81T* jdn vertreten
standard *7* Maßstab, Anforderung, Norm; **~ practice** *93P* gängige Praxis, übliches Verfahren; **~ size** *75* Einheitsgröße, Normgröße; **~ time** *63* Normalzeit; **to follow ~ procedures** *55* übliche Verfahren einhalten
standards *pl 122T* Ansprüche
standardized *51* genormt
standby *8T* Bereitschaft
staple, control ~ *55* Prüfklammer
starting point *26* Ausgangspunkt
to state *38* angeben, erklären, sagen, darlegen, sagen
state laws *pl 19T* Landesgesetze
statement *17* Aussage
statistics *28T* Statistik(en)
status, shipment ~ *43* Sendungsstatus, Versandstatus
stay *26T* Aufenthalt
to stay on *8T* bleiben, dableiben
to steal *57T* stehlen
steel *21* Stahl; **~ coil** *76* Stahlblechrolle; **~ piping** *76* Stahlrohre, Stahlröhren; **~ toe** *28T* Stahlkappe
step by step *73* Schritt für Schritt
sterilizer *76* Sterilisator
stiff *34* steif, starr, fest
stock: ~ management *16* Bestandsführung, Lagerverwaltung; **~ market** *24* Aktienmarkt
stop *26T* Station, Halt; **multi-~** *77* mit Zwischenstopps, Multistopp-; **one-~** *77* durchgehend, aus einer Hand, als Komplettlösung
storage *28* Lagerung, Lager; **cold ~** *36* Kühllager, Kühlhaus; **floor ~** *36* Bodenlager
to store sth *8T* etw lagern; *12* etw (Daten usw.) speichern; *26T* etw aufbewahren

store, convenience ~ *AE 11* lang geöffneter Laden (oft mit Tankstelle), Mini-Markt; **department ~** *97P* Kaufhaus; **DIY ~** *97P* Heimwerkermarkt
storey, multi-~ car park *97P* Parkhaus
storm *83T* Unwetter, Sturm
to stow sth *74* etw stauen, etw beladen
stowage *74* Stauung
straight: ~ ahead *26T* geradeaus; **~ away** *58T* sofort
strategic(ally) *33* strategisch
street sign *35* Straßenschild
strength *122T* Stärke
to stress sth *123P* etw betonen, etw hervorheben
stressful *98* anstrengend, stressig
strict *8T* streng
structure *30* Aufbau, Struktur
to structure sth *7* etw aufbauen, etw strukturieren
to struggle *24* in Schwierigkeiten stecken, zu kämpfen haben
to study sth *39* sich etw genau ansehen
stuffing weight *75* Zuladung, Ladegewicht
sturdy *55* stabil, robust
subcontractor *105* Subunternehmer/in
sub-department *16* Unterabteilung
subject, to be ~ to sth *56* einer Sache unterliegen; **~ line** *38* Betreffzeile
to submit sth *71* etw einreichen, etw vorlegen, etw abgeben
subsidiary *20* Niederlassung; **~ risk** *54* Nebengefahr(en)
to subsidize *8* subventionieren, bezuschussen
substance, infectious ~s *pl 64* infektiöse Stoffe
subtotal *92* Zwischensumme
success, the road to ~ *24* der Weg zum Erfolg
to suggest sth *35T* etw vorschlagen
suggestion *39* Vorschlag
suit *9* Anzug; Kostüm; **trouser ~** *9* Hosenanzug
to suit sb *39* jdm passen
suitable *13* geeignet, passend
sulphur, high-~ *72* mit hohem Schwefelgehalt; **low-~** *72* schwefelarm
sulphuric acid *52* Schwefelsäure
to sum up: to ~ *10T* zusammenfassend (gesagt)
to summarize sth *30* etw zusammenfassen
to supervise sth *17T* etw überwachen, etw beaufsichtigen, etw kontrollieren
supervision *107P* Überwachung, Kontrolle

supervisor *12* Vorgesetzte/r, Chef/in; **training ~** *12* Ausbildungsleiter/in
supplement *119* Zusatz, Ergänzung
supplementary charges *pl 56* Zusatzgebühren, zusätzliche Kosten
supplier *48* Zulieferer, Lieferant, Anbieter
supplies *pl*, **hospital ~** *76* Krankenhausbedarf; **medical ~** *63* medizinische Bedarfsartikel, Sanitätsartikel
supply chain *24* Lieferkette, Versorgungskette; **to reenter the ~** *33* wieder in die Lieferkette gelangen
support *121* Betreuung
to support: ~ sb/sth *15T* jdn/etw unterstützen; *15T* jdn/etw fördern; **~ sth** *31* etw (Argumentation) untermauern; *64* etw finanzieren
surcharge *68* Zuschlag
sure, to make ~ *17T* sicherstellen, gewährleisten, dafür sorgen; **to make ~** *66T* um sicherzugehen
to surf the internet *24* im Internet surfen
surface area *35T* Oberfläche
surname *20T* Nachname
surprised *10T* überrascht, erstaunt
surprising *43T* erstaunlich
to surrender sth *80* etw aushändigen, etw übergeben
to surround sth with sth *35T* etw mit etw umgeben
survey *8* Umfrage
sustainability *64* Nachhaltigkeit
sustainable *43T* nachhaltig
swap body *51* Wechselaufbau
to swap sth *63* etw tauschen
Sweden *66P* Schweden
swinging door *65* Schwenktür
to switch to sth *37T* auf etw umstellen
Switzerland *50* Schweiz
sympathetic *98* mitfühlend, wohlwollend, sympathisch
Syria *12* Syrien

T

T-junction *97* Einmündung
tachograph *114* Fahrtenschreiber
tag, RFID ~ *37T* RFID-Etikett
to tag sth *37* etw etikettieren
tail lift *58* Ladebordwand, Hebebühne
to take: ~ sb on *121* jdn einstellen, jdn übernehmen; **~ sb/sth seriously** *98* jdn/etw ernst nehmen; **~ a left/right** *26T* links/rechts abbiegen; **~ care of sth** *16* sich um etw kümmern, etw bearbeiten, etw erledigen; **~ part in sth** *71P* an etw teilnehmen; **~ action** *112* Maßnahmen ergreifen, handeln;

~ out insurance 68 eine Versicherung abschließen
tally list 15 Abhakliste, Strichliste
tap 37 Wasserhahn
tare 53 Leergewicht, Tara; ~ weight 75 Eigengewicht, Leergewicht
task 17 Aufgabe
taut 51 straff
tax 46 Steuer(n)
taxes pl 87 Steuern
telegraphic transfer 86 telegrafische Überweisung
temperature: ~ level 43 Tempearturniveau, Temperaturbereich; ~ limitations pl 35 zulässiger Temperaturbereich; ~-sensitive 62 temperaturempfindlich
temporary 114 befristet
to tend to do sth 98 dazu neigen, etw zu tun
term 65 Begriff, Fachbegriff; long-~ 11 langfristig
terms pl 86 Konditionen; ~ of delivery 57 Lieferbedingungen; ~ of payment 45T Zahlungsbedingungen; (general) ~ and conditions pl 46 Allgemeine Geschäftsbedingungen; on the ~ agreed 78 zu den vereinbarte Konditionen
text (message) 8T SMS
to text sb 8T jdm eine SMS schicken
theft 77 Diebstahl
theoretical 7 theoretisch, Theorie-
thereafter 87 danach
thereby 55 dadurch
therefore 28T daher, folglich
to think: Come to ~ of it ... 8T Wenn ich es mir recht/genau überlege ...
third party 93T Dritte/r
third-party inspection 93 Fremdprüfung
thoroughly 116T völlig, voll und ganz
though 47T allerdings, aber
throughout ... 7 in ganz ...
to tick sth 58 etw abhaken
tidy, neat and ~ 15T sauber und ordentlich
tile, roof ~ 37 Dachziegel
time, in (good) ~ 19 rechtzeitig; on ~ 33 pünktlich; Coordinated Universal T~ 62 koordinierte Weltzeit; core ~ 117P Kernzeit; daylight saving ~ 63 Sommerzeit; estimated ~ of arrival (ETA) 83T voraussichtliche Ankunftszeit; Greenwich Mean T~ 62 mittlere Greenwich-Zeit, Weltzeit; local ~ 62 Ortszeit; standard ~ 63 Normalzeit; transit ~ 72 Laufzeit, Transitzeit; turnaround ~ 55 Umschlagzeit;

first-~ customer 46 Erstkunde/-kundin, Neukunde/-kundin; full-~ 116T Vollzeit(-); part-~ 11 Teilzeit; multiple ~s 77 mehrfach; to take ~ off (work) 10T sich frei nehmen; ~ clock 114 Stechuhr; ~ period 47T Zeitraum, Frist; ~ zone 62 Zeitzone; ~-clock software 114 Zeiterfassungssoftware; ~-sensitive 62 zeitkritisch
timeline 24 Zeitachse, Zeitschiene
title 15 Titel, Überschrift; job ~ 119 Stellenbezeichnung; document of ~ 78 Inhaberpapier, Traditionspapier, Warenwertpapier
toe, steel ~ 8T Stahlkappe; closed-~ 9 (Schuh:) geschlossen; open-~ 9 zehenfrei
toll 50 Maut; ~ station 50 Mautstelle, Mautstation
tone 98 Tonfall, Ton
tonne 35 Tonne
toppling 74 Kippen
total 46 gesamt, insgesamt; 46 Gesamtbetrag, Summe; ~ charges pl 66P Gesamtbetrag (der Gebühren); ~ weight 68T Gesamtgewicht
touch, personal ~ 28T persönliche Note; to be/get in ~ 83T sich melden
to touch sth 100 etw berühren, etw anfassen
tough 99 schwierig
tour 26 Rundgang; guided ~ 26 Führung
toy 97P Spielzeug
to track sth 17T etw verfolgen, etw nachverfolgen
track, to keep ~ of sth 16 den Überblick über etw behalten
trade 38 Gewerbe, Branche; 55 Handel; domestic ~ 55 Binnenhandel; trade, foreign ~ 55 Außenhandel; global ~ 72 Welthandel; ~ association 64 Branchenvereinigung, Wirtschaftsverband; ~ discount 94 Händlerrabatt, Handelsrabatt; ~ fair 17T Fachmesse, Branchenmesse; ~ magazine 19T Fachzeitschrift; ~ publications pl 64 Fachzeitschriften, Fachpresse
traffic: ~ jam 50 Stau; ~ lights pl 97 Ampel
trailer 51 Auflieger; 57T Anhänger; semi-~ truck AE 51 Sattelzug
to train 7 eine Ausbildung machen; ~ to be a ... 6 eine Ausbildung zum/zur ... machen; ~ sb 16 jdn schulen, jdn ausbilden; ~ sb on sth 37T jdn an etw schulen
trainee 6 Auszubildende/r, Lehrling
traineeship 122T Ausbildung, Lehre

trainer 10 Ausbilder/in
trainers pl 9 Turnschuhe, Sportschuhe
training, vocational ~ 7 Berufsausbildung; weight ~ 55P Kraftsport; ~ company 6 Ausbildungsbetrieb; ~ course 6T Ausbildung, ~ supervisor 12 Ausbildungsleiter/in
transaction 90 (Geschäfts-)Vorgang
transfer 71P Transfer, Transport; telegraphic ~ 86 telegrafische Überweisung
to transfer sth 57T etw (Container usw.) umladen; 78 etw übertragen; 96 etw (Geld) überweisen
transit 35 Transport; in ~ 28T unterwegs, auf dem Transportweg; ~ time 72 Laufzeit, Transitzeit
transparency 29 (Overhead-)Folie, Dia; 43 Nachvollziehbarkeit, Transparenz
transport 16 Transport, Beförderung, Verkehr; air ~ 62 Luftfracht, Luftverkehr; deep sea ~ 24 Hochseeschifffahrt; inland waterway ~ 24 Binnenschifffahrt; intermodal ~ 43 kombinierter Verkehr, intermodaler Transport; overland ~ 50 Landverkehr, Landtransport; public ~ 70 öffentliche Verkehrsmittel, öffentlicher Nahverkehr; rail ~ 50 Schienenverkehr, Eisenbahnverkehr; refrigerated ~ 43 Kühltransport; road ~ 50 Straßenverkehr, Straßentransport; sea ~ 72 Seetransport, Seeverkehr; form of ~ 17T Transportart; means of ~ 111 Transportmittel; mode of ~ 72 Beförderungsart, Verkehrsmittel; ~ documents pl 78 Beförderungspapiere, Frachtdokumente; T~ Emergency Card 54 Unfallmerkblatt; ~ insurance 87 Transportversicherung; ~ link 71T Verkehrsverbindung
to transport sth 17T etw befördern, etw transportieren
transportation 9 Transport, Beförderung
transshipment 42 Umladung
travel ticket 8T Monatskarte, Jahreskarte (ÖPNV)
trial: ~ order 66P Probebestellung; ~ shipment 49 Probelieferung
tricky 97T schwierig
trillion 64 Billion
trip 50 Fahrt; business ~ 8 Geschäftsreise
triplicate, in ~ 78 in dreifacher Ausfertigung
tripod 35 Stativ
trouser suit 9 Hosenanzug

A–Z word list

truck *24* Lastwagen, Lkw; **pallet ~** *36* Palettenhubwagen; **semi-trailer ~** *AE 51* Sattelzug; **~ gate** *74* Lkw-Gate
trucking *20* Lkw-Transport, Spedition
truckload, full ~ *42* Komplettladung (Lkw); **less than ~** *42* Teilladung (Lkw)
true *17* zutreffend, richtig
to trust *92* hoffen(, dass …); **~ sb** *78* jdm vertrauen
tube *111* Röhre
to tuck the shirt in *9* das Hemd in die Hose stecken
tuition fees *pl 11* Studiengebühren
tumble dryer *65* Wäschetrockner
Turkey *12* Türkei
turn, to be one's ~ *19* an der Reihe sein; **in ~** *111* wiederum
to turn: ~ sth into sth *24* etw zu etw machen, etw in etw umwandeln; **~ sth round** *26T* etw (Unternehmen usw.) wieder auf Kurs bringen, etw sanieren; **~ one's back on sb** *31* jdm den Rücken zuwenden
turnaround *115T* Umschlag; **~ time** *55* Umschlagzeit
turning *97* Abzweigung, Querstraße
turnover *28* Umsatz; *115T* Umschlag
to twist sth *74* etw drehen, etw verdrehen
type of goods *35* Warenart
to type sth in *66T* etw eintippen

U

unable, to be ~ to do sth *116* etw nicht tun können
unacceptable *103* inakzeptabel, unzumutbar
unavailable, to be ~ *20T* (Telefon:) nicht zu sprechen sein
unbeatable *43* unschlagbar
underscore *38* Unterstrich
uncomfortable, to be/feel ~ *98* sich unbehaglich fühlen
unexact *75* ungenau
unfinished *67* unerledigt, unfertig
unfortunately *37T* bedauerlicherweise, leider
uninviting *15T* wenig einladend
unique selling proposition (USP) *42* Alleinstellungsmerkmal
unit *55* Einheit; *91* Stück; **on-board ~ (OBU)** *50* Bordgerät, Transponder, OBU; **~ of measurement** *75* Maßeinheit; **~ price** *94* Stückpreis; **U~ Load Device (ULD)** *65* Ladeeinheit (ULD)
universal, Coordinated U~ Time *62* koordinierte Weltzeit

unless *53* außer, außer wenn; **~ otherwise agreed** *87* sofern nicht anders vereinbart
to unload *37T* entladen
unloading *46* Entladung
to unlock sth *77* etw aufschließen, etw öffnen
unpackaged *72* unverpackt
unpaid *10T* unbezahlt
unsuitable *72* ungeeignet
unsure, to be ~ about sth *96T* sich einer Sache nicht sicher sein
up: This way ~ *35* Hier oben
update (on sth) *38* aktuelle Informationen (zu etw), aktueller Überblick (über etw)
to update sth *37* etw aktualisieren
to upgrade *115T* aufrüsten, hochrüsten
to upload *11* hochladen
upper management *112* obere Führungsebene, Chefetage
upset *105* verärgert, ungehalten
to upset sb *99* jdn verärgern
upstairs *26T* (nach) oben
upwind *54* windwärts
urgent(ly) *20T* dringend
use, to put sth to good ~ *123T* etw sinnvoll nutzen

V

vacancy, (job) ~ *123P* offene Stelle
vacation *AE 10T* Urlaub, Ferien
valuable *37* wertvoll
value *68T* Wert; **insured ~** *87* Versicherungswert
to value sth *98* etw schätzen, etw wertschätzen
van *50* Lieferwagen; **box ~** *AE* / **Luton ~** *BE 51* Lkw mit Kastenaufbau und überbautem Führerhaus
varied *118T* vielfältig
various *17T* verschiedene
to vary *11* variieren, sich unterscheiden
VAT *46* MwSt
vegetable oil *72* Pflanzenöl
vehicle *36* Fahrzeug; **articulated ~** *58* Gelenkfahrzeug; **Automated Guided V~ (AGV)** *74* fahrerloses Transportfahrzeug (FTF); **heavy goods ~ (HGV)** *BE 51* Schwerlastwagen; **rigid ~** *58* Einzelfahrzeug, starres Fahrzeug; **~ packing certificate** *53* Fahrzeugpackzertifikat
ventilated *76* belüftet, ventiliert
venue *38* Veranstaltungsort
vessel *53* Schiff; **reefer ~** *73* Kühlschiff; **ro-ro ~** *73* RoRo-Schiff
vest, safety ~ *8T* Sicherheitsweste
via *19T* per; *71P* über

view *13* Aussicht, Blick; **in ~ of sth** *91* angesichts von etw; **point of ~** *123P* Sicht, Perspektive
vignette *50* Vignette
visual(ly) *25* visuell; **~ aids** *pl 31* visuelle Hilfsmittel
visuals *pl 29* visuelle Hilfsmittel
vocational: ~ school *6* Berufsschule; **~ training** *7* Berufsausbildung; **~ training certificate** *119* Berufsabschluss
voicemail *20* Mailbox
void *78* ungültig
volume *52* Volumen
volumetric *66T* volumetrisch
volunteer *113T* Freiwillige/r
to volunteer to do sth *117* sich bereit erklären, etw zu tun

W

to wait: to keep sb ~ing *13* jdn warten lassen
wallet *114* Brieftasche, Portemonnaie
warehouse *16* Lager; **high-rise ~** *28* Hochregallager; **~ receiver** *37* Warenannehmer/in
warehousing *8T* Lagerung, Lagerhaltung, Lagerwesen
warmth *15T* Wärme
warning sign *52* Warnhinweis, Warnschild
Warsaw *106T* Warschau
waste *33* Abfall
wastepaper *24* Altpapier
waterway, inland ~ transport *24* Binnenschifffahrt
way, by the ~ *10T* übrigens; **the right ~ forward** *115T* der richtige Weg; **this ~** *26T* hier entlang; **This ~ up** *35* Hier oben
waybill, air ~ *67* Luftfrachtbrief; **sea ~ (SWB)** *78* Seefrachtbrief
weakness *122T* Schwäche
wear, fashion ~ *62* Modekleidung
wearing apparel *66T* Bekleidung
weather-resistant *76* wetterfest
wedding ring *9* Ehering
to weigh *35T* wiegen
weight, chargeable ~ *66T* frachtpflichtiges Gewicht; **gross ~** *75* Bruttogewicht; **net ~** *75* Nettogewicht; **stuffing ~** *75* Zuladung, Ladegewicht; **tare ~** *75* Eigengewicht, Leergewicht; **total ~** *68T* Gesamtgewicht; **~ distribution** *37* Gewichtsverteilung; **~ training** *55P* Kraftsport
welcome: You're ~. *8T* Bitte (sehr). Gern geschehen.
well, as ~ as *46* sowie, ebenso wie

Westphalia *45T* Westfalen
wheat *62* Weizen
wheel, cheese ~ *49* Käselaib; **four-~ drive** *70* Vierradantrieb, Geländewagen
whether *8T* ob
the whole of ... *112* der/die/das gesamte/ganze ...
wholesaler *32* Großhändler/in
width *55* Breite
willing, to be ~ to do sth *91* bereit sein, etw zu tun
wing *83P* Flügel, Gebäudetrakt
wingspan *65* Spannweite
winner *10T* Sieger/in
wish: Best ~es *39* (*Brief:*) Mit freundlichen Grüßen
to witness sth *101* etw beglaubigen
wonder, it's no ~ ... *43* kein Wunder, dass ...

wood: ~ **shavings** *pl 34* Hobelspäne; ~ **wool** *BE 34* Holzwolle
wooden box *34* Holzkiste
to work *20T* funktionieren; ~ **alongside sb** *26T* mit jdm arbeiten; ~ **closely with sb** *19* eng mit jdm zusammenarbeiten
work, to get on with one's ~ *15T* seine Arbeit machen; **shift** ~ *8* Schichtarbeit; ~ **of art** *62* Kunstwerk; ~ **experience** *18* Praktikum; ~ **placement** *BE 20* Praktikum; ~**-related** *19T* arbeitsbezogen
workforce *28T* Belegschaft, Arbeitskräfte
working: ~ **conditions** *pl 6* Arbeitsbedingungen; ~ **hour** *10T* Arbeitsstunde; ~ **hours** *pl 8* Arbeitszeit(en)
workplace *14* Arbeitsplatz

works council *26* Betriebsrat
worries *pl* **(about sth)** *112* Sorge(n) (um etw)
worth *24* wert
to wrap sth up *116T* etw abschließen, etw zum Abschluss bringen
wrap, bubble ~ *34* Luftpolsterfolie
written *57T* schriftlich
writing, in ~ *8T* schriftlich, in Schriftform

XYZ
x-axis *113T* X-Achse
yet, not ... ~ *28T* noch nicht
yours: Cordially ~, *AE 48* (*Brief:*) Mit herzlichen Grüßen; **Y~ faithfully** *39* (*Brief:*) ... und verbleiben mit freundlichen Grüßen; **Y~ sincerely** *39* (*Brief:*) Mit freundlichen Grüßen

Irregular verbs

be – was/were – been	sein	let – let – let	lassen
become – became – become	werden	lose – lost – lost	verlieren
begin – began – begun	anfangen, beginnen	make – made – made	machen
break – broke – broken	brechen	mean – meant – meant	meinen, bedeuten
bring – brought – brought	bringen	meet – met – met	treffen
build – built – built	bauen	pay – paid – paid	bezahlen
burn – burnt/burned – burnt/burned	(ver)brennen	put – put – put	setzen, stellen, legen
buy – bought – bought	kaufen	read – read – read	lesen
catch – caught – caught	fangen	ride – rode – ridden	reiten, fahren
choose – chose – chosen	wählen	ring – rang – rung	klingeln, anrufen
come – came – come	kommen	rise – rose – risen	(an)steigen
cost – cost – cost	kosten	run – ran – run	laufen, rennen
cut – cut – cut	schneiden	say – said – said	sagen
do – did – done	tun, machen, erledigen	see – saw – seen	sehen
draw – drew – drawn	zeichnen	sell – sold – sold	verkaufen
dream – dreamt – dreamt	träumen	send – sent – sent	senden, schicken
drink – drank – drunk	trinken	shake – shook – shaken	schütteln
drive – drove – driven	fahren	set – set – set	setzen, stellen
eat – ate – eaten	essen	show – showed – shown	zeigen
fall – fell – fallen	fallen	shut – shut – shut	schließen
feed – fed – fed	füttern, ernähren	sing – sang – sung	singen
feel – felt – felt	(sich) fühlen, empfinden	sit – sat – sat	sitzen
fight – fought – fought	kämpfen	sleep – slept – slept	schlafen
find – found – found	finden	smell – smelt/smelled – smelt/smelled	riechen
fit – fit/fitted – fit/fitted	passen	speak – spoke – spoken	sprechen
fly – flew – flown	fliegen	spell – spelt/spelled – spelt/spelled	buchstabieren
forget – forgot – forgotten	vergessen	spend – spent – spent	ausgeben, verbringen
get – got – got (*AE* gotten)	bekommen, erhalten	stand – stood – stood	stehen
give – gave – given	geben	steal – stole – stolen	stehlen
go – went – gone	gehen, fahren	swim – swam – swum	schwimmen
grow – grew – grown	wachsen	take – took – taken	nehmen
hang – hung – hung	hängen	teach – taught – taught	unterrichten, beibringen
have – had – had	haben	tear – tore – torn	(zer)reißen
hear – heard – heard	hören	tell – told – told	sagen, erzählen
hide – hid – hidden	(sich) verstecken	think – thought – thought	denken
hit – hit – hit	schlagen, aufprallen auf	throw – threw – thrown	werfen
hold – held – held	halten, festhalten	understand – understood – understood	verstehen
keep – kept – kept	behalten	wake – woke – woken	wecken
know – knew – known	kennen, wissen	wear – wore – worn	tragen (Kleidung)
lay – laid – laid	legen	win – won – won	gewinnen
lead – led – led	führen, leiten	write – wrote – written	schreiben
learn – learnt/learned – learnt/learned	lernen		
leave – left – left	abfahren, verlassen, weggehen		

Acknowledgements

Karten (Umschlag, S.255): Cornelsen/Carlos Borrell Eiköter
S. 6: Shutterstock.com/kosmos111; **S. 8/1:** Shutterstock.com/wavebreakmedia; **S. 8/2:** Shutterstock.com/Monkey Business Images; **S. 9/1:** Shutterstock.com/Kerry Garvey; **S. 9/2:** Shutterstock.com/takayuki; **S. 9/3:** Shutterstock.com/ASDF_MEDIA; **S. 9/4:** Shutterstock.com/Robert Kneschke; **S. 11/1:** Shutterstock.com/Billion Photos; **S. 11/2:** Shutterstock.com/Dan Kosmayer; **S. 12/1:** Shutterstock.com/Djomas; **S. 12/2:** stock.adobe.com/Photozi; **S. 12/3:** Shutterstock.com/PR Image Factory; **S. 12/4:** stock.adobe.com/contrastwerkstatt; **S. 12/5:** Shutterstock.com/UncleOles; **S. 12/6:** Shutterstock.com/g-stockstudio; **S. 14/1:** Shutterstock.com/Andrey_Popov; **S. 14/2:** Shutterstock.com/Konstantin Chagin; **S. 14/3:** Shutterstock.com/Monkey Business Images; **S. 14/4:** Shutterstock.com/ESB Professional; **S. 14/5:** Shutterstock.com/Stock-Asso; **S. 15/1:** Shutterstock.com/ESB Professional; **S. 14/6:** stock.adobe.com/contrastwerkstatt; **S. 15/2:** stock.adobe. com/ProstoSvet; **S. 15/3:** Shutterstock/Tatiana Popova; **S. 15/4:** Shutterstock.com/MSSA; **S. 15/5:** stock.adobe.com/magneticmcc; **S. 15/6:** stock.adobe.com/electriceye; **S. 15/7:** stock.adobe.com/morganka; **S. 17:** Shutterstock.com/Africa Studio; **S. 18/1:** Shutterstock.com/Travel mania; **S. 18/2:** Shutterstock.com/stockfour; **S. 18/3:** Shutterstock.com/create jobs 51; **S. 18/4:** Shutterstock.com/ESB Basic; **S. 19/1:** Shutterstock.com/BalLi8Tic; **S. 19/2:** Shutterstock.com/Rido; **S. 24:** Shutterstock.com/Dmitry Kalinovsky; **S. 26:** Cornelsen/Oxford Illustrators; **S. 28 Folie:** Cornelsen/vitaledesign; **S. 28/2:** Shutterstock.com/MR. LIGHTMAN1975; **S. 28/3:** Shutterstock.com/Ondra Vacek; **S. 28/4:** Shutterstock.com/Yuliyan Velchev; **S. 28/5:** Shutterstock.com/Petinov Sergey Mihilovich; **S. 28/7:** Shutterstock.com/Matej Kastelic; **S. 30:** Shutterstock.com/ESB Professional; **S. 32/4+8:** Shutterstock.com/pikolorante; **S. 32/5+6:** Cornelsen/Rainer Götze; **S. 34/1, 2, 3, 4, 6:** Shutterstock.com/topae; **S. 34/5:** Shutterstock.com/Lipowski Milan; **S. 34/7:** Shutterstock.com/Aleks Maks; **S. 34/8:** Shutterstock.com/Vahe 3D; **S. 34/9:** Shutterstock.com/Boris Rabtsevich; **S. 35:** Shutterstock.com/laverock; **S. 36:** Cornelsen/Rainer Götze; **S. 40:** Shutterstock.com/hacohob; **S. 42:** Shutterstock.com/twenty1studio; **S. 50:** Shutterstock.com/ekler; **S. 51/1+2:** Shutterstock.com/Nerthuz; **S. 51/3+4:** Shutterstock.com/3DMI; **S. 51/5:** Shutterstock.com/topae; **S. 51/6:** Shutterstock.com/Mechanik; **S. 52:** Shutterstock.com/sonsart; **S. 54/1:** Shutterstock.com/Coprid; **S. 54/2:** Cornelsen/Rainer Götze; **S. 54/3:** Shutterstock.com/WhiteJack; **S. 54/4:** Shutterstock.com/farres; **S. 54/5:** Shutterstock.com/photographyfirm; **S. 54/6:** Shutterstock.com/modustollens; **S. 54/7:** Shutterstock.com/tale; **S. 54/8:** Shutterstock.com/Athapet Piruksa; **S. 54/9:** Shutterstock.com/krolya25; **S. 55/1:** Shutterstock.com/Pro Symbols; **S. 55/2:** Shutterstock.com/Lenka Horavova; **S. 55/3:** Shutterstock.com/brichuas; **S. 57:** Cornelsen/Carlos Borrell Eiköter; **S. 59/1:** Shutterstock.com/topae; **S. 59/2:** Shutterstock.com/sylv1rob1; **S. 59/3:** Shutterstock.com/Pyty; **S. 59/4:** Shutterstock.com/SpeedKingz; **S. 63:** Shutterstock.com/brichuas; **S. 64:** Cornelsen/Rainer Götze; **S. 65/1:** Cornelsen/Rainer Götze; **S. 65/2:** Shutterstock.com/topae; **S. 67:** Shutterstock.com/arogant; **S. 71:** Shutterstock.com/preecha2531; **S. 72/1:** Shutterstock.com/ExpressVectors; **S. 72/3-5:** Shutterstock.com/nexusby; **S. 73/A:** Shutterstock.com/EvrenKalinbacak; **S. 73/B:** Shutterstock.com/Alexyz3d; **S. 73/C:** Shutterstock.com/Darryl Brooks; **S. 73/D:** Shutterstock.com/Oleksandr Kalinichenko; **S. 73/E:** Shutterstock.com/BNK Maritime Photographer; **S. 73/F:** Shutterstock.com/imagineStock; **S. 73/7:** Shutterstock.com/bsd; **S. 74:** Cornelsen/Rainer Götze; **S. 75:** Shutterstock.com/topae; **S. 76/1, 3-6:** Shutterstock.com/topae; **S. 76/2:** Cornelsen/Rainer Götze; **S. 78/Zug:** Shutterstock.com/pikolorante; **S. 78/Grafik:** Cornelsen/vitaledesign; **S. 79:** Shutterstock.com/Studio concept; **S. 83:** Shutterstock.com/ratuszynski photography; **S. 89:** Shutterstock.com/Travel mania; **S. 90:** Cornelsen/Oxford Illustrators; **S. 91:** Shutterstock.com/Daniel-Froehlich; **S. 93/1:** Shutterstock.com/imtmphoto; **S. 93/2:** Shutterstock.com/hans engbers; **S. 97:** Shutterstock.com/hans engbers; **S. 100:** Shutterstock.com/r.classen; **S. 101/Flaggen:** Shutterstock.com/Lana2016; **S. 101/1:** Shutterstock.com/wong yu liang; **S. 101/2:** Shutterstock.com/bulerntevren; **S. 101/3:** Shutterstock.com/ANURAK PONGPATIMET; **S. 101/4:** Shutterstock.com/Flashon Studio; **S. 103/1:** Shutterstock.com/Africa Studio; **S. 105:** Shutterstock.com/Artic_photo; **S. 106:** Shutterstock.com/Bojan Milinkov; **S. 109:** Shutterstock.com/r.classen; **S. 110/A:** Shutterstock.com/Golden Sikorka; **S. 110/B, D, F, G:** Shutterstock.com/Chesky; **S. 110/C:** Shutterstock.com/3DDock; **S. 110/E:** Shutterstock.com/petrmalinak; **S. 110/H:** Shutterstock.com/angelh; **S. 114/A:** Shutterstock.com/Ralwel; **S. 114/B:** Shutterstock.com/Saklakova; **S. 114/C:** Shutterstock.com/Zerbor; **S. 114/D:** Shutterstock.com/Alexey Stiop; **S. 114/E:** Shutterstock.com/Think.A; **S. 114/F:** Shutterstock.com/vpilkauskas; **S. 118/1:** Shutterstock.com/Bojan; **S. 118/2:** Shutterstock.com/CREATISTA; **S. 118/3:** Shutterstock.com/F8 Studio; **S. 120/1:** Shutterstock.com/Christopher Hall; **S. 120/2:** stock.adobe.com/thanksforbuying; **S. 120/3:** Shutterstock.com/Douglas Freer; **S. 120/4:** Shutterstock.com/Sinseeho; **S. 123:** Shutterstock.com/Michal Kowalski **S. 135:** Shutterstock.com/Alex Oakenman **S. 141:** Shutterstock.com/Alex Oakenman

Dank und Anerkennung
Für ihren Rat und ihre Unterstützung möchten wir uns bei Liz Girling (Dangerous Goods Office, Vehicle Certification Agency, UK) herzlich bedanken.

Europe